STONE, I. F. Polemics and prophecies, 1967–1970. Random, 1971.
497p 70-141781. 10.00. ISBN 0-394-46981-X

CHOICE JUL./AUG. '71

Political Science

Stone's latest installment: a collection of his coverage of our national political life as published in his own *Weekly* and in *The New York review of books*, takes up where he left off in *In a time of torment* CHOICE, May 1968). Those who know Stone's work know exactly what to expect: penetrating insight, careful documentation, lively analysis, wit, superior writing by any standards and extraordinary prose for journalism. Stone's position is always clear but while he never abandons his own values, he never permits himself to be blinded to foolishness or knavery in our public life regardless of where his criticism must fall. His material comes from public sources; his ability to see the pattern in it comes from his private and unique ability to order facts in relation to long-range developments in American public affairs. Any student who wants to know what went on in the high reaches of American government during the agony of our national life 1967–70 can ask no better guide and companion than I. F. Stone. Index.

Other books by I. F. Stone

The Court Disposes (1937)

Business as Usual (1941)

Underground to Palestine (1946)

This Is Israel (1948)

The Hidden History of the Korean War (1952)

The Truman Era (1953)

The Haunted Fifties (1963)

In a Time of Torment (1967)

Polemics
and
Prophecies
1967-1970

Polemics and Prophecies

1967 – 1970

BY

I. F. STONE

Random House New York

FIRST PRINTING

9 8 7 6 5 4 3 2

Copyright © 1967, 1968, 1969, 1970 by I. F. Stone

All rights reserved under International and Pan-American Copyright Conventions. Published in the United States by Random House, Inc., New York, and simultaneously in Canada by Random House of Canada Limited, Toronto.

ISBN: 0-394-46981-X

Library of Congress Catalog Card Number: 70-141781

Manufactured in the United States of America by H. Wolff Book Manufacturing Co., Inc.

For my sister Judy

*The author wishes to thank Gerry Bruck, Jr.
for his devoted efforts in selecting
and editing this collection.*

Contents

Part I When Two Equals One

Who Are the Democrats?   3

Party of the Rich and Well-Born   21

A Grateful Patsy Against a Dirty Fighter?   32

The Candidate Least Likely to Make Peace   35

The GOP Convention Was Not Without
    Its Cheering Aspects   43

When a Two-Party System Becomes a
    One-Party Rubber Stamp   44

Why Hubert Is as Tricky as Dicky   49

Part II 'Saigon Afire Now . . .'

The Monster with Little Brain and No Heart   57

The Fraud with Which Bomb Resumption
    Was Excused   60

The Mendacities Go Marching On, Truce or
    No Truce   67

How TV and Press Were Led to Rehash Those
    Tet Supply Lies   70

They'd Do Anything for the Peasant But
    Get Off His Back   72

The Mindless Momentum of a Runaway Military
    Machine   75

If Daddy Keeps at It, Luci, One Day You Won't
    Wake Up   78

None So Blind as Those Who Will Not See   82

Saigon Afire Now—Will It Be Washington in
    April?   85

Part III '. . . Will It Be Washington in April?'

The Fire Has Only Just Begun   93

Billions for Missiles and Pennies for Poverty   96

The Mason-Dixon Line Moves to New York   100

Nixon About to Abolish Hunger "For All
    Time"—Again   109

The Real Meaning of Nixon's Judicial
    Philosophies   112

Part IV Nixon: The Evil of Banality

So What's a Little Isaiah Between Friends?   119

Uncle Sam's Con Man Budget   122

Same Old Formulas, Same Tired Rhetoric   130

Midway to a Nguyen Van Nixon Era   134

Nixon in the Footsteps of Popeye's Elder Statesman   138

Part V The Menace of Militarism

McNamara and the Militarists   145

On National Defense, Space and Foreign Policy,
    the New GOP Platform Reads as If Written
    by General Dynamics for a New Arms Race   159

A Goldwater to Head the Pentagon   162

Nixon and the Arms Race: The Bomber
    Boondoggle   169

Nixon and the Arms Race: How Much Is
    "Sufficiency"?   190

The War Machine Under Nixon   207

Heading for a Bigger Arms Race in the Seventies   230

Part VI Disarmament: A Century of Futility

How Earth Day Was Polluted   237
Why SALT Spells Fraud   241
A Century of Futility   249
Theater of Delusion   260
The Test Ban Comedy   282

Part VII That Barroom Brawl with the Lights Out Revisited

All We Really Know Is That We Fired
    the First Shots   307
McNamara and Tonkin Bay: The Unanswered
    Questions   312
The Supineness of the Senate   326

Part VIII Endless War

Why Not Timbuktu or Easter Island?   343
Playing for Time to Continue the War   347
The Willful Blindness of McGeorge Bundy   350
Why the Casualties Rise as the Peace Talks Go On   354
The Best-Kept Secret of the Vietnam War   360
Immediate Withdrawal Becoming a Bandwagon   366
Lessons for Nixon   369
The Atrocities Nixon Condones and Continues   386
Nixon, Inflation and the War   389
Nixon's Iron Curtain on the Cost of the War   395
Only the Bums Can Save the Country Now   400

Part IX The Mideast

Holy War   411

The Need for Double Vision in the Middle East   433

Part X Pax Americana

How the U.S. Plays Out a Banana Republic
    Comedy in Greece   441

The First Military Dictatorship with a Free
    (but Suspended) Constitution   442

Part XI 'It Wasn't for Lack of Spies . . .'

It Wasn't for Lack of Spies That the Czars Fell   449

The Mujik as the Negro of the Russian Revolution   452

The Rebirth of Freedom—or of Fascism?   459

Who Are the Real Kooks in Our Society?   463

Where the Fuse on That Dynamite Leads   465

Part XII The Streets

The Rich March on Washington All the Time   473

They Pleaded Guilty of Burning Paper Instead
    of Children   478

In Defense of the Campus Rebels   479

Bitter Battles Lie Ahead   483

Index   488

PART I

When Two
Equals One

WHO ARE THE DEMOCRATS?

The two-party system is like those magic black and white squares which look like a staircase at one moment and a checkerboard the next. Sometimes the two parties seem very distinct and sometimes they seem very much alike. This is one of those periods in which they look very much alike, whence the growing disillusion with the two-party system itself. The twin problems of retreat from empire abroad and of conciliating the black revolt at home call for changes of attitude and policy more fundamental than any we have faced since slavery.

The differences between the two parties just aren't that fundamental. To examine the past and nature of the Democratic party, which has normally been the party of change and reform, is to doubt its capacity to cope with the twin crises of our time. In the days of Franklin D. Roosevelt, unlike those of Grover Cleveland, it seemed easy to tell Democrats from Republicans. When we look back on the New Deal now, from the perspective of our present needs, the difference does not look as sharp as it did then. The rhetoric of American political controversy has never prized understatement, and the strategy of the rich has been to scream so loudly at the slightest diminution of their privileges that the sheer decibel count gives the poor the satisfying illusion that a revolution is going on. So it was with the Roosevelt Revolution. When the clamor died down and the smoke of battle began to lift, the Bastilles were still standing.

If one were trying to explain the American two-party system to a visitor from a different political planet, let us say a citizen of a Soviet one-party state, the simplest way to begin would be to say that both American parties were cap-

italist parties. The difference between them has been that
generally the Republicans have represented the interests of
the big property-owners; the Democrats, the small. But
both are equally devoted to private property. After five
years of Lyndon Johnson, it may be hard to recall that in
the Administrations of FDR and Harry Truman the Democrats were tormented by the accusation that they were
crypto-Communist. If a Soviet visitor asked hopefully
whether it was true that in those days the leadership was
secretly inspired by Lenin, one would have to explain that
such charges must be taken in the same sense as when oppo-
sitionists within a Communist state are denounced as agents
of capitalism. This is the universal poetic license of political
controversy. When the Democrats are most heatedly accused of interfering with free enterprise, it usually turns
out that all they have been doing is trying to slow up the
rate at which the big fish of business have been swallowing
the little ones.

Any division of the two parties between big property
and small requires many qualifications. Big landowners
dominate the Democratic party in the Southern states,
which are still pretty much one-party systems; small farmers are the backbone of the Republican party in the Mid-
west and the rural Northeast. There are also big businessmen in the Democratic party and small businessmen in the
Republican. Indeed, Babbitt—the archetype of the Republican standpatter—was a small businessman, from the Mid-
west, let it be noted. It is often said that American politics
stops at the water's edge; it also stops at the oil well's
mouth. The same big oil companies which dominate the Republican party in New York and Philadelphia also dominate the Democratic party in Houston and Oklahoma City.
Depletion allowances are as sacred as the Stars and Stripes.

Wisely managed corporations diversify their political
portfolios by giving to both parties, though not so gener-
ously to the Democrats. In a famous incident during a Federal investigation of the Sugar Trust in the 1890's, a sugar
magnate—or tycoon, as we now say—was asked about the

extraordinary impartiality shown in the benefactions he showered equally on both parties. "The American Sugar Refining Company," he replied genially, "has no politics of any kind. . . . Only the politics of business."

This helps explain why few big businessmen flee the country when the Democrats, as in the 1948 Truman campaign, wage anti-big business campaigns so ferocious as to make Soviet citizens tremble lest the directors of General Motors end up digging uranium in the Far North of an American Siberia. Truman, in a famous speech to farmers at Dexter, Iowa, a few weeks before the 1948 election, sounded like a latter-day Robespierre. "The Wall Street reactionaries," he said in prose as sharp as any guillotine, "are not satisfied with being rich . . . they are gluttons of privilege . . . cold men . . . cunning men. . . . They want a return of the Wall Street economic dictatorship." But when this *enragé* won, the stock market barely yawned.

The style of politics has changed. Trouncing big business, which proved sure-fire stuff two decades ago, has gone out of fashion. We are in a new Era of Good Feeling, in which both parties—and both wings of both parties—share a trusting faith that any problem can now be solved by enlisting private enterprise—so long as it is sufficiently subsidized from public funds. The cynical may wonder whether this is not just another way of buying the acquiescence of the wealthy in social reform by arranging that they make a profit on that, too. Here is a sample of the new rhetoric, as practiced by a present-day radical Democrat:

I do not think we have many real grievances to be urged against bigness in business today. . . . Some Americans hark back before the days of the managerial revolution, back to the days of the "robber barons." But this country and its economy have matured spectacularly since the trust-busting days. . . . The big businesses of bygone generations did, indeed, act in a pattern of savage repression of competition. And current revelations of price-fixing [perish the afterthought!] and other price-holding practices do not help to ease a strong historical suspicion of the motives of great corporations on the part of government

leaders, small businessmen and others. . . . [But] the pluralistic economy of the 1960's bears little resemblance to the economy of the turn of the century that brought forth the first great
trust-busting era. . . . It is high time that the traditional hostility between the intellectuals on the one hand and management
on the other was ended. Doctrinaire thinking has no place . . .
[etc.].

Alert readers may already have recognized the prose style—
as bland as marshmallows, richly garnished with fashionable
literary and political clichés[1]—of Hubert Humphrey. The
quotation is from his last book as a Senator, *The Cause Is
Mankind*. So statesmanlike had he become by 1964, even before his maturing four years as Lyndon Johnson's Vice
President.

   Harry Truman was an unsuccessful haberdasher while
Humphrey has been stigmatized, somewhat snobbishly, because of his family business, as "a drugstore liberal."[2] On

---

[1] Often misconstrued, as in the reference to the managerial revolution.
Apparently Humphrey did not get beyond the title of James Burnham's
book.
[2] Robert Sherrill and Harry W. Ernst, *The Drugstore Liberal* (New
York: Grossman, 1968).
From *The New York Review of Books*, September 26, 1968:

To the Editors:
In I. F. Stone's essay "Who Are the Democrats?" [August 22] he says,
"Harry Truman was an unsuccessful haberdasher while Humphrey has
been stigmatized, somewhat snobbishly, because of his family business, as
'a drugstore liberal' "—and, as his footnote indicates, he bases the second
half of that sentence on the title of the book I co-authored, *The Drugstore Liberal*.
   Shucks, I thought everyone would be familiar with the old saying,
"He's a drugstore cowboy," meaning no cowboy at all; and I thought
everyone would understand that I was just playing on this to say that
Humphrey isn't much of a liberal. The title is only accidentally related to
the fact that Humphrey owns a drugstore—a happy accident, however,
which I hoped would add some humor to the title and therefore to a topic
that is too often painfully dull. In any event, while there are few things
I would not do to show my regard for Mr. Stone, permitting him to in-
flate his reputation as an unsnobbish democrat at my expense is not one
of them.
                                                    Robert Sherrill

I. F. Stone replies:
Sorry, that was dumb of me.

the eve of a new nominating convention, it may be useful to
recall that the great heroes of the party of the common man
have not been of lowly origin. Its four outstanding Presidents were all of the Gracchus type, upper-class leaders of
lower-class upsurge. All the Democratic revolutionaries—as
their fond followers hailed them—were men of comfortable fortune and privileged position. Jefferson and Roosevelt were landed aristocrats. Jackson—the only one of them
born in poverty—amassed a fortune in land and slaves, in
shrewd alliance with the haves against the have-nots of the
frontier. The kind of early hardship Wilson knew was of
the genteel and socially secure variety that afflicts the sons
of ill-paid Presbyterian ministers in well-to-do Southern
small towns.

Except for Jefferson, all were originally of rather conservative views, and none was ever as radical as he sounded.
Even Jefferson, as Richard Hofstadter observed in his perceptive *The American Political Tradition*, confined "the
generous and emancipating thoughts for which his name is
so justly prized" almost entirely to his private correspondence. To their overwrought political opponents, all four
seemed to be traitors to their class, reckless leaders of the
angry dispossessed. But unlike the Gracchi, none of them
ever nourished the tree of liberty with more than a few
drops pin-pricked from the privileged, who bleed easily.
They were revolutionists only in an inflated and metaphori-
cal sense.

Jefferson affirmed the equality of man but never tried to
extend the right to vote beyond the propertied minority.
Jackson was the symbol rather than the leader of the Jack-
sonian Revolution; its battles for universal white manhood
suffrage and free public education were won before he became President. Wilson, like Teddy Roosevelt, began by
being disdainful of the progressive tide they both later rode
to fame and power. The measure of Wilson's New Freedom—how glamorously our liberal patent medicines have
been labeled!—is that its principal surviving monuments are
the Federal Reserve System and the Federal Trade Com-

mission. The former, after all the attacks upon "the Money Trust" which led up to it, merely rationalized our central banking system. The latter, which was to protect the country against the abuses of big business, long ago degenerated into a toothless watchdog.

Though Utopian socialism had as great a vogue among American intellectuals before the Civil War as Communism did before the Second World War, and the American Socialist party was a living force before and for a decade after the First World War, socialistic ideas—as distinct from specific reforms which the Socialists were first to advocate —never penetrated the Democratic party. Even Roosevelt, who was ready to try anything to get the country out of the Great Depression, stopped short at the socialistic. Early in his Administration there was some agitation "to put idle hands and idle machines together"; there was an attempt to do just this in an idle Ohio mattress factory. I can remember my disappointment as a young editorial writer on one of the few pro-New Deal newspapers in the country when the project was so quickly nipped in the bud that it seems to have disappeared from the history books. Production for use—a forgotten phrase—was taboo. The Roosevelt Administration preferred to make jobs by "leaf-raking" and public works rather than disturb production for profit. FDR's celebrated pragmatism ended where the profit system began. His successors show no disposition to go beyond it.

The Democrats, as the party of the agrarian and small property-owner, and of the urban machines based on the proletarian immigrant, have tended to be readier for social reform than the Republicans, but not beyond the framework of the capitalist system. Indeed, the Democrats are super-sensitive to attack as "soft on communism." This is often a major determinant of what they will do in foreign and domestic policy. But the record is full of anomalies. Wilson began the non-recognition policy the Republicans applied to the Soviet Union. Roosevelt broke the diplomatic embargo and extended recognition to Moscow.

Should increased international tension or domestic turbulence bring a flare-up of our characteristic American anti-Communist paranoia, it is hard to tell which party would be first to pander to it. It was the liberal Democrat Wilson who sent Eugene Debs to jail in World War I and the conservative Republican Harding who pardoned him. The first American witch hunt after the Russian Revolution was launched by Wilson's Attorney General A. Mitchell Palmer. But it was the Republicans who revived the Red mania as a political tactic early in the Great Depression under the now forgotten Hamilton Fish, the first sniffer-outer of what came to be known later as "un-American activities." Right-wing Democrats and Republicans carried this on as a weapon against the New Deal and, with covert help from J. Edgar Hoover, revived it again as soon as the Second World War ended.

The purpose was to smear the period of Democratic dominance (in the ugly words later used by Eisenhower's unscrupulous Attorney General, Herbert Brownell) as "twenty years of treason." The Democratic reaction was an attempt to run at one and the same time with the hounds of anti-Communism and the hares of Jeffersonian liberalism. Truman instituted a loyalty purge within the government which put a premium on mediocrity and cast a pall of fear on the capital long before Joe McCarthy. His Smith Act prosecution of the Communists was begun in 1948 as a weapon against the Henry Wallace third-party movement. But his Attorney General, Tom Clark, opposed the repressive Mundt-Nixon bill, and Truman himself vetoed it as an effort at thought control in a message which was in the great tradition of Jefferson's opposition to the Alien and Sedition laws.

Panicky Senate Democratic liberals, among them Humphrey and Morse, had tried to block this bill with a substitute which was in some ways worse—a bill setting up detention camps in time of war or national emergency for persons suspected of being potential spies or saboteurs. This monstrosity marked the debut in American legislation of the idea that a man might be jailed not for something he did but for something it was thought he might do. The right-wingers cheerfully tacked this on to their own bill whereupon these liberals turned about and voted to support the President's veto of the entire measure. But a Congress under the influence of the anti-Red sentiment stirred by the Korean war passed it over Truman's veto. Thanks to this law, America some day may see concentration camps used against black or white radicals.

Humphrey's civil liberties record during this and the McCarthy period followed the standard Democratic pattern. He made occasional speeches against McCarthyism but was himself a junior McCarthy in purging the Farmer-Labor party of Minnesota and investigating the labor movement, particularly the United Electrical Workers, for communistic influence. The high-watermark of Humphrey's cowardice as a liberal, or defensive hysteria as an anti-Communist, was set in 1954, when with the same group of Senate liberals (this time including John F. Kennedy[3]), Humphrey sponsored the outlawry provisions of the Communist Control Act of 1954. These set up standards so sweeping for determining who was a Communist that Humphrey, Morse, and the other sponsors could have been declared Communists too. It was a Republican, John Sherman Cooper, who made the one principled speech against this nonsense, and it was Kefauver who cast the lone vote against it.

Humphrey, as the current villain of the antiwar forces, is being blamed for all this, but his record is no worse than that of Wayne Morse, their current hero, or of many other good liberals like the late Herbert Lehman. They made a shabby record during Joe McCarthy's heyday; it was a Republican Administration and a group of Senate conservatives who finally did McCarthy in. But Humphrey's record has a rich flatulence characteristic of the man; he never does anything by halves, and has a genius for making a fool of himself. "I am tired," he said in 1954, "of reading headlines

[3] He had voted with Nixon in the House to override Truman's veto of the Mundt-Nixon bill and had since been elected to the Senate.

about being a leftist." So in the Senate that year we find him deploring the disbandment of his own little labor witch hunt subcommittee, offering to make its files available to Joe McCarthy, declaring that "rooting out Communist infiltration . . . is priority business" and boasting that his Communist outlawry amendment would force every Senator to stand up and be counted. "We are going to lay the issue on the line," he exulted, "and not on the fringes."

When the Eisenhower Administration, as well as many of Humphrey's old ADA friends, objected that outlawry would be unconstitutional, Morse chortled gleefully, "It now appears that the White House thinks the Senator from Minnesota is a little too hard on the Communists." Morse had lent his prestige as a constitutional lawyer to the Humphrey bill, and still boasts—to show his own political purity—that he once helped father a bill to outlaw the Communists. This whole episode reached its comic climax when Humphrey told the Senate that a man "does not have to become a member of the Communist party to express unorthodox ideas. Let him become a member of other parties, or of the Republican or the Democratic party, if he wants to express unorthodox ideas." Someone should have unfurled a travel-style poster in the Senate chamber at the close of that speech, "Join the GOP and overturn the world."

Marx in his *Eighteenth Brumaire* said history was a form of politics. A corollary needs, however, to be added. The larger the ingredient of politics, the poorer the quality of the history. This is particularly true when the historical estimates reflect immediate rather than long-range political considerations. Judgments made in the heat of a presidential campaign are bad enough; those molded by the passions of a campaign for the nomination are worse. Four years ago in the pages of this same *New York Review* I poked fun at Humphrey's inflated rhetoric and his attempts to ingratiate himself with businessmen, but welcomed as a liberal victory Johnson's choice of Humphrey as running mate. Eugene McCarthy then appeared only as a moribund Senate liberal who had played ball with the oil interests on the Senate Fi-

nance Committee and was the choice of Texas Governor
Connally. Goldwater was the menace; Johnson was not
only the lesser evil but the hope of peace. Humphrey's
more distant past, like Morse's, was forgiven because of the
part Humphrey had played in the fight for a nuclear test
ban, for disarmament, for civil rights, indeed for almost
every social reform measure of the preceding eight years.

Had McCarthy become Vice President, Humphrey might
today be the hero of the peace forces. The reversals of
mood and ideology required, despite the record we are
now emphasizing, would have been no greater than those
which occurred in the case of Robert F. Kennedy, or
Wayne Morse, or of the Americans for Democratic Action,
when that organization of homogenized and certified anti-
Communist liberals—which Humphrey helped to found—
turned against the war and Humphrey himself. Ambition,
conviction, recognition of objective circumstance, may be
more powerful than past position and any desire for con-
sistency. Who for that matter would have dreamed a year
ago that Allard K. Lowenstein could hoist that most lacka-
daisical of all the Senate Democratic liberals, Eugene Mc-
Carthy, onto a white horse?

The historian has the good fortune to begin after fate has
given him the outcome; he can then decide according to his
political philosophy the factors which made it "inevitable"
—no word ever more richly deserved the disparagement of
inverted double commas. The man who must write before
we know what will happen can only rework past history to
fit the outcome his heart fears or desires. Wisely operated
oracles, as far back as Delphi, knew that their only safety
was in ambiguity. But voters and those who presume to advise them face an inescapable test—the need to pick from
two usually ambiguous choices. Which brings us back to
the magic squares of the American two-party system, and
why this system sometimes seems to be government by rou-
lette. You put down your money but you never really
know what you're going to get.

The war. The war. The war. It ruined Johnson. And

Johnson ruined Humphrey. And a Humphrey-Nixon choice this time may ruin the American political system. The hardest part of my pre-convention assignment is to assess the history of the Democratic party and the nature of its seemingly all but certain candidate in the light of the war, and the overwhelming need to end it.

The first thing to be said about the war is that it has become the overriding issue because we are unable to win it. Our past is littered with Vietnams, small countries on which we have worked our will in the name of anti-Communism and, before Communism, of liberty. But the deeds arouse little protest when (as Lady Macbeth urged) done quickly. Johnson was as arrogant in the Dominican Republic, Dulles and the CIA as unscrupulous in Guatemala, but neither brought any widespread revulsion. Our national conscience did not twinge until the military situation hurt. Vietnam would be no issue if the Diem dictatorship had succeeded, if Kennedy's "advisers" had been enough to subdue the revolt against it, if Johnson's bombing of the North had worked, or if Westmoreland's strategy could have gone on to the point where there were no more Vietnamese left, and we could be sure we didn't have to start body-counting the Chinese, too. If the Viet Cong go on causing us enough trouble, any President will have to make peace because victory isn't worth what it would cost, and the wider risks it would entail. This is why John F. Kennedy to his credit drew back twice on Cuba. So we co-exist with Communism 90 miles off Key West but decline to compromise with it 9,000 miles from California. To the fresh eye, the frontiers of freedom must seem downright whimsical.

The second thing to be said is that successful wars, especially if short and profitable, are popular. When Lincoln as a Whig Congressman opposed the Mexican war, the result was his defeat for reelection. Pulitzer and Hearst made circulation, McKinley won reelection, and Teddy Roosevelt earned his glamorous reputation with that "splendid little war" against Spain which marked the debut of American

imperialism in the Far East. The Philippines were our first
Vietnam in Asia, Aguinaldo the first Ho Chi Minh we encountered; there was no lack of enthusiasm when we set
out, in the slogans then current, to "help our little brown
brother," and if he rejected that help to "civilize 'em with a
Krag." The Krag was the M-16 of the time. An Anti-
Imperialist League sprang into action between 1898 and
1900. But a new book[4] which has gone neglected shows
that its leaders were upper-class conservatives and liberal
gentlemen like Godkin of *The Nation*. Perhaps this study
of the first American anti-imperialist movement has attracted so little attention during the current anti-imperialist
agitation because in this it runs so counter to political
clichés. The popular side was pro-imperialist.

A lot of nonsense has to be cleared away if we are to
chart a fresh course. We Americans are neither the benefac-
tors we think ourselves nor the devils our enemies see in us.
Most peoples at some time in their history are expansionist
and the expansion is always carried on in the name of some
benevolent mission. The Czars found this in Pan-Slavism,
the Kaiser in *Kultur*, the French in their *mission civilatrice*,
and the British in the white man's burden, which was heavy
with loot from the darker continents. Revolutionary movements, whether religious or secular, are particularly expansionist. From Mohammed to Mao their leaders have felt the
urge to bestow the new faith as widely as possible, if necessary by the scimitar or gun.

Among the smaller peoples, our current victims, the
Vietnamese, themselves rank high on any scale of aggressive
imperialism. Their acquisition of the Mekong delta, which
they took from the Khmers, goes back only to the eighteenth century, and Black Nationalists who see the Vietnam
war as whitey vs. colored should speak to the darker-
skinned Montagnards, the dispossessed "nigras" of the Vietnamese peninsula.

Among the big peoples we rank high as land-grabbers.

[4] Robert L. Beisner, *Twelve Against Empire—The Anti-Imperialists:
1898–1900* (New York: McGraw-Hill, 1968). I recommend it highly.

We pushed to the Pacific and took half of Mexico as our Manifest Destiny, reluctantly abandoned our designs on Canada, dominated the rest of the hemisphere in the name of Pan-Americanism, set out to make the world safe for democracy under Wilson, and are now rigging elections as far away as Southeast Asia in the name of self-determination. Nations, like gases, tend to expand until stopped and contained by countervailing forces they cannot overcome. We may be headed for containment by China.

Another obstacle to clear thinking is the myth that the people are inherently peaceful. This is part of the democratic ideology. It was born on the eve of the French Revolution, and survived proof to the contrary furnished by the fresh enthusiasm of the Revolutionary and Napoleonic armies. In our own country the Democrats as the popular party have been expansionist from the beginning. They were the agrarian party, and hungered for more land. It was mercantile and capitalist New England which was cold to the War of 1812, even though the war was presumably fought for free maritime commerce; the planters of the South saw the war as a way to solidify their hold on the Floridas while the farmers of the Northwest wanted to annex Canada. The Monroe Doctrine, that first monument of naïve North American imperialism, was a Democratic party accomplishment.

The secret of this unilateral declaration of a protectorate over the hemisphere was that Canning's original proposal for a joint Anglo-American declaration would have included a self-denying ordinance, pledging both powers to seek no territorial aggrandizement. When Monroe consulted Jefferson as the party's greatest living elder statesman, the latter replied, "Do we wish to acquire to our own confederacy any one or more of the Spanish provinces? I candidly confess that I have ever looked on Cuba as the most interesting addition which could be made to our system of States." [5] Jefferson would have accepted Canning's

[5] See p. 98 of the J. Reuben Clark Memorandum on the Monroe Doctrine published by the State Department in 1930 as Secretary of State

invitation, though with this imperialist regret. Calhoun, too, was ready "even if it should pledge the U.S. not to take Cuba or Texas." But the prevailing view embodied in the Monroe Doctrine only barred the transfer of any territory in the Western Hemisphere to a *European* power. Though all this was done in the name of making the Western Hemisphere safe for freedom, we declared our neutrality as between Spain and the colonies in revolt against her. Secretly we often favored Spanish rule.

In the Clark memorandum (see footnote five) the State Department for the first time disclosed instructions sent to our Minister to Madrid in 1829 urging Spain to keep control of Cuba. Bolívar's liberating armies were freeing the slaves and "the sudden emancipation of a numerous slave population . . . could not but be very sensibly felt upon the adjacent shores of the United States." The Vietnamese war is in the pattern set by our relations with Latin America: in the name of liberty, we supported first foreign and then native oligarchies.

On one refreshing occasion our unctuous pretensions were abandoned for plain talk. When Cleveland's Secretary of State warned Britain to keep hands off Venezuela in 1895, he interpreted the Monroe Doctrine with a frank imperial arrogance even Lyndon Johnson in his most brash private moments could hardly equal:

Today [Secretary Olney warned Britain] the United States is practically sovereign on this continent and its fiat is law upon the subjects to which it confines its interposition. Why? It is not because of the pure friendship or good will felt for it. It is not simply by reason of its high character as a civilized state, nor because wisdom and justice and equity are the invariable characteristics of the dealings with the United States. It is because in addition to all other grounds, its infinite resources combined with its isolated position render it master of the situation and practically invulnerable as against any or all powers.[6]

Stimson moved toward a Good Neighbor policy. The documents there printed for the first time from the Department files are the best antidote to the mythology of the Monroe Doctrine.

[6] The Clark Memorandum, p. 159.

Five years after Olney's note, the Democratic party for the first time in its history did indeed campaign against McKinley in 1900 on an anti-imperialist platform, but they were "at a disadvantage," as Robert Beisner's study of the anti-imperialist movement shows, "because they had bellowed for war in 1898 as loudly as anyone." William Jennings Bryan, the party's foremost anti-imperialist leader, "first volunteered to fight in Cuba, then declared himself an opponent of expansion, and finally urged Senate approval of the peace treaty" by which we annexed the Philippines and set out on the course we are still pursuing, of trying to make the Pacific as much a *Mare Nostrum* as the Atlantic or the Caribbean. Indeed our Navy's ambition is to control all the seven seas, and all the Eurasian outlets to them, from the Bosporus to the Formosan straits. Only the rhetoric of anti-Communism keeps us from seeing that no nation in history has ever had such grandiose imperial pretentions, such *hubris, chutzpah,* or brass.

The choice now is between disengagement and disaster. To scale down these colossal ambitions is the first necessity of American politics. But the retreat from empire, as the experience of other great nations has shown, is traumatic. There could be no poorer choice than Humphrey for that task. The first requirement is to disown Johnson's war, and Humphrey cannot disentangle himself, even if he would, from his association with it. Humphrey's nomination would ratify, while McCarthy's would rebuke, the decisions which put U.S. combat troops again on the mainland of Asia. The second count against a Humphrey choice is that his is the very type of spurious liberal evangelism which has provided idealistic cover for our effort to dominate the world. McCarthy's more astringent and sophisticated views offer some hope of a change. We need to recover our cool.

A third count against Humphrey is that he has given no reason to believe that he is any more ready than Johnson to negotiate a compromise in Vietnam. He went far beyond mere loyalty to Johnson when he told *U.S. News & World Report* (May 27), "If Nixon and Humphrey should be the candidates in the general election, I don't think our views of the war would be far apart." This is a war Nixon has wanted us to fight since 1954. Humphrey told students at St. Paul last May 27 we ought to be willing to stay at the conference table "in Paris for months, and if necessary for years, until a satisfactory solution was reached."

This is in accord with the Johnson strategy of defusing anti-war protest with the talks, keeping the fighting at a level the public will tolerate and hoping that somehow we can restore a non-Communist South Vietnam, like South Korea, in our sphere of influence. Humphrey's speech of July 12, supposedly designed to chart a foreign policy of his own, sounds remarkably like the same Johnson-Rusk cracked record. On the one hand Humphrey says, as they do, that "we are not the world's policeman," but on the other hand we must be prepared to fulfill mutual defense commitments where others "violate frontiers and foster local turmoil" as, though he did not say so, in Vietnam. So we are back where Johnson started. Nowhere here is there the necessary recognition that we may only make "local turmoil" worse by the magnitude and clumsiness of our intervention. This is the beginning of wisdom, but Humphrey is a long way from it.

The psychological and institutional obstacles to a retreat, not just from Vietnam but from the future Vietnams that a Pax Americana makes unavoidable, are so great as to make one doubt its possibility. A new President must face up to a military bureaucracy so huge that its weight in the scales of policy is almost insuperable. It is not that the Pax Americana policy has made such a huge machine necessary. It is that the existence of the machine, and all the careers and interests which depend upon it, require continuance of the Pax Americana. We are the prisoners of this machine, which must find work commensurate with its size to justify its existence. The magnitude of the monster is indicated by the growth of the military budget from $12 billion just before the Korean war only eighteen years ago to its current $80 billion and the $102 billion recently requested of Secretary

Clifford by the Joint Chiefs of Staff. This is like trying to keep a dinosaur as a household pet. It will eat us out of house and home. But only McCarthy has even touched on this subject.

The psychological obstacles are as great. The average man approaches the problem of war with simple reactions of anxiety and threatened virility thousands of years old. There is a strong movement for peace, but there is also a strong contingent of cavemen among us, and it is hard to see which is the majority; the same people often belong to both categories. Reagan and Wallace speak for large constituencies, too. In Vietnam as in Korea the Democrats *have* kept the wars limited while Reagan, like MacArthur before him, speaks for a Republican right wing which thinks the whole business can be ended in no more time than it takes to go from the seventeenth to the eighteenth hole by dropping a bomb on Peking and another on Moscow.

The two urgent issues are the Vietnamese war and the black revolt. Both require solutions for which we are poorly conditioned. One is to give way in Vietnam to a Communist, though also nationalist, tide. The other is to deal with the aspirations of the blacks, and the other poor, which can only be met by fundamental changes, a real redistribution of income from haves to have-nots, and an intervention of the State deeper and more far-reaching than anything America has ever known before. The only party less prepared for this than the Democrats, though not much less so, is the Republican party.

The issues, however, are beyond that unspoken ideological consensus within which the two-party system operates. The Democratic party, unlike the Republican, has some legitimate claim to being the party of "the people." But the people for whom it speaks turn out on closer examination to be middle-class owners of property, white-collar workers, or the organized working class. The urban and rural poor, and all but the thin upper strata of the blacks and our other "colored" minorities, are not really a part of its constituency.

They are outside "the people" in whose name it claims to speak. Unfortunately for revolutionary theorists, the more fortunate, those with something to lose, are the overwhelming majority. The poor, white and black, are but a lower fifth of the population. Should the Democratic party move too far in the direction of taking them in, and serving their interests, it is likely to lose much of its white and skilled-worker followers to the Republican party. It is this which makes the Democratic party look so unsatisfactory to the black radicals and the New Left, a purveyor of half measures rather than fundamental change. But in this the party faithfully reflects a majority constituency, and in this sense it is truly *representative*.

The new radicals generally are unwilling to face up to this reality. They prefer to believe that there is something wrong with the party, or with something called "the system," or that society is sick, rather than admit that what they are revolting against is the majority itself. To admit that would be too difficult and too untactful a break with the dominant ideology of democracy. Black nationalist separatism is fantasy based on despair but in one respect it is more realistic than the New Left, for in proposing separation it recognizes that what it is combating is the white majority and not some clique, conspiracy, or perverse ruling elite which has somehow led "the people" astray. In a democratic society it is always assumed that the people are good, as in theology it is always assumed that God is good. Evil is an accident, or the work of the devil. When large numbers of ordinary men commit some outrage against humanity, it is tacitly assumed that somehow they are not part of "the people."

That myth, the Common Man, is the theoretical sovereign of democratic society, and when he turns up in a racist mob or a typical veterans' organization, ideology literally turns off our vision. Democratic political stereotypes remain stalwartly non- and pre-Freudian because you can't win elections by telling voters they themselves are at fault. It is easier to let them off the hook by blaming some abstraction. Adam's sins are still attributed to some serpent which crept

into the Garden. It is the nature of the white majority, and
of man, that brings the two-party system to the verge of
breakdown when faced with the need to swallow a military
defeat and to tax the whites for the benefit of the blacks.
The danger is that the white majority may choose instead to
follow a simplistic demagogy which advocates as the way
out a get-tough policy at home and abroad. Against that
darkening backdrop, McCarthy is a wan hope.

August 22, 1968
*New York Review**

* Those selections not specified as taken from *The New York Review
of Books* appeared in *I. F. Stone's Bi-Weekly.*

PARTY OF THE RICH
AND WELL-BORN

The Republican party began as, and is again, a minority
party. It originated as a third party in 1854, when the slavery issue was splitting the Democrats and the Whigs. It is,
according to Dr. Gallup, really a third party again today. In
1940 a poll of between-election leanings showed that 42
percent identified themselves as Democrats, 38 percent as
Republicans, and 20 percent as independents. When Gallup
repeated the same poll in the fall of 1967, there were more
independents than Republicans. The Democrats still held at
42 percent but the Republicans had dropped to 27 and the
independents risen to 31 percent.

Neither party can win without this floating independent
vote, but the Republicans must get more of it than the
Democrats. It is indicative that the only two men to be
elected President on the Republican ticket in the last forty
years had not been identified with the party when they entered politics. Herbert Hoover had been a strong Wilsonian
while Eisenhower only four years before had been wooed

by the ADA. Both Hoover and Eisenhower won because
their appeal was wider than the party's. To paraphrase
Sholom Aleichem, it's hard to be a Republican in American
politics, a real one that is.

The statistics would seem to show that in 1968 the best
way to elect a Republican President would be to pick a candidate who looks and sounds as little like a Republican as
possible. By that standard the candidate least likely to succeed would seem to be Richard Nixon; the one who best
fills the bill would be John Lindsay. The Republicans
would do best if they went underground, with a crypto-
Republican candidate who could if necessary swear that he
had never really carried a party card.

This is as extraordinary a reversal as may be found in
American history. From 1860 until 1932—a space of sev-
enty-two years, more than two generations—only two
Democrats were elected President, Cleveland and Wilson.
All the others were Republican. A flood of election-year
books seeks to explain or change this history. Most of them
are as dull as the party itself; except in the days of Lincoln
and Teddy Roosevelt, the Republicans have always been the
duller of the two parties. The best books I have found in
this tidal wave of ephemera are George H. Mayer's *The
Republican Party 1854–1966*, a new edition brought up to
date of a book which first appeared in 1964, and Milton
Viorst's *Fall From Grace: The Republican Party and the
Puritan Ethic*. The former is a definitive and scholarly
work, astringently realistic but rather plodding in style, as
if the author himself couldn't help getting bored by his subject; the latter is short and lively, a swift and engaging synthesis of the work in the field, including Mayer's, but with
many fresh insights—Viorst shows real gifts as an historian.

The myths about the Republican party these two books
explode were exploded a generation ago by Charles Beard
in his moving and stately *Rise of American Civilization*.
Mayer and Viorst depict the Republicans as the party of
business and of the WASP. Viorst tries to make the story a
little more interesting by linking the party with the Puritan
ethic, though it is hard to tell where Puritanism ends and

plain acquisitiveness begins. This is no novel thesis. The surprise is that at this late date it should be attacked as "outrageous" and "audacious" by a Republican newspaperman who is a Washington correspondent. In the Washington *Post*, Robert D. Novak called Viorst a "super-liberal" and accused him of overlooking the party's left wing! [1]

In some periods of their history and on some issues, the two parties seem indistinguishable. Foreigners often fail to tell them apart, and Americans in some periods have spoken of them as Tweedledum and Tweedledee. Both parties are loose coalitions, warring multi-party systems, held together by habit and convenience. An operative definition of the Republican party is that it is the one which doesn't have a left wing, but only an occasional, slight and passing protuberance left of center, like a La Guardia or a Wayne Morse. Herbert Hoover, on his return from Europe in 1920 to enter politics, announced that he objected "as much to the reactionary group in the Republican party as to the radical group in the Democratic party." One cannot imagine his reversing this language and attacking the radicals in the Republican party. The last time the Republicans had a faction which could properly be termed radical was a century ago during Reconstruction. The only Republican President whom Wall Street ever regarded as a dangerous fellow was Teddy Roosevelt. In 1904, running against a conservative Democrat, Judge Alton B. Parker, the mercurial and demagogic Teddy sounded incendiary, even if his assaults on "malefactors of great wealth" were largely verbal. In retrospect the first Roosevelt, with his cult of war and masculinity, his imperialist adventures in Latin America and his naïve racism, sounds less like a radical than a premature Fascist, an American Mussolini before his time.

The men who practice politics and those who write about them are two different breeds. The former are concerned with power, and with interests and ideas as means to achieve it. The latter tend to overemphasize the ideas with

[1] Novak collaborates on a syndicated column which sometimes seems to specialize in uncovering hidden left-wing influences nobody else had noticed.

which the scramble for power is rationalized. Our party system calls for treatment by an anthropologist. It is a form of sport, especially a spectator sport. It is a variant of what William James sought when he called for a moral equivalent of war; the party system is an easy way of working off aggressive instincts. It resembles gang warfare, in that it is a means by which the bold and power-hungry, recruiting a handful of followers, can rule the territory they have staked out and enjoy the combat for dominion against rival gangs. They hand out favors and sell protection. Politics is also a form of business; the same division of labor which produces bankers and bus drivers also produces politicians and office holders.

Perhaps the American two-party system seems less mysterious when one observes that traces of two parties can be found in almost all societies, though in one-party dictatorships you may have to look for the other party in jail or concentration camps. The purges in the hierarchies of the communist states reflect the fact that even these One-and-Only parties are really two. Common to all societies are the same two types, the hards and the softs, the standpatters and the reformers, those who believe in coercion and those who believe in persuasion, those who think stability is best preserved by holding fast to the past and those who would bend a little with changing events and aspirations. The Democrats may waver but the Republicans stand with the former in all these pairs.

From the standpoint of interests and classes, the American two-party system may be seen as a division between the more and the less favored, the older stock and the newer immigrant, the businessman and the farmer, the creditor and the debtor, the employer and his workman. The Hamiltonians, the Federalists, the Whigs, and the Republicans appear as the spokesmen for the former, the anti-Federalists, the Jeffersonians, and the Democrats as the spokesmen for the latter. The big money has favored the former but also bought influence in the latter. But it is the Jeffersonian and Democratic strain which has constantly widened democracy and in periods of hard times responded to the needs of the poorer elements. The welfare state is the creation of the Democrats and the bane of the Republicans. This is no small difference.

The Republican party was born of the slavery issue as a sectional party after slavery split both the existing national parties, the Democrats and the Whigs. Most farmers—except for a rich handful, who tended to be Whig—were Democrats until the free soil dispute split the free farmer from the slave farmer. The two could not exist side by side. When the Kansas-Nebraska Act and the Dred Scott decision destroyed the Missouri Compromise and threw open all the Western lands to colonization by slave holders, the Democratic party split. The Western farmer became a Republican. He remained a Republican out of inertia and filial piety until the twenties, when hard times hit the Farm Belt and Republican Presidents vetoed three different attempts to give the farmer forms of crop control which would be the equivalent for him of the protective tariff for manufacturers. These vetoes were to give the West to the Democrats and the New Deal.

To say that the Republican party was born of the slavery issue is not to say that it began as a crusade against slavery. This is a myth Mayer and Viorst easily dispose of. "At no point in its anti-slavery campaign," Viorst writes, "was there any sign that the Republican party was moved by any compassion for the black man." On the contrary, as Viorst points out, "In the Republican constitution of Kansas, adopted by the Yankees in the heat of the anti-slavery campaign, free Negroes were forbidden even to enter the State." Illinois banned Negro immigration by a two-to-one margin in a popular referendum. From Ohio to California, in all that free soil territory, Negroes were excluded from voting. The Republican press in the Northwest, Viorst relates, "proudly supported the politics of what it called with much precision, 'the white man's party.' "

The story is one the black, or Afro-American, must read with despair. The abolitionists were almost as hated in the

North as in the South. The two predecessor parties of the
Republicans, the Liberty and the Free Soil parties, though
they concentrated only on keeping slavery out of the
Western territories, were handicapped, Mayer writes, because "they could not sell the moral arguments for the containment of slavery." The Republican party succeeded by
soft-pedaling the issue of slavery altogether and concentrating on economic issues which would attract Northern businessmen and Western farmers.

"Perhaps the temper of the Republican convention"
which nominated Lincoln "can best be established," Viorst
relates, "by noting that the delegates baldly rejected a proposal to endorse from the Declaration of Independence the
statement that 'all men are created equal.' " Later they reversed themselves "but only after a bitter fight on the convention floor." The platform, with its equivocation on slavery and its espousal of protective tariffs, free homesteads,
and internal improvements, "abundantly demonstrated that
the Republican party had safely made the shift from a coalition held together by the fear of slavery to one united by a
common vision of material gain."

Lincoln, the Great Emancipator, looked to the radicals of
his time—as he begins to look to ours—as the Great Equiv-
ocator. The American Anti-Slavery Society, in comment-
ing on his nomination, saw it as "a convenient hook
whereon to hang appeals at once to a moderate anti-slavery
feeling and to a timid conservatism." Ambition had led him,
Viorst notes, "to align himself with the Whigs, 'the better
people' of the community, rather than the Democrats, the
party of the Southern poor." He became a Republican after
1856. His philosophy of the fluid society "captured the essence of middle class Republicanism." Lincoln summed this
up when he said, "I don't believe in a law to prevent a man
from getting rich. It would do more harm than good. So
while we do not propose to war upon capital, we do wish to
allow the humblest man an equal chance to get rich with
everybody else."

Privately Lincoln felt an abhorrence for the oppression

of the Negro but in public he found it expedient to take an evasive position. In the Douglas debates he denied that he had ever favored "the social and political equality of the white and black races." Viorst completes his portrait of Lincoln by saying, "It is probable that he was at least a step ahead of the Republican party generally in his sympathy for the Negro as a human being. But on one point he was in firm accord with the Republican position. Lincoln would by no means risk war to free the slaves." It was only "the shells which fell on Fort Sumter" which "ended the equivocation." Today's racial turmoil springs from the fact that the Negro was a side issue in a conflict between two classes of propertied white men, the Southern planter on one side and the Northern businessman and farmer on the other.

Lincoln's humanity, imperishably expressed, lifts him beyond detraction. But his compassion was mostly for white men, and only a little for black. "After years of fighting," Viorst writes with painful justice, "he remained faithful to the view that the Negro was less a human being than a divisive factor between the sections." He had no desire "to envenom further the hatred between North and South by emancipating the slaves." His attitude seemed if anything, Viorst goes on, "to have hardened over the course of the war." He spoke of black men "as of a military commodity, of no more intrinsic importance than cavalry horses."

The radical Republicans themselves saw the Negro as an instrument. Viorst quotes a speech by Sumner of Massachusetts in which that radical Senator warned that only through the vote of enfranchised black men "can you save the national debt from the inevitable repudiation which awaits it when recent rebels in conjunction with Northern allies [Democrats] once more bear sway. He is our best guarantee. Use him." The radicals' objective, Viorst writes, "was to make the Negro into a tool, not into a productive, self-reliant human being." Without land the Negro could not attain full citizenship. There was talk for a time "of confiscating major rebel estates for the distribution of parcels among the Negroes, but the Republicans were too

devoted to the sanctity of private property." The conflict
ended with the Negro half serf, half free. We are only now
beginning to pay for the full consequences.

Those sins of the fathers have set our teeth on edge. Suddenly those half-forgotten battles during Reconstruction
over "forty acres and a mule" loom up as the one immediately relevant episode in the dreary and familiar annals of
the party. The years which stretch from Grant to Eisenhower—two victorious and easy-going generals, only dimly
aware of what was going on around them in the White
House—are years of smugness and enrichment. Nothing
more fully discloses the nature of the "party of Lincoln"
than the fact that the Negro made his greatest advances
under the Democrats, and that Franklin D. Roosevelt,
Truman, Kennedy, and Johnson recruited him into the
same party with the Southern white supremacist. Political
history shows few stranger alliances.

The corollary may be a Republican return to power as
the whiter of the two white men's parties. For the first time
the GOP may become the party of the working-class white
and the non-WASP. Recently Richard Nixon envisioned
himself as the leader of a new coalition made up of "the
Republicans, the New Liberals, the New South and the
black militants." No other candidate has gone into so splendid a trance. The "new coalition" will more likely turn out
to be a coalition of white against black.

The Republican party has always seen itself as the party
of the self-made man. Usually nobody is readier to step on
those below him than the man who made it upward on his
own. The psychology of the self-made man now finds its
counterpart in the psychology of whole classes who think
they made it on their own—so why can't the Negro?
Whether they join the Republican party or not, the urban
white working class, the second and third generation of non-
WASP immigrants who have hitherto been Democrats because they felt like underdogs, are acquiring the Republican
outlook with success and turning rightward in reaction
against the rising revolt of the Negro. Their movement up-

ward from proletarian slums to mass-produced suburban villas, their fear of Negro violence and their aversion to Negro neighbors may make them Republican for the first time in their history. The white American working class had been split historically by the prejudices of the native Yankee against the foreign immigrant, whether Irish or East European. The Know-Nothings were the Birchite wing of the first Republicans. The immigrants, while hostile, like white workers generally, to the free Negro and the Abolitionist, stayed with the Democrats as the party which welcomed the new arrival. White workers may now close ranks against the black.

Thus the GOP's failure to reconstruct the South in 1868 and set the Negro wholly free may pave the way for its return to power in 1968. If so this will be the prelude to fresh disasters. It will only demonstrate again the GOP's utter incapacity for any task that requires social revolution. It can no more carry out basic changes at the expense of the well-to-do than an elephant can fly.

With the end of the Civil War, its brief flirtation with idealism was ended. Big business rose to undisputed dominance. The Republican party was its instrument. Politics became secondary to acquisition. Business made the fundamental decisions, helping itself liberally to the public lands and public treasury in the Hamiltonian tradition while recommending laissez-faire and rugged individualism to the worker and farmer it exploited. That era ended in 1929 with the Great Depression, but the mentality of that earlier period not only lives on beneath the surface of the welfare state but is showing signs of revival in the current emphasis among Democrats and Republicans alike on the need to "enlist" free enterprise in the war against poverty.

Babbitt is making a comeback. Viorst quotes from Sinclair Lewis a speech by that archetypal Republican small-town businessman of the twenties to show "how little the Puritan-social-Darwinian ethic had changed after more than a half century of wear." Babbitt angrily tells his children, "The first thing you got to understand is that all this uplift

and flipflop and settlement work and recreation is nothing
in God's world but the entering wedge of socialism. The
sooner a man learns he isn't going to be coddled, and he
needn't expect a lot of free grub . . . the sooner he'll get
on the job and produce, produce, produce. That's what this
country needs." That is indistinguishable from Goldwater
or Reagan.

Neither Nixon nor Rockefeller is quite so naïve, but
both share the belief that somehow "free enterprise" can
again be our salvation, cleaning up the slums and making
jobs for the poor, with subsidies and tax benefits from the
public treasury. So for that matter does Bobby Kennedy, at
least at times and in some sections of the country. Suburbia,
with no desire to be taxed for the benefit of the poor and
blacks, sees this as a painless way out.

But there is no painless and certainly no profitable way to
correct a century of plunder and neglect. A whole spectrum of problems from the slum to air and water pollution
was created by giving free rein to free enterprise to make a
buck any way it saw fit. Those conditions are not going to
be corrected by the same entrepreneurial forces which created them. These exhortations to business to create jobs recall Hoover's pathetic exhortations to business during the
Great Depression. Bank presidents are built to resist evangelism. There has been no rush to invest money in Watts or
Harlem, and in Washington in the wake of the latest ghetto
riots it's suddenly hard even to get insurance in lily-white
neighborhoods. There is no more sensitive plant than the
buck. The party of business is even less likely than the
Democrats to engage in such heretical observations. Not
less but more public funds and social planning are required.
Unfortunately the white middle class is not in the mood and
that mood is determining the minstrelsy of this presidential
campaign.

Rockefeller would no doubt appear in Novack's eyes as
the "Republican left wing" that Viorst perversely overlooked. But there is no sign of a different tune from Rockefeller. On the contrary he has just discovered that no ideo-

logical barrier divides him from Reagan, the TV Tarzan of Republican politics. In foreign policy, Rockefeller has just suggested that we take over the protection of a whole arc of Asia from Iran to Japan, as if we did not already have enough trouble in Vietnam. He is as imperialist as Teddy Roosevelt; counter-insurgency and the Green Berets had their origin in the Rockefeller reports of the 1950's from which the Kennedys borrowed them. In domestic policy Rockefeller is giving ever more emphasis to "crime in the streets," notably, as Sidney E. Zion of the *New York Times* has just shown in *Ramparts* for June 15, 1968, in the shape of a program extraordinarily insensitive to constitutional safeguards, complete with wiretapping and allowing the police to stop-and-frisk, enter without knocking, and shoot-to-kill. So the Grand Old Party from right to "left" is firmly united again.

Recent events have magnified the occupational hazards of prophecy. The only surprise would be if there were no more surprises ahead. Something like a race is on between bigotry and apathy. The latest Gallup poll as this is written shows an almost equal loss of faith in both parties. The answers to the question which party could best handle our problems show that the largest number, 42 percent, see no difference or have no opinion. Thirty percent now think the Republicans would do best, only 28 percent the Democrats. The general lack of enthusiasm for any of the candidates reflects this same mood, compounded of the disillusion created by Johnson's peace promises in 1964—how believe anyone after that?—and an instinctive feeling that the issues raised by the Negro revolt are beyond solution by normal politics. But even Lyndon Johnson may stir nostalgia after four years of Nixon, or a combination of Rockefeller and Reagan. The Republicans are even less prepared than the Democrats to deal with the debacle of American imperialism in Southeast Asia and the beginning at home of racial war.

June 20, 1968
New York Review

A GRACEFUL PATSY
AGAINST A DIRTY
FIGHTER?

We have ourselves a candidate against Lyndon Johnson in the Democratic primaries but unless he picks up steam he's not going to set any voters on fire. Senator Eugene McCarthy was supposed to be the main attraction at the Conference of Concerned Democrats in Chicago last week-end. But his speech—like the one he delivered a few weeks earlier before SANE's national meeting in Chicago for labor leaders against the war in Vietnam—fell flat. He has wit, charm and grace. But he seems to lack heart and guts. This may seem a strange thing to say of the only Democrat willing to step out and challenge Johnson for the nomination. Unfortunately it seems to be true. Watching him at the press conference here at which he launched his candidacy, one began to wonder why he was running at all. A certain cynicism and defeatism seems basic to the man. This is no way to embark on a fight. His hero, Adlai, was a Hamlet. McCarthy gives one the uneasy feeling that he doesn't really give a damn.

The dreadful thing about presidential campaigns is that they make liars of us all. We join up, and stop saying what we think, for the good of the cause. I suppose I'll be swept up in this same kind of nonsense myself. But at least at the beginning a few honest words may be useful. We have to support McCarthy. A poor showing in the primaries for McCarthy will be a poor showing for peace. But he's also got to support us. And himself. It's no easy matter for a politician to challenge the head of his party. It may be political suicide. To embark on so risky an undertaking half-heartedly is the worst possible policy. The only safety lies in shooting the works. There's no other way to a long-shot victory and anyway that's the way to enjoy a wonderful, even if losing, battle in a good cause. If McCarthy couldn't evoke enthusiasm from dissident laborites and dissident Democrats just dying for a new hero to cheer—how's he going to do out in the sticks? Where the audiences are cold? Or half hawk? Or just curious?

One purpose of the intra-party fight against Johnson, as McCarthy and Bobby Kennedy have been saying, is to restore the faith of youth in normal politics and—as they might put it privately—"get them off the streets." McCarthy's going to have to do a lot better than he has so far if he's going to make much of a dent among the disaffected youth and Negroes—though at least he, unlike Bobby, is willing to lay his political future on the line to fight the war. What has to be improved first of all is how McCarthy says it. He just doesn't transmit any sense of passion. Secondly what he does say isn't good enough. The Chicago speech was full of insincere hokum. A sample: "John Kennedy set free the spirit of America. The honest optimism was released." McCarthy doesn't believe it, so why say it? And poor Adlai reduced to the role of Kennedy's UN errand boy would have been surprised to learn that his ideas were revived by Kennedy. Where? At the Bay of Pigs? We would also be glad to spare some of McCarthy's fancy quotes at Chicago from Péguy on Dreyfus and Toynbee on the Punic wars for a little more clarity on Vietnam. It's Ho, not Hannibal, who concerns us now.

McCarthy is remarkably unclear about Vietnam. The Chicago speech showed lazy staff work when he invoked the names of Eisenhower and Bradley among those who had warned us against a land war in Asia—although these two dippy old duffers only a few days before were calling for an invasion of North Vietnam! Most revealing of all were his answers at the Washington press conference. Little attention was paid these by the press because (1) the chief interest seemed to be in politics and personality and (2) most of the Washington press corps is for—or indifferent to—the war.

These answers are pretty appalling. The clearest and simplest appeal McCarthy can make is to say that Johnson broke his 1964 pledges and has adopted more and more of Goldwater's policies. That is true. Everybody can understand it. It's effective. Indeed there's little else he needs to say. But, McCarthy went on to say, "I'm not going to talk about that in the campaign." That one remark really tells the whole story. Is he going to run a cream-puff campaign against as tough and dirty a fighter as Lyndon B.?

McCarthy will stir no enthusiasm if he goes around being a graceful patsy. One of the main functions of the campaign is to educate the electorate and to prepare the way for wiser policies. One main line is evident and needs to be hammered on over and over again. The choice is not between isolationism and internationalism. It's between wasting our blood and wealth in the attempt to enforce a Pax Americana or becoming a loyal member of the United Nations. Somebody has to say out loud that we can't take over the white man's burden in the new Kennedy-era guise of Green Berets and counter-insurgency. Over and over again somebody must say clearly, as the way to peace, "stop the bombing" and "negotiate a coalition government" in South Vietnam.

It is Johnson strategy to ignore the fact that U Thant and others have said over and over again that talks will follow if the bombing ends. McCarthy's reply on bombing was all fuzz. It is also Administration strategy to distract attention from the fact that the new NLF program offers a viable compromise solution. I suspect McCarthy's never even seen it. He needs to do some hard thinking and fresh study if he's to be effective. His most alarming reply was on containment of China. There he said we didn't need Vietnam because we now have a new base in Thailand! That is, a second Vietnam, simmering on the burner?

We enlist in McCarthy's army but we intend to keep stirring up mutiny until the General stops yawning.

December 11, 1967

THE CANDIDATE LEAST LIKELY
TO MAKE PEACE

The question raised by Governor Rockefeller's four-stage plan for peace in Vietnam is whether you can sell the Brooklyn Bridge a second time to the same sucker. Essentially it asks Ho Chi Minh again to call off the war and withdraw his men on the same promise of free elections later. The Rockefeller plan is the 1954 Geneva settlement all over again. Once Ho withdrew his forces after 1954, he had no leverage to make us keep the Geneva promise of elections and reunification. He would be in an even weaker position this time, militarily and politically.

Under the devious wording of the Rockefeller plan, Ho would withdraw all his forces but we would not withdraw all of ours. As he withdrew his forces, we would withdraw "the bulk" of ours. "The small U.S. forces left in Vietnam," the Rockefeller plan says, "would be confined to fixed installations as long as North Vietnam carries out its commitments." [1] Thus an undetermined number of U.S. troops would remain in bases around the country. These forces would not leave until after the elections. Only our side would have the means of enforcing the terms of the settlement. U.S. troops could move into action from their bases on any violation, real, imagined or contrived.

The Rockefeller plan is as lopsided politically. In the 1954 agreement there was no restriction on those who could participate in the promised elections. We decided not to hold the elections because we knew that Ho and the Communists would win. One way to prevent such a victory this time would be to exclude the Communists. The Rockefeller plan says the NLF will be "guaranteed participation in the political life of the country" only when it "ceases

[1] See text *Washington Post*, July 14.

guerrilla operations and agrees to abide by the democratic process." That means the guerrillas would have to give up their arms and then satisfy the governing authority in the South that they would "abide by the democratic process" before they could campaign and vote. This governing authority under the Rockefeller plan would be left to the existing regime in Saigon, with its rigged Constitution and its repressive election laws under which Communists and "pro-Communists" are excluded.

What does the phrase—"to abide by the democratic process"—in the Rockefeller plan mean? Saigon has long had an "open arms" program for Communists and other NLF members who defect. When the Saigon military in charge of the defector camps are convinced the VC have renounced their past views, they are set free to participate in the normal life of the country. Does Rockefeller mean any more than this? In a *U.S. News & World Report* interview June 24, 1968, Rockefeller was questioned about an earlier proposal to broaden the base of the Saigon government. "Are you talking," he was asked, "about bringing in the Viet Cong or the National Liberation Front?" "No," was his answer, "I said democratic elements and I do not consider the Viet Cong a democratic element."

Additional light is thrown on what Rockefeller has in mind by his newly published campaign book, *Unity, Freedom & Peace: A Blueprint for Tomorrow*. In it he says we should "accept in South Vietnam's political life any group that seeks its objectives through the political process, rather than by pursuing them by force *or subversion*" (my italics). On ABC-TV's *Issues and Answers* July 14, the day after his new plan was released, Rockefeller put forward the same formula again. He said the Viet Cong could participate in the election "if they agree to drop military action and subversion." You can stop military action by a cease-fire but how do you stop "subversion"?

At one time Rockefeller said he would accept even a Viet Cong government in South Vietnam if it was the result of truly free elections. Now he says the Viet Cong cannot take part in elections until they give up "force and subversion." What is subversion? The New Deal was constantly attacked as subversive. Even the ADA was labeled subversive during the witch-hunt years of the forties and fifties. In Saigon subversion is anything which threatens the domination of the military junta and the landlord-gentry class. It took a Saigon court only 23 minutes the other day to find the leaders of the new middle-class "Alliance of National, Democratic and Peace Forces" guilty of subversion *in absentia*, and condemn them to death for it. If the NLF has to satisfy the Saigon regime that it has given up "subversion" before it can participate in the political process, it may have to wait a long time.

In the 1954 agreement there was a provision that no one was to be persecuted for the part he had played in the struggle against the French and their puppets. Diem violated it and sparked the rebellion when he began to throw many of the former Viet Minh fighters into concentration camps. This time there would be no guarantee that the Viet Cong, after laying down their arms, might not end up in jail again because they had not convinced the Saigon regime that they had sincerely given up "subversion." Thieu and Ky couldn't have thought up a cuter peace offer.

Nelson Rockefeller is as tricky as Nixon and as glib in his liberalism as Humphrey. For a quarter of a century he has been, if anything, more consistently and ferociously dedicated than either to the cold war and its anti-Communist obsessions. Of all the candidates he is the one least likely to draw back from our costly effort to become the policeman of the world. His position on civil rights is liberal—it could hardly be otherwise to get anywhere in the politics of New York—but liberals fool themselves if they think he would cut down military expenditure for social reconstruction. No major figure in American politics has worked harder than Rockefeller to push ever higher the billions we allocate to the Pentagon. To woo the Kennedy forces and exploit peace sentiment, Rockefeller has reluctantly and belatedly been persuaded to coo like a dove. But his whole record spells hawk.

No one can be more surprised than Eisenhower to hear Rockefeller trying to sound like a peace candidate. During the last Republican administration, Eisenhower was not cold warrish enough for Rockefeller and they split because Rockefeller did not think he was spending enough on the armed forces. In June, 1960, Rockefeller refused to join other Republican Governors in supporting Nixon as Eisenhower's successor. Rockefeller issued an almost hysterical statement at the Governors' conference in which he said we faced a "national catastrophe" unless we quickly stepped up our military efforts. Rockefeller had been urging an increase of at least $3 billion a year in the military budget. He did not come out for Nixon until the latter at a secret meeting in July agreed to support the demand for bigger arms expenditures. "There must be no price ceiling," said the joint statement which sealed their bargain, "on America's security."

Eisenhower in his memoirs, *Waging Peace*, said this statement "seemed somewhat astonishing, coming as it did from two people who had long been in administration councils and who had never voiced any doubt—at least in my presence—of the adequacy of America's defenses." Eisenhower noted that the Pentagon's budget had risen from "less than $12 billion before the Korean war under the Democrats to more than $41 billion in 1960." He pointed to the new supersonic jets of the Air Force and the "revolutionary new submarine-borne Polaris missiles" of the Navy as solid evidence of increased military strength. He related that after Rockefeller's "catastrophe" statement in June, 1960, Eisenhower dryly told a meeting of Congressional leaders at the White House, "I suspect that Rockefeller has been listening too closely to half-baked advisers."

One of those "half-baked advisers" was Dr. Edward Teller. He was the one scientist on the panel which, under Nelson's chairmanship, wrote the famous Rockefeller

Brothers Report on "International Security: The Military Aspect" in 1958. This was a blueprint for a U.S. role as world policeman in the nuclear age. The Strangelovian touch of Dr. Teller was exquisitely visible in the report's most wondrous sentence. "Very powerful nuclear weapons," it said, "can be used in such a manner that they have negligible effects on civilian populations." Such was the Pied Piperism Rockefeller was prepared to follow. The report called for the complete reorganization of the armed forces. One innovation charted the course to a whole series of Vietnams. It called for mobile forces "tailored to the gamut of possible limited wars which may range from conflicts involving several countries to minor police actions." These limited war forces "may require a highly complicated weapons system *including nuclear weapons*" (my italics). This readiness to use nuclear weapons in limited wars anticipated Goldwater by six years; though Goldwater suggested nuclear weapons in Vietnam for defoliation purposes only, not—as the Rockefeller report did—for combat.

Two years before the NLF was organized in 1960, Rockefeller was ready for intervention in Vietnam. "Our security can be imperilled," his report warned in 1958, "not only by overt aggression but also by transformations which are made to appear, insofar as possible, as not aggression at all." Greece, it said, "has furnished one example, Vietnam another." The report invented the phrase "non-overt aggression," i.e., an aggression of which there is no proof in overt acts, only a hunch that something bad is going on. Interventionism never developed a more useful, if paradoxical, doctrine. The report asked us to "realize that non-overt aggression presents issues which are deliberately and intrinsically unclear" and to recognize that "to ask for certainty in these situations is a recipe for inaction." This implies that we must be ready to resolve any doubts in favor of intervention. There is an occult quality about the phrase "non-overt aggression" which recalls the demonology of the cold war and the witch hunt years in their most virulent phase.

The fact is that Rockefeller has always been more comfortable with the cold war liberal Democrats than with the conservative Eisenhower-type Republicans. His "liberalism" is the same mixture of social demagogy at home and military intervention abroad which has characterized Democratic policy from Truman to Johnson and Humphrey. Rockefeller can claim to be the original cold warrior. He boasts in his new book that he was called anti-Russian and pro-Fascist when he fought successfully at the UN organizing meeting in San Francisco in 1945 to admit Fascist Argentina to membership over Molotov's objections—and those of men on our side as diverse as Secretary of State Hull and Walter Lippmann. This signaled the first efforts to use the new organization as an anti-Soviet bloc. Rockefeller also boasts of the part he played in the adoption of Article 51 of the Charter, which allowed for "regional groupings" within the UN. Originally it was represented as an effort to preserve the Monroe Doctrine but it led to the very development the United Nations was intended to avoid—the breakup of the world into hostile military blocs. Rockefeller now boasts that it was Article 51 which four years later made the formation of NATO possible. Article 51 also laid the basis for SEATO.

It is not surprising that in his new book the President for whom Rockefeller expresses the greatest admiration is Truman. Rockefeller admires Truman because he "decided to reverse President Roosevelt's policy of accommodation with the Kremlin, decided to terminate World War II by dropping two atomic bombs on Japan, [and] decided to contain Soviet expansion into the Mediterranean by offering the Truman Doctrine to Greece and Turkey." In foreign policy Rockefeller has always felt more at home with the Democrats. Much of the military program sketched out in the Rockefeller report of 1958 was implemented by the Kennedy Administration: one of Kennedy's first acts was to send Congress a special message boosting military spending;

by fiscal 1962 it was $10 billion more than Eisenhower's
1960 figure of 41 billion. Since, of course, it has been doubled by the Vietnamese war. But Kennedy wasn't belliger-
ent enough for Rockefeller. Rockefeller attacked him for
suggesting that we give up Quemoy and Matsu; these tiny
Chinese offshore islands seemed to Rockefeller "of tremendous significance" to "the defense of freedom." He criticized Kennedy for not being more aggressive in Laos and
Vietnam, accused the new President of mishandling nuclear
defenses in "several secret exchanges of letters" with Khrushchev and after the Bay of Pigs wanted him to make another attempt to topple Castro. He was for intervention in
the Congo to prevent a Communist takeover during the
scare created by poor Lumumba's effort at independence.

Rockefeller is incautious enough in his new book to give
himself high marks for courage because he was dubious
about the nuclear test ban agreement Kennedy negotiated.
He wanted assurances that the treaty "does not prohibit the
use of nuclear weapons to repel aggression anywhere" and
that the Kennedy Administration—rather than use the
treaty as a first step toward broader disarmament measures,
as was hoped at the time—would "take every feasible step
to preserve the ability of our military establishment to deter
and defeat Communist aggression against free peoples
everywhere." Like his scientist mentor Dr. Teller, Rockefeller feared nothing so much as a détente. In this he saw
eye to eye with the military. It is in keeping with this record that Rockefeller in a chapter on "Fiscal Integrity" in
the new book nowhere suggests any cut in military expenditures or in the escalating costs of the Vietnamese war. He
says we will have to "discipline ourselves to set clear priorities and to make hard choices" which will demand "rare
political courage." But he lacks the courage to specify what
are the hard choices he would make if elected. His whole
record shows that for him military strength comes first, and
that military strength is not merely defense but a capacity
for intervention anywhere in the world.

It is not strange that Rockefeller's admiration for John-

son comes through in the new book. He praises Johnson's
"self-sacrifice" in renouncing renomination and sees it as a
"courageous" step toward "the ending of our own, increasingly malignant controversy between 'hawks' and 'doves'
and a long step toward the restoration of national unity."
His only criticism is that Johnson's "peace overtures to
North Vietnam were launched in a manner to stir concern
among our friends in Southeast Asia who now feel themselves directly menaced." He sets out to correct this. He
writes:

I would warn our adversaries not to 'overreact' to our current
discomfiture in foreign relations. In commencing our new quest
for honorable peace in Vietnam, we are expressing a sober reassessment, not seeking peace at any price. At stake in this judgment is not only peace in Vietnam but the chances of peace in
Asia, the Middle East and the whole world. Our adversaries
ought not to conclude that we will be unable to devise an effective strategy against their 'wars of national liberation,' i.e., subversion, or that other peoples less weakened than the South
Vietnamese will not rise up against incursion and intrusion.

These opaque phrases could have come as easily from
Rusk or Johnson. They suggest no more than a tactical retreat. If the military have their way, the retreat will be no
more than enough palaver at Paris to keep the home front
quiet until after the election when they can go on with the
war undisturbed. Rockefeller speaks of a "sober reassessment" but there is no hint that this would extend to the
wisdom of our involvement in land and civil wars in Asia,
much less to the idea of trying to impose a Pax Americana.
On the contrary Rockefeller in a speech in Philadelphia on
May 1 unveiled a grandiose vision of a new regional grouping under American leadership which would ensure "economic progress and political stability" for all the Asian
"hundreds of millions living in the great crescent from
Japan throughout India to Iran." This is a sure way to more
and bigger than Asian Vietnams.

July 22, 1968

THE GOP CONVENTION
WAS NOT WITHOUT
ITS CHEERING ASPECTS

From a Marxist-Leninist point of view, the Republican convention was clearly a victory for the working class. A poor boy grew up to defeat a Rockefeller for the Republican nomination. Those massed millions in last-minute TV and newspaper advertising failed utterly to overcome a militant armed with the correct political line. His proletarian loyalties were so little affected by success that he at once planned to celebrate by visiting Moscow and discussing his future plans in the Kremlin. He was unfortunately dissuaded by nervous bourgeois advisers.

Another cheerful way of looking at the convention is to notice how firmly the party has committed itself to turning power back from Washington to the state and local governments. If anything happens to Nixon after his election, the Presidency will be turned over to a man who only six short years ago had reached eminence no higher than leadership in the Kiwanis Club and the Parent-Teacher Association in a suburb of Maryland, ranking somewhere in the rural hierarchy between a deputy sheriff and a duly elected dogcatcher. The Republicans have proven again that in America anybody is liable to become President.

The convention was a humbling affair altogether for us ethnics. It was hard to listen to Goldwater and realize that a man could be half Jewish and yet sometimes appear to be twice as dense as the normal gentile. As for Agnew, even at a convention where every speech seemed to outdo the other in wholesome clichés and delicious anticlimaxes, his speech putting Nixon into nomination topped all the rest. If the race that produced Isaiah is down to Goldwater and the

race that produced Pericles is down to Agnew, the time has
come to give the country back to the WASP's.

TV is ruining the two-party system. Mayor Daley is
smart to keep that electricians' strike going through the
Democratic convention. The advantage of a national primary would be to shield the American public from too intimate a view of its politicos at work and play. It would take
a comic genius to duplicate some of the ideas Republican
speakers came up with. We remember with special pleasure
that passage in Ivy Baker Priest's nominating speech for
Ronald Reagan in which she said, "We cannot afford the
status quo." The only real sense we could get out of that
remark in that upper bracket assemblage was that maybe
some delegates were falling behind in the payments on their
yachts. We had always assumed that the status quo was
something Republicans could never have too much of. Another oratorical banana peel was dropped by Agnew,
whose style of delivery reminds us strongly of W. C.
Fields. In nominating Nixon, he quoted his hero as saying,
"Right now change rules America. It is time for America to
rule change." This sonorous tidbit sounded as if Nixon
were casting himself as a modern Canute. The GOP has
been trying for years to hold back the tides.

August 19, 1968

WHEN A TWO-PARTY SYSTEM BECOMES
A ONE-PARTY RUBBER STAMP

When a country is denied a choice on the most burning
issue of the time, the war in Vietnam, then the two-party
system has become a one-party rubber stamp. This is the
first and essential point to be made in the wake of the Dem-

ocratic and Republican conventions. The Establishment
and the military have locked the ballot boxes. If the results
are an intensified alienation among the youth who must
fight this war, an increase in resistance to the draft, a rise in
street demonstrations and violence, this is the cause and not
some occult conspiracy. The real conspiracy was the one
which wove together Eisenhower's last inflammatory message to the Republican convention with the iron control
Johnson and Daley exercised over the Democrats. Both parties, both candidates, have been drafted. The Pentagon has
won the election even before the votes are cast.

The second thing which needs to be said is that the country owes a debt of gratitude to the tatterdemalion army of
Yippies, hippies and peaceniks—and to their leaders David
Dellinger, Tom Hayden and Jerry Rubin—who frightened
the Establishment into such elaborate security precautions
in Chicago. They made opposition to the war visible. The
special barbed-wire fences around the Amphitheatre which
turned "Stalag '68" into the favorite joke of the Convention, the system of electronically checked passes so intricate
that it led to a whole series of angry clashes with the delegates themselves, the vast concentration of police, National
Guardsmen and troops, as if in preparation for a revolution,
dramatized for the whole world to see that there was something indelibly undemocratic about this Democratic convention.

Of course security precautions were justified. The Secret
Service, the FBI and the Chicago police had a right to be
fearful of what might happen, especially if Johnson himself
had turned up, and this was the grim eventuality I believe
they had in mind. But the question not to be lost sight of is
why for the first time in American history a convention and
a President required so much protection.

This was the scandal it proved impossible to hide and this
is why the police were so brutal in dealing with the cameramen and the reporters. They *were* the main enemy of the
proceedings, the eyes and ears of the country, the unwel-
come witnesses of the rigging within the Convention and

the repression without. Johnson and Daley, alike in so many
ways, are alike in their obsessive animosity to the press. Daley's big and beefy police seemed to crack the skulls of the
TV and press reporters with a special gusto and as if given
free rein by their masters. Their conduct was in its own
way a resounding tribute to the First Amendment. It also
gave middle-class whites a taste of the police brutality
which is an old story to blacks.

The convention was a triumph of what the Russian
Communists would call "democratic centralism," that submission of "the lower organs of the party to the higher"
which they are reimposing in Prague. The delegates chosen
were less representative of the party rank-and-file than of
the party machines, and the committees were even less representative than the delegates. A Citizens' Committee, to include respected retired jurists, ought to be formed to take
testimony from delegates, demonstrators and the police on
the whole question of how this convention and the protests
against it were handled. It would show I believe that security was used as a way to control the convention. If assassination plots were as thick as Daley and the police now
claim—and Humphrey idiotically echoes them—then it is
strange that no attempts were made, no shots fired, no
bombs thrown. For in the crowded hallways of the main
hotels including the Hilton, it would have been easy for an
assassin to take a potshot at any one of the candidates.
There security was poor.

On the other hand, at the Amphitheatre, guards were
used to harass McCarthy and McGovern delegates. The opposition on the floor was hamstrung by lack of phone communications and by the arbitrary and arrogant rulings that
Carl Albert as Chairman applied to any attempt to protest.
The Johnson steamroller stopped the effort of the Humphrey forces to put a slightly milder face on the pro-war
Vietnam plank. Not the slightest deviation was allowed.
Johnson and Daley are masters of meticulous detail,[1] accus-

---

[1] A sample: In Chicago, unlike Miami, reporters with credentials did
not get assigned seats as usual at conventions. This seemed odd. We

tomed to rule their kingdoms with an iron hand. So it was that a convention strikingly cool—despite its unrepresentative majority—to any mention of Johnson's name was forced to wear his brand in the platform plank on Vietnam and the choice of Vice President. A candidate who might have placated blacks and antiwar delegates was Fred Harris of Oklahoma. But he was the vice chairman of the Kerner commission, whose report Johnson disliked. Johnson and Daley preferred a safe and bridle-broken liberal like Muskie of Maine (Johnson put a saddle on him long ago), with an appeal to Chicago's Polish Americans and an "ethnic" offset to Agnew.

To wander in Lincoln Park among the hippies and Yippies, to drop in on the headquarters of the New Left demonstrators, to talk at random with the youths in Grant Park and the streets was to feel that in revulsion against the war the best of a generation were being lost—some among the hippies to drugs, some among the radicals to an almost hysterical frenzy of alienation. There were a few among them I am sure who sought deliberately by taunts and obscenities to provoke a confrontation with the police, but far more were driven to angry resistance by Daley's unwillingness to let them sleep in Lincoln Park and to grant permits for peaceful demonstrations and parades. These would have let off steam and been far easier to police than crowds which felt their elementary rights were being trampled. Even Joseph J. Lefevour, president of the Chicago lodge of the Fraternal Order of Police, in the middle of a press conference called to defend police tactics, admitted (*Chicago Tribune*, August 30), "Most of the kids in the parks," i.e., Lincoln and Grant parks, "have been orderly. They've obeyed our orders and joked with us. But then their leaders work them up to fever pitch and disappear, leaving the kids to take the consequences." But could they have been worked up "to

---

learned the reason why on the night of the balloting for nominees and the final session, when I and many other reporters were unable to get into the top galleries supposedly reserved for us because they were packed by Daley goons from the Sanitation Department.

fever pitch" without the brutal nightly sweeps at curfew time in Lincoln Park, and the indiscriminate and sadistic way the police beat and tear-gassed not only peaceful demonstrators in Grant Park but onlookers behind the police's own barricades in front of the Hilton?

Daley has long run a one-party state in Chicago, with just that combination of brutality, social welfare handouts and cooperation with big business which is also the essence of Johnson's own conception of personal government. The way Humphrey has stepped out as Daley's apologist, even after the climactic raid on the McCarthy headquarters in the Hilton, is an index of what we can expect from a Humphrey Administration, of what he means by law and order, and of what lies behind his platitudinous evangelism. Another index—to be forgotten at our peril—was his appearance before the Catholic War Veterans on the eve of the convention when he threw away a moderate prepared script and delivered a warmongering address. These two events have finally decided for me that Humphrey is no lesser an evil than Nixon. A vote for Humphrey is a vote for Johnson's war and Daley's police state tactics.

I confess that I do not know what to do politically at this juncture. The three main ways open are Allard Lowenstein's effort eventually to take over the Democrats, Marcus Raskin's attempt to form a New Party, and the New Left's call to go into the streets. To meet the crises of race and war which confront the country, time and patience, faith in persuasion, are required. But how preach these virtues to a youth who may be called up any day for the army? The war is destroying our country as we are destroying Vietnam. Hate and frenzy are poor substitutes for political thinking, yet the *enragés* among the youth, with their romanticism about guerrilla war, may set the tune for the whole country. A handful may provoke the government to such overreaction as to polarize the country between extremes.

The New Left and even its moderate allies are still operating in a fog of misconceptions. The main one is that "the people" are against the war. The people on the contrary are confused and divided. To say that the streets "belong to the people," as Tom Hayden has, is to overlook those people who feel the streets belong to them, too, for the ordinary business of their lives. "Let that party," Raskin said to the Democrats the other day in calling for a New Party, "be the party of the cops, the military, the big city bosses and the non-people." There are an awful lot of "non-people." The need is for dialogue, not monologue, to win them over. If law and order really break down, if democratic processes are abandoned, it is we of the Left, the anti-war forces and the intellectuals who will be the first to suffer. To play with revolutionary talk and tactics as the New Left is doing, when there is no revolutionary situation, is to act as the provocateurs for an American fascism.

The deeper tragedy lies in the increasing abandonment of nonviolent tactics by black and white dissenters alike. To howl down those with whom we differ, to use obscenities instead of arguments, to abandon persuasion for direct action, to dehumanize the other side with cries of "pigs" and worse is to embark on a game the rightists are better equipped to play, and to set examples which American Storm Troopers may some day apply to us. Hate is still the main enemy of the human race, the fuel that heats the furnaces of genocide. How build a better world by relapsing into primitive and sanguinary habits?

September 9, 1968

WHY HUBERT IS AS
TRICKY AS DICKY

It is a delusion to believe that Humphrey is not saying what we want him to say on Vietnam because he is afraid of Johnson. Humphrey's whole record, not just as an anti-Communist on the home front, but on Southeast Asia, leaves

little reason to believe that he would have a different position on the Vietnam war even if freed from Johnson's influence. Humphrey's enthusiasm for American intervention in
Southeast Asia goes back to 1950, when he welcomed Truman's decision to give financial aid to the French and to
their puppet emperor, Bao Dai. When the French were
criticized for not sending troops to Korea, Humphrey defended them on the ground that they were already "fighting for freedom in Indochina." Humphrey was second only
to Nixon in readiness for U.S. involvement. When Nixon
proposed sending American troops into Indochina before
the Geneva conference in 1954, Humphrey was not prepared to go that far, though he told the Senate on April 19
of that year that he thought Nixon's famous off-the-record
speech to the American Society of Newspaper Editors was
"very responsible, considered, mature and intelligent." The
entente cordiale between them far antedates the current
campaign, which is being fought like a gentlemanly boxing
match.

Humphrey *is* a prisoner of the Johnson Administration
and perhaps even more so of the labor movement, his only
organized support outside the party machines. George
Meany is if anything even more hawkish on the war than
Johnson, as Meany was more hawkish than Eisenhower.
Humphrey would take all the enthusiasm out of Meany's
support if he were to shift over on Vietnam. But the essential reason that Humphrey holds back is that he has always
believed in the war, and in the necessity of creating a bulwark in Vietnam against Communist expansion into Southeast Asia. It is indicative that the highly unfair and twisted
attack made on him by Allan Ryskind of *Human Events*,
the organ of the far rightists, in a newly published book,
Hubert, is unable to pin on him any dove-like statement
about the Indochina war. "This is our great adventure,"
Humphrey declared expansively in a talk less than a year
ago to the U.S. embassy staff in Saigon, "and a wonderful
one it is." No one has been more gung ho about this war
than Hubert Humphrey. Eisenhower and Kennedy as well

as Johnson had his support as the escalation continued and the U.S. stakes grew.

The Salt Lake City speech has to be read against this consistent record. Its major disappointment, from the standpoint of the peace movement, does not lie in Humphrey's tricky position on the bombing halt: the fact that like Johnson he links it to reciprocal concessions and goes further than Johnson has in explicitly stating that the bombing would be resumed if we were dissatisfied with the other side's conduct ("bad faith"). This is not unconditional cessation. More important is that Humphrey shows no readiness whatsoever for any political compromise in the peace negotiations themselves. Essentially he, like Johnson and Thieu, call on the other side to lay down its arms and accept "free elections" under South Vietnam's rigged Constitution. Humphrey in no way departs from the clichés of Johnson and Rusk: the view of the war as purely an aggression from the North; the pretense that land reform is going on when South Vietnam's oligarchic legislature, representative of the landlord class and not the peasantry, has already overwhelmingly rejected it; and the old will-o'-the-wisp—that the South Vietnamese army will soon be able to take over the main burden of the war. Without a fresh view of the past and the present, the way cannot be cleared for a political settlement and a genuinely representative government in South Vietnam. This is what Johnson does not want and there is no reason to believe that Humphrey or Nixon is any readier for it than he is.

Humphrey repeated that stupefying nonsense about how on March 31 Johnson "sacrificed his own political career in order to bring negotiations that could lead to peace." Every day makes clearer that just the opposite is the case. Johnson freed himself from the pressures of politics in order to carry on the war. His line has hardened. His latest appointment of a U.S. representative to the UN shows that he no longer bothers to try and fool public opinion at home and abroad by naming men like Goldberg or Ball who are or appear to be doves. Goldberg was himself the victim of Johnson; he really thought the President wanted peace when he stepped down from the Court to go to the UN. Ball's reputation as a dove has always been overblown, and his attack on U Thant for advocating an end of the bombing showed how little reality there was behind the gossip that he was the dove-in-residence of the State Department. I myself never thought his dissent on the war much more than a reflection of his fear that we were paying too much attention to Asia at the expense of his old clients in the Common Market. But of his successor, Russell Wiggins, there is no doubt. Though a liberal in domestic affairs, Wiggins made the editorial page of the *Washington Post* a faithful echo of the Johnson-Rusk line on Vietnam. Johnson no longer needs to pretend.

I am just back from a few days in Paris, where I had a look at the stalemated Paris peace talks. For the newsmen, it is like covering a glacier, except that glaciers sometimes move an inch or so a year. The line of the other side seems to have hardened with our own. There is less emphasis on the *Alliance* as a bridge to the South Vietnamese middle class and a political compromise; the NLF is back in the center of discussion. Apparently Hanoi was preparing last March to make so explicit an offer on peace talks if the bombing ended as to put Washington squarely on the spot. Johnson outflanked Hanoi by making his own offer of a limited bombing pause first. It was a skillful ploy, not a serious proposal, and Washington was surprised when Hanoi accepted it. My impression is that Hanoi did so because of pressure from its own allies. My impression from our own side is that the reason we do not stop the bombing altogether and begin substantive talks is because we have no real negotiating position ready except a Korean solution, i.e., the surrender of the other side. There is a lot more fighting ahead before serious negotiations can be envisaged. The lull is over and the NLF spokesmen exude a quiet confidence.

The outlook is bleak. In South Vietnam, the jails are full of Buddhists and of other non-Communist peace elements. At home it is as foolish to rely on Nixon for peace as on

Humphrey. Johnson has already shown what he thinks of Humphrey in arranging for Marvin Watson to campaign for him. At lunch in Paris some North Vietnamese asked me to explain the election and the two-party system. I said it was a triumph of the dialectic. It showed that two could be one and one could be two, and had probably been fabricated by Hegel for the American market on a subcontract from General Dynamics. The North Vietnamese are Marxists with a sense of humor, but none of us was really laughing.

October 7, 1968

PART II

'Saigon Afire Now...'

THE MONSTER
WITH LITTLE BRAIN
AND NO HEART

Two words sum up the beginnings of our military campaign to subdue the Mekong Delta. One is futility and the other brutality. The first invasion, launched with a tremendous air and naval bombardment, and an equally sensational splurge of publicity, was Operation Dockhouse V. It has just fizzled out. "The ten-day sweep," a sentence buried in the AP's daily military roundup from Saigon admitted (Washington *Star*, January 16, 1967), "proved unproductive." This force of 4,000 U.S. and South Vietnamese Marines could claim no more than 21 Viet Cong killed and 14 captured "during 10 days of slogging through thigh-deep delta mud 68 miles south of Saigon" (*New York Times*, January 17). That is an average of two VC killed a day. We'd like to see McNamara's cost effectiveness figures on this operation. U.S. intelligence must be pretty dismal if such a vast panoply of power was brought to bear in an area where nobody seemed to be around. A companion invasion a few days later 10 miles away by South Vietnam's 9th Division was also preceded by a huge outpouring of firepower and ballyhoo. A detachment of reporters and cameramen were on the heavy missile cruiser *Canberra* as it poured high explosive shells for an hour and a half into the landing area. One of them wrote (*Washington Post*, January 10), "It sounded like a thunderstorm with lightning striking every few minutes." Since nothing more has been heard of that invasion, obviously its results weren't anything to boast of either. Any time the Pentagon runs out of the glamorous names it gives these operations, we'd suggest a code name

suited to this combination of monstrous power with dim intelligence. Why not Operation Dinosaur?

While the Marines were still chasing phantoms in Operation Dockhouse V, 30,000 U.S. troops launched Operation
Cedar Falls, the biggest of the war, against the so-called
Iron Triangle. The name was another triumph for our military men, who seem nowadays to be graduates of Madison
Avenue rather than West Point. The name conjures up the
impregnable fortress. It was another area where the troops
met more peasants than guerrillas. It is or was a fertile 60-
mile-square area of forest, paddy fields, orchards and rubber
plantations long dominated by the Viet Cong under tacit
agreements with French rubber companies and local offi-
cialdom. By the end of the fifth day, U.S. infantrymen had
"fired their rifles only occasionally" and "one intelligence
officer" found it necessary to explain that "he thought it
unlikely that more than 100 enemy soldiers were ever in the
target areas at one time" (*New York Times*, January 13).
But 10,000 peasants live there. It was decided that they were
all "at least passive Vietcong" (*same*) and must be uprooted
and resettled and the whole area razed. To make 10,000
peasants homeless in order to get at 100 guerrillas is the idiot
arithmetic of this war, guaranteed to create 10 new rebels
for every one we kill or capture.

Imagine 30,000 Chinese troops uprooting Iowa villagers
to save them from Republicanism and you get some idea of
how likely this is to win—as our sentimental generals say—
the hearts of the people. This operation in the Iron Triangle
was pictured by the London *Sunday Times* (January 15) in
all its mindless technology. Its correspondent flew over the
scene with the engineer colonel in command. "Below us a
22-ton armored bulldozer named 'Hogjaws' leads a clearing
column on a compass course through the jungle," he cabled.
"Above Hogjaws a 'talkout' helicopter circles, broad-
casting through loudspeakers a tape-recorded message calling on the Vietcong to surrender. Hogjaws is leading a column of two tanks, four 14-ton bulldozers and 12 armored
personnel carriers. As the bulldozers clear a wide road

across the Triangle, the colonel says, 'We are developing a new style of jungle warfare here—we remove the jungle.' " This is not warfare. It's a demolition job.

While bulldozers destroy the jungle, the rubber trees, the rice paddies and the villages, fire rains down on the area from the skies. In seven days, Major General de Puy, commander of the First Infantry Division, had requested and received more than 660 air strikes in support of his troops (*New York Times*, January 15). There were 12 thunderous raids by B-52s and "30 artillery batteries with upward of 130 cannon had been hammering" the area all week (*New York Times*, January 14). It was in this heavy artillery fire that eight American soldiers were killed and 34 wounded, the fourth case of accidental artillery shelling of his own men among the troops General de Puy commands.[1] The South Vietnamese military man who is the province chief told the London *Sunday Times* man he was delighted with the progress of the operation. "The big thing," he said, "is that the Iron Triangle will never threaten Saigon again—within two weeks it will be a big bare field." This recalls that earlier pacification campaign described by Tacitus. We cannot forbear quoting again his familiar condemnation of his fellow Romans, "When they make a wilderness, they call it peace." So do we in the Mekong Delta.

The strategy of the campaign now unfolding is simple and repulsive. An anonymous general explained it to a correspondent in South Vietnam months ago. Mao Tse-tung, in his book on guerrilla war, says the guerrilla lives among the people like a fish in water. "We're going to dry up the water," was how this general put it. We're going to remove the people, and make the area in which the guerrillas have hitherto lived, literally unlivable. This is what we see in the Iron Triangle campaign. Peter Arnett, the AP's prize-winning correspondent, described the process unforgettably in a dispatch published in many Sunday papers January 15: "Burning homes, crying children, frightened women,

[1] This brought to 400 the number of our own troops killed by U.S. bombs and shell-fire, otherwise so surgically precise in avoiding civilians.

devastated fields, long lines of slowly moving refugees." He said it "brought back memories of the resettlement of thousands of peasants during the era of the late Ngo Dinh Diem." That, too, was supposed to "pacify" the countryside. The refugees were herded into camps without latrines or water. "On arriving at the camp," Reuters reported (*Washington Post*, January 15), "a few of the peasants spat in disgust but most were glad to escape the bombs and the defoliation chemicals sprayed from the air." An American official commented complacently, "They don't love us but their attitude is improving." As Lyndon Johnson said in his State of the Union message, "They know that it is possible for them to choose their own national destinies—without coercion."

January 23, 1967

THE FRAUD WITH WHICH BOMB RESUMPTION WAS EXCUSED

The principal excuse for resuming the bombing of the North will turn out, when the full truth is available, to be a fraud. President Johnson said he had "no alternative but to resume full-scale hostilities" because North Vietnam had used the four-day Têt truce for "major resupply efforts of their troops in South Vietnam" rather than to seek a peaceful settlement. In London Prime Minister Wilson went even further and told the House of Commons next day that "the massive southward movement of troops and supplies in the North . . . threatened to create a severe military unbalance." Neither Saigon nor Washington had claimed that troops as well as supplies had been moved south, much less that the movement was such as to create a "severe military unbalance." This would have been too silly an exaggeration for our military to venture. Even if we loaned McNamara and the Seventh Fleet to Hanoi, it couldn't change the military balance of power in the South—in four days yet! Harold Wilson was the foremost victim—and the most far-out echo—of a U.S. propaganda campaign.

This campaign was initiated by Secretary Rusk at his press conference February 9, the second day of the truce. He said, "We have seen large numbers of boats and other vessels dashing south along the coast of North Vietnam to resupply their forces *in the southern part of North Vietnam* and in the demilitarized zone" (my italics). He declared this "indicates that it is their intention to continue the operation." Few stopped to notice that the Secretary did not say the supplies were crossing the 17th parallel. Nor did anyone ask whether supply was a violation of the truce, especially when it occurred on North Vietnam's own territory. The Secretary's remark that the North was resupplying troops in the DMZ was not true. Raymond R. Coffey of the *Chicago Daily News* Service cabled from Saigon next day that "for all the road, sea and air traffic sighted in the North, U.S. officials acknowledge that they still do not have any reports of men or materiel moving into the demilitarized zone of South Vietnam [*sic*]. The farthest south any traffic has been sighted is around Dong Hoi, 20 miles or so [it's closer to 40—IFS], above the zone." [1] But for every reader who saw Coffey's dispatch there were millions who got the intended picture of the Communists crassly violating the truce to move massive supplies across the border. *Time*, for example, said (February 17) that Hanoi used the truce "for reinforcement and replenishment of its troops below the 17th parallel. Army trucks rumbled down canopied jungle trails into South Vietnam and cargo vessels sped down the

[1] This passage was omitted from the dispatch as published in the *Washington Post* February 11. A reader sent me a clipping from the Toronto *Star* February 11 which ran the full dispatch.

coast with impunity. . . ." Like an orchestra leader striking
his baton, the Secretary of State had launched a theme that
was to be repeated and amplified from Washington and
Saigon to prepare the public mind for a resumption of the
bombing.

The day after Rusk's press conference, State Department
spokesman Robert McCloskey was asked whether supply
activities were a violation of the truce. He replied coyly
that he did not want to get into that "since I don't have sufficient information to specify what are violations and what
are not violations in the technical sense." When one correspondent recalled that elements of the U.S. 9th Infantry Division "began to debark during either the Christmas or the
New Year's truce this past time around" and asked whether
that was a truce violation, McCloskey answered, "I can't
say yes or no." Like Rusk, McCloskey created the impression that this was a violation without saying so explicitly,
since that would have been palpably untrue. It was not until
the end of the truce that the AP ticker carried a story from
Bob Gassaway in Saigon saying that both sides had "agreed
only to refrain from staging offensive operations" but "retained the right to continue the movement of supplies."
One has to be pretty gullible to believe that Rusk and Mc-
Closkey did not know this all the time.

According to the Coffey dispatch from Saigon we have
already quoted, "while questioning North Vietnam's activity, U.S. military authorities also were trying to quietly ignore the U.S. movement of men and supplies that has continued all through the cease-fire." Coffey reported that the
first full day of the truce "a new one-day record of 2,762
tons was set for cargo delivered by air to units in the field."
He said the daily Air Force communiqué had in the past
routinely listed the volume of cargo and passengers carried.
But the day after the Rusk press conference—the day the
U.S. military in Saigon first issued its sensational charge that
supply missions in the North were "five times the normal"—
the figures on cargo and passengers carried were missing
from the daily Air Force communique. "When asked for

the figures and why they were missing," Coffey reported, "an Air Force officer said the top U.S. headquarters command had 'told us not to' release them." When Coffey finally got the figures "they showed that U.S. planes—not counting truck and ship movements at all—carried 7,042 tons of supplies and more than 17,000 men during the first three days of the cease-fire."

The most vivid glimpse of U.S. supply efforts was printed in *Le Monde* (February 12–13) that week-end. It said:

While the American services report a considerable intensification of road, rail, river and coastal traffic in North Vietnam, press correspondents Friday were able to verify, on the road from Saigon to Tay-Ninh, that American supply missions had also been able to profit from the Têt truce to increase the re-supply of troops in combat rations and munitions. Long files of trucks belonging to the military transport companies were stretched out along this Northwest road. They were protected by tanks and by helicopters flying along at treetop level. In the town of Tay-Ninh itself, huge trucks and tractors were hauling loads of shells for 105-mm and 155-mm cannons to American units established on the outskirts of the Vietcong's Zone C.

This did not appear in the U.S. press but R. W. Apple, Jr., cabled from Saigon February 12 in the *New York Times* of the same date, that while U.S. briefing officers said resupply efforts in the North "called into question the good faith of the North Vietnamese high command" and "asserted that the allies had made no move to take advantage of the truce"—

Correspondents in the provinces north and northwest of Saigon said, however, that the highways were much more crowded than usual with U.S. convoys. Officers in the American First Infantry Division and 25th Infantry Division confirmed that they were moving extraordinary amounts of food, fuel and ammunition to forward positions." [2]

---

[2] It may be that troops were also moved during the truce. The weekly casualty report issued February 16 in Saigon "also showed," according to a summary in the *Washington Post* February 17, "an addition of 2,000 U.S. troops, bringing the total in Vietnam as of February 11, to 412,000."

But before the truth had thus begun to leak out, the U.S. press was treated to a tidal wave of misrepresentation about what was going on in the North. The day after Rusk's press conference, the U.S. military in Saigon pulled out all the stops. Their propagandistic purpose was faithfully mirrored in the night lead from Saigon by Alvin B. Webb, Jr., on the UPI wire February 10. He cabled that "U.S. scout planes and ships Friday reported helplessly watching North Vietnam take advantage of a 4-day truce to build up their forces with massive supplies," and "American sources said the Communist 'saturation push' has all but killed hopes of extending the cease-fire." The military didn't want the cease-fire in the first place, and were afraid Johnson might somehow be drawn into peace talks. It was not surprising that U.S. officials "added," according to Webb, that "any hopes for extending the truce to allow for peace talks" had "vanished in the dust of the Communist supply convoys." One commander became so alarmed, Webb reported, "that he urged American planes break off their cease-fire 'stand-down' and immediately resume bombing the flood of North Vietnamese ships, trains [this was the only dispatch I saw that implied the trains were again running down the North Vietnamese panhandle] and trucks ferrying arms to South Vietnam's Communist guerrillas." One could almost see the guerrillas waving happily from the ferry slips as the boats came in.

The figures given out in Saigon on February 10 produced headlines that the North Vietnamese were pouring 35,000 tons of supplies "southward" [but still, as few paused to realize, in *North* Vietnam]. The UPI that morning in its enthusiasm even said the barges and the "trucks stacked up at enemy infiltration routes . . . could handle up to 70,000 tons of supplies" but the figure on which the military settled was 35,000. By the time Saigon had to put it in writing this was reduced to 25,000 with many qualifications. But the

That was the third day of the truce. The same communique, according to the AP ticker February 16, showed that South Vietnamese forces declined that week by 3,000. They seem to desert faster than we can replace them.

press generally showed a happy capacity for ignoring the fine print. The traffic was declared to be five times heavier than "normal" but nobody stopped to point out that "normal" has been a condition of constant bombardment in which trucks and ships dared only move under cover of darkness. No American dispatch that I saw raised the question of how the military could be so sure that none of the truck and ship loads carried civilian supplies. There are 17 million people in North Vietnam and perhaps two million live in the area between the 17th and 19th parallels. Keeping them supplied under bombardment cannot be easy. Could it be that *none* of this was food and fuel for civilians? The only dispatch I saw which touched on this point was in the London *Times* February 11. Its man in Saigon said the military "conceded" (apparently when he asked them) that "some of the supplies could be for civilians." "Quite a few people after all," he noted dryly, "live in the southern 'panhandle.' However," he added, "American sources are 'persuaded' they are mostly military."

The Pentagon press office claimed it knew no more than was contained in the communiqué when I tried to raise these and other questions about the figures. The communiqué claims the sighting of 2,200 trucks, though admitting nervously in two places that there may have been duplication. North Vietnam has been getting trucks from Soviet bloc sources, but that is still a lot of trucks. Total U.S. truck *and* bus exports to all of Europe East and West in 1965 was 2,752.

Most of the Soviet trucks are two and a half tons—so I learned at second hand from government sources here—some are four tons. How did military intelligence estimate their loads? In the U.S., where single trucks go as high as 15 tons, the average load per truck carried in 1965 (Motor Truck Facts, 1966) was only 2.65 tons. If they average two tons per load in North Vietnam they are doing miraculously well. This would mean 4,400 tons carried by those 2,200 trucks. Let us make it 5,000 tons to even it off. This still leaves 20,000 tons to be accounted for.

The communiqué says about 1,570 vessels were spotted between the 17th and 19th parallels but admits that 600 were "moving north," while "approximately 970 were observed moving south." Obviously ships heading north were not carrying supplies for the guerrillas in the South. So this leaves 20,000 tons to be carried by 970 vessels. Let us round this off to 1,000 vessels, which means 20 tons per vessel. But from all I can learn most of the vessels in Vietnam are sampans which do well if they carry 500 pounds or a quarter ton. They would have to make 80 round trips in four days to deliver 20 tons. Not even MACV in Saigon claimed these sampans had speedboat motors with which to scurry up and down the 100 miles between Dong Hoi and Vinh that fast.

It turned out in addition that waterborne supply was hampered by bad weather and heavy seas. When the truce ended the U.S. command admitted there had been a "considerable decline" in the southward movement of North Vietnamese supplies but did its best to hide the cause. "This could mean," the AP from Saigon said the military explained (*St. Louis Post-Dispatch*, February 12), "that with extra munitions [nobody had turned up proof of munitions at all] piled up on the border [nor that any shipments had actually been spotted at any border], President Ho Chi Minh's regime did not want its trucks and boats exposed unnecessarily—loaded or empty—after Sunday's dawn" when the truce ended. It was only in William Tuohy's dispatch from Saigon next day in the *Los Angeles Times* that I learned "the level of waterborne shipments down the coast of North Vietnam decreased because of high surf."

Between the high surf and the tall tales, the truth was easily lost to sight. The U.S. military—with the State Department and the White House—have never pulled off a more successful Operation Brain Wash.

February 27, 1967

THE MENDACITIES GO MARCHING ON, TRUCE OR NO TRUCE

The U.S. used the Têt truce in Vietnam to bring up supplies for the biggest ground operation of the war. This is the truth hidden from the American public, which is still being fed the myth that massive supply operations in North Vietnam gave Johnson no alternative but to resume his bombing. The brain-washing that afflicts most Americans was deliciously summed up by a cartoon in the *Montreal Star*. This showed two U.S. officers beside a huge battleship being loaded with troops while cranes swung tanks aboard overhead. One officer says to the other, "Just watch those Congs use the truce for a big buildup."

In last week's issue we exposed the fraudulent campaign about a huge and illegal supply buildup in the North. No sooner had we gone to press than it was announced February 23 that some 30,000 troops had launched "Junction City," a giant search-and-destroy operation against the Viet Cong Zone C in Tay Ninh Province, the biggest yet in this war. Readers will recall that last week we quoted an *Agence France Presse* dispatch from Saigon in *Le Monde* (February 12–13) which described the "long files" of military trucks stretched out during the truce on the road from Saigon to Tay Ninh and the loads of shells for 105-mm and 155-mm cannons being hauled to American units on the edge of Zone C. When the offensive was unleashed from there the following week *AFP* in *Le Monde* (February 25) reported that this offensive "had been prepared during the Têt truce." Not one word of this has appeared in the U.S. press. I managed to break through the Iron Curtain that shelters government propaganda here by making available advance proofs of last week's issue to *The Guardian* in London and Manchester which printed a résumé of our story under a four-column headline on page one, Friday, February 24. This produced so many queries from London that the Pentagon that day was forced to issue a denial, which appeared on the UPI wire but was printed only in London. It isn't much of a denial and it embodies a new falsehood.

The Pentagon denies that it ever charged that the North Vietnamese were violating the truce by their supply activities (all north of the 17th parallel so far as our own reconnaissance observed it) and that it never denied that we were using the truce for movement of supplies, too. Literally this may be so. But the White House, the State Department and the Pentagon certainly did their best to create a contrary impression without explicitly stating a falsehood. Indeed its spokesmen continue to foster that false impression. Senator Russell repeated this myth when debate opened in the Senate February 23 on the supplemental Vietnamese war appropriation. Arthur Goldberg in Tokyo went even further. Three days after the Pentagon issued its denial here, Goldberg was repeating the same myth in Tokyo (*New York Times*, February 28) and adding a new embellishment: he claimed a violation not only of the truce but of the Geneva accord, though even our military did not claim that supplies had actually been spotted crossing the 17th parallel!

It is frustrating to feel so powerless as these myths go marching on. I feel as if I were being smothered under a blanket. The new falsehood in the Pentagon reply was in its smug assertion that all the truce meant to us was higher wages for longshoremen since we have air and naval supremacy "and have no need of a truce of any kind to move supplies." Let us put aside for a moment the Double-Think character of this remark, which implies that any time our bombing of the North stops it is somehow not cricket for people there to breathe freely and move around normally, while the cessation lasts. The hidden falsehood lies in the fact that while we do dominate the air and the sea, we do not dominate the roads in South Vietnam. "Normally"—to use the word our military applies to the constant bombing of the North—we cannot move supplies on most of the roads in the South without a heavy investment of armor and troops.

In the truce, supply was not a violation by either side. To fire upon a convoy (or an air strip) was a violation of the truce. It was therefore easier and less costly for us to move on the roads (and far less dangerous to land and drop supplies upcountry).[1] Tay Ninh has been an air supply area. It is much more costly and difficult to move heavy supplies by air, especially when small air strips ("normally" subject to enemy fire) limit landings to helicopters and the smaller cargo planes. To get from Saigon to Tay Ninh city on the edge of Zone C one goes about forty-five miles northwest on Route 1 and then about thirty-five miles north on Route 22 to Tay Ninh. Few Americans are foolhardy enough to venture very far out of Saigon on Route 1 even by day without a military escort, and fewer still on Route 22, where peasant and commercial traffic—as our military admits—pay road fees to the Viet Cong. Helicopters and tanks protected the trucks which went up those roads during Têt, but they didn't have to fear the kind of traps, ambushes or blocks of "normal" times.

When Saturday's *Le Monde* (February 25) reached me Sunday with its reference to the use of Têt by U.S. forces to prepare the "Junction City" operation, I called this to *The Guardian*'s attention. It published this in London Monday morning. As a result there were questions from Laborite backbenchers in the Commons that day, notably by Sidney Silverman, James Davidson and Michael Foot. Foot asked the Foreign Minister whether the new offensive had not been made possible in part by resupplying during the truce. But this and similar questions drew evasions rather than denials from the foreign minister, George Brown. All this, too, was blacked out in the U.S. press. No one reported either the questions or the answers and it was only by telephoning London that I was able to learn about it in time for this issue. Here the initiation of naval shellfire, river mines

---

1 This may explain the sharp increase in air cargo during Têt which we also reported last week.

and artillery barrages across the parallel is accompanied by
the usual escalation in mendacity. Mr. Johnson summoned
an impromptu press conference to deny that these new
moves constituted escalation at all. He said he wouldn't describe them as *any* kind of step-up because, as he said, "I
wouldn't want to put my credibility in doubt." Nobody
had the temerity to suggest this was a maidenhead he had
lost a long time ago.

March 6, 1967

HOW TV AND PRESS
WERE LED TO REHASH
THOSE TÊT SUPPLY LIES

Just how uncritical, and indifferent to the truth, most of the
press, TV-radio and magazines are, was demonstrated again
by the results of the briefing the Pentagon held March 17
on the eve of the Guam conference. Thirty-two reconnaissance photos and charts (hitherto shown only privately to
equally gullible Congressmen) were released. News stories
and TV-casts thereupon rehashed the myth that we had to
resume the bombing of the North because the Communists
took advantage of the truce for massive resupply to their
troops in South Vietnam. "How Reds Cashed In On Bombing Pause" (*U.S. News & World Report*, March 27) was a
typical headline.

We were not invited to the briefing but were able next
day to see the text and the photos at the Pentagon. Few
reporters seem to have examined either carefully. The heading itself was a giveaway. It said "Briefing by Defense

Spokesman on Tết Resupply Activities *Within* North Vietnam" (my italics). It did not allege a violation of the truce nor deny that we had stepped up supplies during Tết, too. No claim was made, and no photos showed, that supplies had been observed crossing the 17th parallel. The nearest point of heavy supply activity was at Quang Khe, "about 55 miles north of the demilitarized zone." Trucks were shown moving "toward Mugia Pass" but none actually in the pass, which is supposed to be the entrance to the "Ho Chi Minh" trail in Laos.

Perhaps in response to critical analyses like those in this *Weekly*, the Pentagon briefing for the first time admitted, "some of this activity was believed to be associated with the redistribution of food and other non-military products required by various segments of the economy," and to "military forces stationed in that general area of *North* Vietnam" (my italics). No military supplies were identified in any of the photos and caption of the ninth photo said of the "containers, baskets, boxes and bags . . . clustered near the shoreline" that "many of the bags and baskets presumably contained food . . . and other non-military products." It added, "It must be emphasized that this was not all bound for South Vietnam." These admissions were not mentioned in any news stories or TV-casts we saw.

Originally the press was told the North moved 35,000 tons "southward" during the truce. Now the Pentagon scaled this down to 23,000 tons. It appeared from chart number 25 that this 23,000 was "estimated" from "a detailed analysis" of "photographic and visual sightings." Just how the estimate was made was not explained.

Chart number 32 said, "the largest logistic resupply effort ever detected" took place during Tết. This sounded pretty sensational until the figures were examined. Chart number 25 said 1,400 water craft were sighted during the truce, "an average of 350 craft per day or twenty-eight times the daily norm." This puts the "daily norm," i.e., under bombing and shelling, at an average of twelve and a half ships per day.

Traffic "normally" must be almost dead if that is all the ships we sight a day along two hundred thirty miles of coastline between Haiphong and the DMZ.

A second figure claimed "sightings of 2200 trucks," an average "of 550 per day, or twenty-two times the daily norm." That makes the "daily norm" only twenty-five trucks—in a country of 17 million people! This figure gives one some idea of the economic strangulation imposed by our bombing and blockade. The surprise is not that the North took advantage of the truce—as we did in the South—to speed up supplies, but that the volume observed was so small.

March 27, 1967

THEY'D DO ANYTHING
FOR THE PEASANT
BUT GET OFF HIS BACK

On the eve of the Guam conference, Vice President Humphrey delivered a speech to the National Farmers Union in Oklahoma. Nothing better attests the phoniness of Johnson's talk at Nashville and Guam about our "pacification" and "revolutionary development" programs in South Vietnam. For Humphrey, an American liberal speaking to the most progressive of the three big farm organizations in this country, devoted a third of his speech to Vietnam without mentioning the issues most vital to its people, 85 percent of whom are peasants.

The fundamental problem of land reform was not mentioned once. Neither was the problem of the exorbitant rents which absentee landlords continue to exact despite laws more than a decade old which were supposed to limit them to 25 percent of the rice crop. To speak as Humphrey did of the desire to become "free citizens rather than virtual serfs" without mentioning the conditions which keep them serfs marks a new stage in Humphrey's degeneration. He even had the effrontery to quote Tolstoy's famous remark about regimes which are willing to do anything to lighten the peasant's burden except get off his back. That exactly describes the alliance of landlord and militarist we are imposing by force on South Vietnam, and seek only to hide behind a façade of new elections rigged like last year's to keep out any elements not satisfactory to landlord and general. Our "revolutionary development" program is designed to prevent the development of that revolution in distribution of the land we were supposed to have promised Vietnam's landless at the Manila conference. Like everything else in Johnson's program, it must be read in reverse, as the opposite of what it seems to mean.

It will not escape the sharp-eyed that the final communiqué at Guam, instead of repeating the Manila promise of land reform, which implies land for the landless, refers vaguely to "reform of land policies and tenure provisions." This implies only some improvement in the conditions of sharecroppers and tenants. This, too, has been talked of for months without results. It is the scaling down even of the promises which is significant. Equally so is the appointment of Robert W. Komer as the President's No. 2 man for Saigon. Komer was for fourteen years a CIA man before he became assistant to McGeorge Bundy under Kennedy. Last March he was named Johnson's $30,000-a-year assistant for "peaceful reconstruction" in South Vietnam. Six months later he turned in a report on rural progress so spurious in its optimism that even Johnson seemed to be embarrassed by it and denied that "pacification" was going anywhere near so well. The impression Komer has created in Washington and Saigon is of an abrasive opportunist. His razzle-dazzle style of operation accords perfectly with Johnson's own which, ever since he called Diem "the Churchill of Asia" in 1961, has been to lay it on with a shovel. The self-

delusion which has marked official reports on Vietnam since
our involvement began may now be expected to reach ec-
static heights with Komer in charge. If he's an example of
CIA training, the Agency must be run by retired circus
press agents.

Next to land reform, the main question is political liberty. Among the urban middle class, this was the chief
source of dissatisfaction with the Diem dictatorship. "We
do not seek to impose our political beliefs upon South Vietnam," Johnson said grandiloquently at Nashville. "Our Republic rests upon a brisk commerce in ideas." [1]

But the last elections in Vietnam, for the Constituent Assembly, were held reluctantly and only to quiet Buddhist
agitation. There was freedom neither of party organization
nor of nomination, nor of the press. Two reactionary parties, the Dai Viets and the NQQVD, one an old stooge of
the Japanese and the other of the Kuomintang, were the
only ones allowed to operate. Ky promised that for seven
days before the election there would be freedom of the
press—but he never kept that promise. It is a black mark for
American journalism that no reporter seems to have raised
the question of a free press with either Johnson or Ky during the Guam conference.

How do you have a free election without a free press?
When will the censorship be lifted on the Saigon papers?
The most independent English-language paper in Saigon,
The Guardian, was suspended last December after only a
few months of publication when its editor dared question
the official story of how Tran Van Van, Ky's chief civilian
rival for the Presidency, was murdered. Its managing editor, Ton That Thien, was seen, and his cry of anguish "We
have become a nation of thieves and beggars" heard, on the
vivid CBS documentary about Saigon March 14. His life is
believed in danger. His friends are trying to get him an invitation to America. Why does no reporter raise the question

[1] A brisk commerce in standardized ideas—those who have non-
conformist views to offer are lucky to get precarious stalls on the edges
of the market-place.

of his fate and the future of the press with Ky and Johnson? Nothing could bring the ideals of America into greater disrepute among Asian intellectuals than the contrast between our constant talk of defending freedom and our complacent acquiescence in the total absence of a free press.

The chief question raised by the Guam conference is why it was held at all. The first natural reaction is to dismiss it as another publicity stunt were it not for the fact that originally there were no plans to include Ky or the other South Vietnamese leaders; that sounded as if something serious were afoot. Or could this merely have been another instance of Johnson's frenzied desire for "action"?

March 27, 1967

THE MINDLESS MOMENTUM OF
A RUNAWAY MILITARY MACHINE

The central thesis of General Westmoreland's debut on the home front is the oldest alibi of frustrated generals—they could have won the war if it hadn't been for those unpatriotic civilians back home. This was how the Kaiser's ex-generals consoled themselves over their beers after World War I and this was the soothing syrup the French generals spooned up after Dienbienphu. But the former lost the war despite all their monocled splendor because they invited exactly what they had always told themselves they ought to avoid—a war on two fronts, against France and Russia at the same time. The latter lost because their perpetual talk of how they were really winning, when year after year they were losing the finest cadres of the French officer class in the Indochinese morass, finally made the French people realize their generals were first-class liars and their dirty little colonial war not worth the cost. Both cases provide obvious parallels to our own predicament, headed as we are for that major war on the Asian mainland we were always told to avoid, and led by generals who have claimed to be winning ever since 1961, and still claim it, though, as Westmoreland also said, they see no end in sight! We wonder what kind of logic they teach them at West Point.

The heart of General Westmoreland's opening speech at the AP luncheon came when he said the enemy was "discouraged by repeated military defeats" but hanging on because "encouraged by what he believes to be popular opposition to our efforts in Vietnam." One does not need to be a military expert to question this assessment. From the enemy point of view, they are doing far better than they had a right to expect. An undeveloped nation of 30 million people with little industry of its own has defied the world's greatest military power for six years. The rebels have grown from a handful to a formidable army despite (or perhaps because of) the constant step-up in our bombardment North and South. In recent months a whole series of enormously expensive and glamorously named U.S. military sweeps have done little but tear swaths in the jungle. While our casualties have risen sharply, the enemy has managed to elude us, and to strike back at times and places of his own choosing. We are switching troops from the Mekong Delta to handle a swiftly deteriorating military situation in the northern part of South Vietnam. It is no secret that Westmoreland wants more troops and that we are going to need a limited mobilization to get them. Add the billion-dollar losses of our air war, and the growing difficulties of the no longer almighty dollar, as the mounting costs of this "little war" undermine it, and ask yourself whether the other side may not feel downright exuberant, indeed overconfident.

Let us put the case in the most hard-boiled terms. The United States can win this war in Vietnam *if* it is prepared to put in a million men, or more, and then to slug it out patiently year after year until the guerrillas are worn down.

It can win if it deliberately de-escalates the firepower and meets the guerrillas on their own terms, in close combat, instead of alienating the entire population with indiscriminate artillery and airpower. A nation of 30 million cannot defeat a nation of 200 million if the bigger nation cares enough to pay the price of victory and has the patience to pursue it. The key is *patience,* and patience is what the United States lacks. It is not just the signs of popular opposition to the war which encourage the other side. It is the visible impatience. Even our hawks don't like the war and want to get it over with as quickly as possible. For us the war is a nuisance. For them the war is a matter of life-and-death. They are prepared to die for their country. We are prepared to die for our country too—if it were attacked—but not for the mere pleasure of destroying theirs. This is why they have the advantage of morale, and for this General Dynamics cannot provide a substitute.

Self-deception has been the characteristic of our leadership in this war from its beginning. Self-deception is still the key to Westmoreland's presentation. Even after so many years he still refuses to recognize the popular roots of the Vietnamese rebellion. He prefers to see it as something essentially artificial and imposed, which Hanoi can turn off with some magic spigot. First we were going to end the war by bombing Hanoi, but now that we'll soon be running out of meaningful targets in the North, we are in effect promised a quick victory if only we can bomb Berkeley into submission. The general who couldn't defeat the enemy abroad now returns to take it out on the *peaceniks* at home. Our country, he says, is founded on debate. But now, though we may be blundering toward a world war, we are told that debate is treasonable. The greatest issue in our country's history must be decided by momentum and default. Our generals would like to suppress peace sentiment here as they do in Saigon. Free discussion is to be made suspect.

A "high government source" told an equally anonymous *Baltimore Sun* (April 21) reporter (we suspect it was Johnson himself talking to his friend Philip Potter) that the U.S. had to avoid the buildup of a war psychology at home and conduct the Vietnamese war "rather coldly" because our power is so "beyond comprehension" that we mustn't let it get out of hand "if the Northern Hemisphere is not to go up in smoke." This is the awful truth a solemn joint session of Congress ought to hear. Yet Johnson is doing what his better judgment tells him not to. Westmoreland is stepping up war fever at home while abroad the wraps are taken off Hanoi, Haiphong and the Mig air bases in a way which brings nearer that final confrontation with China and perhaps also the Soviet Union. As Senator McGovern told a *Washington Post* reporter (April 26) after a brilliant and courageous Senate attack on the growing war madness, "They [i.e., Johnson and the generals] are really going for broke." As the fog of war closes in, and the drums beat louder, which is patriotism, which is love of country, to fall silent or to try and speak some sobering word?

May 1, 1967

IF DADDY KEEPS AT IT, LUCI,
ONE DAY YOU WON'T WAKE UP

The President's now famous "World War III" bedtime remark to his daughter, Luci, deserves closer examination. The story has been circulating in the press corps on an off-the-record basis for months. Mr. Johnson has told it so often that it is surprising it did not get into print sooner. It seems to have become one of his favorite anecdotes. One can understand a worried President telling his daughter the night of the first air raids in the immediate vicinity of Hanoi and Haiphong, "Your Daddy may go down in history as

having unleashed World War III," adding, in case that was
not enough to get her attention, "You may not wake up
tomorrow." But it is hard to understand the mentality that
can tell and retell the story as if it were some kind of credit-
able escapade. A James Reston column November 4, 1966
quoted Johnson as saying he had been on tranquilizers
since his heart attack in 1955. If this is how lightly Johnson
risks a world war, the rest of the country had better start
taking them too.

The most extraordinary aspect of this affair has gone unnoticed. The day after the remark to Luci, Johnson flew
out to Omaha for a speech in which he told the people of
this country, "Peace is more within our reach than at any
time in this century." This should add a few miles more to
that credibility gap. Ever since Johnson made his first major
escalation in February, 1965, by beginning the bombing of
the North, there have been repeated hints in the press that
Hanoi and Haiphong were to be left alone because Peking
or Moscow or both might intervene if the capital and the
main port of North Vietnam were smashed. It has been impossible to ascertain if these hints reflected discreet warnings from the Russians and Chinese or discreet reassurances
from Washington. Now we learn from the Luci anecdote
that Johnson, in authorizing air strikes for the first time
within the immediate vicinity of Hanoi and Haiphong, felt
that he was risking World War III. The country was neither consulted nor advised on the gravity of that step. On
the contrary, it was deceived. The only sense in which it
could truthfully be said that peace was then "more within
our reach than at any time in this century" was if those air
raids had set off a full-scale nuclear confrontation between
the U.S. and USSR and with it a peace of extinction.

The only charitable explanation is that when Johnson
spoke of peace that day in Omaha and again at Des Moines,
he meant the surrender of the other side and had been sold
the idea by the Joint Chiefs of Staff that these bombings
were worth the risk because they offered a quick victory.
The June 29 raids opened three weeks of savage attacks on

the oil installations in and around Hanoi and Haiphong.
The briefings in Saigon and the press conference held by
Secretary McNamara the day they began created the im-
pression that this was a swift and easy way to dry up North
Vietnam's aid to the guerrillas. McNamara said the raids
were ordered "to counter a mounting reliance by North
Vietnam on the use of trucks and powered junks to facili-
tate the infiltration of men and supplies into South Vietnam." Triumphant headlines appeared next day over the
Navy's claim that two miles from the center of Haiphong
its fliers had hit installations representing 40 percent of
North Vietnam's oil storage capacity and 95 percent of its
tanker-unloading capacity and left them 80 percent destroyed. From these first headlines one would have imagined
that henceforth only a trickle of light arms transportable by
bicycle and foot would reach the South while the economic
life of the North would be crippled.[1]

Now almost a year later, it is clear that the sequel of these
raids was a sharp escalation in the volume and size of the
arms and ammunition supplied. There has been an extraordinary increase in the firepower of the guerrillas. SAM's
have appeared as far south as the demilitarized zone, where
they recently shot down a Skyhawk jet and forced suspension of B-52 flights in that area; the B-52 flies too low and
too slowly to evade the SAM. The 140-mm rocket made its
appearance in the attack on the Danang air base last February and on May 12 as far south as Saigon, where it was used
in the attack on Bien Hoa air base. There six Americans were
killed, one hundred wounded and twenty-nine planes destroyed or damaged. American casualties are increasing.
The number of both guerrilla and conventional clashes
seem to have risen and the so-called "pacification" has had
to be shifted to U.S. military control to save it from collapse. The South Vietnamese have failed to provide secu-

[1] Few noticed, however, that eight days later reconnaissance photos
showed 70 percent of the installations were still in operation (*Facts-on-
File*, July 7). These sober revisions never seem to catch up with the
original claims in this fallaciously precise numbers game.

rity: as against 25 attacks all last year on "pacification" teams there have been "more than 300 attacks this year on pacification teams and more than 500 team members have been killed or wounded" (Raymond Coffey from Saigon in *Chicago Daily News*, May 5). These CIA-trained teams have the job of "rooting out" suspected subversives in the villages; it is easy to imagine the injustice they commit and the hatred they sow.

What all this spells is the coming end of the politically comfortable war Johnson has so far waged—a war without special taxes or wage and price controls, a war of one-year tours of duty, fought by the less fortunate of our society, white and Negro, while the junior executive types of the politically powerful Reserve forces have escaped a call-up. Now the military forces are crying out for more troops or "we'll be here forever," as Hanson Baldwin's anonymous source put it in the *New York Times*, May 17. Here again it is worth looking back at the events of last June 29. Again there is the temptation to "go for broke" in one big new plunge, then at the oil resources of the North, this time perhaps to shut off Haiphong harbor altogether, again at the risk of a confrontation with Russia—anything rather than face the reality of a long, painful war of attrition on the ground against resolute guerrillas. Again Johnson would rather gamble on World War III than face elections next year with a country awakened to the painful costs.

McNamara said June 29 in announcing the new step-up in air raids that one of the purposes was to punish the North for continuing its attempt "to subvert and destroy the political institutions of the South." This is the myth that leads to disaster. If this is not a rebellion but a conspiracy and an invasion, why limit the punishment to North Vietnam? Why not hit at the sources in China and Russia? Why not make it painful for the Kremlin? The theory of the war as an external conspiracy which can be shut off like a faucet leads straight to a confrontation with Moscow. This is the inescapable logic of the Johnson-Rusk-McNamara theory of the war. This is the reason for the fresh outcries in the

Senate. This is why U Thant warns that we may be in the
first stages of World War III. This is why the Pope spoke
in anguish at Fatima. Desperation, impatience, the oversim-
plification of a complex struggle are leading Johnson
straight to a confrontation that would put world civilization in jeopardy.

May 22, 1967

NONE SO BLIND AS
THOSE WHO WILL NOT SEE

A new stage in the Vietnamese-American tragedy began
with the arrests of Dr. Spock, the Reverend Coffin and the
three other leaders of the draft resistance movement. We are
headed for escalation—in repression at home and in war
abroad. The two are the obverse sides of the same process.
There is an historic fitness in the coincidence of the arrests
with the Johnson Administration's campaign to fuzz, confuse and elude the possibility of peace talks opened up by
Hanoi's public declaration that talks "will," rather than
"could," follow an end of U.S. bombing. Our favorite
headline of the period was in the *Baltimore Sun*, January 6,
1968. It said, "U.S. Hunting Signs Hanoi Seeks Peace. Admits Its World-Wide Search Is Without Success." Johnson
and Rusk are cultivating myopia. They wouldn't be able to
see a peace talk offer if Ho Chi Minh brought it personally
to the White House West Gate.

The Administration's search for "assurances" before end-
ing the bombings in a pantomime for the naïve. In a local
New York TV program (WNBC, January 7), Edwin
Newman asked William P. Bundy, Assistant Secretary of
State for Far Eastern and Pacific Affairs, "Now would I be

correct in deducing from what you said, that if we had an assurance there would be no increase in the movement from North to South [i.e., of troops and supplies] that that would be sufficient for us?" To which Bundy replied cryptically, "Well, that's an illustration . . . one good illustration." Newman never got a chance to interrupt Bundy's slippery loquacity long enough to ask just how many "illustrations" would be required before we would agree to talk. Fulbright cut through the fog by telling the AP (*New York Post*, January 9), "The Administration is only interested in surrender."

From the Administration's point of view the alarming reactions to Hanoi's offer were not those which came from friendly and neutral capitals urging us to negotiate but from the U.S. embassy in Saigon. The fear there is that any real possibility of peace talks would lead to the collapse of the South Vietnamese government. Its leading figures would make plans to follow their bank accounts into exile while the lesser men would begin to make their own deals with the NLF. Johnson escalated the war in 1965 by putting U.S. ground troops into the South to avoid a military collapse. The escalations of 1968 will be aimed to prevent a political collapse. The bombings of Russian and Chinese ships in Haiphong harbor, the air attacks on Yunnan from across the Laos border, the itch for hot pursuit into Laos and Cambodia, and the plans for an "Inchon landing" across the DMZ into North Vietnam are the familiar symptoms of that "politics of escalation" with which the Johnson Administration has countered every opportunity for peace talks in the past.

Johnson prefers a wider war to a compromise peace. Only wider war can hide from public view how quickly his pumped-up campaign of optimistic forecast has collapsed. The successful attacks all over the country on U.S. and South Vietnamese outposts and airfields, up to the very outskirts of Saigon and Danang, show how very far the enemy is from military exhaustion. Politically the Saigon government is falling apart even without peace talks. The rigged elections gave the Catholic minority a dominant position in both houses of the new legislature and seemed to assure the military junta a built-in pro-war majority. But the rejection by both houses of the military decree drafting eighteen-year-olds shows how sick of the war even this once die-hard sector of Vietnamese opinion has become. The basic shift was plainly signaled when Saigon's Catholic clergy called for an end of the bombing and assailed the corruption in the regime. A Buddhist-Catholic alliance against the war is now shaping up, and even the labor movement—largely created by the CIA—is swinging against us with the police attacks on the electrical workers' strike in Saigon.[1] The regime's mass base is dwindling to the handful of last-ditch patriots who own the brothels and the bars.

The war this year will become more than ever an American war, and our army more plainly than ever an occupying force. Escalation will require more troops, and perhaps even the dangerous step—already rumored here—of bringing in Chinese troops from Formosa, a step which would inflame Vietnamese opinion and create more tension with mainland China. Indeed the military campaign for "hot pursuit" into Cambodia and Laos seems designed as a roundabout way to force such dangerous expedients and partial mobilization. We are already short of troops to deal with the swarm of attacks all over the country and to shore up the collapsing effort at "pacification." Any serious efforts at "hot pursuit" across the border would soon force Johnson to provide more troops even if it meant higher draft calls and mobilization of reserves in an election year. *U.S. News & World Report* estimated (December 11) that the Cambodian sanctuaries could be "cleaned out" with three U.S.

---

[1] An AP dispatch we saw only in the Washington *Star* January 12 said six labor leaders were arrested by the police as they left a bargaining session with government officials in Saigon. Tran Quoc Buu, chairman of the Vietnamese Workers Federation, predicted the arrests would lead to a general strike by its 300,000 members. "How can we fight against the Communists under these conditions?" he told the AP. "We lose all right to fight against the Communists when things like this happen." Until now Buu and his unions have been faithful creatures of the U.S.

divisions. But to get three more divisions would require a step-up in the draft at home. This means more draft resistance and an intensified struggle in the Negro ghettoes. To shut the door on peace abroad is to invite more racial conflict at home. This is the direction of Johnson's policy and this is the larger dimension of the unfolding tragedy. . . .

January 22, 1968

SAIGON AFIRE NOW— WILL IT BE WASHINGTON IN APRIL?

It is no longer necessary to argue the mendacity of our leaders and the incompetence of our military. Mr. Johnson has assured us that the successful surprise attack on 100 South Vietnamese cities and towns was really a Viet Cong defeat; if they suffer a few more such defeats, we'll be lucky to settle for a coalition government in Hawaii.[1] No nation ever had the misfortune to be led by a bigger team of clowns than those whom Johnson and Rusk, and Westmoreland and Bunker put through their daily capers in Washington and Saigon; their body counts alone are enough to make Bob Hope jealous: these seem to be based on an extension to warfare of installment credit principles—count now, kill later.

[1] Sir Robert Thompson, who ran Britain's successful anti-guerrilla campaign in Malaya and was head of the British Advisory Mission in South Vietnam from 1961 to 1965, wrote of these attacks in the London *Sunday Times* February 11, "In terms of guerrilla and mobile warfare, Gen. Vo Nguyen Giap has achieved a master stroke in South Vietnam and has greatly enhanced his reputation—if such a thing were possible—as an outstanding general and victor of Dien Bien Phu."

We still don't know what hit us. The debris is not all in Saigon and Hué. The world's biggest intelligence apparatus was caught by surprise. Our No. 1 Whiz Kid, the retiring Secretary of Defense McNamara, capped his record of misjudgments on Vietnam by preparing a final defense "posture" statement in which he reported "a drop in [Viet Cong] combat efficiency and morale"! The day he read this report to the Senate Armed Services Committee the Viet Cong made their nationwide raids. Neither under Japanese nor French occupation were the rebels ever able to stage such widespread and coordinated attack. Yet we have 500,000 troops in the country as compared with the 60,000 of the French; our Army is incomparably better supplied with firepower and airpower; and for three years we have been bombing the North so heavily that every town and city except Hanoi and Haiphong is in ruins.

When the bodies are really counted, it will be seen that one of the major casualties was our delusion about victory by airpower: all that boom-boom did not keep the enemy from showing up at Langvei with tanks. Three years of interdiction by airpower and the rebels are steadily better equipped; the days when they depended on weapons captured from our side are long over. Another casualty is the reputation of Westmoreland and our Joint Chiefs of Staff. On TV Westmoreland and Wheeler began to look more and more pathetic as they clung to those inflated body count box scores which only they still take seriously. It is as if they mistake the art of warfare for the demolition and extermination business. Giap is proving that superior military and political skill can win over vastly superior firepower, i.e., brain power over bulk. This is what did in the dinosaur.

Two events during the uprising were deadly. They will never be forgotten as symbols the world over of what the Pax Americana really means for the people we claim to be protecting. One occurred at Bentre after it was shelled "regardless of civilian casualties," as the ordinarily unemotional AP reported February 7, "to rout the Vietcong." A

U.S. major explained, "It became necessary to destroy the town to save it." This will go down in the history books as typical of our whole Vietnamese campaign. The whole country is slowly being burnt down to "save it." To apply scorched-earth tactics to one's own country is heroic; to apply it to a country one claims to be saving is brutal and cowardly. Everywhere we call in artillery and air strikes rather than fight it out hand-to-hand with the guerrillas; this has been characteristic of our intervention from the beginning and this is the secret of why the rebellion grows ever stronger. It is we who rally the people to the other side.

The other incident took place at Khesanh where we turned away not only civilian refugees but allied forces fleeing the fallen camp of Langvei. We not only refused them shelter but disarmed them before driving them away. The best account was a magnificent on-the-spot piece of journalism by Newbold Noyes in the Washington *Star* February 11. The decision was based, it is clear, on two motives. One was an unwillingness to share precious supplies, but had they been Americans our men would have shared their last crust to give them shelter. The other was the suspicion that there might be Viet Cong among them. How can one fight a successful war when mistrust of one's own allies is so deep? Colonel Lownds, the commander at Khesanh, acted only after consulting higher quarters and was in agony over the decision. "This thing," he told Noyes, "can come back to haunt me—all of us. If these people say when the chips were down, after getting us to fight for you, you wouldn't protect us, then the whole civic action business here goes down the drain." The truth is that when the chips are down we feel that the "gooks" (or whatever the similar term of the moment) are expendable. To the darker peoples everywhere this incident will sound (fairly or unfairly) like "whitey" all over again. Don't think it won't rankle.

The idea that we Americans are a superior race, and are justified in using any means of mass killing to save American lives, will be the argument for using tactical nuclear weapons in defense of Khesanh. It is this racial angle above

all which would make it madness for us to add nuclear
weapons to the suffering we have already imposed on the
Vietnamese people. Let just one "little" tactical nuclear
weapon be used at Khesanh and the moral devastation will
be beyond calculation. It will stir race hate among the colored peoples everywhere; they will feel that again they and
not whites are the guinea pigs of these terrible weapons.
The Chinese will bank this away as moral capital for the
day when they can wage nuclear war on us. At home the
awful split among our own people will be vastly deepened.
The alienation among the youth and for every American of
conscience will be beyond anything we have yet experienced. By far the strongest reason for getting out of this
Vietnamese war as soon as possible is because sooner or later
it will carry us to that fatal step, that crime against mankind.

It is time to stand back and look where we are going.
And to take a good look at ourselves. A first observation is
that we can easily overestimate our national conscience. A
major part of the protest against the war springs simply
from the fact that we are losing it. If it were not for the
heavy cost, politicians like the Kennedys and organizations
like the ADA would still be as complacent about the war as
they were a few years ago. A second observation is that for
all the poppycock about the Vietnamese war clashing with
our past traditions, we have long been an imperialistic
people. The Truman Doctrine and the Johnson Doctrine
are only extensions of the Monroe Doctrine, new embodi-
ments of that Manifest Destiny to which our expansionists
appealed in a less cautious day. Bolívar once said that we
plagued Latin America in the name of liberty; today we do
it to a growing sector of the world. Everywhere we talk
liberty and social reform but we end up by allying ourselves
with native oligarchies and military cliques—just as we have
done in Vietnam. In the showdown, we reach for the gun.

And this I fear is what we are going to do at home in
dealing with the rising threat of a Negro revolt. We could
be in the first stage of what Mao has envisaged—a world-

wide colonial uprising against American power, accompanied by a complementary and similar rising of blacks in the racial colonies that our ghettoes have become. It is foolish to dismiss Mao's vision because the guerrilla movements in Latin America and Africa have so far proven unsuccessful and because most Negroes still want only to be accepted fully as fellow Americans. These facts give us time to save our country but only if that time is utilized wisely and quickly. So long as the war goes on it must deepen racial bitterness at home and abroad, because colored peoples are the victims and because colored men make up so disproportionately large a share of our own combat troops while the cry rises to save the white boys from the draft for the graduate schools. And the longer the war goes on the less money we have for the giant tasks of social reconstruction at home. We put $2 billion into the French attempt to hold Indochina. We have spent $65 billion since 1954 on our own. This year the war will easily cost $30 billion. The new "defense" budget has already burst its seams with the *Pueblo* affair, and it was already $80 billion. These stupendous sums are the counterpart of the precious time and energy we waste.

Now Martin Luther King announces a new march on Washington for April. Negro moderates regard it as the last gasp of the nonviolent movement. If it fails, they see race war in our cities. Dr. King, as always, is playing it by ear. He is a mystic. He has no concrete program. He has no clear aim except the full emancipation of his people. The nearest thing to a concrete objective is the Conyers bill, which would spend $30 billion—the cost of one year in Vietnam—for the rehabilitation of our slums and the human beings twisted by life in these urban jungles. That bill hasn't a chance in this atmosphere. The whole trend is to cut rather than to increase welfare expenditures. The emphasis is on repressing crime in the streets, which translates into repressing the Negro. Johnson gave in to that trend by calling in his crime message for enactment of a federal inciting-to-riot bill, which the Administration liberals have fought for two years. The Attorney General, like the new report on the Newark "riots," has stressed that these racial convulsions are due to misery, not conspiracy. But we are moving inexorably to the club, the gun and the jail, to a Vietnam at home.

Troops are being trained to fight urban guerrillas. GI's in Vietnam are being offered discharge 90 days early if they join an urban police force back home. Dr. King promises nonviolence but he also projects a vast sit-down to bring Washington to a standstill unless it prepares to give the Negro what he wants. If he fails, more Negro youth will turn to the revolutionary way. The chances of avoiding some outburst of violence during those April demonstrations will grow slimmer the longer they last. Some shooting, even accidental, may anger even Washington's apathetic Negro population and set off racial fighting here and by chain reaction in other cities. To move toward the end of the war, to show a readiness to spend for reconstruction at home instead of devastation abroad, would change the whole atmosphere. Must we wait until the fires that rage in Saigon set Washington ablaze too?

February 19, 1968

PART III

'... Will It Be Washington in April?'

THE FIRE HAS
ONLY JUST BEGUN

The assassination of Dr. Martin Luther King, Jr., was the occasion for one of those massive outpourings of hypocrisy characteristic of the human race. He stood in that line of saints which goes back from Gandhi to Jesus; his violent end, like theirs, reflects the hostility of mankind to those who annoy it by trying hard to pull it one more painful step further up the ladder from ape to angel.

The President and the Washington establishment had been working desperately up until the very moment of Dr. King's killing to keep him and his Poor People's March out of the capital; his death, at first, promised to let them rest in peace. The masses they sang were not so much of requiem as of thanksgiving, that the nation's No. 1 Agitator had been laid to rest at last. Then a minority of his own people, and not all of them the ignorant and the hungry, celebrated his memory with an orgy of looting while black radicals and New Leftists hailed the mindless carnival as a popular uprising. Since the liquor stores were the No. 1 target, it might sourly be termed the debut of Marxism-Liquorism in revolutionary annals. Those among his own people who sneered at his nonviolent teaching as obsolete now seized upon his death as a new excuse for the violence he hated. Thus all sides firmly united in paying him homage.

Dr. King was a victim of white racism. Its record encourages such murders. Dr. King was only the most eminent in a long series of civil rights victims. The killers are rarely caught, even more rarely convicted; the penalties are light. The complicity, in this case, may go further. It is strange that the killer was so easily able to escape when the motel in which he was killed was ringed with police; some came within a few moments from the very direction of the fatal shot. Violent anti-Negro organizations like the Klan have their cells in many police forces. The Memphis police had shown their hatred in the indiscriminate violence with which they broke up Dr. King's march a week earlier. The Attorney General should be pressed to include the Memphis police in his investigation of the slaying.

Though Dr. King was the greatest Southerner of our time, few Southern political leaders expressed any sorrow over his passing. Most, like Stennis of Mississippi, ventured no more than antiseptic and ambivalent condemnation of *all* violence. In the House on April 8 the few Southerners who spoke deplored the riots more than the killing. The one exception was Representative Bob Eckhardt of Texas, who dared call Dr. King "my black brother." Privately many white Southerners rejoiced, and their influence was reflected in the scandalous failure to declare a holiday in the District the day Dr. King was buried. Though stores closed, government offices were open and Negro mailmen delivered the mail as usual. This is still, despite its black majority, a Southern-ruled town; it shuts down on Washington's birthday, but not Lincoln's.

The most powerful of the District's absentee rulers, Senator Robert C. Byrd (D. W. Va.), went so far as to imply in a Senate speech April 5, that Dr. King was to blame for his own death. Byrd said those who organize mass demonstrations may "in the end . . . become themselves the victims of the forces they set in motion." While Dr. King "usually spoke of nonviolence," Byrd went on smugly, "violence all too often attended his action and, at the last, he himself met a violent end." This should make Byrd the South's favorite criminologist.

Byrd is the Senator to whom the blacks of Washington must come for school and welfare money. As chairman of the Senate Appropriations subcommittee on the District of Columbia budget, Byrd wields far more power than the city's figurehead Negro "Mayor." He has used this key position to block liberalization of welfare rules not only in the District but in the country, since the federal government can hardly apply elsewhere rules more liberal than those he will allow in the District. Byrd has become the national pillar of the "man in the house" rule. This, as the report of the Commission on Civil Disorders protested, makes it necessary for the unemployed father to "abandon his family or see them go hungry." In this sense not a few of the child looters in our gutted ghettoes can trace their delinquency straight back to Robert C. Byrd.

For whites who live like myself in almost lily-white Northwest Washington on the very edge of suburbia, the ghetto disorders might have taken place in a distant country, viewed on TV like Vietnam (which it begins to resemble), or as a tourist attraction on a visit in the bright spring sunshine before curfew to the sullen and ruined ghetto business districts. It was not until five days after the trouble started that two young soldiers turned up for the first time to guard our own neighboring shopping center—"as a precautionary measure," they explained—and tape appeared on its liquor-store windows. Even sympathetic and radical whites found themselves insulated from what was going on not just by the military cordons but even more by an indiscriminate black hostility. Even some liberal and leftist families with children moved out of integrated neighborhoods on the edge of the ghetto in apprehension. These were our first refugees from black power.

Nothing could be more deceptive than the nationwide mourning. Beneath the surface nothing has changed, except perhaps for the worst. The President has called off his address to a joint session indefinitely. His Senate Majority Leader, Mansfield, warns the Congress not to be "impetuous" in reacting to the disorders. How fortunate we should be if all our dangers were as remote as this one! The new civil rights bill, if it passes, is more likely to bring new evils in its anti-riot provisions than reform in housing.

In Washington, as in most cities hit by black violence, the police and the troops have been on their best behavior to the point where business spokesmen are complaining that there has been too much leniency in dealing with looters.

For once, to the Administration's credit, lives have been put
ahead of property. Had police and soldiers begun to shoot,
the killings would have become a massacre and the riots a
black revolution. As it is, in Washington at least, the black
community has been grateful for the protection afforded it.
But this leniency is unlikely to survive when and if white
rather than black areas begin to go up in smoke. There is
little time left for the big multi-billion-dollar program
which alone can rehabilitate the hopeless and bitter generation of blacks that racial discrimination and the slums have
bred. Whites still think they can escape the problem by
moving to the suburbs, and as long as they think so, nothing
will be done. There are already 55,000 troops in our 110
scarred cities—more than we had in Vietnam three years
ago. Already the police talk of guerrilla war. If it comes, a
half million troops will not be enough to contain it. A looting suspect told one reporter at a police station here,
"We're going to burn this whole place. It might take years
but we'll do it." This is the agony of a lost race speaking. If
we cannot respond with swift compassion, this is the beginning of our decline and fall.

April 15, 1968

BILLIONS FOR MISSILES
AND PENNIES FOR POVERTY

The day the poor were driven out of Resurrection City was
the day the Senate voted to approve an anti-missile system.
Monday June 24 deserves to go down in history for its
symbolic significance. Congress turned a flinty banker's
face to the poor but took the first step toward the deployment of an ABM (anti-ballistic missile) network which

could cost more than their most utopian demands. The first installment for Sentinel, the "thin" one, is $5 billion. The total cost of the big one the military-industrial complex wants can easily run to $50 billion. Even that is only the beginning. For the ABM will set off a new spiral in the arms race, as each side builds more missiles to overwhelm the other's anti-missiles, and then more anti-missiles to counter the new missiles. "And at the end of it all," as Nelson of Wisconsin told the Senate that day, the U.S. and the Soviet Union "will be right back where we started, except out of pocket $50 to $100 billion."

While the chief lobbyist of the poor, the Reverend Ralph David Abernathy, went to jail, the lobbyists of the military-industrial complex celebrated their biggest victory. The ABM will prove to be our most wasteful handout. But the lobbyists who sold this bill of goods did not have to live in shanties or confront police lines on their way to the Capitol. The clients of the welfare state ought to get acquainted with the clients of the warfare state. The decision to go ahead with the ABM, the *Congressional Quarterly* said in a special study May 24 of the military-industrial complex, will benefit more than 15,000 companies including such major defense contractors as General Electric, General Dynamics and Thiokol-Chemical. One brokerage firm told its customers last summer that the day Congress approved the ABM was "the day they will shake the money tree for electronic companies." In the last quarter of 1967, after Johnson overruled McNamara and approved the Sentinel, seventy-five mutual investment funds "sold $90 million in other stock holdings [the *Congressional Quarterly* report says] and invested the proceeds in electronics."

The ABM is the latest breakthrough in the arms race, and it is time to recognize the arms race for what it is—the socialism of the rich. It is the welfare system which supports some of our richest corporations. The physicist Ralph Lapp, who did so much to arouse the country to the fallout danger in the campaign against nuclear testing, has provided the best overall view of what the ABM and the arms race

really mean in his new book, *The Weapons Culture*. The
spokesmen for the poor should use it as ammunition. Dr.
Lapp observed that the so-called free enterprise system "has
been distorted into a kind of 'defense socialism,' in which
the welfare of the country is permanently tied to the continued growth of military technology and the continued
stockpiling of military hardware." Dr. Lapp estimates that
since World War II the U.S. has spent about one trillion
dollars—1,000 billions or 1,000,000 millions—on armament! The program has fallen like manna on the country-
club set and—with the related space program—created a
whole new generation of millionaires. We could have
cleaned up every slum and solved every racial and social
problem with a fraction of the money, thought and energy
which went into military hardware, most of it already
junked as obsolete.

Solidarity Day brought a vast throng to Washington and
half a dozen Establishment phonies hastened to address it
from the Lincoln Memorial. But no occasional upsurge of
benevolent feeling, much less spurious oratorical generali-
ties about poverty, is going to change the allocation of
resources between those who grow rich on weaponry and
those who decay on welfare. The swift liquidation of Resurrection City once the visitors had departed was the reflection of a more permanent solidarity among those who
fatten on the waste of national income. Those poor shanties
the police destroyed were the first signs, we hope, of a widening and continued struggle against the inhumanity and
the irrationality of our spending policy. During the House
debate June 26 which ended with sharp cuts in the welfare
budget, a typical Iowa Republican opponent of the poverty
program said the country did not have "money to throw
away . . . on this type of luxury" while a tightwad on the
Democratic side (Flood of Pennsylvania) cried, "What do
you want? Diamonds? What are you going to use for
money? Cigar store coupons?" But when it comes to the
war machine and the space program the billions flow freely.

Mrs. Green of Oregon protested that this same Congress

had voted $4 billion for the space program. "That means," she said, "we are willing to spend more dollars for outer space than we are willing to spend in total amount of tax dollars for the education of fifty million boys and girls in our elementary and secondary schools." But education, unlike the race for the moon, does not rain dollars on Houston, Texas. "It makes me heart-sick," Mrs. Green cried, "to see my nation spending in one day in Vietnam more than the total amount of increase I am requesting that affects two million teachers and the quality of education for fifty million boys and girls." It is not only the blacks nor only the poor who suffer from the huge allocations to the war and space machines. It is the quality of American life. Urban blight and pollution could be ended permanently for what that war in Vietnam has cost us. Abernathy's little army has been fighting a battle for all of us.

Resurrection City is supposed to have been a mess. I found it inspiring. It reminded me of the Jewish displaced persons' camps I visited in Germany after the war. There was the same squalor and the same bad smells, but also the same hope and the same will to rebuild from the ashes of adversity. To organize the hopeless, to give them fresh spirit, to set them marching was truly resurrection. If much went wrong, that was to be expected; what was miraculous was that so much could be accomplished with the supposed dregs of our society. Disorganization is hardly a novelty in Washington; you can find it everywhere from Capitol Hill to the Pentagon. The striking thing about Resurrection City is that there was so much genuine non-racialism. The organizers have been given very little credit for bridging a gap everyone deplores. The Reverend Ralph David Abernathy is not the first man of God to be ridiculed and jailed. The wry humor of the poor he led was summed up for me by that touching sign on one of the mule wagons: "Don't Laugh Folks," it said, "Jesus Was A Poor Man." It would be tragic if their voices were so easily smothered.

The skewed vision which afflicts the respectable in our society was beautifully summed up in the outburst of concern for the twenty-three skinny mules that finally made it to Washington. The first edition of the *Washington Daily News* June 28 carried across its front page a picture of a mule in clover with a caption saying that the mules had been moved to pasture land in Columbia, Maryland, "where the meadows go for $8000 an acre and their next-door neighbors are $15,000 show horses and $20,000 stallions. 'They're going to be treated better than any mules in the history of muledom,' one bountiful lady says." What of the poor hungry human mules who balked at their heavy burdens?

When the Vietnamese war causes inflation, the poor bear the burden in the shape of higher living costs; they eat less. When higher taxes are imposed and the budget cut to save the dollar from inflation, the poor pay again in the shape of fewer jobs and reduced welfare. And now that there is hope the Vietnam war may be ending and more funds available to help them, the Under Secretary of the Treasury tells a Town Hall audience in Los Angeles June 25 that he doubts the end of the war will bring any sizable reduction in the military budget. Mr. Barr estimated that "a cessation of hostilities would result in great pressures to rebuild stock in military supplies and equipment to a more acceptable level." He informs us that "We have been fighting this war on a very, very lean [only $80 billion!] budget." How dare the poor be so obstreperous when the Pentagon is so hungry?

July 8, 1968

THE MASON-DIXON LINE
MOVES TO NEW YORK

On my way into New York City from La Guardia, the taxi-driver told me that his daughter, after a first year as teacher in a black ghetto, had transferred out to Long Island in despair. "The children were wonderful," he said. "The trouble was the parents." An hour later at lunch a Jewish schoolteacher from Brooklyn complained of the black children in her mathematics class for slow learners, but said the black parents, when she called on them for help, were without exception not only cooperative but grateful. But teacher and taxi-driver agreed in blaming Mayor Lindsay, though just for what was not clear. Indeed very little in New York's crisis is clear, perhaps because the real motivations are kept hidden as shameful. More and more people, particularly among the striking teachers, and in the Jewish community, are flailing about in hysteria. A sample: I asked the Brooklyn schoolteacher just what was the issue in the strike. She replied with appalling simplicity, "Anti-Semitism." How do you win a strike against anti-Semitism? By circumcising all gentiles and turning Black Muslims into Black Jews? "What does Mr. Shanker want?" the mayor asked in a similar vein in a radio interview next day. "For the police vans to come into the [Ocean Hill-Brownsville] community, arrest them and send them to New Jersey?" Is the Exodus to be re-enacted, this time with a black cast?

The plain truth is that John V. Lindsay is in trouble because he suddenly finds himself the Mayor of a Southern town. The Mason-Dixon line has moved north, and the Old Confederacy has expanded to the outer reaches of the Bronx. Even without this tide of racism, it would take a genius with two heads to govern the city successfully. Some of its basic problems are universal. One is size. Another is bureaucracy; the educational bureaucracy has entrenched itself in a maze of regulations beyond effective public control. A third is poverty; by next year one of every eight New Yorkers will be on relief. The city is choked with automobiles and people. Even if all eight million were a multiple birth from the same mamma, they would aggravate the hell out of each other. But in New York, as elsewhere, those of a different color, whether black or Puerto Rican, are no longer willing to accept second- or third-class citizenship submissively. They are pushing upwards into the better jobs and the sunnier places. In New York, the world's biggest Jewish city, this has created a special problem—a confrontation between blacks and Jews. This is rapidly turning Lindsay into the world's most down-trodden WASP.

The defeat two years ago of his proposal for a civilian review board to hear complaints against the police was the first disturbing signal in what had been the most liberal city in the country. New York's lower-middle-class whites were reacting like their counterparts elsewhere. In the struggle over schools the fears have now spread to liberal teachers hitherto sympathetic to the civil rights movement. Conflicts in the ghetto with Jewish landlords and storekeepers were relatively easy to contain. But the teachers' strike has churned up fears in an educational establishment that Jewish teachers and principals have dominated for a generation. Now that black unrest seems to threaten union standards and their jobs they are reacting like less liberal and less intellectual "ethnic" groups. The teachers' union is moving closer to the benighted old-line A.F.L. craft unions. A formidable anti-black coalition is shaping up. One of its victims may be the good name of the Jewish community.

If this great city is to be saved from race war, more Jewish intellectuals are going to have to speak up in ways that their own people will resent, just as white Southerners resented those who spoke up for the Negro. The teachers' union is exaggerating, amplifying and circulating any bit of anti-Semitic drivel it can pick up from any far-out black extremist, however unrepresentative, and using this to drive the Jewish community of New York into a panic. Albert Shanker and the teachers' union are exploiting natural Jewish fears of anti-Semitism in order to win the community's support for the strike and for its major objective, which is to prevent effective decentralization and community control of the school system. Unless more Jewish leaders speak up in public and say what they do in private, this manufactured hysteria may prove a disaster for both the black and the Jewish communities. Peoples, like generals, tend to be obsessed by their last war. To hear some New York Jews talk one would think the America of 1968 was the Germany of 1932. They do not see that they themselves are caught up in the backlash which is creating in Wallace the nearest American counterpart to Der Fuehrer, that they are joining the rednecks, that the danger lies in white racism not black. The latter is despairing and defensive; the former holds the potential of a new Nazism in its effort to maintain white supremacy. It would be eternally disgraceful were Jews this time to be among the Brown Shirts.

To visit the black-controlled schools which have stirred such forebodings on both sides of the controversy is like waking from a nightmare. I spent Friday, October 25, in the Ocean Hill-Brownsville district, observing classes and talking with teachers and principals in JHS 271 and its intermediate school neighbor, IS 55, and the visit was therapeutic. It was a day without pickets and I saw only one policeman. The atmosphere was incredibly different from what I had been led to expect. I found black and white teachers, Jewish and gentile, working together not just peacefully but with zest and comradeship. The cleanliness and the neat clothing of the children reflected well on the homes from which they came. The classes were orderly. There was none of that screaming by teacher against pupil, and among the children, which is common in most New York schools. I felt at the end of the day that the racial and union issues were terribly overblown and that the real concern within the embattled district was simply to create effective schools. I saw no reason why this could not be reconciled with proper union standards and I felt it would be a tragedy if this experiment in community control were shut down.

I watched Mrs. Naomi Levinson teach an English class full of eager black children. I read some of the touching poems and essays they had produced. "It's the first time in my eight years as a teacher," she told us proudly, "that I have been allowed to use unconventional teaching methods." I talked with another teacher, Leon Goodman, whose

face lit up with pleasure when he explained the new methods of teaching science he was allowed to apply. "We get
them to think rather than simply to copy down abstractions
from the blackboard." Both impatiently denied that they
had encountered any anti-Semitism.[1] I sat in on a teacher-
team conference of five English teachers, three black, two
white, one of the whites a delicate-featured blonde WASP,
the other an intense and dark-eyed Jew. The two whites
were volunteers. One of them had brought a bongo drum
into the classroom to use with the reading of Vachel Lindsay's incomparably rhythmic "Congo" as a way to awaken
the children to the wonders of poetry. The atmosphere of
this mixed group was wholly devoid of any racial self-
consciousness or tension. One felt their pleasure in working
together. In the corner of one classroom we watched a
young black teacher with a group of children who took
turns at reading "The Prince and the Pauper." On the
blackboard was the assignment, "Write a story about something that went wrong in a person's life" and next to it in a
row there were the helpful hints, "No money. Sickness. No
food. No light. No home. No friends. No job." The words
telescoped the familiar annals of the ghetto.

The only racialism, if it can be called that, was in the
evidence of efforts to awaken black pride. There were some
vivid watercolors produced in a new painting class and ex-
hibited in a hallway as "Soul on Paper." Another hallway
blackboard had "Black Is Beautiful" written not only in
French and Spanish but in Greek, Hebrew, Punjabi, Swa-
hili, Arabic and Esperanto. One room's walls were covered
with pictures and clippings variously headed "Religion,
Statesmen, Musicians, Scientists, Inventors, Diplomats"
showing black achievement in these fields.

In the classroom where Leslie Campbell, an African
gown over his normal clothes, teaches Afro-American
Studies, there were posters showing "Our Homeland" and
"Our Proud and Glorious Past." They reminded me of

[1] About three-fourths of the non-striking teachers in Ocean Hill-
Brownsville are white and about one half of these are Jewish.

Zionist posters in many Jewish Sabbath schools. There were also posters of "The Proud Look" and "Black Pictures of Christ." Campbell after class was friendly and open. He described himself as a black nationalist revolutionary but said he found himself very much in a minority on the faculty. "Most of my black colleagues," he said, "are simply educationists," though they agree on African studies for its psychological value. The other teacher of Afro-American Studies at JHS 271, Alan Kellock, turned out to be a young white man who has studied in Egypt and Ghana and is finishing a doctorate in African history for the University of Wisconsin. He said he had encountered no racial prejudice in Ocean Hill-Brownsville. What purpose did he see in Afro-American history courses? "To get the black children to feel they are worthwhile people. To give them a sense of identity and dignity." Kellock obtained his teaching license last summer. He feels JHS 271 is the most promising place to teach in the entire city.

David Rogers, in his blockbuster of a new book, *110 Livingston Street: Politics and Bureaucracy in the New York City School System*, quotes an authoritative earlier professional study of the city's schools by Strayer and Yavner. "The greatest failing of the schools today," they found as he did, "is the failure to use the creative ability of teachers." When I read this afterwards, I understood the enthusiasm I had found in the two schools I visited. I had thought of community control as a kind of lesser evil, a way of appeasing black dissatisfaction. I did not realize what a dead hand the bureaucracy has fastened on the schools and how much could be done just by lifting it. "Not many teachers come into the system sour," said Percy Jenkins, the Virginia-born Negro who is now principal of IS 55, "but they don't stay long without becoming sour. The kids come in with lively minds but by the fourth grade they too have lost interest." Jenkins himself, a graduate of West Virginia State College, had been in "the system" 15 years and risen to assistant principal before he was chosen to head IS 55 in this community-control experiment. "What you see here," one white teacher explained later, "is a function of the principal, of the fresh directions he maps out and of the commitment brought to this experiment by young liberal arts college volunteers with new ideas."

I spoke with Rhody McCoy, the head of the district; with his assistant, Lloyd Hunter; with the principal of JHS 271, William H. Harris, and with his white assistant principal, John Mandracchia. I have never met a more devoted group of people. All of them are harassed and overworked but sustained by a combination of desperation and joy, desperation because they fear the experiment may soon be wiped out under union pressure, joy in a chance to demonstrate in the little time they have what community control could accomplish. They are enlightened men; one forgets all the nonsense of black and white in talking with them; color vanishes. They fear black extremism as much as white misunderstanding. *And their focus is on the child.*

That cannot be said of their opponents. The child, whether black or white, seems to be the forgotten bystander in the teachers' strike. The union's rallying cry is "due process," i.e., for teachers, and its concern is their tenure. Its alliance is not with the parents for better education but with the employing bureaucracy for the maintenance of their common privileges. The "due process" issue they have raised is a monumental bit of hypocrisy. The best analysis of it may be found in the report by the New York Civil Liberties Union, *The Burden of Blame.* The unsatisfactory teachers were *transferred*, not discharged, and transfers normally are made without hearing or charges; the teachers prefer it that way, to keep their records free from blemish.

The real problem is how to keep teachers *in* ghetto schools. The Board of Education regulations are designed to discourage teachers from fleeing them. The contractual procedures between the Board and the union limit the teacher's freedom to transfer. "Yet," the civil liberties union reported, "in Ocean Hill-Brownsville, the UFT sought to ignore all these procedures and claimed the right for unlimited numbers of teachers to transfer out at will for the duration of the experiment, to abandon the experiment for as long as it continues and then to be free to return, presumably when 'normal' conditions had been reinstated. . . . Significant numbers of teachers did leave . . . Months later, when the Ocean Hill-Brownsville Local Governing Board attempted to exercise a similar unilateral right of transfer, the UFT cried foul."

The Board of Education's notions of "due process" are as one-sided. I have read the full text of the decision handed down by Judge Francis E. Rivers as trial examiner in the case of the transferred teachers. It is by no stretch of the imagination the vindication it appears to be in the headlines.

The hearing, by screening out all but professional witnesses, and barring not only parent testimony but that of para-professional school aides, and by applying strict rules of evidence unsuited to administrative procedures, managed to acquit the teachers without any real exploration of the charges against them.

The Board of Education is past master at manipulating regulations and procedures to achieve the ends it seeks. The Rogers book shows how hard it is even for teachers and principals to find out how it operates. Only a Kafka could do justice to the murk it generates. In a column on due process in the *New York Post* October 24, Murray Kempton provided an incisive glimpse of these operations in the proceedings now underway against four JHS 271 teachers accused of threats, or acts of terror, against attempts to reinstate the transferred teachers. Their attorneys were forbidden to see the reports on which the charges were based. When one attorney asked, "Do you proceed under any rules and regulations?" the reply was "We do not." After all this talk about due process, Kempton commented, "we suddenly discover that in this system there is no protection for anybody except the conscience and good-will of the Superintendent."

All bureaucracies are secretive, none more so than the New York Board of Education. The Rogers book is an eye-

opener, particularly in its account of how desegregation
was sabotaged by the Board. It did not work, Rogers concludes, "because the bureaucracy and the staff made them
fail." It was out of the frustration created by the failure of
integration that black and Puerto Rican parents turned to
community control. This, too, is being sabotaged by the
Board and by the union. They fear the loss of power and
privilege if democracy is substituted for bureaucracy.
They have the support of all the unions which do business
with the educational system, a billion-dollar business. The
New York trade union movement, like its educational establishment, has been a stronghold of white supremacy.
This is where and how the racial issue arises, and the Jewish
community is being enlisted because teaching has been a
Jewish preserve in New York as it was once an Irish Catholic preserve. If community control is crushed, the racial
struggle will take on more violent and hateful forms to the
detriment of both the black and Jewish communities.

The Jews, as the more favored and privileged group, owe
the underprivileged a duty of patience, charity and compassion. It will not hurt us to swallow a few insults from overwrought blacks. It is as right to invoke the better Jewish
tradition against Jewish bigotry as to invoke the better
American tradition against white racism. The genocidal
threat, if any, in this situation lies in the slow death and
degradation to which so many blacks and Puerto Ricans are
doomed in our slums. To wipe out the slums and help save
their occupants would be the truest memorial to those who
died in Auschwitz. When an idealistic young Mayor and
the Rabbi who tried to defend him are howled down in a
synagogue, it is time for the slap that can alone bring hys-
terics to their senses. Lindsay was saying "a Jewish philosopher—" when he was forced to leave. The philosopher he
was about to quote was Spinoza. He, too, was thrown out
of the synagogue in his time. We ought to have better sense
today.

November 4, 1968

NIXON ABOUT TO
ABOLISH HUNGER
"FOR ALL TIME"—AGAIN

On the problems of the poor, as on everything else, the Nixon Administration flounders about like a ship with a broken rudder. In its first months, the word went out that there would be no food stamp program. Then last May [1969] a day before Secretary of Health, Education and Welfare Finch and Secretary of Agriculture Hardin were to appear before the Senate's McGovern Committee on Hunger, the Administration decided it would be too embarrassing to let them go up on the Hill empty-handed. So Nixon sent Congress a food stamp message. The rhetoric had a high caloric content:

That hunger and malnutrition should persist in a land such as ours is embarrassing and intolerable. . . . Millions of Americans are simply too poor to feed their families properly. . . . Something like the very honor of American democracy is at issue. . . . The moment is at hand to put an end to hunger in America itself for all time.

To the hungry this must have sounded like the Prophet Elijah landing with a mandate from Heaven. But the program didn't match the advertising copy. It fit Senator Mondale's capsule history of the food stamp program. He said the government "keeps authorizing dreams and appropriating peanuts." Though "the moment" was "at hand" to "put an end to hunger . . . for all time," Congress is still waiting for the Administration to send up a bill. Even the niggardly Senate Agriculture Committee has reported out a food stamp bill better than Nixon's proposals, and it will be among the main items of business when the Senate reconvenes. Senator McGovern has a bill in (with 31 co-sponsors) which would expand our meager food stamp program to five times its current size. By failing to send Congress a specific legislative proposal, the White House is delaying action in food stamps altogether.

The confusion has been compounded by the President's new message on welfare. Two-thirds of all persons on relief are in dependent families. "For dependent families," Nixon said in his welfare message, "there will be an orderly substitution of food stamps by the new direct monetary payments." The food stamp program he outlined last May would apply only to single persons or childless couples. But, according to an analysis by the National Council on Hunger and Nutrition, if food stamps are eliminated this will cut welfare standards for 87 percent of those in dependent families. Nixon said his program would be "a leap upward for many thousands of families that cannot care for themselves." This would be true only for those living in Alabama, Florida, Mississippi, South Carolina and Texas. Even with a reasonable amount of state supplementation, four-fifths of those in dependent families will end up with less to eat under Nixon's latest program to end hunger.

The principle of a national standard and the principle of a minimum welfare guarantee represent steps forward but the ballyhoo[1] had best be muted until the fine print is available in a legislative proposal. It is not a guaranteed minimum income. "A guaranteed income," Nixon said, "would undermine the incentive to work." Every welfare recipient under Nixon's plan "must also accept work or training provided suitable jobs are available, either locally or at some distance if transportation is provided." At what rate of pay and under what conditions Nixon has yet to answer.

Nixon's New Federalism, in turning over employment training to the states, threatens to reinforce old forms of oppression. In the related field of vocational training, the

---

[1] *U.S. News & World Report* called the proposals "so revolutionary" as to create unrest in Congress while *Newsweek* said they were "so sweeping that even some of his Republican Cabinet officers were left gasping for conservative breath."

states have made a poor record. In welfare administration, most of the states and localities have been unsympathetic to the poor, especially the minorities. "If you feed 'em," one Southern county commissioner told a McGovern committee staff member, "they won't work." Would such officials force welfare recipients to take substandard jobs at substandard wages under threat of removal from the welfare rolls? Could this be used to undermine wage rates? To break strikes, particularly those pitiful stirrings of the unskilled and the unorganized at the rural level?

Nixon has often said it was dangerous to raise hopes that could not be fulfilled. His welfare program violates this favorite precept. Both the poor and the well-to-do taxpayers are in for disillusionment. He promised "a complete replacement" of the present welfare system with its humiliations, but the minimums he proposes are so low that the state welfare systems, snoopers and all, must remain in existence to supplement them. "A measure of the greatness of a powerful nation," he grandiloquently began his welfare message to Congress, "is the character of the life it creates for those who are powerless to make ends meet." How could he then without blushing offer a $65-a-month minimum to the aged, the blind and the disabled? And even less than that to dependent families—$500, or little more than $40 a month, for each adult; $300, or $25 a month, for each child? In what hovel without running water can you feed, clothe and house a family on that income level?

The $1600 minimum is based ultimately on the Agriculture Department's "economy" diet of $1200 a year for a family of four. Any mother who can perform the miracles of cooking, buying and storage this requires should have no trouble obtaining an executive job in industry. The biggest disappointment is invited by Nixon's promise in Madison Avenue prose to replace welfare with "workfare." The AFL-CIO's George Meany, in an unusually sharp criticism of Nixon's plan, pointed out that "contrary to popular conception, the nation's welfare rolls today cover fewer than 100,000 able-bodied men." Even with far more day-care, it is doubtful that enough working mothers can be drawn off relief to make more than a five percent dent in the relief rolls (500,000 off 10,000,000). As for his aid to working fathers paid below the poverty level, a minimum wage of $2 an hour for a 40-hour week would bring them out of poverty faster. Why should the taxpayer subsidize the substandard employer?

September 9, 1969

THE REAL MEANING OF NIXON'S JUDICIAL PHILOSOPHIES

In the general condemnation of the President's outburst over the Carswell rejection, one point seems to have been rarely made, if at all. When Nixon spoke of the right of the South and "its legal philosophy" to be represented on the Supreme Court, few commentators observed that this only referred to the white South. Of the 50 million Southerners, about 10 million are black. For them, the Haynsworth and Carswell appointments, far from being representative, were an affront. The "legal philosophy"—as Nixon so pretentiously called it—of these two mediocre Southern judges is only white supremacy, as reflected in their foot-dragging on civil rights.

It is a very serious matter for the country that in this time of racial crisis, we have a President for whom 10 million Southern blacks are invisible, politically non-existent. This is far less excusable in a northern president than it is in the average white Southerner. Nixon's predecessor, Lyndon Johnson, whatever his other faults, never showed such a blind spot to blacks, though a Southerner, nor to Mexican-Americans, though a Texan. On the contrary, he named the first Negro Judge to the Supreme Court. Johnson would never dare imply, as Nixon did in his statement protesting Carswell's rejection, that the South had a regional philosophy different from the rest of the country's. There is, after all, only one basic American philosophy, as expressed in the Declaration and the Constitution, and imposed on a rebellious South by the Civil War. It is a little late in the day to dignify racial inequality as an alternative American philosophy with a right to a seat on the Supreme Court, and more than strange to watch a Republican President march to the strain of Dixie.

There is today another white South which the President also ignores. It may be a minority white South, but when you add its numbers to the blacks and other minorities of color, it is big enough to elect a Yarborough in Texas and to lead the recent (and integrated!) Democratic state convention in South Carolina to reject a "freedom of choice" school plank. Indeed there are few places left in the South where a candidate for public office can treat blacks as politically non-existent. To act as if the South were still lily-white and monolithic, to key one's whole strategy opportunistically to Wallace, is to undermine that growing, more thoughtful white minority in the South *and on its courts*. When Nixon says the Senate would not accept a Southern nominee he is really saying that it will not accept the only kind of nominee which serves his short-sighted strategy. To nominate a judge like Frank M. Johnson or Elbert Tuttle or Bryan Simpson from the Southern federal bench (as the Reverend Ralph Abernathy suggested here the other night) would not fit into Nixon's plans because this would please the blacks and the non-bigoted whites, and give *their* South another representative, alongside Black and Marshall. The issue is not sectionalism but Nixon's effort—as Reverend Abernathy so well said—"to revive a dead order." Instead of building on a coalition of enlightened whites and blacks, Nixon is playing to the white mob. There could be no

greater disservice to our country, no more serious violation
of his oath of office.

Nixon's other complaint was that Haynsworth and Carswell were rejected because of "their philosophy of strict
construction of the Constitution—a philosophy that I
share." This also will not stand up under closer examination. Hugo Black is a "strict constructionist"—he applies
the Bill of Rights and other constitutional guaranties
strictly. Nixon and Mitchell are the loose constructionists.
Most crime, especially of violence, has always been a state
and local police matter. What could be a looser construction of the Constitution than to bring them under federal
control, as in their recent proposals on dynamiting? In the
past three generations liberals have used the commerce
clause to make possible all kinds of social reform. Nixon
and Mitchell are using it to create a federal police, and to
police not only criminals but the transportation of ideas
across state lines, as in the prosecution of the Chicago Seven.

When the Supreme Court recently held seven to one that
the double jeopardy clause of the Constitution forbids a state
to prosecute an acquitted man a second time on substantially the same evidence, who was construing the Constitution strictly—the majority or the lone dissenter, a Nixon-
style "strict constructionist," his Chief Justice Burger? Or
let us take a favorite proposal of the Nixon-Mitchell era,
preventive detention. What could be a looser construction
of the Constitution than to hold a man in jail before trial
because you think he might commit some other crime in the
meantime? You have to construe the Constitution with extraordinary looseness, in fact you have to ignore its guaranties of fair trial and bail, to arrive at any such result.

Yet the Administration has a bill in Congress to allow preventive detention in federal cases involving "violent" crimes.
It is trying to slip the same proposal through Congress this
year in the District of Columbia crime bill "by hiding it under a misleading title." The quotation is from a speech by a
Southern strict constructionist, Ervin of North Carolina. He
called the attention of the Senate April 8 to a study made

by the National Bureau of Standards for the Law Enforcement Assistance Administration of the Department of Justice. This showed how spurious were Attorney General Mitchell's arguments for preventive detention.

Mitchell claimed that "the pre-trial release of potentially dangerous defendants constitutes one of the most serious factors in the present crime wave." But the study showed that only five percent of those originally charged with a violent crime are rearrested for another violent crime—*arrested*, notice, not proven guilty and convicted. Ervin said the Nixon Administration was ignoring one of the most meaningful conclusions of the study. He said it "clearly shows that speedy trial alone would eliminate almost completely the small number of crimes committed by persons on bail." He told the Senate, "Our task is not to enact an unconstitutional and unwise preventive detention law but to insure that the constitutionally guaranteed right of speedy trial for all criminal suspects becomes a reality." He accused the Administration of using "the law-and-order slogan" to justify a "fundamental negation of America's constitutional traditions."

Behind Nixon's talk of the philosophy of strict construction, as behind his talk of the philosophy of the South, is plain and simple white middle-class prejudice. Preventive detention means putting blacks in jail more easily. His strict constructionism is only a legislative device for restricting the rights of the blacks and the poor generally, as when Chief Justice Burger dissented from a recent decision holding that welfare payments could not be cut off without first granting the recipients a formal hearing. The Nixon-Mitchell-Burger philosophy is to give fewer rights to the disadvantaged. It is the philosophy of the smug, the unsympathetic rich and the Southern white supremacist. That is the kind of majority outlook he hopes to create on the Supreme Court, whether by appointing mediocrities from South or North.

April 20, 1970

PART IV

Nixon: The Evil of Banality

SO WHAT'S A LITTLE
ISAIAH BETWEEN FRIENDS?

The Nixon inaugural must have set a record for the number of invocations. We counted four before Nixon took the oath and one afterward. Indeed it might be said there were six, for Nixon's own inaugural address was in the same genre, so much so that at óne moment when our attention wandered we thought Billy Graham had been elected President. From Nixon's first reference to "the majesty of this moment" to the peroration in which he urged us to build a "cathedral of the spirit," we realized we were hearing a Golden Treasury of the pulpit's most venerable purple phrases. The ministry lost what the country has gained.

Isaiah is our favorite prophet. Ordinarily we would have been pleased when Nixon let it be known that he would take the oath of office on a Bible with its pages open to Isaiah. But we could not forget that Johnson—who could also sound like Billy Graham—started out by leaning heavily on Isaiah, too. His favorite quotation, particularly in his campaign against Goldwater, was Isaiah's "come, let us reason together" but it fell into disuse after he began bombing North Vietnam. Nixon chose that page of Isaiah in which the Prophet spoke of beating swords into ploughshares. This would be heartening if Nixon's speeches on the need for bigger arms spending during the campaign, and his choice for Secretary of Defense, did not seem to suggest that we might have to beat ploughshares into swords. Melvin Laird hasn't been spending his years on the House Appropriations defense subcommittee trying to sell the armed services on Isaiah. Laird has written about a Strategy Gap. Nixon has spoken about a Security Gap, a Submarine Gap and an armament Research Gap. Perhaps it would be safest to put this Isaiah incident down to a Rhetoric Gap, like the

Gospel Gap which enables Billy Graham to denounce materialism—as he did at the Inaugural—while remaining a favorite spiritual back-scratcher of the pious rich.

We would be more impressed with the peaceful sentiments expressed in the Nixon inaugural if they had not become standard fare. Kennedy and Johnson, too, spoke evangelically in their inaugurals of the terrible power of the new weaponry, the need for peace and for diversion of resources to human need. Then they added a "but" about remaining strong, and this—if strength can be measured in more arms—was serious. "Let us cooperate," Nixon said, "to reduce the burden of arms. . . . But to all those who would be tempted by weakness, let us leave no doubt that we will be as strong as we need to be. . . ." Kennedy, too, made the same pledge and then in almost the same words added, "We dare not tempt them with weakness." Kennedy proceeded to step up the arms race and Nixon is pledged to do the same. Nixon announces an era of negotiation as Johnson promised "we will be unceasing in the search for peace." In less than two months he was bombing North Vietnam. Henry Cabot Lodge was then his special adviser and soon to be Ambassador in Saigon, as he will now be Nixon's at the Paris talks. Though the objective circumstances have changed, the parallels are not reassuring.

Our Presidents at their inaugurals have all come to sound like card-carrying members of the Fellowship for Reconciliation. It's easier to make war when you talk peace. They make us the dupes of our hopes, as the newspaper headlines the morning after the inaugural about Nixon's "sacred commitment" attest. Johnson, too, snowed the country with a similar performance when he went up on Capitol Hill for a last boast-in and sob-in among his old cronies, those aged pygmies in aspic, preserved from reality by the gelatinous mutual flatteries which fill the Congressional Record. They are all *g-r-e-a-t* statesmen, like Lyndon and Sam and Gerry and what's-his-name. The surprise was not the last performance of Johnson-playing-Lionel-Barrymore-playing-Lyndon, but the fact that he got away with it; the press by and large acted like sob-sisters in the 1890's covering a society ball to help the poor. Amid the sniffles no one was so uncouth as to peep into Johnson's fantastic exaggerations, like his claim to be spending $68 billion "for such things as health and education" the next fiscal year. More than $35 billion of this is normal expenditure from social security, where the government takes in more from the lower brackets than it pays out, and the munificence is attested by Johnson's proposal to raise the minimum from $55 to $80 *a month*, just enough to keep a beneficiary from dying too visibly.

Johnson, too, talked of peace, but it will be years before we stop paying all the costs—fiscal and social—of his Vietnam war. He said it was "imperative . . . to resist inflation." But it wasn't imperative enough for him to impose taxes on the profits his war inflation created in the upper brackets. The poor and the black will now pay with unemployment to fight that inflation, as they paid disproportionately with their lives to fight his war. He, too, talked of the need "to scale down the level of arms among the superpowers" so that "mankind" could "view the future without fear and great apprehension." But he may have set off a new spiral when he approved the "thin" anti-ballistic missile. And new arms for a fantastically overarmed nation take first priority in his final budget.

In the masterly flim-flam of budgetary accounting, the new estimates gloss over the fact that the war this year will cost $3 billion more than we were told before. A $3.4 billion decline is promised next year (largely due to the saving on planes and explosives if we continue to stop bombing the North). *But* the savings are already whisked away in a $4 billion increase in arms expenditures in the year beginning July 1. Total military spending will be $81.5 billion, nosing past the peak of World War II—how's that for Isaiah!

The poverty program remains just short of $2 billion but arms research and development will go up $850 million to a total of $5.6 billion, including work on such new goodies as missiles which can be hidden on the ocean floor. There's not

a gap Nixon mentioned that the Johnson military budget
does not fill—a "new generation" of missiles (how beautifully they breed!) with multiple warheads, five squadrons
of new FB-111 bombers (to keep Fort Worth and General
Dynamics prosperous), $2.4 billion to give the Navy three
fast new nuclear attack submarines, the quiet variety which
won't disturb sleep in the ghettoes. There is more money
for the Air Force's advanced bomber. Just to make sure we
don't run out of new Vietnams there's three-quarters of a
billion this year and a billion next for those overpriced C5A
carrier planes which can get troops fast to any new trouble
spot and millions more for three of those Fast Deployment
Logistics ships which will take the place of foreign bases
and have heavy equipment ready for the troops when the
C5A's get them there. Even a submissive and somnolent
Congress several years running has turned down the DPL's
as an engraved invitation to more trouble, but Johnson's
budget asks Congress to come and reason together with him
again about the item.

No wonder this is a smooth transition. It's practically one
continuous performance, and better than ever for the Pentagon. So what's a little Isaiah between friends?

January 27, 1969

UNCLE SAM'S
CON MAN BUDGET

It's fortunate for the U.S. government that it is not subject
to the SEC. Any corporation which filed annual financial
reports like the new federal budget would run afoul of
SEC accounting requirements designed to protect the investor.

Let us begin with the claim that it now has a surplus instead of a deficit. If a present-day conglomerate had among its subsidiaries an insurance company, and set up its overall annual accounts in such a way as to make it appear that the legal reserves of its insurance company were available to meet a deficit in its other business operations, that conglomerate would soon find itself hailed into court by the SEC or its own stockholders. Nixon's claim of a $5.8 billion surplus for the coming 1970 fiscal year is based on just such fiction. It is achieved by lumping the surpluses in the government's trust funds with the deficit in its normal operations. Johnson did the same thing in January when he unveiled his 1970 budget and claimed a budget surplus of $3.4 billion. The main source of both claims to a surplus lay in the huge social security funds, the government's public insurance business. These and other trust funds are segregated by law and not usable for any other purpose.

When Johnson presented his budget, Senator Williams of Delaware pointed out that the Johnson calculations of a surplus for both fiscal 1969 and 1970 were based on the existence in 1969 of a $9.3 billion and in 1970 of a $10.2 billion surplus in these trust funds. "Under the law," Williams told the Senate, "no Administration and no Congress can divert these trust funds to defray the normal operating expenses of the Government." Williams said that if this bit of deceptive accounting were eliminated, it would be seen that Johnson had a deficit of $6.9 billion instead of a surplus of $2.4 billion in fiscal 1969 and a deficit of $6.8 billion instead of a surplus of $3.4 billion in 1970. Senator Williams told me after Nixon's budget revisions were made public that all his criticism of Johnson's budget was equally applicable to Nixon's. Nixon's claimed $5.8 billion surplus for 1970 was really a deficit of $4.4 billion if the trust fund reserves were deducted.[1]

Of course this method of federal accounting has been

[1] Williams also criticized Johnson for failing to include in the 1970 budget a $2.7 billion Commodity Credit loss which the government must pay sooner or later. Nixon, too, brushed this same item under the table. To carry on the same metaphor, $2.7 billion is quite a crumb.

going on for years and of course it accurately measures the
net impact on the economy of federal collections and payments from the standpoint of inflation. In earlier days this
was called the "national income account" as distinguished
from the administrative budget. But the administrative
budget is the better index to the government's fiscal sol-
vency, since a deficit in normal operations does not become
visible in the consolidated cash account or "unified budget"
until the deficit has grown so large that it even wipes out
the surplus in the trust funds. The danger signal blinks later
in the "unified budget." Earlier budget messages used to
give both the consolidated account *and* the administrative
budget. But though the basic 1970 budget presentation
takes four separate volumes which total 2,012 pages (and
weigh, even in paperback, seven pounds), there is no place
in it where one can find the administrative budget. Why admit that the operations of the government are still in the red,
if you can make it look as if they are in the black? The $10.2
billion surplus in the trust funds helps to dampen inflation
but it is not available to buy bombs for B-52's or to feed the
hungry.

The "unified budget" has another effect. It understates
the extent to which the war machine eats up public revenues. The first chart in the budget message purports to
show that 41 cents of every dollar in expenditure goes to
the military. But if the trust funds of the government are
separated from the rest of its activities, then the military
share is about 55 cents. The sums Americans pay into social
security trust funds for unemployment, old-age and other
insurance are no different in this sense from the sums they
pay private insurance companies. There is no more reason
to lump public insurance than private insurance funds with
the general revenues of the government in measuring the
impact of military expenditures.

The way to begin to see the real fiscal impact of the war
machine is to begin with the memorandum line on page 526
of the main budget volume where "receipts by source" are
shown. This discloses that of $198 billion in receipts, $51

billion is in trust funds. This leaves available for the general purposes of the government $147 billion. If you next turn to the table on "budget outlay by function," you will find $81.5 billion for national defense. So national defense takes 55 percent of this $147 billion. Then if you look more closely you will see near the foot of the expenditure table $2.8 billion for civilian and military pay increases. The Pentagon's share of that, for its employees in *and out* of uniform (the Pentagon employs nearly one-half of all the *civilian* employees in the government) is $2.5 billion. When that additional pay item is added, the total for national defense is $83 billion, or better than 56 cents of every dollar available. That is a third (actually 36 percent) more than the 41 cents shown in the first budget chart.[2]

At the same time, lumping the trust funds with the general revenues exaggerates the government's contributions to health and welfare. Johnson boasted that outlays for health and welfare in his 1970 budget would be $55 billion, "which is 28 percent of federal outlays . . . more than double the level prevailing in 1964" when his War on Poverty was launched. But $42.9 billion of this was to come "from self-financed trust funds for retirement and social insurance and Medicare." So almost four-fifths of this benevolent munificence was from the beneficiaries. Only the difference, $12.1 billion, represents outlays from the general revenues. That is about 8 percent, not 28 percent.

While the government was to pay $42.9 billion from these insurance and health trust funds, it would collect a total of $45.8 billions in fiscal 1970, or almost $3 billion

[2] I can remember when a feature of the annual federal budget presentation was a chart showing how much was absorbed by past, present and future wars. This added military expenditures, veterans' benefits and interest charges, the last item because past wars are the real reason for the public debt. These three items in the 1970 budget total more than $106 billion and will take more than 70 percent of the general revenues. Secretary Laird said the other day that much of the Soviet Union's space activity was really military. This is also true of our space program. The funds spent on rocket boosters to reach the moon also improve the technology of mass murder by intercontinental ballistic missile. If space is added to the other three items, the total is $110 billion, or almost 75 percent of the $147 billion available.

more than it paid out. This addition to the surplus in the
trust funds is, of course, anti-inflationary, for it cuts down
purchasing power, but this is purchasing power at the bottom of the economic pyramid, taken from those least able
to pay. Regarded as taxation, social security deductions
from payroll represent a savagely regressive—and, unlike so
many income taxes, inescapable—form of taxation. I can remember, when social security legislation was first being
drafted in the early days of the New Deal, writing edito-
rials proposing—as did other liberals and radicals—that it
be financed out of income taxes so as to create a more equitable distribution of wealth, taking funds from the top of
the pyramid to ease poverty at the bottom. The Social Security system adopted, which we still have, essentially takes
from the poor what it gives them, and gives less than it
takes.

The Welfare System and the War on Poverty were admissions that social security was abysmally inadequate. But
Johnson's War on Poverty was made to look far more extensive than it was, and Nixon's revisions use the same deceptive computations. "Our 1970 Revised Budget," says a
Budget Bureau statement of April 14 [1969], "involves *a 10
percent increase over FY '69 in spending for the poor*
[italics in the original]. This reflects our deep commitment
to the under-privileged." The Budget Bureau statement did
not explain, however, that this also represented a cut of $300
million in Johnson's poverty recommendations for fiscal
1970—nor that much of this bloated estimate is padded out
with normal payments from social security.

Johnson claimed he would spend $27.2 billion on "Fed-
eral Aid to the Poor." Nixon out of that "deep commitment" revised this downward to $26.9 billion. The biggest
item in Johnson's, as in Nixon's Federal Aid to The Poor
compilation (at page 47 of the main budget message volume)
is $13.5 billion for "income assistance." My curiosity was
piqued by a discrepancy of almost $10 billion between this
item and a passage at pages 42–3 of the *Budget in Brief*.
This said that federally aided public welfare would in fiscal

1970 provide assistance to a monthly average of 10 million individuals at a total cost of $7 billion. "The federal share," it said, "was $3.7 billion." When I asked the Budget Bureau where the rest of the claimed figure of $13.5 billion came from, I got this compilation (in millions):

600	administrative expenses
6,300	old-age pensions
400	R.R. retirement pensions
500	unemployment insurance
2,100	Veterans Administration[3]
$9,900	Total

The figures given me were "rounded" and so the final totals do not quite match, but this $9.9 billion of "padding" explains how that $3.7 billion in federal welfare income assistance was made to look like $13.5 billion.

It is fortunate that few people on welfare spend their spare time reading the federal budget. It would foment riots. The Budget Bureau "press kit" for Nixon's revisions of the 1970 budget says these involve "hard choices" and are part of the Nixon Administration's "concern for the poor." Nixon added $300 million for dependent children but squeezed $200 million of this out of a projected increase in our pitifully low old-age pensions. "For the aged," the same Budget Bureau explanation says, "a 7 percent social security cost-of-living increase is included in the revised 1970 budget." It does not explain that this is a revision *downward* from the 10 percent increase recommended by Johnson, nor that Nixon also shelved Johnson's proposal to increase the minimum from $55 a month to $80 a month. There are two million Americans—believe it or not—now expected to enjoy retirement on $55 a month! Instead of getting a $25 raise to $80 a month, they will only receive the general 7 percent increase, though I was told this would be

[3] The Budget Bureau, when I asked what the Veterans Administration had to do with the War on Poverty, explained that 80 percent of veterans' pensions, 75 percent of veterans' survivors' pensions and 20 percent of other veterans' benefits had been counted as "Federal Aid to The Poor" in the Johnson table!

"rounded off" so that instead of a mere $3.85, they would get $4 or $5 a month more. This could bring them up to $60 a month. Thanks to the Administration's concern for them, moreover, the revised legislation "includes liberalization of the social security retirement test" allowing them to earn more outside income without having it deducted from their pensions. The liberalization turns out to be $120 a year, about $2 a week,[4] and raises the ceiling on allowed earning to $36 a week! What a *dolce vita!*

Roughly a billion each was cut out of social security and out of the military budget by Nixon. This symmetry of sacrifice is deceptive. Before anyone starts dropping pennies into cups for the Pentagon, I would like to lift the curtain on another murky corner of the budget. To evaluate the Nixon military "economies" you have to go back for another look at the Johnson budget for 1970. This projected a drop of $3.5 billion in the costs of our "Southeast Asia operations." This was to be our first dividend of the road to peace, the money to be saved principally by ending the bombing of the North. Johnson in making up his budget could have allocated this $3.5 billion to welfare or to the rebuilding of the cities. Instead Johnson's budget allocated $4.1 billion more to military spending *unconnected with the Vietnam war*. This accounts for the fact that in his 1970 budget the cost of national defense rose by more than half a billion dollars over 1969 despite the projected $3.5 billion drop in the costs of the Vietnam war.

This favored treatment of the military machine has to be seen against the background of a figure revealed in the Nixon revisions. His revised budget estimates for fiscal 1969, which ends next June 30, disclose that $7.3 billion had to be squeezed out of the normal civilian and welfare opera-

---

[4] The liberalization will allow a maximum of $1800 a year without deductions. By comparison retired professional military men (20 years service) are allowed under the Dual Compensation Act of 1964 to fill Civil Service jobs paying up to $30,000 and still collect their full pensions, a privilege not given other veterans. Under the new pay raise this will mean retired army officers can draw up to $50,000 a year in Civil Service pay and pensions.

tions of the government in this fiscal year to meet the expenditure ceilings imposed by Congress as a condition for voting the 10 percent surtax. This squeeze over and above the original 1969 budget was made necessary by an unexpected rise in certain "uncontrollable" items exempt from mandatory ceilings. *The biggest uncontrollable item was the Vietnam war which cost $3 billion more in fiscal 1969 than had been budgeted for it.* So all kinds of services were starved in 1969 to meet the swollen costs of Vietnam in fiscal 1969. Yet when a $3.5 billion drop in Vietnam war costs were projected for fiscal 1970, the amount saved was allocated not to the depleted domestic sector but to the growth of the war machine.

Nixon's cut of $1 billion in military outlays can only be evaluated properly if you first start by observing that it was *a cut in a projected $4.1 billion increase* in military spending. The cut came out of a lot of fat, whereas the cut in health, education and welfare, and domestic services, came close to the bone and gristle. The second point to be made about the military cuts is that they represent no real overhaul of the bloated military budget. Robert S. Benson, former aid to the Pentagon Comptroller, showed (in the March issue of *The Washington Monthly*) how easily $9 billion could be cut out of military spending without impairing national security. But the three main "economies" cited by the Nixon backgrounders are sleight-of-hand. One is "lower consumption of ammunition in Vietnam." This looks optimistic in view of the enemy offensive and our own search-and-destroy missions; as in other years, this may be one of those preliminary underestimates which turn up later in a supplemental request for funds. The second "saving" comes out of the shift from Sentinel to Safeguard, but the reduction in fiscal 1970 will be at the expense of larger ultimate costs. Indeed, while the Nixon estimates show that Safeguard will ultimately cost $1.5 billion more, McGraw-Hill's authoritative DMS, Inc., service for the aerospace industry puts the final cost $4.3 billion higher, or a total of $11 billion without cost overruns (which DMS expects). The third "economy" cited is $326 million saved (as a *Washington Post* editorial noted tartly April 3) by "postponing procurement of a bomber missile (SRAM) that doesn't yet work." Like all else in the Nixon Administration, the budget revisions represent feeble compromises which give the military machine priority over the growing urban, racial and student crises.

May 5, 1969

SAME OLD FORMULAS, SAME TIRED RHETORIC

In an exchange of toasts at the White House last month, the Australian Prime Minister drew an implied comparison between Lincoln and Nixon. Walt Rostow, too, used to get Lyndon Johnson's juices flowing in the morning by telling him he was just like Lincoln. The Australian got so carried away that he ended up by demonstrating his native talent with the boomerang. If Lincoln had not persevered against the Copperheads and the Horace Greeleys, Mr. Gorton explained, there would today be "a slave autocracy in the South . . . But there would have been no United States." Since Lincoln and the North were trying to reunite the country by force of arms ("aggression") against the wishes of the Southern states for independence ("self-determination"), Mr. Gorton's flattery was clearly beginning to rebound. The more he went on the more it sounded like a toast to Ho Chi Minh.

Mr. Gorton's analogy invites elaboration. If John Brown had succeeded in raising a slave revolt, if the North had helped the rebels, and if England had intervened on the side of the slaveholders (as the Tories later wanted to), the situation would have been comparable to the Vietnamese war. Suppose further that England, tired of a costly distant conflict, had proposed that all "non-Southern" forces withdraw, thus putting Lincoln's Unionist armies in the same "foreign" category as Britain's. Suppose the slaves were asked to lay down their arms while the slaveholders kept their army intact, and trust to "free elections" under a vague promise of international supervision but with the slaveholder regime still in power. Suppose that regime in Richmond were filling the jails with spokesmen for poor white, non-slaveholding and pro-peace elements while Britain—heavily arming this regime in preparation for its own troop withdrawal—piously insisted that its only purpose was to give the South the right of self-determination. That is where Nixon stands today.

For those who wonder just what Nixon was up to in his May 14 peace proposals, the Nixon-Gorton visit offers another source of illumination. Except for New Zealand, with its 150 token soldiers, Australia is the only white country which has put troops beside our own in the effort to revive the white man's burden in Asia. The war is almost as unpopular in Australia as here, and Gorton's opposition—the Labor party—led the protest demonstrations which greeted Ky two years ago in Australia. The conservative coalition Gorton heads was Johnson's faithful junior partner. Gorton was here only a week before Nixon's Vietnam speech. If Nixon were contemplating any real departure in policy, he would be leaving Gorton out on a limb. It would be necessary to prepare Australian public opinion. But nothing in their exchanges reflected any change in policy; they spoke as simple-mindedly as Johnson of their joint effort "to help South Vietnam preserve its independence."

Those who are working themselves into euphoria by wishful exegesis of what Nixon did *not* say in his May 14 address would be wise to pause a moment over what Nixon and Gorton did not say in their exchanges a week earlier. These, as expected, attracted little attention in this country, and did not have to take American peace sentiment into account.[1] The Nixon farewell statement, which Gorton said was framed with his agreement and served as a final communiqué, spoke of their talks on "Vietnam and regional security." A continued U.S.-Australian protectorate over Southeast Asia was implied. Nixon welcomed, and promised to support, Australia's decision to keep troops in Malaysia and Singapore when the British leave two years hence, forever ending the Kipling era east of Suez. But not a single word was said about the negotiations in Paris, or the hope of a turn toward peace.

Nixon, like Johnson, is playing for time. His May 14 address strongly recalls Johnson's at Johns Hopkins in April 1965. Johnson deluded many people into believing that he was moving toward peace at the very moment he was committing the first U.S. combat troops to the South. The only remarkable thing about the Nixon address is that at one point he seemed to be pulling his own leg. When Nixon said "repeating the old formulas and the tired rhetoric of the past is not enough," he seemed to be setting himself up for the cartoonists. If I were running the Secret Service I would find out who wrote that and take him down to the White House cellar for interrogation under the bright lights. For as Senator Gore showed in a devastating analysis on the Senate floor May 20, the speech was full of old formulas and tired rhetoric picked up almost verbatim from Johnson and Rusk. Even Nixon's titillating hints about free elections and a neutral South Vietnam were also uttered, as Gore found, in almost the same words by Rusk in 1966. The parallels with Johnson sound as if Nixon was down on the ranch. If this weren't politics, it would be plagiarism.

The speech is so tricky it has everybody confused except Henry Kissinger. "Proponents leak stories that the President is sending subtle signals to the Reds that he'd let them share in a new Saigon government as part of a peace package," the *Wall St. Journal* said May 23. "Opponents warn this would bring the 'disguised defeat' Nixon had vowed

[1] Indeed the only place the texts are available is in the *Weekly Compilation of Presidential Documents* for May 19.

not to accept. White House aides insist no decision has been made." Never have there been so many hints with so little substance.

You can read in Chalmers Roberts in the *Washington Post* (May 18) that silence gives consent and that what Nixon didn't say May 14 really means he is ready to accept even an interim coalition government. This was "spelled out by persons in a position to know," Roberts wrote ecstatically. But gravitation being what it is, what goes up must come down, and he added a *but*— "The U.S. cannot accept settlement terms which would turn the South over to the Communists and make a mockery of the years of American and South Vietnamese bloodletting." The only sure non-mockery, it would seem, is to maintain in power the same oligarchy we have imposed on the South for 15 years.

On the other hand you may read in David Lawrence (May 21) that the Nixon Administration has "at last" decided that it will not tolerate the continuance of heavy attacks and is not ruling out drastic reprisals which "could mean the resumption at any moment of the bombing of North Vietnam and even a blockade of Haiphong harbor." Obviously the White House is handing out different lines of poop. Richard Wilson (Washington *Star*, May 21) reports jubilantly that before Nixon went on TV May 14 he gave an extemporaneous résumé to his top-level officials. They not only applauded but "there was no doubt what they were applauding." The main emphasis was on "not quitting" and on Nixon's "unpleasant options" if Hanoi does not accept mutual withdrawal. These include "a massive fire-bomb raid to destroy Hanoi." We'll put 'em back in the Stone Age yet. Senator Hugh Scott, the GOP whip, dropped hints of the same kind after Senator Kennedy—in the wake of "Hamburger Hill"—attacked the bloody nonsense of charging up any hill a well dug-in enemy baits for U.S. attack.

In the blizzard of hints, there is also a preview of what Nixon may say to Thieu on Midway June 8. It is hinted that if one reads the fine print closely one will see that Saigon holds a secure veto over the international supervisory body to verify withdrawals "and for any other purpose *agreed upon* between the two sides." The elections, too, would be held under "agreed procedures" and agreed means the agreement of the Thieu regime. While Nixon takes the high road, Thieu will have the low, and when domestic opinion gets tired of seeing the Reds reject Nixon's "generous" offers, the iron will be hot and the Pentagon hopes it can strike again.

June 2, 1969

MIDWAY TO
A NGUYEN VAN NIXON ERA

Two decades ago Karl Mundt and Richard Nixon were comrades in arms on the House Un-American Activities Committee. Long before Joe McCarthy, they were our foremost practitioners of McCarthyism. When Nixon said at Beadle State College in South Dakota on his way to Midway, "In public life, we have seen reputations destroyed by smear . . . We have heard . . . sly voices of malice, twisting facts" he was providing a perfect description of their own activities in those years. A satirist, seeking savagely to caricature America, could not have done better than Nixon preaching the virtues of a free society at a ceremony dedicating a library named for Mundt. The only time Mundt ever came close to a book was to see whether or not it might have been written by a Red. Their main achievement was the creation, for the first time in our history, of an official agency designed to police public thinking. Their Mundt-Nixon bill, fathered up a dark alley by the U.S. Chamber of Commerce, was fought as unconstitutional by conservative leaders of the American bar and opposed by Tom Clark, then Attorney General. It was vetoed by President Truman as an attempt at "thought control."

Thanks to the anti-Red hysteria which marked the early months of the Korean war, Congress passed it over his veto. It created a Subversive Activities Control Board—the very name is redolent of Inquisition rather than free society—but Supreme Court decisions have left it an empty shell. It was supposed to set up a blacklist of Reds, to force them to put a Scarlet Letter label on their publications and broadcasts, and to deny them the right to travel abroad. All these efforts have been struck down as unconstitutional. The SACB is a ghostly reminder of the fascistic ideas which were written into American law under the guise of fighting Communism. Mundt and Nixon were a long way from Jefferson in those years. There is little reason to believe them much closer today, when Nixon has appointed three heroes of the witch-hunters to key posts: Burger, the defender of "faceless informer" testimony, to be Chief Justice; Roger Robb, the prosecutor of J. Robert Oppenheimer, to the Court of Appeals for the District of Columbia; and Otto Otepka, the pet State Department stool pigeon of congressional inquisitors like Eastland, to a $36,000-a-year job on the Subversive Activities Control Board. It may be no accident that Nixon's little lecture on freedom never once mentioned the Bill of Rights.

Nixon had to find a very out-of-the-way college to get away with a commencement address which claimed for itself "the honesty of straight talk" without saying a word about the war. He also had to be a long way from nowhere to get away with his description of black demands for open admission to such schools as New York's City College. "Instead of seeking to raise lagging students up to meet the college standards," Nixon said, "the cry now is to lower the standards to meet the students. This is the old familiar self-indulgent cry for the easy way." This was extraordinarily insensitive. Whatever its merits, the demand for open enrollment for graduates of ghetto high schools is hardly a form of self-indulgence. On the contrary it reflects the desire of the blacks fortunate enough to be in college to open the doors wider to the less fortunate, and to force better teaching in ghetto high schools. The C.C.N.Y. proposals, for example, are only a more modest variant of the open enrollment to all high school graduates which exists in many state colleges.[1] It was unfair so to misrepresent black demands in that faraway lily-white forum. If "passionate concern," as Nixon said, "gets nowhere without dispassionate analysis," it was his obligation to speak soberly of his own plans for higher education. But that would have gotten him back to the war, and the whole web of lies would come apart if one strand were treated honestly.

Nixon's commencement address next day at the Air Force Academy was another example of his tendency to sound like Billy Graham while practicing the below-the-belt in-fighting he perfected in the House of Representatives. The real issues now raising a storm in Congress over military spending and military power cannot be seriously discussed with a man who talks of "unilateral disarmers" and "neo-isolationists." This is the old smear-and-run tactics of the old Nixon. The speech was low demagogy, full of *non sequiturs* and floosy historical analogies. But what it said is clear enough. Nixon is determined to pursue the course of the Pax Americana. This means no reduction in military spending or military power, and it reveals, as in a lightning flash, how illusory it is to expect any move toward disarmament from this Administration. He speaks rather of "control of arms" and only "in the context of other specific moves to reduce tension around the world." That is the old Dulles dream of forcing political concessions as the price of arms negotiations.

The Air Force speech is the best key to the charade on Midway Island. A President who believes that the U.S. must be the world's policeman is headed for more Vietnams, and is unlikely (as he said) to accept a "disguised defeat" in getting out of this one. The token withdrawal,

[1] Including, as I learned by phone, Beadle State itself.

which may prove to be largely support or kitchen troops, is aimed to appease and mislead opinion at home. The best guide to the realities lies in the astringent comments of the two Senators closest to the military. Russell said the withdrawal of 25,000 men "is of no great significance" and "will not substantially reduce American casualties." Stennis said he had no "high hopes" that the South Vietnamese army would soon be able to take over the war. If Nixon has his way we may keep troops in Vietnam indefinitely, as we have in Korea and Western Europe, to man "the frontiers of freedom."

This is the meaning of Pax Americana, and if it leads to unrest at home, he is ready for it. "We have the power to strike back as need be," he said at Beadle State. "The nation has suffered other attempts at insurrection." Though he proclaims an era of negotiation abroad, he is preparing for confrontation at home. That helicopter spraying 50 pounds of CS gas indiscriminately over campus demonstrators, nearby elementary schools and hospital facilities in the Berkeley People's Park clash may be a preview of what can be expected elsewhere. Reagan, the National Guard and the police treated fellow Americans with the mindless and mechanical brutality we mete out in Vietnam. We are beginning to repeat here all the errors we made there. Nixon is as little responsive to his opposition as Thieu is to his. Thieu returned from Midway so emboldened that he held a press conference threatening that anyone who even advocated a coalition with the NLF would be "severely punished." Instead of spreading freedom to Vietnam, Nixon may soon be reducing it here. Instead of de-Americanizing the war, we are beginning to Vietnamize America. We may be moving toward a Nguyen Van Nixon era, combining the worst of both regimes.

June 16, 1969

NIXON IN THE FOOTSTEPS OF
POPEYE'S ELDER STATESMAN

A President with troops scattered around the globe can always find some excuse for action "to protect them." The successful assertion of Congressional authority over the war-making powers of the President is not a constitutional problem. The real problem to which Congress and the country should address themselves lies in the nature of our foreign policy and the size of our military establishment. As long as we have navies on every sea, bases on every continent, Green Berets for intervention and C-5A's for swift intercontinental transport, the chances of stumbling into new Vietnams and Cambodias—or worse—will remain high.

This basic question was hardly touched upon in the Senate debate over the Cooper-Church amendment. The rationale for the expansionist course we have been pursuing since the Truman Doctrine was put by one of Nixon's Republican supporters, Senator Clifford P. Hansen of Wyoming. He said World Wars I and II had taught us the "hard lesson" that we had to maintain an active role in keeping the peace "or we will be forced to fight big wars." To pull out of the war in Southeast Asia, *or anywhere else that the President thought our involvement necessary*, "would be," Hansen said, "to abdicate our responsibilities as a great nation and as a force for justice and liberty." This is the basic premise of our disastrous involvement in Indochina but it was not challenged. The supporters of the Cooper-Church amendment were too busy splitting enough constitutional hairs to muster a majority.

The real lesson of the two world wars was just the opposite. The lesson was that no single power, or combination of powers, was strong enough to keep the peace, that only a world organization could save mankind from a fresh catastrophe. It was this realization which led to the League of Nations and afterward to the United Nations. If the UN fails, it is unlikely that mankind will have another chance. These vital truths are receding from public consciousness. When the UN held its twenty-fifth anniversary on June 26 in San Francisco, neither the President nor the Secretary of State put in an appearance or bothered to send a message. This was the first anniversary not addressed by an American President. Truman, Eisenhower and Johnson each honored the UN's birthday. This may well be dismissed as hypocrisy but at least the sinners turned up in church. This time the affair was ignored. Even in the rebellious Senate no one marked the occasion. U Thant's anniversary address was hardly noticed in the press, though its insight and humanism shine like secular Gospel beside the inanities and evasions of Nixon's efforts to represent his Cambodian search-and-destroy operation as an Indochinese Stalingrad.

In his TV interview on Cambodia, Nixon conjured up the danger of a "rampant isolationism" if we were forced out of Indochina. A President who says he fears isolationism ought to be a supporter of the UN. But when people like Nixon speak against isolationism they are not advocating internationalism. What they fear is a revulsion against militarism and imperialism. The Pax Americana is the "internationalism" of Standard Oil, Chase Manhattan and the Pentagon. Nixon is, it is true, trying somewhat to cut down American commitments abroad under irresistible fiscal pressures, White House briefers speak of abandoning our world policeman role, but the alternative they offer is not a revitalized UN but the so-called Guam Doctrine. This is imperialism by proxy. We may be on the verge of imposing quotas against the Orient's low-wage textiles but we are eager to buy its low-wage soldier-power. The Guam Doctrine will be seen in Asia as a rich white man's idea of fighting a war: we handle the elite airpower while coolies do the killing on the ground.

Unfortunately, faith in victory by airpower and combat-by-coolie is so deeply ingrained in American thinking that it was sometimes hard to tell doves from hawks in the Cooper-Church debate. "The argument has been made," Cooper said, "that our amendment scuttles the Guam Doctrine." He said its purpose was merely to require Congressional approval before extending the doctrine to Cambodia again. "Nothing in the Cooper-Church amendment," Church assured the Senate, "would prevent Asians from helping Asians." He called this "a viable and valid cause." Helping is quite a euphemism for what we have been getting Asians to do to each other. Church said the amendment would not prevent the Thais or the South Vietnamese from fighting "for the Lon Nol government." It would merely require prior Congressional approval for "the kind of undercover arrangements that were used to make it so profitable for Thailand, South Korea and the Philippines to send their forces to Vietnam." It may sound to Asians as if the doves merely wanted to drive a harder bargain for their services.

The Cooper-Church restrictions on U.S. airpower over Cambodia may also prove too subtle for the Oriental mind. The amendment does not prohibit U.S. bombing of Cambodia nor U.S. close air support of South Vietnamese or Thai forces *in* Cambodia. It only forbids "direct" air support to Lon Nol's forces. The word "direct" was added on motion of Senator Jackson (D. Wash.). It was foreshadowed by Secretary Laird's earlier explanation that while we were only going to bomb enemy supply lines in Cambodia, Lon Nol troops who just happened to be in the same area might derive "ancillary benefits" from it. No Secretary of Defense has shown a finer genius for semantics.

The Guam Doctrine may be traced back to that elder statesman, Wimpy, in the Popeye comic strip. Wimpy in a crisis always manfully suggests, "Let's you and him fight." In trying this out on Asia, Nixon hardly pays a compliment to the astuteness of its ruling classes, the world's oldest merchants. They were taking customers tenderly to the cleaners in their bazaars when the progenitors of Anglo-American civilization were still painting themselves a bright baby blue. The first time we tried Wimpy-Nixon statecraft was in

China. There the Asians on our side ended by making business, not war. They sold whole armies to the Asians on the other side and retired with the swag to Taiwan. SEATO's latest meeting, like that of "free Asia" in Djakarta a few weeks earlier, indicates no rush to man the Cambodian "frontier of freedom." Indonesia, the pride and joy of our anti-Communists, flatly turned down Pnom Penh's request for arms. SEATO's final communiqué "expressed understanding" for Lon Nol's appeal. The Thais are waiting to see how much we are willing to pay. If the price isn't high enough, they'll come to terms with China. To them this may not seem to be the fate worse than death we proclaim it. Japan deals with China. So does Burma. No Chinese planes, after all, are devastating Asia. Mao's Little Red Book doesn't look as scary as a B-52. Why be an American-style anti-Communist if you can't make an honest buck on it?

"The prospect suddenly loomed," Nixon said in his formal report explaining his latest *incursion*, "of Cambodia's becoming virtually one large base area for attack anywhere into South Vietnam along the 600 miles of the Cambodian frontier." What happens when that prospect suddenly looms up again? This is the question he never answered in his TV interview. Do we go back in, bomb Hanoi, invade the North or commit some larger folly? The least Congress can do is pass the McGovern-Hatfield bill and set a firm date on our withdrawal from the Indochinese morass. Not enough Asians are going to fight Asians for us even if the price is right.

July 13, 1970

PART V

The Menace of Militarism

McNAMARA AND
THE MILITARISTS

The catchword most often associated with Robert S. Mc-Namara's seven years as Secretary of Defense was "systems analysis." Yet the greatest deficiency in his book, *The Essence of Security*, which brings together his most important public papers during those years is his incapacity for analyzing systems, though of another order. No one would guess from these antiseptic pages that there are such things as militarism, or a military-industrial complex, or just plain politics, and that they represent *systems*, i.e., inescapable relationships which affected the problems McNamara faced in the Pentagon and the decisions he made.

McNamara voices all the stereotypes of liberal humanitarianism, but he keeps them free from the grime of reality. He argues for wider public knowledge and participation in defense problems, and says we must not be frightened away by their complexity. But the only complexity with which he deals is the minor one of weaponry. He omits the other and greater social complexities in which decisions of weaponry are enmeshed. He reminds one of a mid-Victorian novelist writing without mention of sweat or sex.

Let me cite two simple but fateful decisions—one at the very threshold, the other at the end of his stewardship. Both sharply raised the tempo of the arms race, and involved—as he himself admits—billions of wasted dollars without in any way adding to national safety; indeed, they magnified the dimensions of peril. One was his surrender to Kennedy on the missile gap, the other was his surrender to Johnson on the anti-ballistic missile. Both represented the victory of politics over reason, and of military-industrial interests over real considerations of security. An informed public would have been a powerful ally against both decisions; and McNamara tried in some degree to marshal it. But how can an effective opinion be created if men as able as McNamara are squeamish about telling the full truth?

There is a striking difference between this farewell message by the ablest civilian manager our military establishment ever had and those of our two greatest soldier presidents. That difference in the end may prove a disservice, outweighing all the managerial and budgetary reforms with which McNamara is credited. Washington in his Farewell Address warned against the danger to liberty in "an overgrown military establishment," and Eisenhower provided a graphic new term for an old problem when he warned against the "military-industrial complex." These two warnings provide fundamental insights into basic institutional dangers, and the warnings were given weight because they came from such honored military men.

But McNamara after seven years of wrestling with the military bureaucracy nowhere even uses the term or touches on the meaning of militarism as a social phenomenon. On the contrary, he is so blind to the intrinsic nature of military establishments and the mentality they develop that he advocates new social missions for the Pentagon, particularly in education! He seems unaware of the social consequences when he proposes to apply on a larger scale at home those "civic action" military programs we have helped to launch in Latin America. "Quite apart from the projects themselves," he says of this Latin experience, "the program powerfully alters the negative image of the military man as the oppressive preserver of the status quo." This is public relations, not social engineering. It may change the image in glossy North American publications, but not the reality in Latin America.

McNamara seems unaware that the fruit of all this civic action our Marines began to launch a half century ago has been a succession of Neros like Somoza, Batista, and Trujillo. The same tough-guy types and the same authoritarian temperaments are bred by our own—and every—military establishment. It does not speak well for McNamara that after so many turbulent years of close association with these men McNamara seems to have missed the point. This master of quantification seems poorly equipped for factors which escape measurement—like the quality of men and institutions. His proposal that the Pentagon move into social problems has now been taken up by his successor, Clark Clifford, a better political operator but without McNamara's enormous energy and grasp of detail. In a speech September 26 [1968] Clifford said he had asked his aides to draw up for the new administration plans under which the military services could help "in alleviating some of our most pressing domestic problems." This is the road to Argentina and Peru.

The most striking example of McNamara's shortsightedness in this area lies in his attitude toward the concept of the military-industrial complex. A certain complacency, perhaps conceit, leads McNamara to gloss it over. Several years before Eisenhower launched the famous phrase, Lieutenant General James M. Gavin, after his retirement in 1958 as Chief of Research and Development in the Pentagon, touched on the fierce pressures the arms manufacturers, with their allies in Congress and the military, are able to exert. In his book *War and Peace in the Space Age*, he said it took "the judgment of Solomon and no little political fortitude" to resist them. McNamara seems so confident that he possessed both that, in a farewell newspaper interview he gave the Associated Press (Washington *Star*, February 4, 1968), he dismissed the dangers against which Gavin warned. His interviewer, Saul Pett, asked McNamara whether he shared Eisenhower's concern about the military-industrial complex. "I don't," McNamara replied, "as long as the Secretary of Defense operates as he should, examining all the factors of a problem and making decisions on his own analysis, regardless of the pressures applied to him." [1] The reply is not re-

[1] McNamara's successor has taken a step further in the process of dulling public awareness. "I am convinced today, after six months in this office," Secretary of Defense Clifford said complacently on September 26, "that the dangers General Eisenhower warned against were real dangers. But I am also convinced that they have been avoided through

ally responsive. It does not touch on the problem—the pressures which *prevent* the Secretary from operating "as he should."

The military-industrial complex has been a reality ever since war, in the latter part of the last century, became big business. It made its debut in the naval rivalry which enriched steel and shipbuilding companies in England and Germany and helped to bring on World War I. The power of the military-industrial alliance has grown with the cost of armaments and the magnitude of military spending since World War II. It is embodied in a network of trade associations that link the defense industries to the Pentagon. Like many of the corporations themselves, these organizations are staffed by a multitude of retired generals and admirals. Their pressures distort military decision and national policy. No doubt McNamara overcame these pressures in many intra-mural controversies, as in the shelving of the nuclear powered airplane, the Skybolt missile, the RS-70 supersonic bomber, and the Dynasoar program. But from an overall point of view, the military-industrial complex never had it so good as in the McNamara years. Eisenhower's last military budget was $44 billion; McNamara's last was almost twice that amount. The monster fattened even as McNamara strove mightily to keep its nose clean in public. It might even be said that he saved it from its own excesses. He was more its nursemaid than its master.

If the President backs the Secretary of Defense, McNamara asked his AP interviewer in what was intended to be a clincher, "how can the military-industrial complex get to

the checks and balances of our governmental system." This soothing bit of banality came in an address to the National Security Industrial Association, perhaps the most powerful single component of the armament lobby, and in the midst of many signs that the military-industrial complex was riding higher than ever, including Clifford's own abandonment, on *Meet The Press*, September 29, of McNamara's long effort to make the country understand that the concept of nuclear superiority was meaningless. One would be tempted to say that the sky's the limit now on the arms race, if the skies of space were not the very scene of its coming intensification.

him?" He said he was backed by both Kennedy and Johnson, as no doubt on many occasions he was. But he did not
mention their failure to back him in two of his most momentous decisions. It was the political power of the military-
industrial complex operating through the Presidency, which
forced McNamara against his better knowledge and judgment to acquiesce, when he took office, in the costly fraud
of the "missile gap," and which also forced him, as he left
office, to participate in the nonsense about building a "thin"
anti-missile defense against China. Yet nowhere in the index
nor in the chaste pages of *The Essence of Security* is there
any reference to the military-industrial complex. The
nearest that McNamara comes to this indelicate fact of life
in the Pentagon is when he writes, "Every hour of every
day the Secretary is confronted by a conflict between the
national interest and the parochial interests of particular industries, individual services, or local areas." This is flutter-
ingly vague. No one would guess from that pallid little
sentence, or anything else in the book, what enormous
pressures the arms lobby can generate or the major occasions
on which they overwhelmed McNamara himself. Yet to
repeat the phrase McNamara chose as title of his book, "the
essence of security" lies not so much in any external enemy
as in controlling these interests and the momentum of the
arms race from which they profit. This is what we most
need defense against.

It may be urged on McNamara's behalf that these are
official speeches in which he could not afford to be wholly
candid. But so were Washington's and Eisenhower's. In any
case the excuse implies that the Secretary was unable, as a
prisoner of forces stronger than himself, to tell the whole
truth. But this excuse attests to the power of the institutional forces whose potency he disparages. Now that he is
out of the Pentagon, he could have touched upon them in a
preface, but perhaps the admission would have been too
much for his pride. McNamara is at bottom a bright school-
boy who hates to have anything less than A-plus on his report card; his idealized image is the No. 1 Whiz Kid. To

admit the realities would be to admit that he was not wholly capable of mastering them.

The fact is that McNamara arrived in Washington an innocent country lad from the bucolic simplicities of the automobile business. He seemed never to have heard that dirty eight-letter word *politics*. He discovered on reading the secret reports when he took office that there was no missile gap, and proceeded in all fresh innocence and enthusiasm to tell this to the press as if it were glad tidings, as indeed it was or should have been. Had he done a little systems analysis of the kind which comes easily to politicians who never heard of computers, he would have realized that he was stepping into a complicated situation in which the facts and the truth were minor considerations. He was giving aid and comfort to the enemy, i.e., the Republican party. McNamara's press conference put Kennedy's new Secretary of Defense squarely behind Eisenhower, who had declared only three weeks earlier in his last State of the Union message, "The 'bomber gap' of several years ago was always a fiction, and the 'missile gap' shows every sign of being the same." It also undercut one of Kennedy's principal campaign themes, and, as any sophisticated observer would surmise, threatened to upset a network of understandings between the Democratic party and the aviation lobby, "contracts"—as the politicians say—whence many campaign contributions had flowed.

The roof fell in on McNamara. Next day Pierre Salinger told the press that he was speaking with Kennedy's approval in terming McNamara's finding "absolutely wrong." It is a pity there is no record of what went on between Kennedy and McNamara. The latter must have been startled to discover that in Washington facts counted for so little; his discovery, after all, was far from sensational. Even my little *Weekly*, in an issue which went to press a week before the McNamara backgrounder (which was restricted to a select few) had called attention to evidence that there was no missile gap, including a report by Britain's Institute of Strategic Studies. This credited Russia with only thirty-five ICBM's, as against the 400 to 500 figure given in the exuberant leaks to the press from Air Force Intelligence and the aviation lobby. Perhaps the facts marshaled by McNamara in a White House showdown explain why Kennedy himself, the day after Salinger's "absolutely wrong," scaled down his own rebuke to "premature." But six weeks later in his first budget message to Congress, Kennedy unabashedly declared, "It has been publicly acknowledged for several years that this nation has not led the world in missile strength," and launched a huge missile buildup, though authoritative figures from the outgoing Republicans showed we were not only ahead in long-range missiles but had ten times as many vehicles (missiles and bombers) capable of reaching Russia with nuclear weapons as Russia had capable of reaching the U.S. Now in his new book McNamara lifts the curtain just a little on that farce and ever so gingerly calls it a mistake. This is in the chapter based on his San Francisco speech of September, 1967, which was supposed to be sensationally candid. McNamara said of that 1961 decision:

Our current numerical superiority over the Soviet Union in reliable, accurate and effective warheads is both greater than we had originally planned and much more than we require. How this came about is a significant illustration of the intrinsic dynamics of the nuclear arms race. . . . In 1961 when I became Secretary of Defense, the Soviet Union had a very small operational arsenal of intercontinental missiles. However, it did possess the technological and industrial capacity to enlarge that arsenal very substantially. . . . We had to insure against such an eventuality by undertaking a major buildup of our own Minuteman and Polaris forces. . . . But the blunt fact remains that if we had had more accurate information about *planned* [my italics] strategic forces, we simply would not have needed to build as large a nuclear arsenal as we have today. . . . I am not saying that our decision in 1961 was unjustified; I am saying that it was necessitated by a lack of accurate information.

This apparent candor covers a network of deceptions. If the reader will go over McNamara's passage carefully, he will see that he not only admits there was no missile gap but admits he knew it at the time. He falls back on the excuse that we had no "accurate information" on what the Soviets *planned* in the way of *future* production. But that is not how the Kennedy Administration told it at the time. The public was told that we were behind; that there *was* a missile gap. Ralph Lapp, in his penetrating new book *The Weapons Culture*, puts it plainly when he writes, "There was no missile gap but it was not politically expedient to admit this fact. Instead, the myth was perpetuated and the arms race accelerated." Kennedy, "having campaigned on a missile gap platform apparently found it politically necessary to commit the nation to more missiles than Mr. McNamara believed to be enough for strategic deterrence." All this was due to the power of the military-industrial complex, which Lapp's book explores and whose potency McNamara denies.

The inadequacy of McNamara's account becomes more striking if one checks back on those given in Sorenson's *Kennedy* and Schlesinger's *A Thousand Days*. The former says that the U-2 flights disclosed that Khrushchev's first ICBM had proven "too costly, too cumbersome and too vulnerable a weapon for mass production," and that he had settled "for a very few of these missiles" while he tried to develop a better ICBM. Schlesinger writes that while the "missile gap" had "withered away" by the time the first Kennedy budget was prepared, it nevertheless provided for more missiles than did the extensive program already launched under Eisenhower. Schlesinger says "the White House staff . . . wondered whether the new budget was not providing far more missiles than national security required." He is protective of Kennedy and blames McNamara for the increase. Schlesinger says that McNamara

did not believe that doubling or even tripling our striking power would enable us to destroy the hardened missile sites or missile-launching submarines of our adversary. But he was already engaged in a bitter fight with the Air Force over his effort to dis-

engage from the B-70, a costly high-altitude manned bomber
rendered obsolescent by the improvement in Soviet ground-to-
air missiles. After cutting down the original Air Force missile
demands considerably, he perhaps felt that he could not do more
without risking public conflict with the Joint Chiefs and the
vociferous B-70 lobby in Congress. As a result, the President
went along with the policy of multiplying Polaris and Minuteman missiles.

This shift of blame to McNamara strains one's credulity.
But what it adds up to is that Kennedy and McNamara
built more missiles than they thought we needed in order to
appease the Joint Chiefs and the aviation lobby for the cancellation of the B-70. This is a very different decision-
making process than that portrayed by McNamara in the
Pett interview and in *The Essence of Security*. "The blunt
fact," to use McNamara's phrase, is that it was not lack of
accurate information, nor in this case "the intrinsic dynamics of the arms race," but the dynamics of the political
system and the military-industrial complex which led us to
overbuild.

Another point and another revelation is in order before
we leave this McNamara account of what happened. Mc-
Namara went on to another misleading half-disclosure:

Furthermore, that decision in itself, justified as it was, in the end
could not possibly have left unaffected the Soviet Union's future nuclear plans . . . the Soviet reaction is in part a reaction
to our own buildup since the beginning of the 1960s. Soviet
strategic planners undoubtedly reasoned that if our buildup
were to continue at its accelerated pace, we might conceivably
reach in time a credible first-strike capability against the Soviet
Union. That was not, in fact, our intention. . . . But . . . the
result has been that we have both built up our forces to a point
that far exceeds a credible second-strike capability.

This is only half the story. The whole story is that, after
the U-2 incident, the Russians knew that we knew the truth
about the missile gap. They hoped the new Administration
would not unleash a new phase in the arms race by acting as

if there were a missile gap. They tried to open talks with the new Administration on this problem but met with what may have sounded to them like nuclear double-talk. We owe this revelation to another passage (page 301) in Schlesinger's *A Thousand Days*. McNamara's account has to be read against Schlesinger's:

The Soviet Union watched the arrival of the new administration with marked interest. Khrushchev, who had given up on Eisenhower after the U-2 incident and the collapse of the Paris summit in May, 1960, seized several opportunities to semaphore his hopes for Kennedy. His messages to Harriman and others after the election were followed by a Pugwash meeting on disarmament in Moscow in December [1960]. . . . Walt Rostow and Jerome B. Wiesner, who were among the Americans at the Moscow meeting, saw V. V. Kuznetsov of the Soviet Foreign Office. . . . In the course of their talk Kuznetsov mentioned the campaign furor about a "missile gap" and suggested that, if the new administration went in for massive rearmament, it could not expect the Russians to sit still.

So Kennedy and McNamara knew at the time they made their decisions that they were choosing between the appeasement of military-industrial pressures at home and a chance to avert a sharp and costly step-up in the arms race with the Russians. The American public may have been in the dark but both sides understood the cost entailed if the new Administration gave in to the missile gap propaganda. This again is very different from the picture drawn by McNamara.

Rostow's reply to the Russians, as reported by Schlesinger, must have made the Russians feel that we took them for fools. "Rostow replied," Schlesinger writes, "that any Kennedy rearmament would be designed to improve the stability of the deterrent, and the Soviet Union should recognize this as in the interests of peace; but Kuznetsov, innocent of the higher calculus of deterrence as recently developed in the United States, brusquely dismissed the explanation." It is hard to know whether Schlesinger wrote this tongue-in-cheek. The "higher calculus of deterrence"

must have seemed to Kuznetsov sheer cant, a highfalutin
new synonym for the low arithmetic of domestic arms-
lobby politics, which was threatening to develop a U.S. first-
strike capacity rather than a stable deterrent. This, and not
the lack of accurate information, is why both sides find themselves with far more destructive capacity than they need.
McNamara's account is far from being as candid as it appears to be.

This is even more true when McNamara comes to discuss
the ABM, the anti-ballistic missile. The definitive and final
word on the missile-to-shoot-down-a-missile was said by
General Omar Bradley in a little-noticed and undeservedly
forgotten speech he made at St. Alban's[2] in Washington, in
1957. "Missiles will bring anti-missiles," General Bradley
predicted, "and anti-missiles will bring anti-anti-missiles"
until this "whole electronic house of cards" collapses; the
only way out is "accommodation in a world split by rival
ideologies" even if at the cost of "such sacred traditions as
absolute national sovereignty." McNamara's argument
against the ABM is on a less lofty plane. It is in the realm of
hardware rather than philosophy. McNamara argues that
the enemy may easily overwhelm our batteries of anti-
missiles by adding to the number of attacking missiles or the
number of warheads they carry. Both sides would step up
their missiles and anti-missiles in this mad arithmetic and still
find themselves where they started. McNamara's powerful
presentation of this argument may be found in Chapter
Four, as reprinted from his San Francisco speech against the
ABM.

But if the text of the speech as delivered is compared with
the text reprinted as Chapter Four of the book, one finds
that the book omits—almost as if he were ashamed of it and
preferred to forget it—that portion of the speech which
embodied his backdown under pressure from Johnson, and
his acquiescence in a "thin" ABM system, ostensibly aimed
only at China. That portion of the speech has been rele-

[2] The only place the text was ever published was my *Weekly* of
November 18, 1957.

gated to an appendix, which includes the admission in the original speech, "The danger in deploying this relatively light and reliable Chinese-oriented ABM system is going to be that pressures will develop to expand it into a heavy Soviet-oriented ABM system. We must resist that temptation firmly." The advice seems ironic from a man who had just succumbed to the first step away from his own better judgment and in the direction of a new and destabilizing chapter in the nuclear arms race.

Few readers of the McNamara book will realize that Chapter Four is the relic of a retreat from the very argument it presents and a surrender to the pressures of the military-industrial complex. These had been building up for years. In 1959, Eisenhower rejected a recommendation by the Joint Chiefs of Staff that the U.S. build an anti-ballistic missile defense. The wisdom of that rejection had been underscored by McNamara himself only nine months before his backdown. On January 23, 1967, at the annual Senate "military posture" hearing, he testified that if Eisenhower had gone ahead with that ABM system, the Nike-Zeus, in 1959, at an estimated cost of $13–$14 billion, "most of it would have had to be torn out and replaced, almost before it became operative, by the new missiles and radars of the Nike-X system." The lesson he tried to drive home was, "By the same token other technological developments in offensive forces over the next seven years may make obsolete or drastically degrade the Nike-X system as presently envisioned." A few weeks later, to emphasize the point, the Defense Department disclosed that the U.S. had spent $20 billion since World War II on missile systems never completed or out of service because of obsolescence. Their military value was nil but the social waste and the private profit were enormous.

In that portion of the San Francisco speech which remains in Chapter Four, McNamara cites the fact that the science advisers of Eisenhower, Kennedy, and Johnson, and the directors of research and engineering at the Pentagon under his secretaryship and those of his two Republican predecessors had all advised against the deployment of an ABM system. They all saw in it "a senseless spiral upward of nuclear arms." But in 1967 Nixon and the Republicans in Congress, allied with the Joint Chiefs of Staff, were pressing an ABM gap against the Democrats as the Democrats and the military had pressed a missile gap against the Republicans six years earlier. Johnson gave in to that pressure. Ralph Lapp in his book says of this what McNamara should have said in his: "If a U.S. president authorizes a $5-billion Sentinel system to protect himself from Republican charges of failing to insure the nation's security, then one might just as well junk all the elaborate systems of defense analysis that we possess."

It is these systems on which McNamara's reputation is based. He betrayed them by acquiescing in the ABM in 1967 as he acquiesced in the missile gap buildup in 1961. This man, who prides himself on objective considerations of cost-effectiveness and at the same time tries hard to live by liberal precepts, could have ended his term in office with honor by resigning on the ABM issue, as he might have resigned on the even more compelling issue of the continued bombing of North Vietnam. But Vietnam, his most traumatic experience and the scene of his most disastrous misjudgments, is barely mentioned in passing. The noblest effort of his career, his testimony of August 25, 1967 before the Stennis subcommittee of the Senate, in which he cogently argued the case against the bombing of the North, is not even included in his book, again as if he would like to forget it and to have it forgotten. McNamara is capable of writing that worldwide student unrest springs from "the fear that somehow society, all society—East and West—has fallen victim to a bureaucratic tyranny of technology that is gradually depersonalizing and alienating modern man himself." How inspiring an example he might have set if he had himself defied this "bureaucratic tyranny" and resigned in protest against the bombing of the North, or the decision to embark on the ABM, with all the fateful consequences

against which he himself warned! If loyalty to the bureaucratic and political team is to outweigh loyalty to mankind,
what hope can there be? Certainly nothing McNamara can
possibly do at the World Bank can begin to match what he
might have done by a resignation on either or both of these
issues.

The elaborate reasons McNamara gives in the appendix
as to why it is all right to build a "thin" system against
China though not a big one against Russia are a subterfuge.
The advocates of an ABM regard the decision to build a
"thin" $5-billion defense as the entering wedge for a big
one which will cost from $40 to $70 billion. The idea of an
ABM defense against China is best judged by comparing
our nuclear power with theirs. "Our alert forces alone
carry more than 2,200 weapons" averaging more than one
megaton apiece, McNamara disclosed in the San Francisco
speech. As against this nuclear armada, the debates in Congress have revealed that our intelligence believes that by the
mid-seventies the Chinese may have four or five intercontinental missiles! The best reply to McNamara's Chinese argument was the comment of Senator Russell, who favors a
big ABM. "The Chinese are not completely crazy," he said.
"They are not going to attack us with four or five missiles
when they know we have the capability of virtually destroying the entire country. . . . I don't like people to think that
I am being kidded by this talk of a defense against a Chinese
nuclear attack."

The ABM will prove the biggest military-scientific gravy
train yet. A few days after the San Francisco speech, announcing that we would build the "thin" ABM against
China, Senator Clark of Pennsylvania called the Senate's attention to what happened in the stock market. He said the
story was there. "Where is the ABM money going to go?
Raytheon, up 4⅛ to 91⅛ on Monday, September 18, the
day of the McNamara speech; Aerojet General, up 4⅜ to
33¼ on the same day. Strong rising trends have been just
as visible in other major ABM contractors—Thiokol, Martin
Marietta and Sperry Rand. The vast new defense pork lunch

wagon—maybe the biggest ever—has begun to roll, and the investors on the stock market know it." The money needed "to rebuild our cities and heal the wounds in our society," Clark protested, "is being drained off to build Armageddon instead." These are the realities one will not find in McNamara's book.

November 7, 1968
New York Review

ON NATIONAL DEFENSE, SPACE AND FOREIGN POLICY, THE NEW GOP PLATFORM READS AS IF WRITTEN BY GENERAL DYNAMICS FOR A NEW ARMS RACE

All political platform-writers cultivate amnesia. This beneficial affliction is evident in that portion of the new Republican platform which deals with National Defense. "All the world was respectful," it says, "of America's decisive strategic advantage over the Soviets achieved during the Eisenhower Administration." On the contrary, the Eisenhower Administration was accused by the Democrats and the aviation lobby of allowing first a bomber gap and then a missile gap to develop. Both turned out to be figments of the armament salesman's imagination. But eight years ago the Democrats were accusing the Republicans of endangering national security by falling behind in the arms race. This time the Republican platform makes the same accusation against the Democrats. Kennedy called Eisenhower's term in office "years of the locust" in which "we obtained economic secu-

rity at the expense of military security." This time the Republicans charge that "advanced military research and development have been inhibited and stagnated by inexpert,
cost-oriented administrators" (my italics).

One difference between 1960 and 1968 is that we were
then spending some $40 billion plus at the Pentagon while
this year it will be $80 billion plus. This year's requests by
the Joint Chiefs of Staff, before Secretary Clifford pared
them down, was $102 billion.

But the Republicans do not think those who administer
the military budget ought to be "cost-oriented." It is they
who now talk of "gaps." Though the Democrats are spending twice as much as did the Republicans, the Democrats are
accused of "frittering away superior military capabilities"
by "standing still" and "enabling the Soviets to narrow their
defense gap, in some areas to outstrip us, and to move to
cancel our lead entirely by the early seventies." The Republicans picture the Navy saddled with "second-best weaponry" (the TFX), submarine improvements delayed while
"the Soviets have proceeded apace," anti-submarine warfare "left seriously inadequate, new fighter planes held up
and new strategic weaponry left on the drawing boards."
In the platform plank on science, they also "deplore the
failure of the Johnson-Humphrey Administration to emphasize the military uses of space." The Republicans "regard
the ability to launch and deploy advanced spacecraft as a
military necessity." The platform reads as if written by
General Dynamics.

The Republican concern for the military is again evident
in the platform plank on a healthy economy. The Republicans say "such funds as become available with the termina-
tion of the Vietnam war *and upon recovery from its impact
on national defense* will be applied in a balanced way to
critical domestic needs and to reduce the heavy tax burden"
(my italics). The first priority will be to rebuild our
"starved" armed forces. In our July 8, 1968 issue we called
attention to a series of Johnson Administration speeches
which tried to prepare public opinion for the news that even

if the Vietnamese war ended there would be little money available for domestic needs because the money would be needed by the military to cope with backlogs of delayed weapon improvements and depleted inventories. Did not the Under Secretary of the Treasury on June 25 explain that the military had been fighting the Vietnam war "on a very, very lean budget?" Only after these military needs are met will the Republicans apply what is left, if anything, "in a balanced way" to "critical domestic needs" and to "reduce the heavy tax burden." The suffering poor will be helped equally with the suffering rich, but only after our suffering military has been taken care of.

In its special study last May 24 of the military-industrial complex, *Congressional Quarterly* reported, "One Pentagon source told *CQ* that any increment over $40 billion in the post-Vietnam defense budget will be purely due to pressures by the military-industrial complex rather than to the defense needs of the nation." *Congressional Quarterly* in that same study said, "Several highly placed Administration and industry sources said cuts totalling $10 to $15 billion could be made in the defense budget while retaining or improving the current level of national security." That saving alone would be enough, according to a report made some weeks ago to Governor Rockefeller, to scrap our present welfare system and initiate a system of guaranteed minimum income for the poor. But the platform's long and lachrymose platform plank on the poor says not one word about any income guarantee. On the poor, the Republicans are "cost-oriented."

One paragraph in the foreign policy plank endorses "limitation" of arms provided there are "trustworthy guarantees" against violation. But a major section of the national defense plank is devoted to specific areas in which the Republicans would step up the arms race. They want to build more missile-armed nuclear submarines and to stimulate military research in an effort to find "major innovations" in weaponry. They pledge "to assemble the nation's best diplomatic, military and scientific minds for an exhaustive reassessment of America's worldwide commitments and military preparedness." There is no sign, however, of any retreat from a Pax Americana. In a passage of the foreign policy plank which sounds exactly like Rusk, the Republicans say, "We do not intend to conduct foreign policy in such a way as to make the United States a world policeman." But the very next sentence, again exactly like Rusk, says, "However, we will not condone aggression or so-called 'wars of national liberation.'" In the plank on Vietnam the party does express its concern over "hastily extemporized undeclared wars which embroil massive U.S. Army forces thousands of miles from our shores" but the solution favored seems to be the use of more airpower. For the next sentence says, "It is time to realize that not every international conflict is susceptible of solution by American *ground* forces" (my italics). Our colonial cops will travel in B-52's.

If there is any doubt about the GOP's commitment to Pax Americana, Nixon made it clear at his August 6 Miami Beach news conference when asked whether he now thought the Vietnam war unwinnable, "I do not think that the war is not winnable and I should state further that I certainly do not seek the Presidency for the purpose of presiding over the destruction of the credibility of the American power throughout the world." This paraphrases Churchill's famous last stand for British imperialism.

August 19, 1968

A GOLDWATER
TO HEAD THE PENTAGON

As show business, Nixon's introduction of his Cabinet was shallow and banal. He himself seemed like a bush-league Ed

Sullivan. No less than 10 times the TV audience was assured that there was some mysterious "extra dimension" enveloping what seemed to be a random assortment of the kind of businessmen to be met at any Rotary Club luncheon; the only extra dimension visible in their records was the size of their bank accounts. This is another Cabinet of millionaires. At first glance the weakest appointment was Nixon's law partner, John Mitchell, to be Attorney General. At a time when that office requires the deepest insights, we get an Attorney General who has spent his professional career as a municipal bond expert! The best appointment was that of William P. Rogers to be Secretary of State; the most alarming, that of Melvin R. Laird to be Secretary of Defense. Unfortunately Rogers, who was a first-rate Attorney General under Eisenhower and gave us some of the best federal judges ever to sit in the South, knows next to nothing about foreign affairs, while Laird is all too well equipped to be effective at the Pentagon in terms of his own outlook. He is a more competent and less open Goldwater. The prize in the Nixon package has gone to the military-industrial complex. . . .

Nixon has tried to create the image of a non-ideological Cabinet; he has called his Cabinet "pragmatic centrists." The man he would put in the Pentagon is no centrist. His legislative score for 1967 was rated at 100 percent by the U.S. Chamber of Commerce, 85 percent by the conservative Americans for Constitutional Action, and 7 percent by Americans for Democratic Action; he is liberal on health legislation. "A steely and shrewd politician . . . at the center of our largest conservative apparatus," was the summation of the National Committee for an Effective Congress.

Neither is Laird a pragmatist. I was wrong last week in saying that he would be as surprised to be called a practitioner of geopolitics as Babbitt would have been to be called a guru. This small-town Wisconsin lumber dealer is quite at home with the swamis of the cold war. His one book, *A House Divided: America's Security Gap* (Henry Regnery, 1962), warms up to a climax in which he calls Christianity and communism irreconcilable but says, "positivism, not communism, is the philosophical virus that causes our paralysis." In his native Marshfield, Wisconsin, just using such words in public would be enough to mark a man down as suspect. "It is a profound lesson of history," Laird writes in a peroration worthy of his fellow Presbyterian, John Foster Dulles, one of Laird's heroes, "that as any nation increases its dedication to materialistic, positivistic criteria at the expense of dependence upon God and the truths beyond history, that nation has begun its downward course." This deep-seated opposition to materialism does not keep Laird from worrying about "the present profit squeeze" nor from suggesting as mandatory "a major overhaul of the tax system," by which he means a shift from income to more direct taxes, i.e., from the rich to the poor, who are presumably better adapted to a less materialistic way of life.

The book carries a modest acknowledgment "for able editorial and stylistic assistance" to Karl Hess, who surfaced to fame two years later as Goldwater's ghost writer. The "strategy gap" the book seeks to fill is the lack of an offensive posture. The book suggests that the U.S. take the initiative, among other places (1) in ridding Cuba of communism, (2) in any future East German or Hungarian uprising, and (3) in effecting "the unification of Germany." A Pentagon chief with such aims will rarely have a dull moment. These are high-wire examples of the brinkmanship Laird so admires in Dulles. The basic axiom of the book is "better dead than Red," though expressed in the fruitiest and most full-bodied Goldwaterite prose. "Is the fact that more lives are involved in decisions today," Laird asks in sententious reference to nuclear war, "sufficient in itself to make the condition of life [i.e., liberty] second to the primacy of biological preservation?" The answer, in the finest tradition of extremism in the defense of liberty, is "no." This overreadiness for the ultimate sacifice was considered too dangerous for the White House in 1964. It would be no less dangerous in the Pentagon today.

At his Pentagon press conference Friday, December 13,[1] when a reporter asked, "May I read some of your words back to you from your book?" Laird replied, "I was afraid someone might do that." The words read back to him were that "the credible announcement of first-strike initiative is the sole way to effective disarmament discussions with the Soviet Union." Laird claimed this was the thesis not only of his book but of a report concurred in six years ago by all the members of the House Defense Appropriations subcommittee, on which he has served since 1953. He said that was "written in a period of confrontation. We are now in a period of negotiations, and I think that that should be considered as we face the future."

Yet Laird doesn't seem to be facing the future very differently now than then. The ability, if necessary, to take the nuclear initiative and strike first is implicit in the insistence on nuclear "superiority" which is a central theme not only of the book but of Laird's major expositions of defense policy since and indeed of the Nixon campaign. The Nixon task force report on National Security made the maintenance of nuclear superiority its main recommendation. It assailed "the euphoric hope" that peace could be reached by replacing superiority with parity. It said the U.S. "must be prepared to crush all *threats* to the peace with force if required" (my italics) including nuclear weapons. This implies first strike and preventive war. Negotiation in this context becomes another form of dictation through intimidation.

The full significance of the Laird appointment becomes clearer if one goes back and has a fresh look at the kind of men on the task forces which prepared Nixon's position pa-

[1] In his book (p. 134) Laird cites as an example of Khrushchev's "mastery of the psychological techniques of political warfare" his announcement that a 50-megaton bomb would be set off on Halloween eve." He thus became the first American statesman to discover that the Kremlin so finely tuned its moves to exploit the superstitious twinges of the West (perhaps as an echo of the Pumpkin Papers in the Hiss case?). We hope no brooder over a crystal ball in Moscow finds in the day and date chosen for Laird's first Pentagon press conference a similarly ingenious way to frighten the U.S.S.R.

pers on defense and foreign policy. These were heavily weighted with the military and apocalyptic rightists. The task force on national security "was made up primarily," *Congressional Quarterly* noted in a study December 4 which predicts a sharp rise in military spending under Nixon, "of military and civilian officials associated with the 'massive retaliation' doctrine of the 1950's and members of Congress who favor a 'tough' military line." Many of them are men whom Laird salutes as his mentors in his book—Admirals Arleigh Burke and Arthur Radford on the defense task force, and on the foreign policy task force Professor Robert Strausz-Hupé of the University of Pennsylvania and Professor Gerhart Niemeyer of Notre Dame, both mighty Druids in the dark forests of geopolitics. Other kindred spirits on the defense task force were Craig Hosmer, Dr. Edward Teller's faithful mouthpiece on the Joint Congressional Committee on Atomic Energy, and Senator Tower of Texas. On the foreign policy task force, just to keep it from slipping too far left, were also Robert Amory, who lost his job as deputy director of the CIA in the wake of the Bay of Pigs; Robert C. Hill, who distinguished himself as Eisenhower's last Ambassador in Mexico by indiscreet relations with the right-wing *Sinarquistas;* Professor David N. Rowe of Yale, and Walter Judd. The last two have been as stalwart as Mao himself, though on the other side, in resisting revisionism in America's China policy.

These task forces and their composition do not fit that mask of moderation the Nixon public relations strategy has fashioned for his debut. Any idea that the work of these Republican troglodytes on defense and foreign policy can be dismissed as a mere campaign exercise will be dispelled by a closer look at Laird's record, his book and his associations. He is one of them. Along with Henry A. Kissinger, the new White House foreign affairs expert, and Kissinger's deputy, Richard V. Allen, Nixon's foreign affairs expert during the campaign, they belong to a closely knit mutual admiration society. The accolade from Kissinger's colleagues of the Harvard liberal establishment on his appointment as Nixon's mentor has served to distract attention from his less well-known but more significant ties with these right-wingers. Laird's book is complimentary in its references to Kissinger, as it is to Niemeyer and Strausz-Hupé. Laird told the Washington *Star* in a full-length interview December 18 that in 1964, as chairman of the Republican platform committee, "he relied more heavily on the views of Henry Kissinger than those of Barry Goldwater," while Allen in an interview with the *New York Times* December 14 disclosed that during the Nixon campaign he "maintained discreet contact with Dr. Kissinger, then foreign policy adviser to Governor Rockefeller." Such political dexterity must be close to genius.

Laird in his book also acknowledges the inspiration of David M. Abshire, who, with Allen, edited a huge 1,000-page right-wing symposium on *National Security: Political, Military and Economic Strategies in the Decade Ahead* (Praeger: 1963) for the Georgetown Center for Strategic Studies and the Hoover Institution on War, Revolution and Peace. Allen himself moved from the first to the second and is now on leave to the White House. The volume carries an introduction by another of Laird's heroes, Admiral Burke. Among the contributors are Kissinger and such seers as Herman Kahn, Edward Teller, Senator Jackson and Walt Rostow. When Allen three years later published a study for the American Bar Association, *Peace or Peaceful Co-Existence?*, Laird praised it in the *Congressional Record* (August 26, 1966) as proving "conclusively" from a study of 3,000 Communist documents (no less!) that co-existence was only a more deceitful way of seeking world domination through "a many-pronged offensive." This is back to the bogeyman view of the fifties. Laird, Kissinger and Allen will prove a formidable team in fashioning foreign policy.

Whether prongs or tentacles, Laird sees them everywhere. His world-view, like that of Niemeyer and Strausz-Hupé, is equally compounded of demonology and melodrama. During the hearings on the fiscal 1966 budget in March, 1965, when the bombings of North Vietnam had just begun, Laird told McNamara (page 121, Part 3 House appropriations hearings), "I think there is a good possibility that we will have a breakout under Communist pressure in some other place in the world within the next six or seven weeks. It seems that the Communists operate this way. At the time of the missiles to Cuba, Red China attacked India. At the time of the Bay of Tonkin, that incident, when we were completely diverted on the situation taking place in the Vietnamese war, the Communist-backed rebels marched and took over Stanleyville [in the Congo], which was a very strategic place." It takes a wide-angle vision to link together in one cosmic plot the Cuban missile crisis, the Indo-Chinese border war, the Tonkin Gulf bombings and the rebellion in the Congo.

Had Laird been Secretary of Defense in the past eight years, history might have been very different. He thinks we should not have backed away at the Bay of Pigs. He sees Rostow as naive, Rusk as soft and McNamara as a positive menace. He believes President Kennedy made a cardinal mistake when he said we would never strike first. He advocates a policy of nuclear reprisal along the lines of "a policy called 2X" which he says Dulles considered in the fifties. This would involve a steady escalation in nuclear reprisal to "the point at which the cost to the enemy would outweigh the gain" and show him that aggression was "unprofitable." Though an opponent of McNamara's cost-effectiveness approach, Laird seems to have a touching faith that such reprisals would lead an enemy calmly to sit down and balance gains against losses and decide that crime doesn't pay, like a businessman soberly contemplating a poor investment.

Something of this approach is evident in Laird's own shift away from support of Johnson in the Vietnam war. Laird began to lose enthusiasm after Johnson in the Johns Hopkins speech announced a readiness to negotiate. Laird has no faith in the Saigon regime and believes the Communists will take over if our troops pull out. This is also the view of the Joint Chiefs of Staff, who would like (from distant echoes we have picked up) to keep a garrison force of U.S. troops there indefinitely. They may find Laird easy to convince. Laird warns in his book that past mistakes have been due to our failure to listen to the military in political discussions. He describes the military as "highly intelligent citizens with a broad grasp of our military potential and future needs . . . well-equipped to make meaningful recommendations for policy." There is no trace in this description of that astringent eye required to keep the military within bounds.

Not to examine Laird's views and record fully in the hearings and the confirmation debate would be a gross neglect of senatorial duty. If the appointment cannot be blocked, at least the country should be put on notice as to what it may expect. Laird at one point suggested in the House that the Peace Corps be renamed the Freedom Corps because "freedom is the important issue" and "mere survival under peace is not the important message we wish to deliver to the world." To confirm Laird as Secretary of Defense is to risk the likelihood that in the next four years the Pentagon's course will be set on higher goals than "mere survival."

December 30, 1968

NIXON AND THE ARMS RACE: THE BOMBER BOONDOGGLE

The No. 1 question for the new Nixon Administration is what it will do about the arms race. If it opts for higher military spending, the consequence will be intensified social conflict. If the new President's policies in office follow his campaign pledges, the decision has already been made. Nixon has begun by promising to perpetuate one of McNamara's greatest errors and to undo his greatest accomplishment. The error is that miscarriage of an airplane, the TFX, now known as the F-111, which has already cost the country several billion dollars. His accomplishment was to make the country realize that at a certain point in the awful arithmetic of nuclear power, superiority in weapons became meaningless.

In his Security Gap speech over CBS on October 25, Nixon said that one of his major aims would be to "correct its [the Pentagon's] over-centralization" in order to give greater weight in decision-making to the military as against the top civilians. "I intend to root out the 'whiz kid' approach, which for years," Nixon said, "has led our policies and programs down the wrong roads." But he is following McNamara down his most costly wrong road, just when the military have been proven right and the top civilians wrong, and indeed—as we shall see—on the one issue where the "whiz kids" sided with the military against McNamara. On the other hand, Nixon has set out, in the search for nuclear superiority, to follow the military down a dead-end path where the military are demonstrably wrong and the "whiz kids" are demonstrably right. To examine these two divergent courses is to see the trouble which lies ahead, on many different levels, for the new Administration and the country.

Let us begin with the TFX and with the speech Nixon made November 2 at Fort Worth, Texas. Fort Worth is where General Dynamics builds the TFX or F-111, the plane that was the focus of the longest and bitterest controversy of McNamara's years in the Pentagon. "The F-111 in a Nixon Administration," the candidate said at Fort Worth that day, "will be made into one of the foundations of our air supremacy." This pledge, which received too little attention, may prove to be the biggest blooper of the campaign, and the beginning—if Nixon tries to keep that pledge—of the biggest fight between the Nixon Administration and the very forces he might have counted on for a honeymoon, the Senate conservatives who specialize in military policy and who were most critical of McNamara in the

TFX affair. It is startling that a man as cautious as Nixon should have made so unqualified a pledge to a plane which has become a tragic joke.

Last May, when the Senate Appropriations subcommittee on the Department of Defense was holding hearings on the budget for the fiscal year 1969, the Chairman, Senator Russell of Georgia, booby-trapped the Air Force Chief of Staff, General McConnell, with what appeared to be an innocent question on this plane, the F-111:

SENATOR RUSSELL: Would it be a very serious matter if one of these planes were recovered by any potential enemy in a reasonably good condition?

GENERAL McCONNELL: Yes, we have quite a few things in it that we would not want the enemy to get.

SENATOR RUSSELL: That is mainly electronic devices.

GENERAL McCONNELL: That is true of practically all the aircraft we have.

SENATOR RUSSELL: Of course the Russians got a B-29 when they were one of our allies. They fabricated a great many of them as nearly comparable to the B-29's as they could. I was hoping if they got a F-111 they would fabricate some of them as near ours as they could and see if they had as much trouble as we did. It would put their Air Force out of business.[1]

Neither General McConnell nor his civilian superior Air Force Secretary Harold Brown dared say one word in reply to Senator Russell's cruel jibe.

Russell's sardonic view of the F-111 is shared on both sides of the aisle in the Senate. On October 3, Senator Curtis of Kansas, a senior Republican, a member of the Aeronautical and Space Sciences Committee, delivered a devastating attack on the F-111 in the Senate, in which he said McNamara's "obstinacy" in producing the F-111, "will be a major problem that the new Administration must face." Just one month later Nixon began to face it by pledging himself at Fort Worth to make this plane "one of the foundations of our air supremacy."

[1] Senate Appropriations Committee Hearings on the 1969 Defense Department budget, Part I, Department of the Air Force, p. 103. Released September 19, 1968.

Either Nixon and his staff do not read the newspapers, much less the *Congressional Record* and the hearings, or Nixon like McNamara is determined to override military judgment and keep the billions flowing into General Dynamics for this jinxed plane. The difference is that when McNamara overrode the military, it was difficult for outsiders to judge so complex a technological controversy—especially when so many of the facts were still classified. Newspapermen like myself, who start with a strong bias against the military, assumed that McNamara was probably right. But 1968 is the year when the F-111 finally went into combat; the results have led many people inside and outside Congress to look at the old controversy with a fresh eye.

Nixon's reckless pledge was the only bright spot for the F-111 in the year 1968. The latest, 1969, edition of *Jane's Aircraft*[2] says succinctly,

The 474th Tactical Fighter Wing at Nellis [Air Force Base, Nevada] was the first to be equipped with the F-111As [the Air Force version of the F-111]. Six aircraft from Nellis arrived at the Takhli base in Thailand on 17 March 1968 and made their first operational sorties over Vietnam on 25 March. Two were lost in the next five days.

The foreword, which went to press later, says "Three of the first 8 F-111A's dispatched to Vietnam were lost in a matter of weeks and the type was grounded shortly afterwards." No mention was made of these losses by Secretary of the Air Force Brown when he read his prepared statement to the Senate appropriations defense subcommittee in executive session last May 6. On the contrary, he said the F-111 "is proving, in its tests and operational units, to be an outstanding aircraft." By then three of the original six had been lost, as may be seen from the following colloquy, where the reader will notice Secretary Brown's squeamish reluctance to use the word "lost":

SENATOR RUSSELL: How many of these have we sent over to Southeast Asia?

2 John W. R. Taylor, ed., *Jane's All the World's Aircraft, 1968–69* (New York: McGraw-Hill), p. 279.

SECRETARY BROWN: We sent six and have sent two replacements.

SENATOR RUSSELL: You have lost three, so you have five?

SECRETARY BROWN: There are five there now.

SENATOR RUSSELL: Do you have any information on these three that were lost? Do you know whether any of them fell into the hands of the North Vietnamese to be sent to Moscow along with all the secret equipment of the Pueblo?

GENERAL MCCONNELL [Air Force Chief Staff]: No, sir.[3]

In his Senate speech of October 3, Senator Curtis disclosed, "Thus far, 11 F-111 aircraft have crashed with a number of fatalities." He revealed that the wings were broken off one plane during a "static ground test" just six weeks before the first six planes were deployed to Southeast Asia, and that the week before his Senate speech another F-111A had crashed during a training flight owing to "a fatigue failure in the wing carrythrough structure."

If rightists treated Nixon and the Defense Department the way he treated the State Department in the days when he was a practicing witch-hunter, a proposal to make such a plane, with such a record, a foundation stone of American air supremacy would have been adduced as proof positive that the Pentagon had been infiltrated with Red and pinko saboteurs.

Last January the British Royal Air Force canceled its order for 50 F-111K's. In March Congress ordered work stopped on the F-111B's, the version for the U.S. Navy. On October 7, Senator Symington followed Senator Curtis with a speech suggesting that production of the F-111's for the Air Force also be stopped: he said that "the series of crashes in the past five months" makes it doubtful that it will ever prove to be "a truly reliable airplane" and declared that its future should "receive highest priority upon convening of the new Congress."

The strangest discovery which turns up in studying Nixon's pledge at Fort Worth is that he and his staff were either unaware of, or ignored, his own famous "position pa-

[3] Senate 1969 Defense Appropriations Hearings, *op. cit.*, pp. 102–3.

pers." The one on "Research and Development: Our Neglected Weapon," [4] which was made public in May, 1968, says of the F-111:

The effort to transform the TFX (F-111) into an all-purpose all-service aircraft has created serious problems. Against military advice, the F-111 was selected as a superior, yet economical, weapons system . . . The aircraft were to cost approximately $2.4 million each. Now they are priced at more than $6 million each . . . In view of the recent decision that the F-111B, the Navy version, is unacceptable, and a substitute aircraft be initiated, the final cost of the program will increase enormously coupled with years of delay. The program has resulted in the Air Force having a new aircraft that does not meet the original requirements . . . The F-111B has been found unacceptable and the F-111 Bomber version does not meet Air Force requirements for an advanced bomber in the 1970 time frame.

Nixon devoted one of his main campaign speeches to "the research gap." The Fort Worth speech showed his own research gap. Did he and his staff fail to read their position papers? Another of these papers, "Decisions on National Security: Patchwork or Policy?" is also in conflict with his Fort Worth speech. That paper says "a notable example" of how the top civilians overrode military judgment in the McNamara years was the original award of the contract for the F-111. "The contractor unanimously recommended by both the military analysts and the Weapons Evaluation Systems Group," it says, "was rejected." The rejected bidder was Boeing. The contractor McNamara chose was General Dynamics. Nixon at Fort Worth affirmed the same choice.

We are not dealing here with a minor item. General Dynamics is the country's biggest weapons producer. A Defense Department press release of November 18 on the nation's top 10 defense contractors showed General Dy-

---

4 All these position papers have been reprinted in a one-volume compilation, *Choice for America: Republican Answers to the Challenge of Now*, published July, 1968, by the Republican National Committee, 1625 Eye St. N.W., Washington 20006.

namics as No. 1. In the fiscal year ending last June 30, it received $2.2 billion in arms contracts, or 5.8 percent of the total awarded in those 12 months. More than 80 percent of the firm's business comes from the government. The TFX represented the biggest single plum in military procurement. The original contract was for 1,700 planes at a total cost of $5.8 billion, or about $3 million per plane. These figures have since skyrocketed. This year, before the Navy contract was cancelled, the Pentagon admitted the cost of the Navy version would be $8 million apiece and of the Air Force version $6.5 million. As usual these, too, were understatements. Senator Curtis disclosed that the contractor's cost information reports put the average cost of the Navy plane at $9.5 million and that internal budgeting projections at the Pentagon put the Air Force plane at $9.1 million each. The original contract would have run up in the neighborhood of $15 billion.

Even with the cutbacks, more than $6 billion has already been spent and at least between $3 and $4 billion more "will be added in succeeding years," Senator Curtis said, "if present Defense Department plans are carried to completion." If Nixon keeps his word, they *will* be completed, perhaps expanded. But if he tries to do so, he will almost certainly find himself embattled with the Air Force buffs in Congress. For Curtis, Symington, Russell, and McClellan speak for a group of Senators who feel that the Air Force has been starved and stunted while all this money has been wasted on the TFX. We are in the presence of a wide-open split not only between the proponents of General Dynamics and Boeing respectively but within the Air Force and the whole military-industrial complex.

History is repeating itself, and it is the history of subordinating military efficiency to moneyed and political pressures. The only difference is that Nixon will find it harder than did McNamara to hide the realities, now that the F-111 has finally begun to fly—and fall. When the Kennedy Administration took over, General Dynamics was drifting close to receivership. It lost $27 million in 1960 and $143 million in 1961. *Fortune* magazine in January and February of 1962 published a fascinating two-part story of its misjudgments and its business losses by Richard Austin Smith. Smith said its losses on its civilian plane business had been so disastrous that its working capital had dropped below the minimum required by its agreement with its bankers and that if the bankers had not reduced the minimum this "technically could have started the company down the road to receivership." Smith wrote that the output of the General Dynamics plant at Fort Worth in 1962 would be half what it was in 1961. *Fortune* said, in its strangulated prose, that General Dynamics would have to shut down its facilities "unless it gets contract for joint Navy-Air Force fighter." This was the TFX.

The TFX contract saved General Dynamics in 1962. The cancellation of the F-111 could ruin it in 1969. The effect of cancelling the Navy version of the plane was already reflected in a third quarter deficit, as of September 30, 1968, amounting to $1.51 a share compared with a net profit of $1.13 a share in the third quarter of 1967. *Moody's News* showed General Dynamics had to write off $39.6 million in contracts in 1968 as against only $12 million in 1967. Its net after taxes for the first nine months of 1968, after allowing for sales of assets which made the accounts look better than they otherwise would have, was only $9 million as compared with $36 million for the same period the previous year.

Standard & Poor's Outlook, October 7, 1968, said the stock of General Dynamics was "a speculation in the success of this F-111 program" and that "the most important price determinant over the near term will be developments in this trouble-plagued F-111 program." *The Value Line*, October 18, said, "Since our July review the ever-sensitive stock market has sold these shares down to a two-year low." It said that if the problems of the F-111 were not soon resolved, it was "vulnerable to further procurement cutbacks." This was the bleak outlook two weeks before Nixon's speech at Fort Worth. McNamara saved General

Dynamics in 1962. Nixon promised on November 2 to save it again.

McNamara's error on the TFX is worth close study because it shows the diminishing relationship between military procurement and genuine considerations of defense. It demonstrates the growing extent to which procurement is determined by military-bureaucratic and industrial considerations. The prime determinants were to save the largest company in the military-industrial complex financially and to appease the bomber generals, who simply will not admit that their expensive toys have grown obsolete. Billions which could do so much for poverty are squandered to maintain these favorite Pentagon clients on the military relief rolls in the lush style to which they have become accustomed.

General Dynamics, behind its glamorous front, is almost as much a creature of the government as the Air Force. In 1967 some 83 percent of its sales were to the government. *Moody's* observes of the huge Fort Worth establishment, where Nixon gave so much solace to this peculiar form of free and private enterprise, that the "plant, including most machinery and equipment, is leased from the U.S. government." The chief asset of General Dynamics seems to be its ability to wangle contracts out of the Pentagon.

The error in the TFX affair occurred on three levels, which have had varying degrees of attention, in inverse ratio to their importance. McNamara was wrong—so events seem to have proven—(1) in giving the TFX contract to General Dynamics instead of Boeing, (2) in insisting that the same basic plane be adopted for the diverse needs of the Air Force and Navy, and (3) in surrendering to the pressure of the Air Force for a new bomber and the Navy for a new missile weapons system to meet a nonexistent Soviet bomber threat just so they could go on with their expensive bomber game.

The first, the least important, got the most attention in

earlier years, since it promised Republican and conservative Democratic critics of the Kennedy and Johnson Administrations a scandal. But the shock of the Kennedy assassination cut short the McClellan committee investigation. A key figure was Roswell Gilpatric, a corporation lawyer who has done two tours of duty at the Pentagon, the first as Under Secretary of the Air Force in 1951–53 and again as Deputy Secretary of Defense in 1961–64, returning on each occasion to the famous Wall Street law firm of Cravath, Swaine and Moore, with which he has been associated since 1931. Through Gilpatric's efforts the firm became counsel for General Dynamics in the late fifties, and Gilpatric has combined his law work with activity in foreign and military policy in the Council on Foreign Relations and as a member of the Rockefeller Brothers Special Study project, which called for a sharp increase in military expenditures in January, 1958. In 1960 he was named as adviser on national security affairs by Kennedy during his campaign for the Presidency and after the election became Deputy Secretary of Defense, No. 2 man to McNamara at the Pentagon. There he played a major role in awarding the TFX contract.

General Dynamics has always been adept at having friends at court. It chose for its president in the fifties a former Secretary of the Army, Frank Pace. The $400-million losses of its Convair division during his incumbency make one wonder whether his chief qualification for the job was that he knew his way around Washington. Similarly it did not hurt General Dynamics to have its ex-counsel as No. 2 man in the Pentagon while it was fighting for the contract which could alone save it from receivership. Nor was General Dynamics hurt by the fact that Fred Korth, whom the Kennedy Administration had for some unfathomable reason made Secretary of the Navy, was a Fort Worth, Texas, banker, a past president of the Continental Bank, which had loaned money to General Dynamics, "and that Korth had kept an active, though not a financial, interest in the activities of this bank"[5] while in public office.

[5] Robert J. Art, *The TFX Decision* (Boston: Little, Brown, 1968), p. 4.

Korth told the McClellan committee "that because of his peculiar position he had deliberately refrained from taking a directing hand in this decision [within the Navy] until the last possible moment." [6] But it was "the last possible moment" which counted. Three times the Pentagon's Source Selection Board found that Boeing's bid was better and cheaper than that of General Dynamics and three times the bids were sent back for fresh submissions by the two bidders and fresh reviews. On the fourth round, the military still held that Boeing was better but found at last that the General Dynamics bid was also acceptable.

It was at this last moment that the award was made to General Dynamics. The only document the McClellan committee investigators were able to find in the Pentagon in favor of that award, according to their testimony, was a five-page memorandum signed by McNamara, Korth, and Eugene Zuckert, then Secretary of the Air Force, but not—interestingly enough—by Gilpatric. Senator Curtis charged in his Senate speech on October 3, that some months after the contract was announced in November, 1962, "a team of experts was assembled in the Pentagon to review the designs . . . The experts were directed to find strong points for General Dynamics and weak points for Boeing so the decision could be defended in Senate hearings."

During the McClellan committee hearings in 1963, Senator Ervin of North Carolina focused on another angle to this contract when he said to McNamara, "I would like to ask you whether or not there was any connection whatever between your selection of General Dynamics, and the fact that the Vice President of the United States happens to be a resident of the state in which that company has one of its principal, if not its principal office." The reference of course was to Lyndon Johnson, to Texas, and to Fort Worth. McNamara answered, "Absolutely not." [7] In the dissolute atmosphere of Washington there were few to believe such political virginity possible. When General Ac-

[6] *Ibid.*, p. 5.
[7] *Idem.*

counting Office investigators asked McNamara how he
came to override military judgment, "The Secretary said
that, after finding the Air Force estimates inadequate for
judging the cost implications of the two proposals [i.e.,
General Dynamics' and Boeing's], he had made rough
judgments of the kind he had made for many years with the
Ford Motor Company." The most charitable comment is
that the TFX, then, proved to be the Edsel of his Pentagon
years.

Under normal circumstances one would have expected
all this to be aired in the 1968 campaign. But the military-
industrial complex plays both sides of the political fence,
and the defense contractors are an easy source of campaign
funds. Nixon not only kept silent but pledged himself to the
very same plane. The same cynical charges made behind the
scenes about the original TFX contract will no doubt be
made again about Nixon's reaffirmation of it. The first
point in favor of General Dynamics was and is its financial
weakness. Boeing, with a better record for engineering and
on costs, is in good shape; half its business is commercial, a
testimony to its reputation. Why let the weaker company
go down the drain? The TFX affair illustrates the survival
of the unfittest in the military-corporate jungle.

The second point in favor of General Dynamics was and
remains political. General Dynamics is in Texas, a swing
state with twenty-four electoral votes, and its biggest sub-
contractor on the F-111, Grumman, is in New York with
forty-five electoral votes. Boeing would have produced the
plane in Kansas, with eight votes, which go Republican anyway, and in the state of Washington with nine. Nixon's
November 2 pledge shows that any major new plane must
show it can fly successfully through the electoral college.
Nixon's pre-election speech at Fort Worth recalls two
other comparable appearances there, one *opera buffa*,
one tragic. The former occurred on December 11, 1962, a
month after General Dynamics won the TFX contract,
when Johnson made a triumphant visit to the plant at Fort
Worth and was greeted by union members waving banners

which said "LBJ Saved the Day" and "We're Here to Say Thanks to LBJ." [8] The other was the morning of November 22, 1963, a few hours before he was assassinated, when President Kennedy addressed a rally in Fort Worth and paid tribute to the TFX as "the best fighter system in the world." [9] For Johnson and Kennedy, as for Nixon, in the TFX contract electioneering and defense were inextricably mingled.

A key word in the TFX controversy was "commonalty." McNamara wanted a plane which could be used by the Air Force and the Navy in common. With the cancellation of the contract for the Navy's version of the F-111, the battle for commonalty between the two services was lost. But Nixon's pledge on the F-111 shows that commonalty still exists in defense politics. For Republican as well as Democratic administrations, what is best for General Dyamics is best for the country.

This mention of "commonalty" brings us to the other two misjudgments involved in the TFX decision. One was to try to build one plane for many diverse Air Force and Navy missions. The other was to counter a Soviet bomber threat which does not now exist and is unlikely ever to come into being. With these misjudgments[10] we come to technological details which must become part of public knowledge if we are to understand the expensive and nightmarish nonsense in which the arms race has engulfed us.

President-elect Nixon, as we have seen, pledged himself to "root out 'the whiz kid' approach" to national defense. As it happens, the "whiz kids" were as opposed to the TFX as generals and admirals were to the idea of trying to build a

[8] Fort Worth *Star-Telegram*, December 12, 1962, quoted in McClellan Committee hearings on the TFX, Part X, p. 2658.

[9] *Public Papers of the Presidents: John F. Kennedy 1963*, p. 887.

[10] I venture to speak so dogmatically not only because of what has happened this year to the F-111, but because among men at the Pentagon devoted to McNamara I have found no one who does not feel the TFX was a mistake.

common plane for both services. "Pressure within the Defense Department for a single sophisticated multimission aircraft [using the new swing-wing design] came from the Office of Defense Research and Engineering, which .was headed in the early 1960s by Harold Brown, the present Secretary of the Air Force," *Congressional Quarterly* reported last February 16. "Although the concept was opposed by the young systems analysts that Defense Secretary McNamara had brought with him to the Pentagon, they were not then in a position to conduct a running battle with Brown. At the time the Office of Systems Analysis was subordinate to the Pentagon comptroller, which was one level below Brown." Nixon to the contrary, this mistake might not have been made if the "whiz kids" had had more influence.

McNamara had been trying to cut down duplication in supplies among the three services, a source of enormous waste, and he accomplished substantial savings in this field. His critics in Congress say privately that to an automobile man, accustomed to mounting various kinds of cars on much the same chassis, the idea of using the same "chassis" in military planes must have seemed a natural. Indeed to an outsider there seems to be little reason why the same plane should not be used by the various services for the same type of mission. Why—for example—can't the Air Force and the Navy use the same dogfighter?

The trouble in the case of the TFX or F-111 is that the Air Force and the Navy had such diverse missions to be performed by the common plane on which McNamara insisted. It is being built for a tactical fighter, a long-range strategic bomber, a reconnaissance plane, and—until the Navy contract was canceled—a new weapons system, a plane carrying a new type of missile.

The Navy wanted the plane to be light enough for a carrier but big enough to carry a special missile—the Phoenix —and a big load of radar equipment. Its Naval mission would be to loiter hour after hour over the fleet to protect it from a nuclear supersonic bomber attack; the radar would enable the plane to detect an incoming plane and hit it with the missile far enough away so that the fleet would be safe from nuclear blast and radiation. The Air Force wanted the plane to be able to fulfill a very different mission. It was to be able to fly at supersonic speed under the radar defenses around the Soviet Union and then, after unloading its nuclear bombs on target, make altitude swiftly enough to elude not only enemy ack-ack or fighter planes but the effects of the nuclear blast it had set off. To fit one plane to two such diverse purposes would seem to require the ingenuity of a Rube Goldberg. This particular mistake has been thoroughly debated, since it serves intra-service animosity. There's nothing the Navy hates worse than losing a battle to the Air Force.

A second level of misjudgment, the most basic of all, has hardly been discussed at all, at least in public. Here one is led to question the good sense of both the Air Force and the Navy. The Navy is still as full of bomber admirals as the Air Force is of bomber generals. They started the bomber gap nonsense in the fifties and still suffer from the obsessions which the arms lobby exploits so skillfully. "In the early 1950's we were told the Russians were going to build thousands of supersonic bombers," Senator Symington commented ruefully last May during the Senate hearings on the 1969 defense budget. "They did not build any long-range bombers of that type." [11] Symington was himself once the captive and spokesman of those inflated fears, as he was several years later of the "missile gap" campaign, which he later helped to expose as fraudulent.

In the hearings last April on "The Status of U.S. Strategic Power," which reflected the views and fears of those who favor a bigger arms budget, Chairman Stennis said of the present Soviet bomber fleet, "I have never looked upon these bombers as a serious threat to the U.S. unless we just let our guard down completely. They are the same old bombers, the Bear and the Bison." These are the subsonic bombers whose appearance in Moscow in the fifties set off the

[11] 1969 Senate Defense Appropriations Hearings, Part V, p. 2664.

bomber gap scare. The Russians just aren't spending money on long-range supersonic nuclear bombers when the same delivery job can be done so much more cheaply and quickly by missiles.

When Stennis's Preparedness Subcommittee of Senate Armed Services filed its report October 4 on the U.S. Tactical Air Power Program, it said, "The F-111B [i.e., the Navy version of the F-111 armed with the Phoenix missile—IFS] was designed primarily for fleet air defense against a Soviet supersonic bomber. But that threat is either limited or does not exist." Yet the Navy, having got rid of the F-111B, is planning its new VFX-1 to carry a Phoenix missile for use against the same non-existent supersonic Soviet bomber attack. The Navy insisted in the fiscal 1969 hearings that the Phoenix-armed plane "is the only system that provides the Navy with an acceptable level of Fleet Air Defense for the 1970–80 era, particularly for any missile threat against the fleet." [12]

This assumes that the Soviets will play the game our way and build the supersonic nuclear bombers the Phoenix is designed to counter. In chess, when one sees the other side concentrating his forces in one sector, one attacks in another. But our Joint Chiefs of Staff do not seem to play chess. *Congressional Quarterly*, which has good sources in the Pentagon, reported last May 3 that many Navy aviators were hostile to both the F-111B and its successor, the VFX-1 project, for a Phoenix-armed plane. It quoted a Pentagon source as saying the whole program was based on a false premise. It said Soviet doctrine envisioned the use of fighters, submarines, and missile-launching patrol boats instead of nuclear supersonic bombers for attacks on carriers and battleships. Obviously an attack would come where the other side can see we are least prepared. The Phoenix is likely to prove not only a waste of funds but an impediment to genuine defense by concentrating on a threat which does not exist now and is not likely to exist later.

12 *Ibid.*, Part IV, p. 1426.

The main Air Force mission for the F-111 is a reflection of the same bomber delusions, but on a larger scale. To see this in perspective one must step back and observe that we now have three major ways of destroying the Soviet Union. One is the ICBM, the intercontinental ballistic missile. The second is the submarine-launched nuclear missile, the Polaris. The third is the intercontinental bomber force of the Strategic Air Command. Any one of these three forces can itself deliver much more than the 400 megatons which McNamara estimates would destroy three-fourths of the Soviet Union's industrial capacity and 64 million people, or one-third its population.

Of the three mega-murder machines, the only one which can be stopped is the bomber fleet. It's an expensive luxury, a toy on which the bomber generals dote, and which the aircraft industry is only too happy to supply. High-flying bombers cannot get through the Soviets' radar and SAM (surface-to-air) missile defenses. So the F-111 is designed to duck low under Soviet radar defenses, drop nuclear bombs, and make a high, fast getaway, all at supersonic speeds. The basic argument against the F-111 is that if we ever want to hit major targets in the Soviet Union, we would do so with missiles which can reach their targets in thirty minutes with fifteen-minute warning time instead of planes whose flight and warning time would be measured in hours. If we tried to use bombers first, they would only warn the enemy and provide plenty of time for retaliatory missile strikes against our cities. If these bombers were to be used for a second strike *after* a Russian attack on us, the bombers (if any were left) would arrive hours after the missiles, and there would be little if anything left to destroy anyway. The intercontinental bomber is a surplus and obsolete deterrent but one and one-third billion dollars is allocated to the F-111 in the fiscal 1969 budget, much of it for these bombers.

But this is not the end of this expensive nonsense. The

military always assumes that the enemy will do what we do,
that anything *we* produce *they* will produce. This is sometimes but not always true. The geographical and strategic
situation of the Soviet Union is not the same as that of the
United States; this dictates differences in weapons systems.
In addition—no small consideration—the country which is
poorer and has fewer resources to waste will be more careful in its expenditures. But we always estimate that the
enemy will spend as prodigally as we do. This is how the
bomber and missile gap scares originated. So we are spending billions to "keep ahead" of Soviet bombers and bomber
defenses. We are also assuming that the Soviets will be as
silly as we are and also build a fleet of F-111's to "get
under" our radar defenses. So Congress has already embarked on another multi-billion-dollar program of building
new radar "fences" and new types of interceptor planes to
deal with these hypothetical Soviet F-111's.

To make all this plausible, the Air Force does its best to
hide from the Congress the true facts about the Soviet air
force. Twice during the past year Senator Symington, who
feels that the billions spent on this bomber are diverting
funds which could more sensibly be spent on new fighter
planes, has asked Pentagon witnesses for the numbers of the
various Soviet bombers. "Do you believe," he asked Dr.
John S. Foster, Jr., Director of Defense Research and
Development, "that the Soviet Union poses a serious
bomber threat to the United States today?" The answer
was "Yes, Senator Symington, I do." Symington replied in-
credulously, "The Soviets have not built a bomber for
years, except the Blinder—and the latter's performance is
not as good as the B-58 which we abandoned. In spite of
that we now have to spend billions of dollars defending
against bombers also."

He then asked Dr. Foster to supply the Appropriations
Committee with the numbers of each type of Soviet
bomber. The numbers were deleted by the censor.[13] But if
one turns to McNamara's final statement in the same hear-

[13] See p. 2362, 1969 Defense Department Budget Hearings, Part IV.

ings[14] he gives the number of Soviet intercontinental bombers as 155, as compared with our 697. These Soviet bombers are mostly the old subsonic Bear and Bison bombers, neither of which could possibly duck under U.S. radar defenses in the way the F-111 is supposed to duck under the Soviet Union's.

Even the report on *The Status of U.S. Strategic Power* filed last September 27 by the Senate's Preparedness Subcommittee under Senator Stennis, which argues for larger arms expenditures, says, "There is no evidence that the Soviets are proceeding with the development of a new heavy bomber and, should they elect to develop one, it is probable we would see indications of the program three to four years before the aircraft becomes operational."

To counter this, the Air Force sophists have come up with a new argument. When Senator Symington asked Dr. Foster, as head of Pentagon research and development, why they were planning new types of bomber defense against non-existent types of Soviet planes, Dr. Foster replied, "discouragement of Soviet aspirations to develop a more advanced bomber." [15] But why spend billions to discourage the Soviets from building a bomber they show no signs of building anyway?

Another favorite reason often used by the Air Force may be found in Air Force Chief of Staff General McConnell's presentation to the Stennis hearings on strategic power last April. "A bomber force," the general said, "causes the Soviets to continue to develop bomber defenses rather than concentrating their expenditures just on missile defenses." [16] *So we waste money to make them waste money.* Though we are richer, this may be worse for us than them, because our planes are far more elaborate and expensive.

Since the Air Force thus admits that there is no sign as yet of a new supersonic Soviet bomber able to penetrate

[14] *Ibid.*, Part V, p. 2718.
[15] *Ibid.*, p. 2719.
[16] "Status of US Strategic Power," Preparedness Investigating Subcommittee of the Senate Committee on Armed Services, 90th Congress, 2nd Session, April 30, 1968, Part II, p. 169.

our existing defenses, why does it go on talking of a Soviet
bomber "threat"? As usual, it turns out that this simple
word has an unexpected meaning in the special language developed at the Pentagon. This prize item of military semantics may be found in the testimony of Air Force Secretary
Brown to these same Stennis committee hearings. Dr.
Brown was explaining to the committee that if Soviet anti-
aircraft defenses were improved and we had to build in additional "penetration aids" to get past more efficient radar
devices, we would have to build bigger bombs than we now
have. "Otherwise," he said, "we will find ourselves carrying
many penetration aids and comparatively few weapons."
Dr. Brown went on to say there was "general agreement"
at the Pentagon that such an advanced U.S. bomber "probably will be needed at some time in the future" but just
when would depend on "how fast and far the Soviet threat
is likely to evolve." Then he explained, "By threat here we
are principally talking about Soviet defenses against bombers." [17]

The threat, in other words, is not that they might be able
successfully to attack us with their bombers but that they
might build up their anti-bomber defenses to the point
where we might not be able to attack them successfully
with *our* bombers! It would be only a short step from this
to defining aggression as the building of defenses to discourage an enemy attack.

The *reductio ad absurdum* is in a passage I found in the
fiscal 1969 defense budget hearings before the House Ap-
proriations Committee. Mahon of Texas, the able chairman of the defense subcommittee, was questioning Air
Force officials about the Soviet bomber menace. Here is the
colloquy which spills the whole and final truth about this
costly nightmare:

MR. MAHON: Officials of the Department of Defense have
not indicated to this committee that they think the Soviets
will go very strong on the manned bomber. They will rely
principally on the ICBM. Is that right?

[17] *Ibid.*, p. 179.

GENERAL MCCONNELL [Air Force Chief of Staff]: That is the consensus.

MR. MAHON: The Air Force has a little different view?

GENERAL MCCONNELL: [Deleted by censor].

MR. MAHON: [Deleted by censor].

GENERAL MCCONNELL: [Deleted by censor].

MR. MAHON: How long have the Soviets had, Secretary [of the Air Force] Brown, to develop a follow-on[18] bomber?

SECRETARY BROWN: They have had ten years.

MR. MAHON: Have you seen any evidence?

SECRETARY BROWN: I see no evidence of it, Mr. Chairman. The Air Force view is at least as much a view that "they ought to have one" as it is "they will have one." [19]

Billions in contracts for new bombers and new bomber defense are threatened should the Russians stubbornly persist in not building a new bomber force. In extremity perhaps Congress might be persuaded to add the Soviet Union to our foreign aid clients and give them an advanced bomber force to keep the U.S. aircraft business strong and prosperous. Or General Dynamics and the other big companies in the military-industrial complex might pass the hat among themselves and buy Moscow a new bomber. Should those old obsolete subsonic Bears and Bisons stop flying altogether, it would be a catastrophe for Fort Worth, a form of economic aggression in reverse. Ours—the rich man's strategy—is to make the Russians waste their resources by wasting ours. Theirs—the poor man's strategy—might be to strike a mortal blow at the arms business here by cutting their own expenditures to the minimum the balance of terror requires.

Nothing so terrifies the military-industrial complex as this notion of a *minimum* deterrent, as we shall see when we analyze Nixon's pledge to restore that crucial notion of "nuclear superiority," about which McNamara had finally succeeded in making the country see a little sense.

January 2, 1969
New York Review

[18] Air Force lingo for a new bomber.

[19] House Appropriations Committee Hearings on the Fiscal 1969 Defense Budget, Executive Session, February 26, 1968, Part I, p. 751.

NIXON AND THE ARMS RACE:
HOW MUCH IS "SUFFICIENCY"?

The annals of the Nixon Administration, in so far as arms are concerned, must begin, like the Gospel of John, with The Word. But Nixon has changed The Word at the very outset. In the campaign it was "superiority." At his first press conference this was changed to "sufficiency." The two words seem to move in different directions. One implies an endless arms race. The other seems to promise that at some point we will have enough. . . .

Sufficiency was the Eisenhower Administration theme in fighting off the demands for higher defense spending from the military and its industrial allies. Is Nixon, faced with budgetary problems and an unstable dollar, coming back to it now? That is the question which will soon be answered by his decision on the anti-ballistic missile and by the results of the review he has ordered of the military budget, which is due the latter part of March.

The shift from "superiority" to "sufficiency" may prove to mean little or nothing. But the shift, even if only semantic, offers new leverage to the peace movement. For it raises the question of how much armaments is enough, and it raises it on the highest level and in the broadest forum. When the new President himself adopts the term "sufficiency," he invites public discussion of the military budget in the simplest and most graphic terms. How much is enough? If Secretary Laird has his way, the budget review will find present military appropriations *in*sufficient. Perhaps the peace movement ought to set up a public hearing board of its own to take testimony from experts on this problem of "sufficiency" and publish both the testimony and the final report. In what follows we will try to give a preliminary sketch of the military monster.

The real word for America's nuclear arsenal is not sufficiency but lunacy. When the Rathjens report says "the strategic forces of both sides are too large," that is the understatement of the millennium. Briefly, we have three and one-half times as many nuclear warheads as the Soviet Union, and ten times as many as we need—not just to "deter" but to destroy it. The first figure is from Clark Clifford's final posture statement on the fiscal 1970 budget (page 42) last January 15. This says we can launch 4,200 warheads with our ICBM's, Polaris submarines, and bombers, while the Soviet Union can launch 1,200. The second figure is from a table (page 57) of McNamara's final posture statement for the fiscal 1969 budget dated January 22 of last year. This for the first time gave figures on the number of 1-megaton warheads (one megaton = 1,000,000 tons of TNT) needed to wreck the Soviet Union. The *maximum* is 400.

As McNamara explains, "Further increments would not meaningfully change the amount of damage because we would be bringing smaller and smaller cities under attack." McNamara figures this would kill 74 million people, or more than three times the total Soviet losses in World War II, and destroy 76 percent of Soviet industry. Give or take any reasonable number for error, this is no longer war as man has ever known it before, but instant cremation. Seventy-four million people will be "only" 30 percent of the Soviet population in 1972, the year to which this table is projected. But a footnote (page 52) of an earlier McNamara posture statement in January, 1967 still applies to these estimates of lethality. The footnote explains that they cover only "prompt" deaths from blast and fallout—"they do not include deaths resulting from fire, storms, disease, and general disruption of everyday life." So add to the immediate deaths any number for the slow deaths, and then ask yourself again how much is enough? What is sufficiency?

The assumption behind these computations is as distant

from human realities as the numbers. Never has so much precision been attached to so much spurious rationality. The assumption is that war is a kind of game on which nations embark after consulting a computer to see who would come out ahead. Not the least dangerous aspect of our war machine is that it is based on so fallacious a theory as to why and how wars occur. Starting from so abstract and mechanistic an axiom, the planners have developed a series of corollaries which seem designed to confuse not only us but even our computers.

The first corollary is that if it looks to the attacker as if the damage to himself in any war would be "unacceptable," he will be "deterred." The second corollary is that the way to confront your enemy with "unacceptable" damage is to have an "assured destruction capability," which you can impose on him in a "second strike" of retaliation if he attacks first. The third is that to do this you need a nuclear arsenal which is so large and so invulnerable that the enemy cannot destroy it—or enough of it—in a first strike to save himself from destruction in return. The fourth and final corollary is that you have to keep building more and better weapons to be sure of maintaining that second-strike capacity. This is what keeps the nuclear rat race going. Those who work within the military bureaucracy are doomed to serve its purposes. The proliferation of doctrine furthers the proliferation of armaments. The finely spun concepts of deterrence and second strike give a rational appearance to an essentially irrational process, the mindless multiplication of weaponry.

The arms race is based on an optimistic view of technology and a pessimistic view of man. It assumes there is no limit to the ingenuity of science and no limit to the deviltry of human beings. Thus so-called "conservative" military planning assumes the best of the enemy's laboratories and the worst of his intentions. It seeks to ensure against all possible contingencies, like an insurance salesman selling protection against the possibility of blizzards in the tropics.

The proliferating corollaries of deterrence having conditioned us to mega-weapons and mega-deaths, the sheer numbers of nuclear weaponry no longer surprise us. They numb and comfort. When Clifford reports that we have 4,200 deliverable warheads as compared with the Soviets' 1,200, we are instinctively cheered to hear that we are so far "ahead." No one any longer asks where they would be "delivered" or how many times we might find ourselves killing the same peasant woman and her cow. Such talk is "old hat." It is hard to realize that less than a decade has passed since a one-time Chairman of the Joint Chiefs of Staff like General Maxwell Taylor could argue that 200 missiles would be a sufficient minimum deterrent. It is odd to be reminded by General LeMay himself in his new book[1] that "as few as 17 large-yield Soviet ICBM's could severely damage the 17 densely populated urban complexes in the United States that contain over one-third of our population."

By the same calculation, three large-yield U.S. ICBM's could destroy Moscow, Leningrad, and Kiev while thirty much smaller ones could wreck the Soviet Union's thirty other cities with a population of 500,000 or more. Surely this should be enough deterrence. LeMay himself proceeds by a series of splendid non sequiturs to prove that this means we need more missiles! He goes on to say, "The Soviets have 40 ICBM's for each U.S. urban complex. The U.S. on the other hand, to cover some 175 dispersed Soviet cities, would need 7,000 missiles to provide the same ratio of 40 per target. Yet we plan to have only 1,054 from now on." If one large-yield Soviet ICBM is enough to damage severely a whole U.S. urban complex, why do they need 40? And why do we need 40 each for every one of 175 Soviet cities, though 175 gets us down to places like Kirovsk, half the size of Hiroshima (about 100,000) which we destroyed with a "primitive" A-bomb so small (less than 20 kilotons) we no longer consider that size a strategic weapon?

---

[1] General Curtis E. LeMay, *America Is in Danger* (Funk & Wagnalls, 1968), p. 88.

Our 4,200 warheads average out—to adopt LeMay's standard—to twenty-four each for those 175 Soviet cities. But apparently this is insufficient. We are on the verge of expanding the number of warheads eightfold, and soon after, ten- or twelvefold. A table appended to McNamara's last posture statement (page 214) shows that during the eight years in which he presided over the Defense Department we spent over $68 billion on our strategic forces.[2] And now we are told, in effect, by McNamara himself, that it is not enough![3] Our weapons have to be MIRVed.

The acronym stands for Multiple Independently Targeted Reentry Vehicle. The subject has long been a deep secret. It was first described publicly by Secretary McNamara, when he said in his final posture statement on January 22 of last year, "Now, in the late 1960's, because the Soviet Union *might* [the italics were McNamara's] deploy extensive ABM defenses, we are making some very important changes in our strategic missile forces. Instead of a single large warhead, our missiles are now being designed to carry several small warheads and penetration aids, because it is the number of warheads, or objects which appear to be war-

[2] For the morbid it is worth adding that despite this vast nuclear arsenal we also allocated more than $190 billion to our general purpose forces during the same eight years. The total assigned in those eight years to "defense" (surely it deserves quotation marks in this context) was more than $500 billion or half a trillion dollars!

[3] At the same time McNamara warned, " 'Superiority' is of little significance. For even with . . . any 'superiority' realistically attainable, the blunt, inescapable fact remains that the Soviet Union could still effectively destroy the United States, even after absorbing the full weight of an American first strike. . . . Under these circumstances, surely it makes sense for us both to try to halt the momentum of the arms race which is causing vast expenditures on both sides and promises no increase in security" (pp. 52–53, final posture statement, 1969 budget). In a similar vein Clifford warned in his final posture statement for fiscal 1970 (p. 49), "We stand on the eve of a new round in the armaments race with the Soviet Union, a race which will contribute nothing to the real security of either side while increasing substantially the already great defense burdens of both." No such sentiments have ever been expressed by their successor, whose book, *America's Strategy Gap: A House Divided*, is a Goldwaterite "better dead than Red" manifesto.

heads [i.e., the so-called "penetration aids"—IFS] to the defender's radars, that will determine the outcome in a contest with an ABM defense."

Last August, sixteen MIRV's were tested successfully for the first time in an ICBM, the Minuteman, and in an underwater ballistic missile, the Poseidon, which will replace Polaris. A vast expansion in the number of our warheads is now under way. McNamara's final budget set in motion the conversion of 31 of our present 41 Polaris-carrying submarines into carriers of Poseidon. The remaining 10 are of a type it would be too expensive to convert; it would be cheaper to replace them with new Poseidon submarines. The number of warheads the Poseidons can carry is still classified. The number generally given is 10 warheads per missile, though I have been told by one informed source that the Poseidon can carry as many as 14.

Each Polaris sub now carries 16 Polaris missiles, or a total for the fleet of 656 missiles, each with one warhead. But as Poseidons replace the Polaris on 31 ships—with a total of 496 missiles—and if each Poseidon missile can carry 10 warheads, that is a total of 4,960 warheads. In addition we are replacing Minuteman I and Minuteman II, our main intercontinental ballistic missiles, with Minuteman III, which will also be MIRVed. Again the figures are classified but it is generally believed that each Minuteman III will carry three warheads.

In his final posture statement McNamara projected for the period 1969–73 a nuclear missile force made up of:

$$
\begin{array}{rl}
1,000 & \text{Minutemen} \\
496 & \text{Poseidons} \\
160 & \text{Polaris} \\
54 & \text{Titans} \\
\hline
1,710 & \text{missiles}
\end{array}
$$

This was the same size as our nuclear missile force last September when we estimated our own nuclear long-range missile force at 1,710 and the Soviet's at 945. But MIRVed up, this would become, in warheads:

$$\begin{array}{rl}
3,000 & \text{Minutemen} \\
4,960 & \text{Poseidons} \\
160 & \text{Polaris} \\
54 & \text{Titans} \\
\hline
8,174 & \text{warheads}
\end{array}$$

This would change the disparity in nuclear missile warheads from less than two-to-one in our favor (1,710 to 945) to almost nine-to-one (8,174 to 945). It would mean we could aim several of our missiles at each one of theirs, threatening a possible first strike. To see how this expansion of nuclear power must look to the other side we need only read a passage in Clark Clifford's final posture statement last January, and substitute U.S. where he said Soviets. "It is quite evident," Clifford wrote, "that if the Soviets achieve greater accuracy with their ICBM's, together with a MIRV capability, our land-based strategic missiles will become increasingly vulnerable to a first strike."

The most alarming aspect of this vast expansion of American striking power, as seen from the other side, must be the fact that it is accompanied by a new propaganda campaign designed to make the U.S. feel insecure—to sell the idea that all this still is not enough. A new numbers game is being played similar to the ones which accompanied the bomber- and missile-gap campaigns. Its principal spokesman is the man Nixon picked to be Secretary of Defense, Melvin R. Laird. Through him and its multifarious lesser mouthpieces, the military-industrial complex is trying to make it appear that new "gaps" are developing, one in strategic offensive power, the other in anti-ballistic missiles, and that these threaten to change the balance of power and to create what Nixon in the campaign melodramatically called a "survival gap," a phrase he may regret if he should now seek to hold the military budget down.

This new campaign focuses first of all on the sharp increase in the number of Soviet ICBM's in recent years. The latest U.S. intelligence estimates, as given by Clifford in January, credit the Soviet Union with a steep increase in ICBM's in two years: from 250 in mid-1966 to 570 in mid-1967 to 900 in September, 1968, as compared with the 1,054 ICBM's we have had since we decided to freeze their numbers at that level in November, 1964.

It is possible that by next fall the Soviets will actually have more ICBM's than we do. By focusing simplistically just on these numbers, a new wave of near-hysteria may be whipped up. But ICBM's are not the only component of the strategic forces. And numbers are not the only thing that counts. The cryptic remark with which Clifford followed this revelation is a good starting point for assessing the realities. "We have been anticipating for some time," Clifford reported, "a Soviet deployment of a solid-fuel ICBM. We now believe the deployment of such a missile has started, although at a relatively slow rate." These quiet words light up an extraordinary technological missile gap in our favor. Liquid-fuel missiles are obsolete. They take about fifteen minutes to load, and they are so full of valves and controls, the chances of a misfire are high. The solid-fuel missile can be fired in less than a minute. We have only fifty-four liquid-fuel ICBM's left in our arsenal, the huge Titans, still useful as big city-killers, though vulnerable to a first strike. We began to phase out the liquid-fuel Atlas and to deploy the solid-fuel Minuteman as far back as the autumn of 1962. It is startling to learn that we only now "believe," in Clifford's words, that the Soviets have begun to deploy a solid-fuel missile of their own, though "at a relatively slow rate." "Their new solid-fuel ICBM," Clifford added (page 46), "appears to be no better than our earliest Minuteman missiles, first deployed in fiscal 1963." Fiscal 1963 began July 1, 1962. U.S. intelligence estimates of Soviet power are not given to understatement. If that is the best the intelligence men can say, the lag is serious indeed.

The fact is that during the past six years we have not only replaced all our liquid-fuel Atlases with solid-fuel Minutemen but introduced two new and improved models of Minuteman; the missile industry, like the automobile, believes that the way to maintain sales is to get the customer to trade in his old car every few years for a new model. Our present force consists of 600 Minuteman I's and 400 Minuteman II's, and the Minuteman III—with MIRV, i.e., multiple warheads—is already being phased in.[4]

To go from Minuteman I to Minuteman III, as we have seen, is to increase the number of warheads by at least three for the same number of missiles. Even the Senate group closest to the Pentagon in outlook, the Preparedness Subcommittee of Senate Armed Services under the chairmanship of Stennis, said in its report last September 27:[5]

Instead of an increase in numbers of missile launches, we have planned to meet the greater and still growing Soviet threat by qualitative improvements such as *Poseidon, Minuteman III, MIRVs,* increased accuracy, penetration aids and silo hardening. *The Joint Chiefs themselves have not recommended a quantitative increase in missiles to meet the current threat* [emphasis added].

The numbers game is discounted on this more sophisticated level of discussion. What the Joint Chiefs ask, says the Stennis report, is not more missiles but "the phasing in of an advanced ICBM, which they believe would provide for the modernization [a lovely word, in two or three years a missile model is already "ancient"—IFS] of the force while increasing our total missile throw weight. Technical improvements which the Joint Chiefs foresee include better warhead design and increased reliability, survivability, penetrability and accuracy." What the Stennis report might have added, but doesn't—the Pentagon does not like to mention the subject—is that more "throw weight" would presumably make it possible for the new ICBM to carry more warheads than Minuteman III, further multiplying our striking power.

---

4 *Status of U.S. Strategic Power. A Report by the Preparedness Subcommittee of the Senate Armed Services Committee,* 90th Congress, 2nd Session, September 27, 1968, p. 11.
5 *Ibid.,* pp. 11-12.

If we MIRV, the Soviets will eventually MIRV their missiles, too. In the letter submitting his report to the full Armed Services Committee, Senator Stennis says, "Of major importance in the strategic nuclear field, are the apparently well-documented press reports that the Soviets have flown a multiple re-entry vehicle. This compounds our concern. . . ." But these "press reports" apparently were not "well-documented" enough to be confirmed in this year's posture statement. In any case we are several years ahead in this technological breakthrough and have already begun to deploy Poseidons and Minuteman III's.

Lest it stupefy the reader, we will touch only in passing on two other components of the nuclear equation in strategic offensive forces which the new numbers game omits— the intercontinental bomber (we have 646, or four times the Soviet fleet of 150), and the underwater missiles carried by nuclear submarine. We have 656 missiles (in process of being MIRVed, as we have seen, into ten times as many warheads) as against the Soviets' forty-five. When all these numbers and the technological factors are added in, the imbalance is so great that it makes talk of a new missile gap— even if the Soviets pass us in the number of ICBM's—a colossal deception. The gap in our favor is enormous.

Much the same holds true of the strategic defensive. It is true that the Russians have already built some elements of an anti-ballistic missile system around one city, Moscow, while we have yet to deploy our Sentinel at all. But their ABM system is already obsolete, and it would be to America's advantage if the Russians wasted scarce resources in deploying it. "Their GALOSH ABM system," Clifford reported in January, "resembles in certain important respects the Nike-Zeus system which we abandoned years ago because of its limited effectiveness." It is the same system Eisenhower wisely vetoed when the Joint Chiefs recommended its deployment in 1959. Even the Stennis report (page 10) says, "The fact that it has not been deployed at other cities probably indicates that Soviet officials have reservations about its effectiveness."

Perhaps they are at last readier to learn from our experience than the present advocates of the Sentinel ABM system in this country. "Had we produced and deployed the NIKE-ZEUS system [which GALOSH resembles] proposed by the Army at an estimated cost of $13 to $14 billion," Deputy Secretary of Defense Cyrus Vance told a Senate inquiry[6] two years ago, "most of it would have had to be torn out and replaced almost before it became operational, by the new missiles and radars of the NIKE-X system. *By the same token, other technological developments in offensive forces over the next* . . . [deleted by Pentagon censor] *years make obsolete or drastically degrade the NIKE-X* [Sentinel] *system as presently envisioned*" (my italics).

Even here our planned ABM program is many times the size of the Soviets'. They are wasting money putting an already obsolete system around one city. We are on the verge—if we go ahead with Sentinel—of wasting many times that amount by deploying a soon-to-be-obsolete "thin" ABM system big enough to give a dubious "area defense" to the whole country and "point defense" to more than a dozen cities. Even in folly, we may insist on being "ahead."

Even before the Russians finish deploying GALOSH around *one* city, we are preparing a further expansion of striking power big enough to overwhelm a much more extensive and up-to-date Soviet ABM when and if they deploy one. Such is the endless see-saw of the nuclear arms race.

In any discussion of "sufficiency" it is essential to take a close look at what our military thinks sufficient. To see the dimensions of the expansion projected for the next four years it is necessary to go back to McNamara's final posture

[6] *U.S. Armament and Disarmament Problems. Hearings before the* [Gore] *Subcommittee on Disarmament of Senate Foreign Relations*, February 3 to March 3, 1967, 90th Congress, First Session, p. 58.

statement of last year and read the section entitled "Capability Against the 'Highest Expected Threat' in the NIE." The NIE stands for the National Intelligence Estimates. These are agreed upon by the U.S. Intelligence Board (of twelve separate intelligence agencies, no less!). The Board provides a range of estimates as to Soviet power in the next few years. A McNamara footnote explains (page 57) that the "highest expected threat" is actually higher than anyone really expects, since this "is actually composed of the upper range of NIE projections for *each* element of the Soviets' forces" (italics in original). That is, strategic missiles, missile-armed submarines, and bombers. "In many cases," the footnote continues, "these represent alternatives and it is highly unlikely that all elements would ever reach the top end of the quantitative range simultaneously. Therefore, the 'highest expected threat' is really a greater threat than that projected in the NIE."

With that in mind, the reader may be prepared more fully to grasp the stupendous multiplication of our retaliatory power sketched by McNamara when he says,

Even if the Soviet strategic forces by 1972 reach the higher end of the range of estimates [these are classified—IFS] projected in the latest NIE's and even if they were to assign their entire available missile force to attacks on our strategic forces (reserving only refire missiles and bomber-delivered weapons for urban targets), about one-half of our forces programmed for 1972 would survive and remain effective.

Then McNamara says,

If the Soviets expand the Moscow ABM defense and deploy the same or a similar system around other cities at the highest rate projected [again the figures are classified—IFS] in the latest NIE's, about three-quarters of our surviving weapons would detonate over their targets.

Apparently—though McNamara does not say so explicitly—some 1,600 1-megaton warheads could under those circumstances reach their target. That is four times the 400 1-megaton warheads we mentioned earlier as enough to

wreck the Soviet Union. Here McNamara inserts the table
to which we earlier referred. It purports to show Soviet
population and industry destroyed in such an attack in
1972, assuming a total Soviet population of 247 million, of
whom 116 million would be urban. This is the horrendous
table:[7]

WARHEADS 1-mt	FATALITIES millions	%	INDUSTRIAL CAPACITY DESTROYED %
100	37	15	59
200	52	21	72
400	74	30	76
800	96	39	77
1200	109	44	77
1600	116	47	77

We see in this table that even if only 100 warheads got
through it would destroy 59 percent of Soviet industry and
kill 50 percent more people in one blow than the Nazis did
in the four years of World War II. If the Soviet Union
published a table of this kind we would accuse them of trying to terrorize us into giving up the nuclear arms race altogether.[8]

As if to pile horror on horror, McNamara added, "Even
if the Soviets deploy a substantial number of [additional]
ABM interceptors by 1972 our strategic missile forces alone
could still destroy more than two-fifths of their total popu-

[7] Line in original because, as McNamara explains, "beyond 400 . . .
would not meaningfully change the amount of damage."

[8] A more than adequate substitute is provided—with majestic objectivity—by McNamara himself in a table on p. 64 showing the number of
fatalities on both sides in the event of an "all-out strategic exchange" in
the mid-1970's. This shows that even if the U.S. built up offensive and defensive forces to a maximum so-called Posture B, including an anti-missile
defense, which he says would probably end by costing $40 billion, the
Soviets, by a maximum program of their own, adding MIRV's and penetration aids, plus 550 mobile ICBM's, could kill 90 million Americans even
if we struck first! Mobile ICBM's, constantly moving around on vehicles, would be almost impossible for an enemy to target.

lation (more than 100 million people) and over three-quarters of their industrial capacity." What an arsenal we must be building up!

McNamara goes on to explain that "these results, of course, reflect the decisions we have taken in recent years to enhance the future capabilities of our 'Assured Destruction' forces." These, he says, include (1) the replacement of Polaris by Poseidon with MIRV's, (2) improved missile penetration aids, i.e., chaff and decoys to confuse the radars which set in motion the other side's ABM's, (3) an increase in the planned number of Minuteman III ICBM's with MIRV's, (4) development of new small re-entry vehicles "to increase substantially the number of warheads or penetration aids which can be carried by a single missile," and (5) "the development and production of SRAM's for our strategic bombers." This last is an acronym for Short Range Attack Missiles. These would enable our intercontinental bombers to stop short of Soviet bomber defenses and fire nuclear missiles into Soviet territory.

In addition to the SRAM, the Air Force has begun a campaign for a new weapon system called SCAD (see the *New York Times*, February 5). These add a new horror to our alphabetical military nightmares. SCAD stands for Subsonic Cruise Armed Decoy. These are small pilotless but nuclear-armed aircraft which could be launched from a carrier plane toward enemy targets from beyond the Soviet Union's defense perimeter. One enthusiastic planner was quoted as saying, "SCAD does for bombers what the multiple warhead does for missiles—it makes the enemy's defense problem virtually impossible." It would take a new and larger intercontinental bomber to carry SCAD's, and this is what the Air Force hopes for. The cost, of course, will be in the billions.

In the meantime SCAD is one of ten "Advanced Development Projects" for which Clifford asked almost a quarter billion dollars in additional research and development funds in the new fiscal 1970 budget. One of these is a new ABM to succeed Sentinel and a new "Underseas Long-Range Missile System" in case Soviet anti-submarine capability becomes a threat to Polaris and Poseidon. Another is an Ocean Engineering project which may take us one step further toward the new idea of hiding ICBM's under the ocean floor. The armed forces also have not yet given up the idea of using the MOL (the Manned Orbital Laboratory) as a step toward weapons in space, despite an international treaty against it. This, dear reader, only skims the surface of what is on the drawing boards and in the laboratories; we have only touched the highlights of the unclassified material on strategic weapons. We have not even touched the plans in the works for counter-insurgency, which promises new Vietnams, or such goodies as new bacteriological and chemical weapons.

For the military, there will never be "sufficiency."

I would like to make three grave observations in conclusion.

(1) With MIRV, we are entering a new period of darkness. The U-2 and the SAMOS satellite dissipated the missile gap nonsense because we could actually see and count how many ICBM's the other side had. There is no way to see from afar, or to be sure, just how many MIRV's there are on each missile. This may bring us back to that atmosphere of panicky conjecture and exaggeration so useful to the arms lobby and the military.

(2) The deployment of an ABM will make each side fearful lest the other venture a first strike, calculating that the ABM, if improved sufficiently and buttressed by fallout and blast shelters, may cut down casualties to an "acceptable" level. Each side will become more fearful of adventurism on the other.

(3) MIRV's open a new era in the arms race, and raise the threat of a first-strike capacity. If one side can, by MIRV's, obtain, let us say, a tenfold advantage over the other, it may have enough to destroy the other's missiles—

or think it has. This will take the balance out of the "balance of terror."

McNamara implies that the MIRV was developed as an answer-in-advance to a Soviet ABM. But there is evidence that MIRV was first developed to provide capacity for a first or preemptive strike. At last year's Senate hearings on the fiscal 1969 military budget, Senator Mansfield put a series of questions to Dr. John S. Foster, Jr., whom Laird has retained as the Pentagon's Director of Research and Engineering. These have gone almost unnoticed but deserve close attention. Question No. 10 asked, "Is it not true that the U.S. response to the discovery that the Soviets had made an initial deployment of an ABM system around Moscow and possibly elsewhere was to develop the MIRV system for Minuteman and Polaris?" The unexpected answer was:[9]

Not entirely. The MIRV concept was originally generated to increase our targeting capability rather than to penetrate ABM defenses. In 1961-62 planning for targeting the Minuteman force it was found that total number of aim points exceeded the number of Minuteman missiles. By splitting up the payload of a single missile [deleted] each [deleted] could be programmed [deleted] allowing us to cover these targets with [deleted] fewer missiles. [Deleted.] MIRV was originally born to implement the payload split-up [deleted]. It was found that the previously generated MIRV concept could equally well be used against ABM [deleted].

In 1961-62 our strategic force was far greater than the Soviet Union's. If we then sought a MIRV in order to cover more aim points, this could only have been for a counterforce or preemptive strategy. That was the time when McNamara, as shown by his famous Ann Arbor speech of June 16, 1962, was moving in that direction. "For a short time," General LeMay says in his new book, *America Is in Danger* (page 269), "I thought we had convinced Mr.

[9] *Senate Appropriations Committee Hearings on the Department of Defense Budget for Fiscal 1969*, 90th Congress, 2nd Session, Part 4, p. 2310. All the deletions are in the original, as made by the Pentagon's censors.

McNamara, but I soon learned how wrong we were. To be successful, such a counterforce strategy requires a clear nuclear superiority because it takes more than one missile to destroy another." MIRV, by increasing the number of warheads manyfold (Dr. Foster admitted to Mansfield), might soon give us in the neighborhood of 10,000 warheads, in place of our present 1,700 or so single-headed missiles.

At present the U.S. has three strategic forces, each of which is big enough to strike a mortal blow at the Soviet Union even if the other two were destroyed in a first strike. If we add SCAD's to our bombers and MIRV's to the Minuteman and to the nuclear submarine (Poseidon), we will have what must begin to look from the other side, with its present level of forces, like three separate strategic forces, *each with a first-strike capacity*. The MIRV is incomparably more unsettling to "the balance of terror" than the ABM. The MIRV is the great leap forward of the nuclear arms race. McNamara put it very quietly in this colloquy before the House Appropriations Committee hearings last year on the 1969 military budget:[10]

MR. MAHON [D. Tex., chairman of the committee]: I am concerned lest the Soviet Union make some kind of "quantum jump" in the development of their strategic forces. . . . Is it your view that neither the United States nor the Soviet Union in the next few years will come up with an entirely new weapon which will outmode present weapons?

SECRETARY MCNAMARA: I think it extremely unlikely. There will be continued development in such weapons. The true significance of more recent developments are obscured somewhat by the fact that they did not involve as dramatic a *physical* change as took place between the bomber and the missile. I, myself, do not agree with your statement that there are not changes going on today as important in terms of strategic capability as those that occurred between the bomber and the missile. *The fact is that the destruction capability between the Atlas and the Poseidon or between the Atlas and Minuteman III, in my opinion, was substantially more than between the B-52* [our last intercontinental bomber] *and the Atlas* [our first intercontinental missile] [my italics].

[10] *Op. cit.*, Part I, pp. 251–2.

Such are the incredible dimensions projected for our military machine. Unless some new agreement puts an end to the endless spiral and proliferation of new weapons and anti-weapons, it will devour an ever-increasing share of the material and scientific resources on both sides and make war, should it come, many times more destructive. . . .

March 27, 1969
New York Review

THE WAR MACHINE
UNDER NIXON

In government the budget is the message. Washington's heart is where the tax dollar goes. When President Nixon finally, and very tardily, presented his first budget proposals in mid-April in a mini-State of the Union message, he said, "Peace has been the first priority." But the figures showed that the first concern of the new Administration, as of the last, was still the care and feeding of the war machine.

Only Nixon's style had changed. "Sufficiency" rather than "superiority" in nuclear armaments remained the new watchword. But in practice it was difficult to tell them apart. Administrations change, but the Pentagon remains at the head of the table. Nixon's semantics recalled John F. Kennedy's eight years earlier. The Eisenhower Administration had waged battle for four years against the bomber gap and the missile gap with the slogan of "sufficiency." "Only when our arms are sufficient beyond doubt," was Kennedy's elegant riposte in his inaugural, signaling a new spiral upward in the arms race, "can we be certain without doubt that they will never be employed." The rhetoric was fresh but the idea was no different from John Foster

Dulles's "position of strength." This is the *plus ça change* of American government and diplomacy. It emerged intact after Nixon's first three months in office, too.

At a press conference four days after his budget message, Nixon said again that "sufficiency" in weaponry was "all that is necessary." But a moment later he was clearly equating it with nuclear superiority. He said he didn't want "the diplomatic credibility" of a future President in a crisis like that over Cuba's missiles "impaired because the United States was in a second-class or inferior position." A press corps obsessed with the latest plane incident off North Korea did not pause to consider the implications. Was "diplomatic credibility" to be measured in megatons? Were we preparing again to play a thermonuclear game of "chicken," to see who would blink first at the prospect of instant incineration? Was this not the diplomacy of brinkmanship and the strategy of permanent arms race?

No correspondent asked these questions, and Nixon did not spell out the inferences. His tone was softer, his language more opaque, than that of the campaign, but the essential "security gap" theme had not changed. The main emphasis of Nixon's first months in office, the main idea he tried to sell the country, turned out to be that it was in mortal peril of a Soviet first-strike capacity. The new Administration sought to overcome a mounting wave of opposition to the ABM, and to the military generally, by ringing the bells of panic.

True, the Secretary of State often seemed to deny the perils the Secretary of Defense painted. Which was the party line? It was indicative that when visiting editors were given a press kit on the ABM April 7, with a covering letter on White House stationery signed by Herbert G. Klein as Nixon's "Director of Communications," the only thing new in that kit, the only news it contained, *and the one bit on which nobody commented*, was the "document" the Administration had chosen as the first item. It was a reproduction of a column in which Joseph Alsop three days earlier had exuberantly portrayed the "grim" (a favorite Alsop word) dangers of a first strike from Laird's new monster, the Soviet SS-9. The leading journalistic pied piper of the bomber gap and the missile gap had been enlisted by the new Administration to help it to propagate a new gap. If the White House stationery and the Klein signature were not enough to make Alsop's nightmare official doctrine, the reproduction of the column carried at the bottom of the page this imprimatur: "Prepared under the direction of the Republican National Committee, 1625 Eye St. N.W., Washington, D.C." The candor was dazzling.

The Budget Bureau fact sheets which accompanied Nixon's spending proposals sought to create the impression that on the military budget, as on so much else, Nixon in power was reversing the course set by Nixon on campaign. "Military and military assistance programs account for 1.1 billion (27 percent) of the $4.0 billion outlay reduction [for fiscal 1970]," said one fact sheet, "and $3.0 billion (55 percent) of the cut in budget authority." But, as we shall see, while the cuts in domestic civilian programs proved all too real, those in the military budget were either dubious or deferrals.

There was in the Nixon budget one complete and dramatic about-face—on the FB-111. Six months earlier, just before the election, at Fort Worth, where General Dynamics was building this new strategic bomber, Nixon had promised to make the F-111 "one of the foundations of our air supremacy." Now it was put permanently on the shelf. Procurement of the bomber was cut back sharply for fiscal 1969, which ended June 30, and abandoned altogether for fiscal 1970. Only the F-111D, the Air Force fighter version of this plane, was to stay in production a while longer.

Thus *finis* was soon to be written to the career of the multipurpose, multiservice plane originally known as the TFX, one of McNamara's most costly misjudgments. But on this, as on almost every other item of apparent economy in the Nixon-Laird revisions of the Pentagon's budget, the few hundred millions saved in fiscal 1969 and 1970 were linked to commitments which would cost literally billions more in the decade ahead. Every short step back hid another leap forward in expenditures.

The TFX was McNamara's effort to stall off the drive of the bomber generals to commit the country to an entirely new manned bomber in the missile age. He gave them the FB-111, the bomber version of the TFX, instead. Laird reduced FB-111 procurement in fiscal 1969 by $107 million and eliminated altogether the planned outlay of $321 million in fiscal 1970. But he then added $23 million for fiscal 1970 to speed "full scale engineering" of the new intercontinental bomber AMSA (Advanced Manned Strategic Aircraft) for which the Air Force and the aviation industry have been lobbying for years. "The FB-111," Laird told the Senate Armed Services Committee March 15, in an echo of the lobby's arguments, "will not meet the requirements of a true intercontinental bomber and the cost per unit has reached a point where an AMSA must be considered to fill the void."

It will be quite a void. The cost overruns, which had more than doubled the price of the FB-111, now became the excuse for going ahead with a far more expensive bomber. The net saving of $405 million in fiscal 1969 and 1970 ($107 plus $321 minus $23 million) will commit the country to a new plane which Senator Proxmire told the Senate April 22 will cost at least $24 billion during the next decade. Such illusory economies place heavy first mortgages on the future in favor of the military and at the expense of social needs.

Even so, there was hidden in the F-111 cutback a $200 million consolation prize for General Dynamics. The formal budget document[1] carried an increase of $155.7 million for "Production of F-111D at minimum sustaining rate related to FB-111 cancellation." I was puzzled by this reference to a "sustaining rate." What was being "sustained"— military needs or General Dynamics?

[1] House Document No. 91–100, 91st Congress, First Session. *Reductions in 1970 Budget Requests. Communication from the President of the United States*, p. 17.

I found a fuller explanation when *Aviation Week &
Space Technology* arrived for May 5. It said the revised
Nixon procurement plans for General Dynamics F-111D
provided $599.8 million for aircraft "plus $56 million for
advance procurement and $71.4 million to cover excess
costs generated in fiscal 1968." It said the total of $727.2
million "represented a sharp increase over original fiscal
1970 plans of $518 million." Indeed this is an increase,
though *Aviation Week* did not say so, of $209.2 million
rather than the $155.7 specified in the budget message.

The increase had been approved by Deputy Defense Secretary David Packard—a director of General Dynamics
until his Pentagon appointment—to counterbalance a cut of
$320.9 million in the FB-111 program. It would "enable
General Dynamics to retain its present production facilities." Not only did thirteen of these fighter planes crash in
their twenty-six months of operations[2] but Senator Curtis
of Kansas, in a comprehensive Senate speech last October 3,
said they were not maneuverable enough as fighters. They
are effective only as tactical bombers against enemy forces
like those in Vietnam, which have no air cover of their
own. Yet the government was not cutting back on its original plan to buy 331 of these F-111D's.

This is only one of many examples in the budget of how
easily the Nixon Administration finds millions for such dubious military purposes but not for urgent social needs. The
$200 million consolation for General Dynamics is the same
amount—a very inadequate amount—Nixon set aside in his
budget message for riot-devastated cities. Nixon got a lot of
publicity out of his order to give this urban program priority, but it didn't have enough priority to be a $200 million
addition to the budget. It was just deducted from the
meager amounts already available for other urban purposes.

Those who still look for the "shape" of the Nixon Administration are bound to remain bewildered. Shape is another

2 AP in Omaha *World Herald*, March 7, 1969.

word for policy, and policy requires the substitution of decision for drift. The campaign promised decision from one direction, the right. The situation requires decision from another direction, which might be called the left. Nixon turns out to take his stand—though that is too strong a word—in the middle of makeshift compromises. Whether on electoral reform or tax reform or poverty, feeble and inadequate half-measures are the rule. This shapelessness is the shape of the new Administration.

Hand-to-mouth decisions are standard in all governments, and inertia is basic in politics as in physics. But drift is only safe in quiet waters; to let inertia have its way in stormy seas is to risk disaster. Richard Nixon in the sixties is beginning to resemble Calvin Coolidge in the twenties, when the country kept cool with Cal, just before going over the brink with the stock market crash and the Great Depression.

To let inertia reign in the American government is also to let the military dominate. The sheer size of the military establishment, its vast propaganda resources and its powerful allies in every business, locality, and labor union affected by the billions it spends every year, gives it momentum sufficient to roll over every other department and branch of the government. In the absence of a strong hand and hard choices in the White House, the Pentagon inevitably makes the decisions.

But there is more than default, and more than meets the eye, in the military budget. The readiest source of campaign funds and political support for nomination and election as President lies in the military-industrial complex. It is also the most skillfully hidden source. I suspect that the 1968 campaign, like the 1960, was preceded by deals which called for a buildup in military procurement. This would help to account for the steep increase in appropriations by the Kennedy Administration despite its discovery on taking office that the "missile gap" did not exist.[3]

---

[3] Carl Kaysen, who was Kennedy's Deputy Special Assistant for National Security Affairs, has given us more precise figures than I have ever

The two plums the military-industrial complex most wanted on the eve of the 1968 campaign were the ABM and AMSA, a new advanced strategic bomber. In 1966 the Armed Services Committees of both houses recommended extra funds to speed both projects. A Congress still comatose on military matters dutifully voted the money. But McNamara refused to spend it. Johnson made two moves during the following year which cleared the way for both projects. In September, 1967 he forced McNamara to swallow the bitter pill of advocating a "thin" ABM system in which the Secretary of Defense clearly disbelieved. Two months later Johnson made the surprise announcement—as much a surprise to McNamara as to the press—that he was shifting the redoubtable Pentagon chief to the World Bank. That cleared the way for AMSA, too, and with both projects it also cleared the way for the 1968 campaign.

As late as January, 1968, in his last posture statement as Secretary of Defense, McNamara was still fighting a rearguard action against AMSA. He argued that the principal problem lay in the growing sophistication of Soviet air defenses. "Repeated examination of this problem," he told Congress, "has convinced us that what is important here is not a new aircraft but rather new weapons and penetration devices."

AMSA began to inch forward when Clifford replaced McNamara. In Clifford's first posture statement last January, he struck a new note when he declared the FB-111 would be too small to carry the new weapons and penetration devices McNamara had in mind. One wishes one knew

---

seen before in the chapter on "Military Strategy, Military Forces and Arms Control" in the Brookings Institution symposium, *Agenda For The Nation* (Doubleday, 1969). He wrote (pp. 562–3) that the decisions of 1961 and 1962 by Kennedy "called for the buildup by 1965 of a U.S. strategic force of nearly 1,800 missiles capable of reaching Soviet targets; somewhat more than a third were to be submarine-launched. In addition, some 600 long-range bombers would be maintained. *This was projected against an expected Soviet force of fewer than a third as many missiles and a quarter as many bombers capable of reaching the United States*" (italics added). The "overkill" was worth billions to the aviation and electronics industries.

more about this, since it seems unlikely that McNamara would have overlooked so simple a point. While Clifford said "we are still uncertain whether a new intercontinental bomber will be needed in the 1970s," he more than doubled the research and development funds for AMSA, increasing them from $30 million in fiscal 1969 to $77 million in fiscal 1970, "to keep the program moving."

The Nixon-Laird revisions two months later went further. They not only added $23 million more for AMSA but authorized the Air Force to move into the engineering phase, the last stage in R and D before procurement. "Now, after a very careful review," Laird told the Senate Armed Services Committee March 27, "we have decided to cut off the FB-111 program . . . and concentrate our efforts on the development of a new strategic bomber, AMSA." General Dynamics, which lost out when Nixon phased out FB-111, will be one of the bidders on AMSA.

ABM and AMSA together could spell $100 billion in electronic and aviation contracts in the years ahead. AMSA itself may prove a bigger gamble and a far more costly error than the TFX. *Space/Aeronautics* for January published a special issue plotting future trends in strategic warfare. It pointed out some of the pitfalls which may lie ahead for AMSA. About eight years elapse between concept definition and actual production in developing a new bomber. But Pentagon intelligence has never been able to come up with estimates of enemy threat valid for more than two or three years. "Thus," this Conover-Mast publication for the aerospace industry concluded, "there is no way of telling, the critics of AMSA claim, whether we would be committing ourselves to a system we really need or to what will end up as an immensely costly mistake."

The survey admitted that AMSA would be "less vulnerable than the B-52 and perform better," but added philosophically that "in a nuclear exchange time is too important an element for bombers to have any real effect." In other words even the fastest bomber may have no targets left after the far swifter missile exchange is over. One firm intelligence forecast emerged from the survey. "If AMSA is built," *Space/Aeronautics* said, "it will probably be our last strategic bomber. Once the present generation of Air Force commanders is gone, the top-level manpower will not be there to produce the sort of pressure that has kept AMSA alive for so long." Once the bomber admirals are dead, the clamor for a new bomber will die out, too. But the last fly-by will cost plenty.

AMSA is only one of many new military projects hidden in the new 1970 budget which will add billions to the future costs of government. "The present inflationary surge, already in its fourth year," Nixon said in his April 14 message, "represents a national self-indulgence we cannot afford any longer." But the principal beneficiaries of that indulgence are the military and their suppliers. And they seem to be exempt from anti-inflationary measures.

Fully to appreciate what the military is getting one has to begin with a disclosure made in the Budget Bureau's presentation of Nixon's budget revisions. Nixon had to squeeze $7.3 billion out of the normal civilian and welfare activities of the government in fiscal 1969 in order to meet the expenditure ceilings imposed by Congress when it enacted the 10 percent surplus income tax. This reduction over and above Johnson's budget for fiscal 1969 was made necessary by certain "uncontrollable" items. An example is the interest on the public debt, which rose by $300 million. But the biggest uncontrollable item, ten times that much, or $3 billion, was an increase in Vietnam war costs over and above those originally estimated by Johnson.

So all sorts of civilian services during the current fiscal year have had to be pared to meet the unexpected increase in the cost of the Vietnam war. Now let us couple this revelation about the 1969 budget with a basic decision made by Johnson in the 1970 budget. In that budget Johnson for the first time, on the basis of his decision to end the bombing of the North, which was very costly, and perhaps in expectation of less combat on the ground in the South,[4] forecast the first sharp cutback in Vietnam war costs. This was estimated as a saving of $3.5 billion during fiscal 1970.

This was to be the country's first "peace dividend." But instead of applying this $3.5 billion in the 1970 budget to starved civilian and welfare services, or to reduction of the deficit, Johnson added this $3.5 billion *and $600 million more* to the money available for the Pentagon to spend on procurement and activities other than those connected with the Vietnam war. *The total increase in the non-Vietnamese military budget as projected by Johnson was $4.1 billion more, even though he estimated the Vietnam war was going to cost $3.5 billion less.*[5] In his April 14 message, Nixon said of our domestic needs, "What we are able to do will depend in large measure on the prospects for an early end to the war in Vietnam." The Johnson 1970 budget projected the first slowdown but proposed to use the savings entirely for military expansion. Nixon went along with that decision.

From the Pentagon's point of view there could not have been a smoother transition than the shift from Johnson to Nixon. Nixon revised Johnson's social and welfare programs downward but left his military budget essentially untouched. It read like the handiwork of the Johnson who

[4] According to a little-noticed press release by Senator Stephen M. Young (D. Ohio), a member of the Senate Armed Services Committee, which has access to much information otherwise secret, Johnson had originally planned a cutback of troops in Vietnam. Young asked Nixon to recall two divisions before July and more later with an announcement, "We have accomplished our objectives in Vietnam. Our boys are coming home." Young said Johnson had decided on a similar announcement last year but was talked out of it by the Joint Chiefs of Staff.

[5] Since I have been challenged on this "peace dividend" by some colleagues, and others have wondered by what elaborate computation I arrived at it, I give the source, p. 74 of *The Budget of the US Government for Fiscal 1970.* It says, "As shown in the accompanying table outlays in support of Southeast Asia are anticipated to drop for the first time in 1970—declining by $3.5 billion from 1969. This decline reflects changing patterns of combat activity and revised loss projections. *Outlays for the military activities of the Department of Defense, excluding support of Southeast Asia, are expected to rise by $4.1 billion in 1970, to provide selected force improvements*" (my italics).

was the ally of the military and the armament industries as chairman of the Senate Preparedness subcommittee during the fifties. Johnson's last defense budget was not only the highest ever sent Congress—$81.5 billion as compared with the World War II peak of $80 billion in fiscal 1945—but laid the basis for a huge expansion in spending during future years. It gave the go-ahead signal to a wide variety of projects the armed services had long desired.

Nixon had campaigned on a "security gap," but Johnson left few if any gaps to fill. "The number of new programs spread through the new defense budget," *Space/Aeronautics* commented in its February issue, "is astounding in comparison with the lean years from fiscal 1965 to 1969." Among them were $400 million for "major developmental activity on no fewer than six new aircraft" and—biggest item of all—an increase of $1.64 billion to a total of $2.85 billion for the Navy's surface ship and submarine building program. Arms research and development was boosted $850 million to a total of $5.6 billion, including work on such new monsters as missiles which can be hidden on the ocean floor.

This farewell budget also put Nixon in a bind. As *Space/ Aeronautics* pointed out in that same editorial, if Nixon tried to cut back appreciably on the Johnson budget, he would open himself to "security gap" charges. On the other hand, "If he doesn't defer or cancel at least some of them, and if the war in Vietnam cannot be brought to an honorable close some time next year, he will face a crushing arms bill in fiscal 1971, when many of these starts begin to demand more money." That was the risk Nixon and Laird preferred to take.

Nixon claims to have cut $4 billion from 1970 outlays, and taken $1.1 billion, or 27 percent, from the military. Critics have protested that he took $3 from civilian needs for every $1 he took from the military. But even this is illusory.

From another point of view, even if we accept the Nixon cuts at face value, the military will have $3 billion more in fiscal 1970 for non-Vietnamese war purposes than it had in fiscal 1969. We have seen that Johnson budgeted a $3.5 billion cut in Vietnam war costs for fiscal '70 and then added $4.1 billion to the military budget for projects unconnected with the Vietnam war. If you deduct Nixon's $1.1 billion from that $4.1 billion, the Pentagon is still ahead by $3 billion.[6] If Nixon had applied the whole projected saving of $3.5 billion on Vietnam to civilian use or deficit reduction, the fiscal 1970 total for national defense would have been reduced to $97,499 million. All Nixon did was to *cut the Johnson increase* by a fourth. Even this may turn out to be—at least in part—a familiar bit of flim-flam. Since 1965, when Johnson began to bomb the North and take over the combat war in the South, almost every annual budget has underestimated Vietnamese war costs. These have had to be covered later in the fiscal year by supplemental appropriations. The under-estimate in fiscal 1969, as we have seen, was $3 billion. The fiscal 1970 budget is running true to form.

The biggest "economy" item in the Nixon military budget is $1,083.4 million, which is attributed to "reduced estimates of ammunition consumption rates."[7] Just how much of the estimated $1.1 billion "saving" in outlays for fiscal 1970 will be the result of lower consumption of ammunition in Vietnam was not made clear. The $1,083.4 million is given as a net reduction of obligational authority in fiscal 1969 and 1970. It is one of the three main items in that

6 Even that understates the case. Down near the bottom of the budget outlays table of the Nixon revisions is $2.8 billion more for "civilian *and military* pay increases" (my italics). Laird in his April 1 presentation said this would add $2.5 billion but failed to make clear whether this was for the whole government or only for Pentagon civilian and military employees—almost half the civilian employees of the government work for the Pentagon. Clifford in his 1970 statement gave a figure of $1.8 billion for Pentagon pay increases but did not make clear whether this included the civilian employees. So pay raises will add between $1.8 billion and $2.5 billion to this $3 billion figure.

7 See page 17 of House Document No. 91–100, 91st Congress, First Session.

$3 billion cut in obligational authority for fiscal 1970 which make it possible for the new Administration to claim that 55 percent of the total cut in obligational authority for 1970 ($5.5 billion) came from the military. Obligational authority is not necessarily or entirely translated into actual outlays during the fiscal year in which it is granted.

This projected cut in the rate of ammunition consumption is in addition to Johnson's projected cut of $3.5 billion in Vietnam war costs. Though Laird does not blush easily, even he seems to have been embarrassed by this particular "economy." "To be perfectly frank," said Laird, who rarely is, when he first broached this item to the House Armed Services Committee on March 27, "I think the ammunition consumption rates for Southeast Asia are based on rather optimistic assumptions, particularly in view of the current Têt offensive." Yet, under pressure from the White House to show more economy, the optimism rose sharply in the next four days. The following table shows the change in estimated savings for ammunition and its transportation in millions of dollars in those four days:

	March 27	April 1
Ground Munitions	−$380	−$460
Ammo. Transport	− 34.4	− 34.4
Air Munitions	− 417.9	− 511.9
Ship Gun Ammo.	− 47.1	− 77.1
TOTAL CUTS	879.4	1,103.4

These figures are for total obligational authority for fiscal years 1969 and 1970. Perhaps the Administration hesitated to make public its actual outlay estimates for these two years, since they may easily turn out to be higher rather than lower, and may have to be met later in the year by a supplemental appropriation. Between March 27 and April 1 Laird boosted the estimated reduction in total military outlays for fiscal 1970 from "about $500 million" to $1,113 million. Most of the increased "economy" seems to have come from this ammunition item.

There are several indications in the official presentations

themselves which lead one to think Laird was right to be queasy. The original 1970 budget projected consumption of 105,000 tons a month in ground munitions through December, 1970. Actual consumption in January was given as 96,000 tons, but that was before the recent enemy offensive got under way. The consumption of ammunition must have risen sharply with the fighting in February, March, and April, but when I asked the Pentagon for the monthly figures since January, I was told they could not be given out. "We can only say," an official spokesman told me, "that the Secretary's projections are being borne out." If that is true our troops must have been meeting enemy attacks with switchblades.

Another indication—how I love tracking down these liars!—appears in what we know about the volume of bombs dropped on South Vietnam and Laos since we stopped bombing the North. The Pentagon's own figures on total tonnages dropped show little change. Total tonnages dropped in September and October last year, before the bombing of the North stopped, were almost 240,000. Total tonnage dropped in January and February of this year, when it was dropped only on Laos and South Vietnam, was more than 245,000. There was an increase of 5,000 tons. That increase makes the estimate of a saving of more than a half billion dollars in air munitions for fiscal 1969 and 1970 look very phony indeed.

Laird himself said consumption of air munitions was rising. On March 27 he told the House Armed Services Committee that while consumption had been estimated at 110,000 tons per month for the twenty-four months from January 1969 to December 1970—that doesn't sound like much deescalation ahead, at least in the air!—"actual consumption is now running at about 129,000 tons per month." Yet he projected a saving of $42.5 million on air munitions in fiscal 1969 and $375.4 in fiscal 1970. When he got back to the committee four days later, he placed actual consumption even higher, at 130,000 tons a month, but also projected higher savings! Now he was to save $89.5 million on air munitions in fiscal 1969, or twice the figure four days earlier, and $442 million for fiscal 1970, an increase of $47 million over the earlier estimate. Yet Laird said he saw "no indication that consumption will decline by very much during the next twelve-to-eighteen months." How then were expenditures on air ammunition to be lower than expected when the tonnage of bombs dropped was running higher than expected? Non-Euclidean geometry is not half so exotic as Pentagon arithmetic.

The ammunition figures for Vietnam are stupendous. The original Johnson-Clifford budget in January projected the cost of ammunition in Vietnam during fiscal 1970 at $5.2 billion. This expenditure of shot and shell over Vietnam is two-and-a-half times the total 1970 revised Nixon budget of $2 billion for the Office of Economic Opportunity (down $132 million), and more than twice the revised elementary and secondary education outlay for 1970 which he set at $2.3 billion (down another $100 million).

After this razzle-dazzle on ammunition, the next largest item of military saving in the Nixon-Laird budget revisions is the ABM. Let us return to the formal document sent Congress by the President. There on page 17[8] are given "principal changes in 1970 budget authority resulting from 1969 and 1970 Defense program changes." The second largest of these is $994 million for "reorientation of the antiballistic missile program to the new Safeguard system." This and the ammunition item make up almost $2.1 billion of that $3 billion cut in military obligational authority on which the new Administration commends itself.

A businessman in financial difficulties who thought up such savings for his stockholders would soon be in jail for embezzlement. The "reorientation" of Sentinel into Safeguard may reduce spending in fiscal 1970 but only by add-

[8] House Document No. 91–100. Reductions in 1970 Appropriations Request. Communication from the President . . . together with details of the changes. 91st Congress, First Session.

ing at least $1.5 billion and possibly $5.5 billion more in the next few years. This is an expensive rebaptism or, better, if we consider the phallic significance of these monsters, re-circumcision. Nixon had an easy way out of the ABM fight if he wanted one. He could have announced that like Eisen-hower he had decided to keep the ABM in research and development until he was sure it would not be obsolete be-fore it was deployed.

If he had been a little more daring and a little less be-holden to the military-industrial complex, he might have cut billions[9] from the military budget immediately by offering a freeze on all new deployment of strategic defen-sive and offensive missiles, if the Russians did likewise, as a preparation for strategic arms negotiations. This would not only save at least $5 or $6 billion in the new fiscal year but ensure our present nuclear superiority and fully guarantee against first-strike nightmares.[10]

Nixon chose instead a tricky stretch-out. This offered some reductions in the new fiscal year, as compared with Johnson's ABM proposal, but at the expense of higher costs later. This ingenious compromise made it possible to offer an apparent saving to the taxpayer *and* larger eventual or-ders to the electronics and missile industries. This not only fulfilled the Administration's promise of New Directions but enabled it to move in opposite directions at the same time. Johnson's Sentinel was estimated to cost $5.5 billion, Nixon's Safeguard from $6.7 to $7 billion, or $1.5 billion more. This may prove another official underestimate. An

[9] The Johnson budget for 1970 placed the expenditure for strategic forces at $9.6 billion as compared with $9.1 in 1969 and $7.6 in 1968. Much of this is for deployment of new weaponry.

[10] "Such a freeze," Senator Percy declared in a speech April 17, "should be acceptable to the Defense Department. Secretary Laird has testified that our missiles on land and under the seas as well as our long-range bomber force present an overwhelming second-strike array. If a freeze—fully verifiable by both nations through satellite reconnaissance as well as other intelligence sources—is put into effect, the U.S. deterrent will remain credible into the foreseeable future." But if the deterrent remains credi-ble, what will the poor missile salesmen do?

authoritative service, which covers all developing major weapons and aerospace systems for industrial and governmental subscribers, places the total cost of Safeguard much higher.

This is DMS, Inc. (Defense Marketing Service), a ten-year-old service now a part of McGraw-Hill. I had never heard of it until an anonymous reader sent me a reproduction of its report on Nixon's Safeguard. I checked with its Washington office by telephone and was given permission to quote it. Its detailed analysis places the total cost of the system at $11 billion and ends by warning that "in a program as complex as Safeguard, historical experience indicates costs in the long run are likely to be considerably higher." When Senator Cooper put the DMS analysis into the *Congressional Record* May 8, he noted that it did not include "about $1 billion AEC warhead costs." This would bring the total cost of Nixon's Safeguard past $12 billion.

The DMS report notes that we have already spent $4.5 billion on the ABM from fiscal 1956, when the Army started the Nike-Zeus program, through fiscal 1968, and that the research efforts which made Nike-Zeus obsolete before it could be deployed are still going on, at a cost of $350 to $500 million annually. "A number of new concepts as well as hardware," the report said, "are currently under investigation." These threaten Safeguard with obsolescence too. "Preliminary research," DMS said, "has pointed the way toward the following types of advances." One was radars of much higher frequency, so the interception "would be made with either a much smaller nuclear warhead or even a conventional high explosive charge." Another was a new third stage for Spartan, so the missile could fly out at greater ranges and "maneuver through a cloud of decoys to find and destroy the real warhead." A third—most expensive of all—was "defensive missiles carried either in ships or large aircraft deployed closer to the enemy's launching sites."

We give these details to show that in embarking on the

ABM we are embarking on a wholly new sector of the arms race with a high rate of obsolescence to gladden the hearts of the electronics companies and of AT&T, whose Western Electric has long been the main contractor. The reader should note that the three advances cited in the DMS report are relatively simple and foreseeable developments. All kinds of "far-out" possibilities are also being investigated. The secret hope which lies behind all this Rube Goldberg hardware is that some day somebody will turn up a perfect ABM defense and thus enable the possessor to rule the world because a power so armed can threaten a first strike, knowing it will be immune to retaliation.

The most candid expression of this viewpoint was made by Senator Russell during the defense appropriations hearings in May of last year. "I have often said," Senator Russell observed, "that I feel that the first country to deploy an effective ABM system and an effective ASW [anti-submarine warfare] system is going to control the world militarily." [11] This control of the world, however, may be on a somewhat reduced basis. Six months later, during the Senate's secret session on the ABM (November 1, 1968), Senator Russell admitted, "There is no system ever devised which will afford complete protection against any multiple firing of ballistic missiles . . . we will have no absolutely foolproof defense, I do not care how much money we spend on one, or what we do." Senator Clark replied that casualties would be so high as to destroy civilization "and if there are a few people living in caves after that, it does not make much difference." To which Russell made his now famous rejoinder, "If we have to start over again with another Adam and Eve, I want them to be Americans and not Russians" (*Congressional Record*, E9644, November 1, 1968). Thus we would at last achieve an unchallengeable Pax Americana! And thus the ABM turns out to be another variant of the military's unquenchable dream of an Ulti-

[11] Department of the Army, Senate Hearings, Department of Defense Appropriations for fiscal 1969, 90th Congress, Second Session, Part II, page 868.

mate Weapon, to leap some day like a jackpot from a slot machine if only they go on pouring money into R and D.

I would ask the reader's indulgence for one more foray into the labyrinthine depths of the Pentagon budget. Deeper knowledge of these recesses is necessary if we are ever to hunt down and slay the dragon. I want to deal with the next largest source of the Nixon military "economies." These involve deferrals of expenditures amounting to about $480 million. Most critical comment has been content to note that mere deferral of spending is not real economy, since what is saved in fiscal 1970 will be spent later. There is a more important point to be made. These deferrals, if closely examined, provide additional proof of how recklessly and wastefully the Pentagon dashes into production before full testing and evaluation have been completed, before it knows, in other words, that these expensive weapons will work. We will see how much pressure it takes to make the Pentagon admit this elementary error.

To grasp the full significance of these so-called "economies" of Nixon and Laird we must see them against the background of revelations by two Senators, one the leading pillar of the military in the Senate establishment, Senator Russell, the other a former Secretary of and long-time spokesman for the Air Force who has turned against the military-industrial establishment, Senator Symington.

During the secret debate on the ABM last November 1, Russell told the Senate one of the "most serious mistakes" he had ever made as Chairman of the Armed Services Committee, which passes on all military requests for authorization, and as chairman of the Senate subcommittee, which passes on all defense appropriations, "was in allotting vast sums to the Navy for missile frigates before we knew we had a missile that would work on them." He said "we built missile frigates, we built missile destroyers and missile escort ships" on the basis of "unqualified" testimony of "everyone in the Department of Defense and in the Navy" that effective missiles were being developed. "It probably cost the taxpayers," Russell said, "$1 billion, because they have had to rebuild those missiles three times."

A more comprehensive statement of the same kind was made to the Senate by Symington on March 7 of this year. He put a table into the *Congressional Record* (at page S2464 that day) which showed how much had been spent in the past sixteen years on missiles which were no longer deployed or never had been deployed, because of obsolescence. The total was fantastic. Symington gave the names, the expenditures, and the life-span of each missile. The total cost of those no longer deployed was $18.9 *billion*, and the cost of those which were abandoned as obsolete or unworkable *before* deployment was $4.2 billion. The total was $23 billion. Imagine what those wasted billions could have done for our blighted cities!

Symington's table was introduced to underscore his point —buttressed by past testimony from McNamara—that the ABM would soon be another monument to this kind of expensive obsolescence. Another inference to be drawn from this table is how many billions might have been saved if the Pentagon had not rushed so quickly into these miscarriages. Behind the glamorous names which flashed through the appropriations hearings and the ads in the aeronautical and military trade journals—Navaho, Snark, Dove, Triton, and even Plato (what did he do to deserve *this* honor?)—lies an untold story of beguiling missile salesmanship and drunken-sailor procurement methods. It might be worth billions in future savings if a Congressional investigating committee really dug up the full story and its lessons.

The need for such an investigation becomes plain if one examines the funny thing which happened to SRAM (acronym for short-range attack missile) on Secretary Laird's way to and from the budget forum on Capitol Hill between March 27, his first appearance before the House Armed Services Committee, and his second appearance on April 1, just four days later. SRAM is one of the new missiles which have been under development. It is supposed to be mounted on a bomber so it can be rocketed into enemy territory from a position more than a hundred miles away from the enemy's defense perimeter. The idea is to circumvent the enemy's defenses by stopping the bomber out of their range and lobbing the missiles over them.

SRAM has had several predecessors, all expensive, of course; it is not a simple contraption. The predecessors appear in Senator Symington's table. Crossbow, Rascal, and Skybolt were earlier attempts at a stand-off missile; they cost a total of $962.6 million before they were abandoned prior to deployment. Hound Dog A, which cost another $255 million, is another missile in the same family which is no longer deployed. SRAM is very different in capability, range, and complexity. SRAM is intended to do for the bombing plane what penetration aids do for the ICBM. SRAM is supposed to carry all kinds of devices to confuse the radars of the enemy defense.

When Laird appeared before the House Armed Services Committee on March 27 he referred, without further explanation, to "delays experienced in the SRAM development production program." The original Johnson-Clifford budget last January for fiscal 1970 called for the modification of all seventeen B-52 squadrons of series G and H at a total cost of about $340 million to enable them to carry SRAM. The "modification kits," as Laird described them, were to be bought from Boeing "at a total cost of about $220 million," and it was planned to buy kits for twelve squadrons in 1970, leaving the rest to be modified in 1971. Laird proposed to save $30 million in fiscal 1970 by equipping only ten squadrons in 1970 and the remaining seven in 1971. He said "This change will give us a smoother program."

But the White House and the Budget Bureau, desperate for ways to cut, put pressure on the Pentagon, and four days later Laird was back before the Armed Services Committee. Now instead of $30 million he proposed a deferral of the SRAM program amounting to $326 million. It now appeared that he had been less than candid with the committee. The cryptic references to "delays" turned out to be quite an understatement. He came forward with new changes in the SRAM program, all of them—he explained —"related to the difficulties encountered in the development of this Short Range Attack Missile." Now it was not "delays," but "difficulties."

Laird went on to quite a revelation. "We have now reached the conclusion," he told the committee, "that procurement of operational missiles should be deferred until the test program conclusively demonstrated that they will work as intended." So "we have deleted most [but not all!] of the missile procurement funds" from fiscal 1969 and 1970, for a total cut in the two years of $153 million.

Then he proposed to defer not only the missiles but the modifications designed to enable the B-52's to carry them. "Inasmuch as we do not know when operational missiles will be available," Laird said, "we have also deferred all special SRAM modification work on the B-52's and FB-111's." The total net deferral—after adding $17 million to R and D for "a greater portion of the overhead cost" (another consolation fee?)—was to be $326 million.

This shows how much pressure it takes to squeeze the fat out of the military budget, and a little more candor out of the Pentagon. Why didn't Laird tell the committee on March 27 what he revealed on April 1? But for the extra pressure, the Pentagon would have gone on with procurement of the SRAM before knowing whether it would work, and with modification of the strategic bombers to carry the missiles before it was sure that it would have the missiles. What if further testing modifies the missile, and this requires a change also in the kits which modify the planes to carry these missiles? Why risk the waste of millions?

The SRAM story raises similar questions about Laird's rather cryptic references in his budget presentation to a similar deferral of "about $160 million" in the Minuteman ICBM program. The most important part of that "saving"

is due, as Laird told House Armed Services on March 27, to
"a slowdown in the deployment of Minuteman III." This is
the Minuteman which will carry MIRV—"multiple independently targeted re-entry vehicles," i.e., additional warheads independently targeted. It was tested for the first time
last August 16 with three warheads.[12] "While we are confident," Laird said, "that the Minuteman III will perform as
intended, we believe it would be prudent to reduce somewhat the previously planned deployment rate, at least
through the FY 1970 procurement lead-time." Why only
"somewhat," and what does "somewhat" mean for the whole
program? "This delay," Laird went on, "would serve to reduce the amount of overlapping of R and D and production
and provide more time for production." Why risk overlapping altogether until testing has been completed? Laird
himself said he was planning to accelerate operational testing "to help ensure that the missile is working well before
we return to the originally planned rate in fiscal 1971." "Mr.
Chairman," Laird said, patting himself warmly on the back,
"this reflects our determination to minimize cost overruns
resulting from R and D modifications after production has
commenced." But perhaps more serious cost overruns could
be avoided if Minuteman III, like SRAM, were subjected to
further deferrals.

A franker if ironic account of the Minuteman III cuts
appeared May 5 in *Aviation Week*. It says, "The reason for
the reduction is fear of reliability problems with the new
missile." It said the Air Force had "decided 'to reduce the
concurrency of development and production' of the missile
in order to insure reliability of all components." Even the
Foreign Service could not have hit upon a smoother phrase
to equal that "concurrency of development and production." *Aviation Week* added, "The cutback was publi-
cized by some Defense Dept. sources as evidence of U.S.

---

[12] "On August 16," said a special survey in *Space/Aeronautics*, page 88,
last January, "Poseidon and Minuteman III were launched with ten and
three warheads respectively."

willingness to reduce strategic offensive armaments prior to arms reduction talks with the Soviets, but that was not the reason."

This effort to make the Minuteman cuts look like evidence of Pentagon enthusiasm for arms talks originated in Laird's own presentation on April 1. In a super-slick conclusion he told the committee, "Our decision to slow the Minuteman III deployment—though necessitated for other reasons—provides a period of time in which arms limitation agreements could become effective at a lower level of armaments. . . . It remains to be seen, of course, whether our potential adversaries will similarly indicate with actions that they, too, are serious about desiring meaningful arms limitation talks." These are the moments when Laird sounds as if he were dreamed up by Molière.

June 5, 1969
New York Review

HEADING FOR A BIGGER
ARMS RACE IN THE SEVENTIES

Despite euphoric reports about the SALT talks and the $5.9 billion cut in the final defense budget this fiscal year, the military monster is far from being subdued. It takes a long time before cuts in congressional authorization and appropriation bills actually lead to cuts in expenditure. The best guide to actual expenditures is the daily U.S. Treasury statement. Its January 2 statement covering all but the last two days of the first half of the 1970 fiscal year is not encouraging. The cash deficit for the six months was $12.4 billion as against $7.8 billion in the same period last year. To this deficit the military establishment was a prime contributor, despite the first withdrawals from Vietnam and talk of reduced commitments. In the first half of the fiscal year the military drew more than half a billion ($685 million) *more* from the Treasury than in the corresponding period a year ago. The *rate* of increase seemed to be going up. In December alone military spending was more than $1 billion higher than in December a year ago. The tempo of military spending is still feeding the fires of inflation.

The Tax Foundation estimates that in 1970 the average tax burden per American family for defense will be $1,250. For those families lucky enough to be on the gravy train of the military-industrial complex, this tax is easily outweighed by their earnings. Indeed from an economic point of view the arms race is a device for taxing the poor to the profit of the well-to-do. The prospect for a change in the seventies is dim. The Arms Control and Disarmament Agency estimates that the world has spent $4,000 billion on arms since 1900, and at the current rate of increase will spend that much again in the coming decade alone. That, too, will not help our chronic inflationary fevers.

There is little reason to believe that the Strategic Arms Limitation Talks (SALT) will change the picture much, if at all. The two biggest escalations which lie ahead are those to be sparked by MIRV and the ABM. There is no sign that Washington or Moscow is prepared to halt either. The constant and pleased assurances from the State Department and the Pentagon that the Russians at Helsinki were behaving splendidly and avoiding "propaganda" are—in our opinion —cause for depression, not optimism. If Moscow were militantly for disarmament or arms control, we may be sure this would be stigmatized as "propaganda."

Disarmament buffs had naïvely assumed that a main purpose of the SALT talks was to block MIRV, for once the missiles on both sides are outfitted with the multiple warheads, it will be impossible for either side to know by aerial surveillance how many warheads there are atop each missile on the other. The fog and the fear will come down again, and it will be hard to keep the arms race within any bounds at all. But the Pentagon is now leaking the revelation that there has never been much if any intention on our side to curb MIRV. William Beecher, who covers the Pentagon for the *New York Times*, reported in a dispatch to that paper December 31 that while the Johnson Administration in the summer of 1968 was prepared to propose a freeze on strategic weapons, there was to be no limitation on "improvement of systems within the limited numbers," including MIRV's. This was the first public disclosure of the Johnson negotiating position. George C. Wilson, who covers the Pentagon for the *Washington Post,* reported (January 1) from a similar briefing with unnamed officials that "the Nixon Administration view is that multiple-warhead submarines are a fact of life already," so MIRV discussion would focus on the land-based missiles "but, according to informed sources, the Soviets showed little interest at the SALT talks in calling off the flight tests of MIRV missiles." Clearly the Nixon Administration shares this lack of interest.

The second biggest item of future arms spending is the ABM. The Pentagon is beginning to leak stories designed to build up support for its escalation. Beecher reported in the *New York Times* January 2, "Administration Expected to Back ABM Expansion." The AP was given a similar backgrounder, "Soviet Buildup Spurs New Anti-Missile Plans" (Washington *Star*, January 3). This was an effort to revive the first-strike scare of last spring. The AP was told that if the Russians continue building SS-9's at the current rate they will have 420 by 1974–75, and that these 420 would then be able to wipe out 95 percent of our 1,000 Minutemen in a surprise attack. The arithmetic sounds like pure Pentagon Munchhausen. Unanswered is the question of why anyone would risk a first strike at our Minutemen when this would expose the Soviet Union to destruction from our submarine missile fleet. Another question no one raised at the backgrounder was, if land-based missiles are now so vulnerable to first attack, are they not obsolete? Indeed the House Appropriations Committee report on the new defense budget (December 3, page 78) suggests that instead of spending millions to bury the missiles in "very costly" hard-rock silos and in defending them with more ABM's, it would be better to replace them altogether with submarine or mobile land missiles. "The final argument for expansion," the AP account said, with unintended irony, "is that it would cost less now than later in the face of rising prices and inflation."

The House report noted that the fiscal 1969 military budget was 7 times the military budget of 1948, just two decades ago. It may easily double and redouble within the next ten years. The reductions in the 1970 budget were mostly cuts in fat and waste. Old ships were mothballed, headquarter staffs—military and civilian—were cut down. Development contracts were stretched out. The budget cuts were a tactical retreat. In that retreat the Pentagon saved the major new weapons systems, whose costs will proliferate into billions during the next decade. Senator Hatfield (R. Ore.) spelled out a few of them in his speech on final passage December 15. There was $100 million for AMSA, the new strategic bomber; it will eventually cost from $8 to $23 billion. The $450 million for the new F-14 plane launches a program that will cost from $15 to $30 billion. The $425 million for a new nuclear attack aircraft carrier will give us 15 such task forces eventually; each costs $1 billion. The $5 million for the new Navy underwater missile system (ULMS) is another item which will escalate into billions. These are but a few samples of the spiraling expenditures ahead.

Most important of all, despite talk of cutbacks the new troop level strength next June will still be 3.2 million men, down only 260,000 from the previous June, and three quarters of a million men higher than in the first Kennedy year, when the military buildup began. This huge force is the embodiment of a continued Pax Americana, "a projection of threats and contingencies," Hatfield said, "that are far overdrawn and bear little relation to the contemporary realities of international affairs." This year's appropriation, though reduced somewhat, still "allows us to station troops on foreign soil throughout the globe, where their mere presence often contributes more to the undermining of our relations with foreign nations than to our own security."

January 12, 1970

PART VI

Disarmament:
A Century of
Futility

HOW EARTH DAY
WAS POLLUTED

The week the devoted band of youngsters who ran the Vietnam Moratorium gave up in despair was the week in which other youngsters all over the country, with the full support of the Establishment and its press, celebrated Earth Day. On the grassy slopes of the Sylvan Theatre in the shadow of the Washington Monument, where so many anti-war teach-ins have been held, a predominantly youthful audience jumped with joy as the rock bands played. Looking out at that tumultuous sea of sweet faces, in their long hair and bizarre costumes, I felt that just as the Caesars once used bread and circuses so ours were at last learning to use rock-and-roll, idealism and non-inflammatory social issues to turn the youth off from more urgent concerns which might really threaten the power structure. And I said so in my speech.

The pollution issue is real enough, though a little exaggerated, but it cannot be solved in isolation. From one viewpoint, the Earth Day affair was a gigantic snow job. Here was the country slipping into a wider war in Southeast Asia. Even as we spoke the news was leaking that U.S. officers in civilian clothes, either CIA or military, were directing a South Vietnamese offensive into Cambodia, and that six days earlier the U.S. had already promised the new Cambodian regime a few thousand rifles but had asked them (*New York Times*, April 23, 1970) to keep the shipment secret. Two days before the Earth Day rally, Secretary of Defense Laird had made a speech to the AP which can only be read as a deliberate effort to sabotage the SALT talks, but here we were talking as if we had nothing to worry about but our drains.

The anti-pollution campaign was saved providentially

from a Nixon message, but half the Cabinet were on the day's soap-boxes. The only bright note was provided by the oldest section of the American revolutionary movement, the DAR. Their convention denounced anti-pollution as a subversive movement. The clear proof: it was being entertained by Pete Seeger, "a documented Communist." "It's strange, isn't it," one DAR speaker noted astutely (ah, if only the CIA and the FBI were as sharp as these old dowagers!), "that today is Lenin Day and Earth Day." If it was anybody else in the White House but Richard Nixon they'd have been calling him Vladimir Ilyich.

The Nixon budget should clear him of suspicion. He called air and water pollution a "now-or-never" task, but turned in a budget which allocates 52 cents of every general revenue dollar to the military and space, but only four-tenths of one cent per dollar to air and water pollution. New weaponry alone gets $5.4 billion while air and water pollution get $569 million. Senator Tydings at the University of Maryland Earth Day said we ought to be spending on pollution what we are spending on the Vietnam war. But nobody knows what that is. Laird said months ago it would be $17 billion, but this year for the first time in history part of the military budget is blacked out, and no figures are given for certain items, Vietnam among them.

Unless there is a sharp change of course we are already in the first stages of a wider and more costly Second Indochinese War. Our secret services brought it on, upsetting the status quo in Cambodia by encouraging the anti-Sihanouk coup, as they upset the Laotian status quo with their Plain of Jars offensive last year. The enemy took up the challenge, and now Nixon's latest Vietnam message has raised the stakes by putting Cambodia and Laos squarely into the area of our concern. We must either get out altogether or plunge in further, for the military consequences otherwise would leave South Vietnam outflanked. You can kiss goodbye to any hope of controlling inflation if Nixon takes the plunge.

What a time to talk about pollution! What a time to fill the campuses, the press, the radio and TV with Earth Day talk when such momentous secret decisions are being made. Education on the complex tasks of air and water control are all to the good, and should be sharpened to a fundamental discussion of governmental and corporate policy the Establishment doesn't want. But how much more urgent and important to educate the public, while there is still time, to the more critical issues of the widening war in Southeast Asia and the SALT talks in Vienna. On both Nixon is waging a con game, and Earth Day distracted from it. In the former he remains a prisoner of the terrible power of inertia. He still wants to avoid humiliation. How to avoid some humiliation for so many disastrous mistakes? He still wants victory of some sort; indeed he speaks as if it were possible and imminent. And what is the meaning of the message leaked through James Reston (*New York Times*, April 22, 1970) that he will use "any" weapon to prevent a major military defeat as and when more troops are withdrawn? Are we back in desperation to the lunatic nonsense of threatening to use nuclear weapons?

The campuses and the communications media should be full of these questions, as they should be full of discussion about SALT. There the battle to curb the arms race is being lost even as it begins. The day the SALT talks opened, Nixon had leading Senators in for a snow job. What Nixon is really trying to pull off was indicated four days earlier when Nixon won the support of Mendel Rivers and the House Armed Services Committee for a $1.4 billion expansion of the ABM in return for $300 million more for the Navy. The ABM expansion was cleared publicly the day the SALT talks reopened. Seen from the other side this signals a U.S. drive for an area defense and an area defense is a necessity for a first-strike strategy. The night before the SALT talks opened, Secretary Rogers chose the significant vehicle of an interview with Radio Free Berlin to declare again our intention to go ahead with MIRV. Add MIRV to

ABM and there is nothing for SALT to do but ratify a new spiral in the arms race. That has been Nixon's intention from the beginning.

Senator Jackson, whom Nixon wanted as Secretary of Defense, is working hard on the Hill, and Laird, whom Nixon took as second choice, is working hard out of the Pentagon to make sure that SALT does not succeed. The Laird speech to the AP April 20 is the most mendacious performance by a U.S. official since the days of John Foster Dulles. The Soviets are several years behind us in nuclear proficiency. They have just begun to deploy a solid-fuel equivalent of Minuteman. They have just begun to develop MRV (multiple warheads). We had it several years ago and are already developing MIRV. The latest report of the London Institute of Strategic Studies, released April 11, showed that thanks to MIRV our present total of 4,200 deliverable warheads (as against the Soviet's just under 1,900) would become 11,000 by 1975—a stupendous imbalance, clearly raising the threat of a first strike. Yet Laird told the AP editors we had been standing still for five years while the Russians have been forging ahead!

Laird achieved this bit of trickery by ignoring the enormous qualitative advances we have made in those five years and focusing on the Soviet's effort to make up in numbers and in megatonnage (which is wasteful) for their lag in accuracy, multiple independently targeted warheads *and* numbers. He continued to impute to the Russians a desire to achieve what our Air Force has long sought—first-strike capacity. If the roles were reversed and a Soviet official were to present so false and inflammatory a picture of the power balance we would decide that it was time to pack our bags and head for home. Let pollution buffs notice Dr. Panofsky's testimony that we already have enough weapons between us to make the entire Northern Hemisphere unlivable in one swift nuclear exchange. If SALT fails and we up the firepower, we may wake up one morning and find there is nothing left of Earth to pollute.

May 4, 1970

WHY SALT SPELLS FRAUD

The folly of competition in arms was recognized by philosophers in the eighteenth century and statesmen in the nineteenth. The first disarmament conference was held at The Hague in 1899. Except for the period of the two world wars, there has hardly been a year in which disarmament negotiations of some kind have not been going on. These have become a ritual, and almost a comedy, punctuating the pauses and fresh starts of the arms race. The military machines and their allies have learned to turn them into an elaborate kind of game, designed to befuddle public opinion into believing that something was being done about the ever-growing expense and danger.

Not only the State Department but the Pentagon and the Joint Chiefs of Staff have developed subdivisions skilled in "arms control," that is, talk about arms control. This gamesmanship has been perfected to the point where it may actually be used to cover up a new spiral in the arms race, or indeed even to sell the public on the need for new weapons and higher expenditures. This is the only safe, if cynical, perspective from which to view the Nixon Administration's preparations for new talks on strategic weapons. The men named to direct these talks and the negotiating positions being mapped out in advance are not calculated to restrain or reduce the arms race but to move it forward into the higher and more dangerous levels represented by the ABM and the MIRV. SALT—Strategic Arms Limitation Talks—will prove a fraud.

Some apparent motion toward arms talks was essential to the Nixon Administration on the eve of the Senate battle over ABM. This was a political necessity to convince wavering Senators that the ABM is just a bargaining card to use in negotiations, and to keep alive the hope that this dangerous and expensive new development will be made unnecessary by joint agreement. But if you look closely you will see that nowhere has the Nixon Administration explicitly said it would forgo an ABM if the Russians did likewise. On the contrary, you will see that the Nixon Administration is not prepared to negotiate *whether* there will be an ABM but only *how much* of one.

This was implicit in a hint dropped by the President March 14 at the original press conference announcing the ABM, when he was asked whether he would "be willing to consider abandoning the ABM program altogether if the Soviets showed a similar willingness or, indeed, if they showed a readiness to place limitations on offensive weapons?" Nixon replied that "the arms talks that at least preliminarily have been discussed, *do not involve limitation or reduction.* They involve only freezing where we are" (my italics). Then Nixon went on to say that he "would imagine that the Soviet Union would be just as reluctant as we would be to leave their country naked against a potential Chinese Communist threat," and added, "So the abandoning of the entire system, particularly as the Chinese threat is there, I think neither country would look upon with much favor." Moscow must have been startled to hear Nixon speaking for it.

The full meaning of Nixon's remarks begins to be spelled out by a pamphlet, *Safeguard: What Are the True Answers?*, sent out recently to editors all over the country by Nixon's Director of Communications, Herbert G. Klein. The answer to the question, "How would Safeguard affect prospects for arms control?," after spelling out various possibilities, concludes by saying—

However, those parts of the Safeguard program designed for defense against China, small countries with a strategic delivery capability or accidental or unauthorized attacks from any source would not be affected by arms control agreements with the Soviet Union, nor do we expect the Soviet Union to forgo deployments designed for similar purposes.

This means the only part of the Safeguard system open in negotiation is that small part designed specifically to protect our Minuteman bases. This leaves out the major part of the system, the Spartans and the computer-radars which go with them and the Sprints to protect the computer-radars.

Indeed, from the rest of the reply to this question it is not even clear just how much of our Minuteman defenses would be negotiable. It says, "If the Soviet Union slows down or stops its deployment of the large payload SS-9 missile or if the likelihood that these missiles will be armed with accurate multiple warheads is materially reduced, we can readily *limit* that part of the Safeguard program which is designed to defend our land-based missiles." The italics are ours, to emphasize what is here offered is limitation of planned deployment and not reduction.

But what if the development of the Soviet SS-9 is an answer to our MIRV, as it seems to be? This does not say that we would give up our MIRV if they did not develop theirs. It says we would limit our ABM missiles if they slow down or stop the deployment of the SS-9 and "materially reduce" the "likelihood"—whatever these terms mean—that they will be armed with "accurate multiple warheads." So we are proposing to bargain our ABM's against their MRV's instead of negotiating ABM's against ABM's and MIRV's against MIRV's to put a stop to both monstrous developments. (MRV's are multiple warheads; MIRV's are multiple *and* independently targeted.)

This slick stance becomes clearer in the next sentence— "Even more favorable reductions in the Soviet offensive and defensive threat could be matched by further restraints in our ABM deployment." There is no indication of any readiness to put our own MRV's and MIRV's on the table, nor even to go beyond "further restraints" in our ABM deployment.

The Administration's negotiating position on MRV's and MIRV's is less clear. But there are clues in an article Harold Brown, former Secretary of the Air Force, wrote in *Foreign Affairs* last April. Brown is one of six men picked for the negotiating team in the SALT talks. Brown is regarded as the most dovish of the six, and Brown is not much of a dove, as we shall see. The others are Major General Royal B. Allison, former arms control specialist for the Joint Chiefs of Staff; Paul H. Nitze, a Dean Acheson hard-liner from way back, Deputy Secretary of Defense under Johnson, more recently picked by the new Pentagon team as "consultant" to prepare for the new talks; Llewellyn Thompson, former Ambassador to Moscow; and two standard-model State Department types who were once assistants to John Foster Dulles—Gerard C. Smith, now head of the Arms Control and Disarmament Agency and Philip J. Farley, deputy assistant Secretary of State for political-military affairs.

At first glance Brown's article seems to be in favor of arms control, but reading it closely one can see that it is for arms control *after* and not before the construction of anti-ballistic missiles and the deployment of multiple warheads on each side. If this is to be the position of the Nixon Administration, then the effect of new arms talks—even if successful—would be *to initiate rather than prevent a new spiral in the arms race.*

Insofar as ABM is concerned, Brown says a limit of 100 would be enough protection against "small accidental strikes" but 1,000 would be "much more satisfactory . . . against third-country attacks." He admits that 1,000 "might begin to threaten the stability of the U.S.-Soviet deterrence, since it might give the attacker the capacity to eliminate most of the retaliatory weapons that would survive a first strike employing improved MIRV technology." Brown then suggests a limit of several hundred launchers for city defense "as opposed to missile site defense," for which he gives no concrete number. So this envisages city defense *as well as* missile site ABM's, though not as many as 1,000 altogether. An agreement on these lines would thus open and vastly enlarge this new ABM sector of the arms race.

Insofar as MIRV is concerned, Brown at first seems to be against its deployment. "Clearly," he writes, "an agreement to ban the deployment of MIRV's would be desirable to forestall erosion of the capability to deter." But this soon begins to blur. For Brown goes on to say, "But the agreement *should* allow multiple re-entry vehicles that are *not* capable of being individually guided." The italics are Brown's. But then Brown admits by implication that once we move into multiple warheads it is difficult if not impossible to tell by aerial surveillance how many there are atop each missile and whether they are independently guided or not. As Brown says, "Unfortunately a check on deployment of different types of payload clearly requires on-site inspection of a very obtrusive kind." A "very obtrusive kind" is presumably the kind we, as well as the Russians, would object to.

The one clear answer to this problem is to negotiate an agreement banning both MRV's and MIRV's while there is still time to prevent this new and destabilizing development. Brown suggests instead a murky compromise. "It is possible," he suggests, "that even without on-site inspection we can tell enough about each other's missiles to obtain reasonable assurance." He says, "This is so because the probable number of warheads per missile is proportionate to the payload of the missile, and payload, in turn, is directly related to the gross volume, which we may be able to determine unilaterally," i.e., by aerial reconnaissance.[1]

"Thus," Brown goes on, "a ceiling on numbers and sizes of missiles could also limit MIRV's to a number less than that needed for an effective first strike, *and yet permit enough re-entry vehicles to penetrate missile defenses*—as required for deterrence" (my italics). If we need multiple warheads to overcome ABM, why not negotiate an agreement to deploy neither?

Brown's further suggestions admit that once ABM's and MRV's are allowed, policing such an agreement would be difficult. He says we would not only need an agreement to limit the number of ABM's and missiles but "to ban com-

[1] For a startling revelation of how much we can now learn by aerial reconnaissance see Jeremy J. Stone's chapter, "Can The Communists Deceive Us?," in the symposium on the ABM edited by Abram Chayes and Jerome B. Weisner.

pletely any mobile land-based missiles, since they would make it easier to conceal illicit increases in a missile force." Once the horse was stolen, any number of locks would be needed for the stable door. "A subsequent agreement," Brown continues, "should then be worked out to limit the size of missiles and thus prevent the *unlimited growth* of the MIRV threat through development of larger and larger missiles" (my italics). But even this is not enough because, as Brown writes—

All deterrence systems tend to obsolesce. Thus, the increasing accuracy and miniaturization of missile warheads reduce the survivability of missiles in silos; improved antisubmarine warfare techniques have the same effect upon Polaris; improved FOBS or submarine-launched missiles lessen the effectiveness of the bomber; and new ABM or anti-aircraft techniques might seriously affect weapons penetration—all without an increase in the quantity of weapons.

This opens the prospect of an endless arms race in quality if not quantity once ABM and MIRV are accepted. To meet the menace of perpetual improvement, Brown adds another rickety device to his Rube Goldbergian arms control structure. "In order to attain a lasting treaty," he writes, "we might need an understanding on exactly what sort of improvements would or would not be allowed." This in turn would "also require some form of relatively simple on-site inspection to ensure compliance." The inspectors would have no easy time of it. For Brown would design the treaty limits "to control the first-strike threat," but he says they "should not inhibit the countermeasures which must be taken against gradual improvements in the other side's forces or against illicit improvements." Finally Brown admits that "the problem is complicated by the fine line between first-strike and second-strike capabilities." No wonder we are already being told cheerfully in backgrounders from the Pentagon that the negotiations might take years! How achieve stability once you embark—as Brown would have us embark—on two such destabilizing developments as ABM and MIRV?

There is a hidden ploy in the recesses of this negotiating position. An agreement to limit the number and size of missiles would freeze U.S. superiority. We are ahead of the Russians in miniaturization and accuracy of warheads as well as in the development of MRV and MIRV. The MRV's in clusters of three are already deployed in Polaris A3 missiles, possibly even in Minuteman III, though the latter is not certain. We have already budgeted $2 billion for the coming fiscal year to deploy Poseidon and Minuteman III, both MIRVed. The Russians have only tested cluster MRV's. We began to deploy MRV's in Polaris as far back as 1966. Thus the Russians, in accepting an agreement of this kind, would have to settle for a position of inferiority in which the U.S. might achieve a first-strike capacity without violating any of the various agreements set forth by Brown. After all, we are putting 10 or more warheads in each Polaris submarine with Poseidon and three or more in each Minuteman without any significant increase in the size of the missile and no increase in their numbers. These MIRV's will soon increase our capacity to the point where the Soviets would have reason to fear a first strike.

Such corkscrew negotiating positions, almost certain to ensure failure and thus excuse a further surge in the arms race, suits the solidly Goldwaterite chain of command which will oversee the talks for the Pentagon. The new Deputy Secretary of Defense for Policy Planning and Arms Control is Dr. Yuan-li Wu, originally a refugee from Communist China, more recently a scholar at that cold war citadel, the Hoover Institute of War and Revolution at Stanford. Goldwater welcomed the appointment in a Senate speech June 5 and attended Dr. Wu's swearing in, where the Senator found himself among old friends. Dr. Wu's superior is Dr. G. Warren Nutter, the new Assistant Secretary of State for International Security Affairs. The ISA is the Pentagon's own little State Department and Dr. Nutter has been described (by Karl Hess, Goldwater's famous ghost writer) as "the anchor man" of Goldwater's "think tank team" in 1964. And Nutter's superior, of course, is

Secretary of Defense Laird, who presided over the writing
of Goldwater's platform in 1964, and whose inflammatory
campaign for the ABM is hardly calculated to make the
Russians feel they are dealing with an Administration soberly and sincerely anxious for arms talks and détente.

This sour impression will not be corrected by the political complexion of the General Advisory Committee Nixon
has just appointed to the Arms Control and Disarmament
Agency. The most prominent appointee is Dean Rusk,
whom Nixon greatly admires; no Secretary of State ever
cared less about disarmament. The most disquieting appointee is that same William J. Casey, the lawyer-public relations man who is chairman of the Citizens Committee for
Peace with Security which was organized out of the White
House basement and has already distinguished itself by a
highly dubious poll showing 84 percent—why not 99 percent?—of the American people in favor of the ABM. There
is not one strong voice for disarmament on the advisory
committee; the doves are weak, the hawks are strong. This
should be no surprise. A President who wanted Senator
Jackson as Secretary of Defense and settled for Laird, and
whose most influential mentor seems to be Major General
Strom Thurmond, is not likely to negotiate an end to the
arms race.

July 14, 1969

A CENTURY OF FUTILITY

For almost a century and a half there has been agitation for
disarmament. For almost a century there have been few
years in which disarmament of one kind or another has not
been under negotiation. During those tumultuous years
every other movement for social reform has made striking
progress. It has been a century of futility for the struggle

against the arms race. As the strategic arms limitation talks (SALT) open in Vienna, it is time to cast up this account and ask why.

It was not for lack of understanding or of leadership. The principal arguments we make against the arms race today are the same as those that thoughtful men have used for more than a century. That it raises tension, but it does not change the balance of power but only the level of destructiveness and cost, that it wastes resources needed for social reconstruction—these arguments were as familiar in the nineteenth as in the twentieth century, and proved as futile.

The guns of Waterloo had hardly fallen silent before the first peace societies began to urge disarmament in Britain and America. The Napoleonic Wars, like the two world wars, had a sobering effect, but then as later this soon wore off. "What is the advantage of one power greatly increasing its army and navy?" the British Prime Minister, Sir Robert Peel, asked in a once-famous speech against the arms race in 1841. "Does it not see that if it proposes such increases for self-protection and defense, the other powers would follow its example?" The consequence, he went on, is "no increase of relative strength" but only "a universal consumption of the resources of every country in military preparations." One hundred and twenty-eight years later, Secretary of State Rogers made exactly the same appeal in his speech last November as the preparatory SALT talks were about to begin in Helsinki:

Competitive accumulation of more sophisticated weapons would not add to the basic security of either side. Militarily it probably would produce little or no net advantage. Economically it would divert resources needed elsewhere. Politically it woud perpetuate the tensions and fears that are the social fall-out of the nuclear arms race.

In the intervening years, only the level of danger and of cost has changed. But these have grown enormously.

The United States, the most powerful nation of the twentieth century, is repeating the experience of Britain, the most powerful nation of the nineteenth. Despite the H-bomb and the ICBM, a British Victorian statesman would find himself quite at home in our current debate over arms policy. The industrialization of war and the growing militarization of industry, which we now call the military-industrial complex, began in England in the middle of the last century. To dip back into the history of armament agitation before World War I is to experience a strong feeling of *déjà vu*.[1] Then as now we see the defeat of reason over and over again by the same alliance of primitive instinct, private interest, and technological momentum, in a world without law.

The most powerful and the most respected political leaders of the time were unable to prevail over this still irresistible combination. The most extraordinary manifesto against the arms race was issued in 1857, when the two great rivals of nineteenth-century British politics, Disraeli and Gladstone, joined Lord John Russell and Richard Cobden, the century's foremost advocate of disarmament, in an appeal for a reduction in military expenditures. These had soared in the just-ended Crimean War. All their popularity and influence, however, could not keep Parliament that very year from raising naval appropriations 50 percent above prewar levels. On two occasions statesmen of the first rank —one Tory, one Liberal—resigned from high office in equally impotent protest against rising arms expenditures: Lord Randolph Churchill (Sir Winston's father) as Chancellor of the Exchequer in 1886, and Gladstone as Prime Minister in 1892, after a false war alarm led Parliament to more than double the Admiralty budget.

Such heroic resignations have yet to occur in our time. In all else armament politics remain substantially the same: the hopes and fears, the contending principles in which they are

---

[1] For the period to 1907 the best account I have come across, and to which I am indebted, is Merze Tate's *The Disarmament Illusion*, published by Macmillan and Harvard in 1942, long out of print but soon to be reissued by Russell & Russell, which has just republished her later book, *The US and Armaments* (Harvard, 1948), on which I have also relied. Miss Tate is a professor of history at Howard University.

rationalized, even the tactics and the cast of characters. Nineteenth-century Britain had its "gaps" and its Joe Alsops, too. Recurrent appeals to lift the burden of armament and divert the funds to eradicate slums and other social evils were countered with recurrent panics about enemy buildups. In these the British Admiralty, the shipbuilders, and the gunpowder manufacturers played a hidden part, making use of frenetic newspapermen in their orbit of influence, as the Air Force lobby with the aviation, electronics, and shipbuilding industries do today. Antiwar political leaders and journalists exposed these scares then as now, but with no permanent effect.

The strongest and safest country in the world, and the one with the largest navy, was a victim of the worst invasion nightmares, just as today the strongest nation on earth seems to spend more time than any other worrying about its security. There were six "panics" between 1847 and 1892, all fomented for their beneficial effect in boosting military and naval expenditures. The earliest exposé of these hobgoblins was Richard Cobden's *Three Panics* (third ed., 1862). The last, on the eve of World War I, was *The Six Panics* (1913), by F. W. Hirst, then editor of *The Economist*. They still make instructive reading.

These panics illustrate the tactic, still in use today, of projecting some fantastic possibility and treating it as if it were a reality. The earliest precursor of our latest equivalent, the Nixon-Laird scare about the Soviet SS-9, was the panic created by Lord Palmerston and the Duke of Wellington in 1847 when they seized on some dockyard expansion in France to picture England in danger of what we would now call a "first strike." Palmerston insisted that the shift to steam navigation had "thrown a bridge across the Channel," suddenly filling the ancient moat which had so long protected England from invasion. The seventy-seven-year-old Duke of Wellington, then doddering, said 50,000 men could be moved across this bridge undetected in a single night from Cherbourg and make a surprise attack on London the next morning! This "bridge of steam" was the first of many graphic but wholly fallacious metaphors which have supplied the melodrama for armament scares ever since.

Experts were mobilized by the peace forces to explain away and to ridicule these fears, as patiently as a psychiatrist trying to deal with a paranoid patient, or a present-day anti-ABM scientist from MIT disentangling fact from fancy in one of Laird's latest. Of the six synthetic panics between 1847 and 1892, the first five were aimed at France, the last at Germany, which after 1870 replaced France as The Enemy. Sir William Harcourt, who tried unsuccessfully to stem the panic of 1892 as Chancellor of the Exchequer, summed up the techniques still in use today. "The principle of the alarmists," he said, "is to pile up every conceivable contingency, probable or improbable, on one side and to admit no possible contingency on the other."

Then as now no level of preparation was enough to satisfy the military. "If you believe the doctors," Lord Salisbury said of these ever-more-costly apprehensions, "nothing is wholesome; if you believe the theologians, nothing is innocent; if you believe the soldiers, nothing is safe." So it is now, when weapons systems like Minuteman are sold to us as marvels of invulnerability one day and declared the next to be so weak as to be in peril of instant destruction. However egregiously mistaken the generals and admirals have proven in a century of warfare, they have never failed to earn their medals for salesmanship.

Alfred Vagts, to whose solid and passionate *History of Militarism* I owe these quotations from Lord Salisbury and Sir William Harcourt,[2] tells us how these tactics spread to the parliamentary politics of the Continent. What he says of Western Europe in the half-century before World War I applies as well to our presidential campaigns since World War II. "Either allied with the bureaucracy or on its own motion," he writes, "the party in opposition often produced

[2] Lord Salisbury is quoted on p. 362 and Sir William on p. 364 of Vagts, *A History of Militarism, Civilian and Military* (Meridian, rev. ed., 1959), which deserves a better fate than the remainder counter on which I found it.

an alarm by accusing the party in power of neglecting the country's defenses." These were the tactics of the Democratic party's alarms about a Bomber Gap in 1956 and a Missile Gap in 1960, and of Nixon's about a Security Gap in 1968. Their precursors were the Battleship Gaps fomented by Navy leagues in Britain and Germany before 1914. Their assiduity in exaggerating the other side's naval strength and in publicizing every aggressive statement on the other side, however obscure or unrepresentative its source, played a major role in bringing on World War I. Their counterparts today could push us down the slope to World War III.

In an effort to reverse the tide before World War I, the first international disarmament conference was held at The Hague in 1899 and a second in 1907. The military and their allies quickly developed the expertise to frustrate them. Both conferences were called on the initiative of the Czar, and this gave hostile propaganda an opportunity along lines which have a quite contemporary ring. The Russian proposal was portrayed as a plot to undermine the security of Western Europe, or alternatively as an effort to halt arms competition in the West in order to free Russian energies for further expansion in Asia at the expense of China.

When the Russian Foreign Ministry proposed to forbid the development of more powerful explosives, Secretary of State John Hay objected that this would restrain "the inventive genius of our people." [3] As a brake on pacifist enthusiasm, Captain Alfred T. Mahan, whose *Influence of Seapower Upon History* was the Bible of American imperialism, was named to the U.S. delegation. When the Czar proposed an agreement to abstain from the use of "asphyxiating or deleterious gases," Captain Mahan argued as a cheerful old salt that it was no more cruel to asphyxiate

[3] Similarly a French admiral at the Washington Naval Conference in 1921 defended the continued use of submarines by saying, "You could not stop the progress of humanity" (Vagts, p. 403).

one's enemies than to drown them by torpedoing a vessel.[4] Present-day advocates of chemical and bacteriological weapons speak with the same tender impartiality.

Though the first Hague Conference succeeded in setting up the International Court of Arbitration, and the second reached an agreement against the use of poison gas in time to be broken in World War I, both managed to avoid even a weapons freeze, much less arms reduction. "All the great powers," Miss Merze Tate wrote in her authoritative *US and Armaments*, "considered the Czar's proposals troublesome, but felt that they had to express their attitudes cautiously in view of the pacific tenor of public opinion." [5] In the private sessions Captain Mahan said "his government will on no account even discuss the creation of any limitation of naval armaments" since the U.S. needed a larger navy "in the struggle for Chinese markets." [6]

Loftier considerations were invoked publicly against the popular cry for arms reduction. Teddy Roosevelt, a skeptical and unwilling participant in the 1907 conference, cautioned that venerable liberal, Carl Schurz, a leader of the disarmament movement, that peace must be "second to righteousness"—quite in the manner a half-century later of that secular parson of the cold war, John Foster Dulles. At the second conference the delegates managed, by tacit agreement, a triumph of diplomacy. They succeeded in limiting discussion of disarmament to twenty-five minutes and their only action to passage of a resolution declaring that because arms expenditures had risen considerably since the first Hague conference, it was "eminently desirable that the governments should resume the serious examination of this question." This was adopted by unanimous acclamation.[7]

After these arduous efforts the conference, before adjourning, resolved to meet again in seven years. The out-

[4] Tate, *US and Armaments*, p. 43.
[5] *Ibid.*, p. 44.
[6] Tate, *Disarmament Illusion*, p. 292.
[7] Tate, *US and Armaments*, p. 58.

break of war in 1914 made a repetition of the comedy unnecessary. Yet the war itself, the long stalemate in the
muddy trenches, and the unprecedented butchery seemed
at last to promise the triumph of disarmament when the war
was over. As early as 1915 a consensus began to appear,
ranging from the Socialist movement to men in power like
Sir Edward Grey, that the arms race had been a major cause
of the war, and that disarmament was necessary if a new
war were to be avoided.

In January 1917, Woodrow Wilson in a special message
to the Senate termed this "the most immediately and intensely practical question" facing mankind, and said there
could be "no sense of safety" among nations if the arms
race continued. The fourth of his famous Fourteen Points
for peace specified "that national armaments will be reduced to the lowest point consistent with domestic safety,"
i.e., to what was needed for internal order. A League of
Nations was to create a framework of enforceable world
law for the settlement of international disputes. To prevent
the machinations of the munitions makers, which played so
malevolent a role in the prewar arms race, Wilson's first
draft for the Convenant of the League also provided "that
munitions and implements of war shall not be manufactured
by private enterprise."

But as the war drew to a close, these brave beginnings
soon turned into another comedy on a grander scale. In the
Paris peace negotiations the phrase about reducing armament
to the lowest point consistent with "domestic safety" was
changed to "national safety," which made it meaningless
and opened the door to a new arms race. The British Admiralty—loyal to the shipbuilding and armorplate industries—
led the objections to abolishing private manufacture of arms.
Article 8 of the Covenant was diluted to read that members of the League agreed "that manufacture by private
enterprise of munitions and implements of war is open to
grave objection." Therefore the Council of the League was
to "advise how the evil effect attendant upon such manufacture can be prevented," but with "due regard" for "the

necessities of those members of the League which are not
able to manufacture" the war materials "necessary for their
safety." It would take a Swift or a Voltaire to match such
splendid satire.

The price was the resurgence of a militaristic Germany
and World War II. The disarmament of Germany was predicated on general disarmament by the victors. "In order to
render possible the initiation of a general limitation of the
armaments of all nations," the Treaty of Versailles said,
"Germany undertakes strictly to observe the military, naval
and air clauses which follow." While German power was
sharply cut back, negotiations for general disarmament proceeded at a pace which exasperatingly recalled one of the
Eleatic paradoxes that deny the reality of motion. Negotiations seemed to be moving—for one could see the experts
rustling papers and watch the documentation piling up in
the League archives—but when one looked again, the
crowded train seemed still to be in the station.

In 1920 the League set up a Permanent Advisory Commission to which each member of the Council named an
Army, Navy, and Air officer. These soon created a technical thicket calculated to keep exploratory discussions running around in circles. It took six more years before the
Conference for the Reduction and Limitation of Armaments finally convened in Geneva in February, 1932. The
day it met the Japanese bombardment of Shanghai was already signaling the breakdown of the postwar order. To
this conference, President Herbert Hoover—for once sub-
limely quixotic—proposed the abolition of tanks, chemical
warfare, and aerial bombardment. But though the smaller
countries applauded, England and France would not support what now appears as a last wan hope. Within a few
months Hitler had come to power and begun the rearmament of Germany in preparation for World War II.

German rancor and cynicism over the failure of the other
great powers to keep their promises to disarm were ingredi-

ents in the witch's brew of National Socialism. In justice to the German people, it must not be forgotten that despite the terrible inflation of 1923, the rankling inequality imposed by Versailles, and the world depression, they never gave Hitler a majority in a free election. Had there been general disarmament in the early twenties, had the Powers then proceeded to set up the machinery of military and economic sanctions the League Covenant envisaged for the punishment of any international lawbreaker, the Weimar Republic might have survived and World War II been avoided. Who has imagination enough to grasp the magnitude of the suffering which might never have happened *if . . . ?*

Will the same heartbreaking question some day be asked about the pledges made by the two nuclear superpowers in the Nuclear Non-Proliferation Pact? Will the fanfare with which it has just been ratified in Washington, London, and Moscow some day appear to have been another bit of sour "theater"? Will a parallel some day be drawn with the disarmament pledges of the Versailles Treaty? Will it be said that some new monster like Hitler might never have arisen, that World War III might never have occurred, if the United States and the Soviet Union had fulfilled the pledge they gave *unwillingly* in Article VI of the Non-Proliferation Pact? Article VI says—and every word should be read carefully—

Each of the parties to the Treaty undertakes to pursue negotiations in good faith on effective measures relating to cessation of the nuclear-arms race at an early date and to nuclear disarmament, and on a Treaty on general and complete disarmament under strict and effective international control.

This Article VI was put into the treaty at the insistence of the non-nuclear powers. It was not in the drafts submitted by the two nuclear superpowers. Those contained similar pledges but only in the preamble. Perhaps the non-nuclear powers recalled that the pledge of general disarmament in the Versailles Pact was also in a preamble, and the jurists held that preambles did not embody specific obligations. "One of the most attractive features of this much maligned class of experts," Salvador de Madariaga once wrote of this quibbling over the 1919 disarmament pledges, was "their natural tendency to put a minimum value on their own words." [8] The non-nuclear powers are as cynical about the NNPP as the Germans were about Versailles. When the U.S. and Soviet drafts were first presented to the eighteen-nation disarmament conference in Geneva in 1965, the UAR delegate commented caustically that a non-proliferation treaty should do more than "bless and perpetuate the nuclear monopoly and supremacy of the five Powers which possess the bomb." M. Messmer, the French Defense Minister, said with cruel but precise wit that it was aimed merely to castrate the impotent. [9]

While most of the nations of the earth have signed the pact (the count was 97 as this went to press) and half of them (49 at last count) had ratified it, the half-dozen non-nuclear powers within reach of achieving the bomb on their own are delaying signature or ratification until they see in the SALT talks whether Article VI is to be—in a once-famous phrase of sinister history—another scrap of paper. Their cynicism is not allayed by the recollection that almost nine years ago the U.S. and the USSR in a joint report to the United Nations General Assembly on the result of the McCloy-Zorin negotiations had already pledged themselves to general and complete disarmament down to only enough non-nuclear forces sufficient "to maintain internal order" and "provide agreed manpower for a UN peace force," words which recall Wilson's original proposals. The McCloy-Zorin agreement today is as vaguely remembered as the law tablets of Hammurabi.

---

8 Quoted in Tate, *US and Armaments*, p. 70.
9 Quoted in Elizabeth Young's Adelphi Paper, *The Control of Proliferation* (London: Institute for Strategic Studies, April 1969), pp. 6 and 11, respectively.

The amnesia of the superpowers is only matched by the prodigality of their pledges. Among other goodies the Mc-Cloy-Zorin agreement promised to bring down the nuclear chimney for Christmas were "disbanding of armed forces . . . [and] bases," cessation of arms production, "elimination of all stockpiles of nuclear, chemical, bacteriological and other weapons of mass destruction," and cessation of their production, "elimination of all means of delivery of weapons of mass destruction," abolition of military organizations and training, and "discontinuance of military expenditures." [10] One can only wonder how many bottles of vodka were consumed before these top-level negotiators signed on the dotted line for the millennium. The morning after, it was all forgotten! Obviously disarmament talks take place in a realm of discourse in which no words, however solemn and specific, can be taken seriously. Article 26 of the UN Charter adopted a quarter-century ago is as monumental a dead-letter. It provided that—

In order to promote the establishment and maintenance of international security with the least diversion for armaments of the world's human and economic resources, the Security Council shall be responsible for formulating, with the assistance of the Military Staff Committee referred to in Article 47, plans to be submitted to the Members of the United Nations for the establishment of the regulation of armaments.

This, too, has for all practical purposes vanished from memory.

The SALT talks will be the fourth, and possibly the last, real opportunity since World War II to bring the nuclear arms race under control.

April 9, 1970
New York Review

[10] *Facts on File*, 1961, p. 407.

THEATER OF DELUSION

The Strategic Arms Limitation Talks (SALT) now re-opening in Vienna may best be seen as the latest in a series of fumbling attempts by mankind to pick up the pieces in the wake of Hiroshima. A month after that first atomic bomb dropped, Einstein said what is still the last word of wisdom on the subject, though we are as far as ever from applying it. To a UPI reporter who tracked him down in a forest cabin near Lake Saranac, Einstein said "the only salvation for civilization and the human race" now lay in "the creation of a world government. As long as sovereign states continue to have separate armaments and armament secrets," he warned, "new world wars will be inevitable." [1]

This idea, like so much else in the repetitive and frustrating history of the struggle against the arms race in the last hundred years, was not new. It appeared at least as early as 1913, in a novel by H. G. Wells, *The World Set Free*. Wells predicted the splitting of the atom—by some stroke of luck or intuitive genius placing the event in 1933, when it actually occurred. He also forecast the use of nuclear energy in a world war so catastrophic it shook men and nations out of their accustomed habits and led them to form a world government as their only assurance henceforth of survival. [2]

[1] Otto Nathan and Heinz Norden, eds., *Einstein on Peace* (New York: Schocken, 1968), p. 336.

[2] In a recently published fragment of autobiography, the late Leo Szilard, discussing the origins of the atomic bomb, wrote of the impression made on him by the Wells novel. It is to the Szilard memoir in *The Intellectual Migration: Europe and America, 1930–1960* (edited by Donald Fleming and Bernard Bailyn, Belknap Press of Harvard University Press, 1969) that I owe my knowledge of Wells's prophetic book. Szilard first read the novel in Berlin in 1932 and thought of it again in London in September of the following year after hearing Lord Rutherford tell the British Association for the Advancement of Science it was "the merest moonshine" to look for sources of power on a commercial scale from nuclear fission!

For a fleeting moment, since forgotten, the dropping of the first bomb did push the American government in the direction of world government. The horrors of Hiroshima and then Nagasaki, the realization of what a third and nuclear world war would do to mankind, shocked American political leaders and scientists into a project whose novelty and magnitude began to be commensurate with the peril they foresaw. But the Baruch-Lilienthal-Acheson plan for the international control of atomic energy they then presented to the United Nations proved to be the first of four lost opportunities since the war to bring the nuclear monster under control; the SALT talks represent another chance, and I fear it too will be lost.

The Baruch plan, as put forward in 1946, would have set up a kind of world superstate for the nuclear age. Unfortunately the plan seems to have passed through three stages, in which the original idealistic impulse was successively revised to make it more "practical" politically. In the process it also grew less magnanimous. It ended up looking—from Moscow's point of view—like a plan for domination of the world and the economy of the Soviet Union by the United States, as Acheson now admits in a section of his newly published memoirs which has escaped attention.[3]

Dean Acheson, then Under Secretary of State, was chairman of a committee appointed by President Truman after the war to draw up a plan for the international control of atomic energy. This committee in turn set up a consultative group of scientists and big-business executives[4] under David E. Lilienthal and including J. Robert Oppenheimer. The

[3] I was struck by it because I made a similar criticism of the plan when it was first presented a quarter century ago with no knowledge of the intramural misgivings and differences of which Acheson now provides a glimpse. I was then Washington editor of *The Nation*. See my three Washington letters in that publication: "Atomic Pie in The Sky" (April 6, 1946), "Atomic Report: Second Reading" (April 13, 1946), and "The McMahon Bill" (April 20, 1946). Lilienthal, because of his association with the TVA, was then a hero of the liberals and the left, and my colleagues were shocked that I should criticize a plan which bore his magic name.

[4] From New Jersey Bell Telephone, General Electric, and Monsanto Chemical, companies which had played key roles in the making of the bomb.

original sketch for a world authority to take over all sources of uranium and to control all nuclear production facilities came from the Lilienthal group.

This was at least twice revised before publication by the Acheson committee. The others on his comittee were General Leslie R. Groves, who headed the Manhattan Project which built the bomb; Dr. Vannevar Bush, who organized science for war in World War II; Dr. James B. Conant, then president of Harvard; and John J. McCloy, Assistant Secretary of War under Henry L. Stimson. Stimson recognized very early that the secret of the bomb would soon vanish and had best be shared while it might still be used to build a more stable world.

The main drawback in the original Acheson-Lilienthal plan was that it asked the Soviet Union and all other countries to hand over control of their uranium deposits and open themselves to geological survey at once in return for a promise at some unspecified future date to cease our own production of bombs and hand over their secret to an international authority—if Congress did not change its mind when the time came.

The hedges not only became more onerous but began to seem deliberate pitfalls by the time the plan was revised again by Bernard Baruch, whom Truman named in March, 1946, as U.S. representative on the United Nations Atomic Energy Commission. The group Baruch chose to work with him in revising the Acheson-Lilienthal plan for presentation to the UN contained neither liberals, idealists, nor scientists. It was the earliest official postwar collection of cold warriors: John Hancock of Lehman Brothers; Ferdinand Eberstadt, another Wall Street banker with strong military ties; Fred Searls of Newmont Mining, a concern of imperial dimensions and worldwide cartel connections; and Herbert Bayard Swope, the journalist who had become Baruch's personal public relations man.

The Baruch plan, as it became known when it was submitted to the UN, must have seemed to Moscow the blueprint for a world capitalist superstate in which the U.S.

would retain its atomic monopoly behind the façade of an international organization under U.S. control. In *Present at the Creation* (Norton, 1969), Acheson discloses publicly for the first time that he felt the plan as transformed by Baruch contained provisions "almost certain to wreck any possibility of Russian acceptance" because Moscow would see them "as an attempt to turn the United Nations into an alliance to support a U.S. threat of war against the USSR unless it ceased its efforts" to develop an atom bomb, too.[5]

Even the earlier pre-Baruch version would have been hard to sell a ruler of Stalin's ferocious suspicions and primitive Marxist views. The Baruch plan was enough to have frightened off even a gentle Menshevik. It would have eliminated the veto in the UN Security Council to assure, in Baruch's words, "swift and certain punishment" of any violator. It would have thrown the war-torn and terribly weakened Soviet Union open to Western inspection, and at the mercy of a U.S.-led majority in the Security Council. Baruch was no fool and he knew the Russians well. His rhetoric in presenting the plan matched the occasion. The choice, he told the UN, is "world peace or world destruction." But his draftsmanship ensured a Russian *nyet*. So the first opportunity was lost.

In retrospect the failure transcends the personalities who took part. Mankind just was not ready. The U.S. was not generous enough. The Soviet Union was not trusting enough. If the roles had been reversed, it is hard to believe that the Russian regime, self-righteously Communist and deeply nationalistic, would even have made the gesture. If the view from the Kremlin had been of a war-wrecked U.S.A., their hard-liners would have dismissed such idealism as weakness and seized the opportunity (as our hard-liners did) for an attempt at world domination. Even if the U.S. had been more generous, the Soviets would have been too mistrustful. Even if Russia had not been Communist, even if it had been a capitalist ally, the realities of domestic politics would still have kept the American government from being

[5] p. 155.

magnanimous enough to relinquish the atomic secret without attaching strings intended to maintain its control.

The proof of this lies in our nuclear relations with our closest ally, Britain. The production of the world's first atomic weapons was a joint Anglo-American achievement. But by 1945 Britain found itself excluded from information and control despite specific Roosevelt-Churchill agreements for sharing them. Britain was forced to go it alone at Harwell and produce its nuclear weapons on its own. In April, 1946 (two months before the Baruch plan was presented to the UN) Congress went a step further and in the McMahon Act forbade the sharing of atomic secrets with Britain or any other nation.[6] Nations and men as the last war ended just had not reached the necessary stage of understanding. Wells, if he were still alive, might have said that the shock of atom bombs falling on two cities was not enough. In his novel, men came to their senses only after an all-out nuclear war had destroyed every city on earth.

After each lost opportunity for nuclear disarmament since the war, a new monster of destruction has been born. When the Baruch plan failed, there was only the A-bomb. It had been dwarfed by the H-bomb when the second lost opportunity arrived almost a decade later. This was what Philip Noel-Baker, the grand old man of the world disarmament movement, still active in his eighties, called "The Moment of Hope: May 10, 1955."[7] On that date Moscow made a dramatic about-face at the UN disarmament subcommittee meeting in London and substantially accepted

[6] This was most recently recalled in The Adelphi Paper, *The Control of Proliferation*, by Elizabeth Young (*op. cit.*).

[7] In his indispensable book, *The Arms Race* (New York: Oceana Publications, 1959). As a Labour MP and British delegate Noel-Baker has been a figure at most of the disarmament conferences since World War I. Among his earlier books, which deserve the attention of a new generation, the most important is *The Private Manufacture of Armaments* (1937), the most complete account of the intrigues of what we now term the military-industrial complex before and after World War I. It has long been out of print, and should be made available again.

Western proposals for general and nuclear disarmament it had long derided. It offered to lift the Iron Curtain and permit international inspection on a wide scale as part of that scheme, only to have the West suddenly lose interest.

The proposals of May 10, 1955, were part of a larger reversal in Russian policy which followed the accession of Khrushchev to power in February of that year and the confidence generated by successful detonation of a Soviet H-bomb. The Soviet disarmament proposals in London were the second of three dramatic about-faces in Soviet foreign policy in the space of little more than one month. The first was the announcement on April 15 that the Russians, after nine years of fruitless negotiation by the West, had agreed to withdraw their troops from Austria and to sign a four-power pact guaranteeing its independence. The third was the arrival of Khrushchev and Bulganin at Belgrade airport on May 26, where Tito impassively heard them declare that they "sincerely regret" Stalin's efforts to overthrow him. This Canossa was the most dramatic manifestation of the new regime's eagerness for a fresh start in foreign policy.

The May 10 disarmament statement was as big a surprise. For years the West had complained that the Soviet Union's disarmament proposals would "ban the bomb" but deny inspection and maintain its superiority in conventional arms. The Western powers were for "total prohibition" of nuclear arms but insisted that it had to be accompanied (1) by reduction of the conventional armies of the U.S., the USSR, and China to a figure between one and one-and-one-half million men and those of Britain and France to about 650,000, and (2) by "the establishment of a control organ" with powers "adequate to guarantee the effective observance of the agreed prohibitions and reductions." [8]

On May 10, 1955, the Russians tabled a draft treaty accepting the West's ceilings on the size of conventional armies, its proposed cut-off by stages in the production and stocks of all "weapons of mass destruction," and the estab-

[8] From the Anglo-French memorandums of June 11, 1954 and March 29, 1955, quoted on pages 15 and 18 of Noel-Baker's *The Arms Race*.

lishment of an international control organ. This organ, in
the Soviet draft treaty, would have had a staff of internationally recruited inspectors residing permanently in all sig-
natory states. The inspectors would have had "within the
bounds of the control functions they exercise, unimpeded
access at all times to all objects of control." They would
also have had "unimpeded access to records relating to the
budgetary appropriations of States for military needs," and
the "rights and powers to exercise control, including inspection on a continuing basis, to the extent necessary to
ensure implementation of the above-mentioned Convention." [9] The Russians added a new proposal of their own:
the establishment of "Control Posts" at large ports, at railway junctions, on main motor highways, and at air fields to
guard against the danger of surprise attack.

The Western delegates in London were startled. M. Jules
Moch for France said, "The whole thing looks too good to
be true." The U.S. delegate to the disarmament talks declared himself "gratified to find that the concepts which we
have put forward over a considerable length of time, and

[9] Conventional Western writers on disarmament and standard Western
news compilations like *Keesing's* in London, our own *Facts on File*, and
even the new *Yearbook of World Armaments and Disarmament* issued by
the Stockholm International Peace Research Institute (compare its feeble
account on p. 152 with Noel-Baker's and the new material presented in
this article) have all joined in brushing this draft treaty and the moment
of hope it represented under the rug as if not in accordance with the
Western "party-line" on disarmament, much as historians do in the Soviet
Union with matters which run counter to theirs.

The text is hard to come by. Noel-Baker quotes it from Cmd. [British
parliamentary "command papers"] 9639, pp. 33–42. For those who do
not have access (as I didn't) to this British document in the famous series
issued by HMS Stationery Office, the full text is also available as Document 89, p. 382, of *Disarmament and Security: A Collection of Documents, 1919–1955* published sixteen years ago by the Senate Foreign Relations Committee subcommittee on disarmament "pursuant to Sen. Res.
93, and Continued by Sen. Res. 185, 84th Congress," U.S. Government
Printing Office, 1956, now very rare but invaluable.

If I may be pardoned a personal note, I had the joy of finding it while
working on this article after a frantic search through a small mountain
of documents in my garage. A new generation of revisionist historians
may also be interested in an immediate contemporary reaction to the
May 10, 1955, draft treaty, "Russia Offers to Lift Its Iron Curtain for
Peace," in the May 16, 1955, issue of my weekly newsletter.

which we have repeated many times during the past two months, have been accepted in a large measure by the Soviet Union." The British delegate said he was glad the Western "policy of patience" had "now achieved this welcome dividend" and that the Western proposals "have now been largely, and in some cases entirely, adopted by the Soviet Union." [10] Even John Robinson Beal's official biography of John Foster Dulles, which is as slick and corkscrew as its subject was, admitted that "the new Soviet proposals actually were plagiarized from the French and British and *were by no means acceptable,* but for the first time there were signs of Russian movement"! [11] (The exclamation point and the italics are added.)

But Washington was curiously unmoved. The State Department, which knows how to orchestrate the press, played the news down, and so did the news media. The day after the news from London the President was asked about it at a press conference by Walter Kerr of the New York *Herald Tribune.* The colloquy was less than jubilant:

Q: Mr. President, I wonder if you have had an opportunity to see a report on the latest Soviet disarmament plan.

THE PRESIDENT: On what?

Q: On what has been described as the recent Soviet disarmament plan submitted to the summit.

THE PRESIDENT: You mean the one submitted through the Disarmament Commission in London?

Q: Yes, sir.

THE PRESIDENT: Well, I have just had a chance to glance at it.

Q: Do you care to comment on it, sir?

THE PRESIDENT: No, not at the moment. The whole question is so confused. It has still some of the elements they have always had in it. They want to get rid of one kind; we would like to get rid of everything. It is something that has to be studied before you can really comment on it.[12]

---

[10] *The Arms Race,* pp..21–22. Citing Cmd. 9650, pp. 607 *et seq.,* where the subcommittee's discussion of the Russian proposal may be found.

[11] John Robinson Beal, *John Foster Dulles* (New York: Harper & Row, 1957), p. 298.

[12] *Public Papers of the Presidents, Eisenhower 1955,* pp. 497–8.

Not until his press conference of July 6 did Eisenhower give any indication of his thinking and then both the question and answer indicated that the American government was cooling off on its own proposals now that they were in danger—that seems to be the only word for it—of being turned into reality by the unexpected Soviet acceptance of them. This was the implication when Edward P. Morgan asked the President that day if he could give the press the benefit of his "personal thoughts" on the subject of disarmament. "For instance," Mr. Morgan prompted, "do you feel that we, the American people, are going to have to move away somewhat from the concept of total drastic disarmament toward a sort of standoff?" The question, I suspect, knowing how the State Department operates, reflected "backgrounders" downgrading the significance of the breakthrough in London.

Total "drastic" disarmament had been the declared goal of U.S. policy since the "Essential Principles for a Disarmament Program" had been tabled by the U.S. at the UN in April of 1952. Inspection, the U.S. had then and has since stressed, was the heart of the problem. But now Eisenhower wondered aloud whether we really wanted inspection. This was Eisenhower's answer to Mr. Morgan in that rambling but revealing way Eisenhower had of talking to the press:

I wouldn't want to have anything I now say taken as authoritative, for the simple reason that the more one studies intensively this problem of disarmament, the more he finds himself in a kind of squirrel's cage. . . . Everything comes back, as I see it, to acceptable methods of enforcement. How do you enforce such things? This brings us instantly to the question of examinations, of inspections. Now, one way to approach this problem is what would we, in the United States, [sic] suppose took a vote of this body today or we started as a committee of the whole to study it, what kind of inspection are we ready to accept? Are we ready to open up every one of our factories, every place where something might be going on that could be inimical to the interests of somebody else?[13]

13 Ibid., pp. 676–7.

Eisenhower did not complain—as he could have—that the Soviet proposals on inspection did not go far enough, that they did not define "objects of control" or more fully spell out the powers of the inspectors, or that they left enforcement unclear since the control organ presumably would operate under the UN Security Council where the Soviet Union had a veto. Instead, now that a workable system of inspection seemed within reach of negotiation, he was worrying about how much inspection *we* would stand for. It was now we who were suspicious of intrusion, fearful for our secrets, hesitating to lift our own "curtain." [14]

In London, where the Soviet delegation wanted to go on with the negotiations, the Western governments insisted on a recess. The debates were not resumed until August 29. After one week, the U.S. delegate Harold Stassen made a surprising announcement. He wiped the slate clean of all past U.S. proposals and freed his government from commitment to them:

The United States does now place a reservation upon all of its pre-Geneva substantive positions taken in this sub-committee on Disarmament or in the Disarmament Commission or in the UN on these questions in relationship to levels of armament.

In other words, as Noel-Baker points out, the manpower ceilings, the cut-off arrangements on nuclear stocks, "the detailed plan for inspection and control, all the other proposals urged with such vigor and persistence only three months before—all were withdrawn."

In the meantime, at the summit conference in Geneva on July 21, Eisenhower had come up with a wholly new plan that Nelson Rockefeller, always a cold warrior and never a

[14] Noel-Baker writes (*The Arms Race*, p. 545) that the mutual inspection safeguards later established by the West European Union treaty and Euratom, the West European Nuclear Energy agency, show that Western "General Staffs are still reluctant to accept the 'sacrifices' of sovereignty such inspection must involve" and cites as an example in a footnote a London *Times* report (Oct. 12, 1956) that "under the WEU system five days' notice must be given of any inspection, and that component parts of armament were excluded" from inspection. "These restrictions," Noel-Baker comments, "would make inspection a farce."

friend of disarmament, had helped to draw up, the so-called
"open skies" proposal.[15] Rockefeller was then Eisenhower's
Special Assistant for Cold War Strategy.[16] "I have been
searching my mind and heart," Eisenhower said as he unveiled the new plan at Geneva with more than a touch of
schmaltz, "for something that I could say here that could
convince everyone of the great sincerity of the U.S. in
approaching this problem of disarmament." [17]

It is indicative that he felt it necessary at that point to
prove U.S. sincerity. He then proposed to Bulganin and
Khrushchev that the U.S. and the USSR "give each other a
complete blueprint of our military establishments, from beginning to end" and "provide within our countries facilities
for aerial reconnaissance to the other country . . . where
you can make all the pictures you choose."

It is hard to believe that the same man who was so hesi-
tant on July 6 about the lesser measures of inspection proposed by the Russians was now sincerely ready two weeks
later to exchange "a complete blueprint" of all military establishments with them. The plan looked more like public
relations razzle-dazzle to cover a U.S. retreat on disarmament. It must have been put forward only because Washington was sure that Moscow would reject it. For years we
had accused the Russians of proposing disarmament without inspection. Now it looked as if we were proposing inspection without disarmament. Though it was presented as
a way to prevent surprise attack, it would obviously have
provided the Strategic Air Command with exactly the maps
its bombers needed. The response could not have been a
surprise. In his memoirs Eisenhower writes that Khrushchev rejected the "open skies" plan as "nothing more than a
bald espionage plot against the USSR." [18]

Though negotiations went on interminably, hope of an
agreement had disappeared. The U.S. line had so far reversed

15 Dwight D. Eisenhower, *Mandate for Change* (New York: Doubleday, 1963), p. 519.
16 *Ibid.*, p. 511.
17 *Facts on File*, 1955, p. 245.
18 *Mandate for Change*, p. 521.

itself that by May 4 of the following year (1956) Stassen was telling the UN disarmament subcommittee, "It is the U.S. view that low force levels and drastic reduction in armaments—even though carried out under an armaments agreement—would not, if they were not accompanied by progress in the settlement of the major political issues, be in the interest of any country represented at this subcommittee table. These reductions would increase the danger of the outbreak of war. . . ." [19] Arms reduction had become a menace to peace! The major political issue which is one key to the 1955 failure was the future of Germany. Washington wanted a reunified and rearmed Germany free to join the Western camp. The May 10 disarmament proposals would have ended the hope of this by liquidating both the NATO and Warsaw pacts with their forward bases and paving the way for a Germany that would be reunited but neutral ("the Austrian solution") and with limited military forces.

One crucial date must not be forgotten. Five days before the dramatic Soviet about-face on disarmament, West Germany had joined NATO. Today the Bonn Federal Republic has 460,000 men under arms, NATO's largest European contingent. If the Western proposals for ceilings on conventional armies had been put into effect after their acceptance by the Soviet Union, West Germany would not have been allowed to mobilize anywhere near that number of men.

It is May 5 that explains May 10. Germany was to be our main military bulwark in Europe, as we now hope to make Japan our main military bulwark in Asia. German rearmament was the stumbling block to general disarmament. But it is hard to avoid the conclusion that even if there had been no German problem, some other excuse would have been found to keep the arms race going. Not until Kennedy took office was there another real chance to bring it under control, and by that time a new monster had made its appearance, the Intercontinental Ballistic Missile,

[19] *The Arms Race*, p. 23.

able to carry an H-bomb warhead in thirty minutes in either direction between the U.S. and the USSR.

The opportunity at the beginning of the Kennedy Administration for a fresh start in curbing the nuclear arms race was not so dramatic as the Baruch plan or the May 10, 1955 Soviet draft treaty, but was nevertheless substantial. It was lost, and while it was lost two new monsters were secretly being gestated, the ABM and the MIRV, the latter a new ICBM with multiple heads like some terrifying Hindu god of destruction.

Basically the opportunity was missed because Kennedy as president, like Kennedy as senator and as candidate, tried to ride two horses at once in two opposite directions, rearmament *and* disarmament. I can recall an occasion in the Senate when in the short space of one week he made two speeches, one idealistic and eloquent on the need to end the arms race, the other alarmist on the need to fill that nonexistent missile gap. This might have been fallacious logic but it was—as they say—practical politics. It served to keep his lines open to two antagonistic constituencies, the powerful armament makers with their allies in the military bureaucracy, and a public increasingly anxious about the mounting cost and danger.

In justice to John F. Kennedy it must be said that the effort to please both at once was characteristic of all the great powers before World War I, as it has been of every U.S. administration since World War II. This was the trap that private interest, the sheer inertial mass of the military bureaucracy, and the ancient instincts of mankind had set, and in which we are still caught. The result has been to make disarmament negotiations nothing more than an exercise to disarm the public, while the arms race spirals ever upward.

A lovely sample of the Pied Piper rationalizations supplied by intellectuals in every generation for this ultimately suicidal political strategy may be found in the little book which Arthur Schlesinger, Jr., wrote for the 1960 campaign, *Kennedy or Nixon: Does It Make Any Difference?* [20] Schlesinger wrote that Kennedy promised "creative idealism," but Schlesinger's formulation of it in the sphere of disarmament only offered the same old glamorous but opportunistic rhetoric. "A new spirit arising within our nation," he wrote—

will lead to a reconstruction of our approach to foreign affairs. Instead of responding interminably to the initiatives of others, we will begin to take the initiative ourselves in the fight for a decent peace. Disarmament, instead of being an occupation for clerks, will receive the top priority it deserves in the conduct of our foreign affairs.

But, Schlesinger goes on, as if the Kennedy of the two faces were looking over his shoulder as he wrote—

Pending the establishment of a reliable disarmament system, of course we have no choice but to remove the existing gaps in our own defenses; *indeed, only by showing that we can stay in the arms race as long as they,* can we convince the Russians of the imperative need for arms control. But we will arm in order to disarm (my italics).

This was the same old Kennedy tactic. What greater nonsense than this idea that the richest nation on earth had to prove to a contender with less than half its resources that we could stay in the arms race as long as the Russians could? Every sophisticated observer knew that the insiders in Washington had long rationalized the arms race as a form of economic warfare, which—in wondrous asymmetry—kept them poor while it kept us rich, or at least that portion of us who drew benefits from arms production and research. To this day it has been a cardinal axiom of U.S. policy that by forcing the diversion of the Soviet's more limited natural resources, productive capacity, and skilled manpower from its enormous backlog of consumer needs to armament we were imposing burdens so heavy we could exact a political price for lifting them in arms negotiations.

[20] New York: Macmillan, 1960, p. 42.

It is enlightening to test Schlesinger's final proposition "we will arm to disarm"—the dialectic in the service of the arms race!—against his own later account, in *A Thousand Days*, of what happened behind the scenes in the new Administration. He writes[21] that "the Soviet Union watched the arrival of the new Administration with marked interest." Khrushchev "had given up on Eisenhower after the U-2 incident and the collapse of the Paris summit" in 1960 and had "seized several opportunities to semaphore his hopes for Kennedy." Khrushchev's "messages to Harriman and others after the election were followed by a Pugwash meeting on disarmament in Moscow in December." Walt Rostow and Jerome Wiesner were among the Americans who took part, and they saw V. V. Kuznetsov of the Soviet Foreign Office to urge the release of two American RB-47 fliers shot down over the Arctic. "In the course of their talk," Schlesinger's account reveals—

Kuznetsov mentioned the campaign furor about a "missile gap" and suggested that, if the new Administration went in for massive rearmament, it could not expect the Russians to sit still.

Both sides knew by then that what Schlesinger calls "the campaign furor" about a missile gap was a fake; this is indeed implicit in the disparaging phrase he chooses for it. What follows shows what spurious rationalizations intellectuals will indulge in when they take service with political leaders—

Rostow replied that any Kennedy rearmament would be designed to improve the stability of the deterrent, and that the Soviet Union should recognize this as in the interests of peace . . .

Kuznetsov must have felt that he was being taken, that he was dealing with a con man. Now let us return to Schlesinger's narrative—

. . . but Kuznetsov, *innocent of the higher calculus of deterrence as recently developed in the United States*, brusquely dismissed the explanation.

21 Houghton Mifflin, 1965, p. 301.

The italics are mine. They make the reader realize what a great humorist was lost when Schlesinger turned to history.

Here was the genesis of the stepped-up arms race in the sixties, from which the SALT talks are now supposed to deliver us. Here was the test of the proposition that we were only arming in order to disarm. When Schlesinger 200 pages later in his narrative comes to explain why the new Administration embarked on a huge missile buildup even though it knew there was no missile gap, he forgets this slick poppycock about "the higher calculus of deterrence." He gives us instead an intramural picture of decision-making which, despite its subtle court-historian apologetics, is immensely valuable. For it begins to uncover the real motivations and the real difficulties which have hampered every attempt to curb the arms race during the past century.

"There remained for a moment," Schlesinger begins his account of how Kennedy formulated his first budget, "the question of the 'missile gap.' Though disowned by McNamara in February, the gap had persisted as a center of intraservice argument, with the Air Force continuing to claim that the Russians had 600 to 800 ballistic missiles while the CIA estimated 450 and the Navy 200." [22] Schlesinger does not say so, but each service was, as usual, tailoring its intelligence estimates to support its own budgetary demands. The Air Force overestimated because it wanted more planes and missiles. The Navy set a low figure because it wanted more money for ships.

It is curious that Schlesinger does not give us the estimate Army intelligence put forward. General Maxwell Taylor, just retired as U.S. Army Chief of Staff, had been recalled to active service by Kennedy in July 1961 as "Presidential Military Adviser for foreign and military policy and intelligence operations." [23] Taylor was an advocate of a "minimum deterrent" of from 100 to 200 ballistic missiles as a sufficient umbrella against general war while allowing the Army to carry on "limited" and brush-fire war. The point

[22] *Ibid.*, pp. 499–500.
[23] *Facts on File*, 1961, 237E2.

of his book *The Uncertain Trumpet* (Harper, 1960) was a plea to spend more money on the Army's general purposes forces and less on strategic nuclear weapons. The Kennedy decision to build 1,000 missiles went directly contrary to the views of the man he had chosen as his military adviser. I wonder if Schlesinger would now explain why he left the Army point of view out.

Let us return to his narrative at the point where we broke off. "But on Thanksgiving week-end," Schlesinger continues, "when the President convened his defense experts for a meeting at Hyannis Port, the weight of evidence was plainly against the Air Force, and the issue finally withered away." Withered away? That is a strange phrase to use in view of what follows immediately after. "The budget nevertheless," Schlesinger goes on, "contemplated a sizeable increase in missiles; *and the White House staff, while favoring a larger Minuteman force than the original Eisenhower proposal, wondered whether the new budget was not providing for more missiles than national security required*" (my italics).

How did Kennedy react to that? "The President," Schlesinger continues, "though intimating a certain sympathy with this view [perhaps a vestige of that creative idealism Schlesinger had promised?], was not prepared to overrule McNamara's recommendation." But was it just McNamara's recommendation? I showed in an earlier article for *The New York Review* (November 7, 1968) that the White House slapped McNamara down when he, an innocent to armament politics, let slip the truth about the missile gap to the press as soon as he caught up with the facts in his new office as Secretary of Defense. The White House next day insisted that there *was* a gap. It would seem more reasonable to assume from this incident alone that it was Kennedy, not McNamara, who insisted on building more missiles.

To see how far Schlesinger distorts history in the service of Kennedy one need only check the contemporary public accounts. Unless Rostow and Wiesner were incredibly ill-informed, they must have known that U.S. nuclear power was overwhelmingly superior to the Soviet Union's. Five days before Kennedy's Inaugural, the well-informed Pentagon correspondent of the conservative Washington *Star* reported (January 15), "New national intelligence estimates of Soviet missile production indicate the 'missile gap' may have disappeared." Two years before, at the height of the missile gap scare, it was estimated that by 1961 the Soviet Union would have 50 to 100 missiles operational "but intelligence officers," said the *Star*, reflecting what we later learned were actual counts by aerial reconnaissance, "cannot find nearly that number."

A report reaching Washington before Kennedy's Inaugural (by the British Institute of Strategic Studies, which depends ultimately on U.S. intelligence) credited the Soviets with about thirty-five operational ICBM's and about 200 long-range bombers. The Russians then, as now, did have more intercontinental land-based missiles than the U.S. But the imbalance of total power was stupefying. It turned out that we had ten times their total nuclear delivery capacity.

This was made public in the House of Representatives five days after the inaugural, by the Republicans. They were smarting under Kennedy's implication that eight years of their rule had somehow left the U.S. with inadequate defenses. The main presentation that day was made for the Republicans by—of all people—Representative Melvin Laird, now Nixon's Secretary of Defense. Two years later, he was himself to join the alarmists with his book *America's Strategy Gap*. But here are the figures he gave that day, without rebuttal from the Democrats or the new Administration. These declared that we had:

—about 16 Atlas ICBM's.
—two Polaris submarines with a total of 32 missiles capable of reaching Russia.
—"over 600 long-range B-52 jet bombers, each carrying more destructive, explosive power than that used by all the combatants in World War II."
—nearly 1,400 B-47 medium-range jet bombers based abroad

and at home with a 4,500-mile range "and distances beyond
with air-to-air refueling."
—the first of SAC's B-58 Hustlers, supersonic medium-range
bombers.
—"14 aircraft carriers able to launch more aircraft than the
entire Soviet heavy bomber force."
—"18 wings of tactical aircraft, each wing with a substantial nuclear attack capability deployed globally."
—64 IRBM's [intermediate-range ballistic missiles] in England,
capable of reaching Russia, and 30 Jupiter IRBM's being deployed in Italy, "from which Russia can be hit."
(Or "well over 2,000 nuclear carrying vehicles capable of
reaching Russia.")

In addition, the Republicans pointed out that under the
final Eisenhower budgets, there would be 600 Minuteman
missiles by the end of 1964; 129 Atlas and 126 Titan ICBM's
by the end of 1962; 4 more Polarises in service by the end
of 1961, with 64 more missiles; and that 15 Jupiter IRBM's
were being erected in Turkey.[24]

Dr. Ralph Lapp, the outspoken atomic physicist, estimated on the basis of the figures disclosed in the House that
we were in a position to dump more than 30,000 megatons
on the Soviet Union. The USSR, he further computed, has
about three million square miles of inhabited territory. It
takes about one megaton, he said, to render 1,000 square
miles uninhabitable. At that rate it would take 3,000 megatons, evenly spread, literally to wipe out the Soviet Union.
We could deliver more than ten times that much!

In the light of those figures, the contrast of tone between
Eisenhower's farewell and Kennedy's debut was hardly
creative idealism. Eisenhower finished with a series of warnings against the forces making for a stepped-up arms race.
His final State of the Union message, January 12, said the
bomber gap "had always been a fiction, and the 'missile gap'
shows every sign of being the same." He said U.S. power
was sufficient to deter "and if need be to destroy predatory

[24] *Congressional Record*, Jan. 25, 1961, pp. 1227–37.

forces." In his TV farewell of January 17 he sought to put the country on guard against the growing influence of "an immense military establishment and a large arms industry" which he termed the military-industrial complex.

Kennedy, instead of joining in that warning, demonstrated the political power that the complex could exert. The inaugural invoked Isaiah—as Johnson did, too, four years later, before taking us into a new war. Kennedy called on the Russians to negotiate disarmament since both nations were "overburdened by the cost of modern weapons and both rightly alarmed by the steady spread of the deadly atom." But his first State of the Union message, January 30, stepped up the arms race immediately. He spoke of "an hour of national peril," implied that the country was in danger because of inadequate defenses and, though he did not mention the missile gap, he said he was giving orders to accelerate the missile program, to step up the construction of Polaris submarines, and to increase our airlift capacity so our conventional forces would be better able "to respond with discrimination and speed to any problem at any spot on the globe at a moment's notice." These were the trumpets of Pax Americana and imperialism, premonitions—if the country had but known—of Vietnam and the Bay of Pigs.

How gullible does Schlesinger expect his readers to be? Against this background, his account of the discussion later that year about the first Kennedy budget is incredible: that Kennedy showed "a certain sympathy" for the White House staff view that we were building more missiles than we needed but that he was "not prepared to overrule McNamara's recommendation."

Implicit in Schlesinger's opaque account is a damning revelation. This can be seen if one looks closely enough at his explanation of why McNamara recommended more missiles than he thought we needed. "As for the Secretary," Schlesinger writes, "he did not believe that doubling or even tripling our striking power would enable us to destroy the hardened missile sites or missile-launching submarines of our adversary." To any knowledgeable readers this means that Kennedy and his advisers were not discussing deterrent but *first-strike* capacity.

The targets of deterrence are Russian cities and industry; the purpose is to let the enemy know that if he hits us, we can destroy him. But the targets of first strike are the missiles and the missile-carrying submarines of the enemy. A first strike, to be successful, must first destroy these lest they destroy our cities and industry in retaliation. Apparently the Air Force, in asking for more missiles, wanted a first-strike capability, and McNamara was arguing that we couldn't hope to achieve a first-strike capability even if we doubled or tripled our striking force. This is Schlesinger's unwitting revelation.

Eisenhower, we have seen, had ordered a build-up of Minutemen to 600 missiles. The Air Force wanted 3,000, according to a recent revelation by Dr. Jerome Wiesner, who was a Kennedy science adviser.[25] McNamara settled for 1,000 Minutemen and eventually for forty-one Polaris submarines with sixteen missiles each or a total of 256 seaborne missiles, 160 more than Eisenhower had projected.

Schlesinger implies that McNamara and Kennedy upped the Minuteman program from 600 to 1,000 and the Polaris program from six to an eventual forty-one even though McNamara knew this increase was not needed for deterrence and was not—*could never be*—big enough for a first strike. Why? Schlesinger says McNamara "was already engaged in a bitter fight with the Air Force over his effort to disengage from the B-70, a costly high-altitude manned bomber rendered obsolescent by the improvement in Soviet ground-to-air missiles. After cutting down the original Air Force missile demands considerably, he perhaps felt that he could not do more without risking public conflict with the Joint Chiefs and the vociferous B-70 lobby in Congress. As a result," Schlesinger concludes, "the President went along with

25 Dr. Wiesner revealed the figure on a national educational television show, *The Advocates*, Sunday, March 1, 1970.

the policy of multiplying Polaris and Minuteman missiles." [26]

Schlesinger expects us to believe that Kennedy merely "went along with the policy of multiplying Polaris and Minutemen" in order to let McNamara appease an Air Force angry over the loss of the B-70! This, even if true, was not "the higher calculus of deterrence," much less the dialectic of "arming to disarm." But I find it impossible to believe decisions which cost so many billions—and were so profitable to the arms industry—were merely the result of intramural bureaucratic bargaining and appeasement.

There may be a better clue in a cryptic passage of Kennedy's first State of the Union message. "We are moving into a period of uncertain risks and great commitment," he said, "in which both the military *and diplomatic* possibilities require a Free World force so powerful as to make any aggression clearly futile" (my italics). The bomber generals and their friends in Congress had long argued that the best card in military *and diplomatic* confrontations was the existence of a first-strike capability. This too was Laird's theme in *America's Strategy Gap*, two years after Kennedy's inaugural. Kennedy may well have agreed. He may indeed have felt, after the Cuban missile crisis, that fear of an American first strike was the card with which he had won.

The final touch of bitter irony is that 1961, the year Kennedy stepped up the arms race even though there was no missile gap, was also the year in which Kennedy joined Khrushchev in pledging general and complete disarmament. Their special representatives, McCloy and Zorin respectively, even submitted a signed joint agreement to the UN General Assembly on September 20 of that year in which the two superpowers agreed to the total abolition of all weapons of mass destruction, the reduction of conventional forces to the minimum necessary for internal order, and the establishment of an international control agency under the UN but free of the veto, so that inspectors could have "unrestricted access" for "effective verification." What more

[26] *A Thousand Days*, p. 500.

does one need than this gap—an abyss wide—between word
and deed to see that disarmament negotiations had become a
form of political theater, a theater of delusion?

April 23, 1970
New York Review

THE TEST BAN COMEDY

Our last installment ended by calling disarmament negotiations a theater of delusion. The outstanding example is the
Limited Nuclear Test Ban Treaty. In appearance it was one
of the few successes in the history of armament negotiations
and the great achievement of the Kennedy Administration.
It seemed to promise that we were at last to bring the nuclear monster under control. Logically, the SALT talks
could—and should—have begun seven years ago in 1963
after that treaty was signed, with so much mutual congratu-
lation, in Moscow. It was the first time the two superpowers had reached a major formal agreement. It signaled a
thaw in the cold war. In the manic-depressive cycle of the
sick relationship between Washington and Moscow, it was
the "up" phase after the terrifying "down" of the Cuban
missile crisis the year before. It seemed a most propitious
moment for the kind of strategic arms limitation talks now
belatedly beginning in Vienna.

In a television address the night after the treaty was
signed, the youthful President addressed the country and
the world with jubilation and hope. He put the moment in a
perspective of grandeur. "Since the beginning of history,"
Kennedy said, "war has been mankind's constant companion." Now, when war "would not be like any in history,"
when it could kill 300 million people in America, Europe,
and Russia in "less than 60 minutes," there was a chance "to
turn the world away from war."

Let us, the President said, "make the most of this opportunity . . . to slow down the perilous nuclear arms race, and to check the world's slide toward final annihilation." Yet this was, as a Hindu philosopher would say, all delusion, a dream which bore little resemblance, as we shall see, to the Kennedy Administration's waking and working plans for the aftermath of the treaty.

When one goes back into the records to try to understand how and why the opportunity was lost, one comes upon a deeper mystery and falls into a worse despair. Though the treaty contained no concrete measure of disarmament, and though it banned nuclear testing in the atmosphere, underwater, and in outer space, but not underground, it did seem a first limit at least on testing and on the nuclear arms race. The real question is how and why it proved to be a curtain-raiser instead on a new and more intense period of competition and expenditure in atomic weaponry.

The arms race merely moved underground. What seemed a minor loophole opened, metaphorically and literally, into an enormous cavern. The total volume of testing *increased* instead of decreasing. The magnitude reached the point where two years ago we began to test underground in the megaton range. By miracles of ingenuity, we learned to do underground almost everything which scientists once thought could only be done in the atmosphere: the development and testing, for example, of those "penetration aids" designed to let loose a fusillade of deception in combat between whole fleets of missile and anti-missile. In this intensified testing the two new monsters, MIRV and ABM, were perfected and are still being improved. What looked like the peace movement's greatest triumph in 1963 proved to be a bonanza for the military and its industrial allies.

The signing of the limited test ban, the fourth major lost opportunity since World War II to curb the nuclear arms race, differed in one vital respect from the others. The treaty was the culmination of a worldwide campaign against atmospheric testing. It mobilized overwhelming majority support in the United States, Japan, and every other country aware of the danger from the radioactivity those atmospheric tests released.

For the first time the opponents of the nuclear arms race had an issue more effective than a generalized, albeit cataclysmic, danger. Suddenly, in the shape of strontium 90, the menace turned up in the baby's milk bottle and in cancer statistics. Hypochondria was mobilized in the service of idealism and the combination worked. Adlai Stevenson put the issue on the political map in the 1956 campaign by calling for an end to H-bomb tests, while Nixon, in a Republican chorus of derision, called any restriction on testing "a fearful risk." In Kennedy's 1960 campaign the issue was muted, but it was there.[1]

The hypochondria which made the campaign against atmospheric testing so effective proved a weakness in victory. Support evaporated rapidly when the treaty was signed and atmospheric testing stopped. It proved impossible to keep a full head of steam in the boiler of the disarmament campaign when all one had left was the more familiar issue of the danger in continuing the nuclear arms race, even if it no longer threatened baby's milk. Somehow talk of universal holocaust proved not half so effective as being able to tell the individual he or his child might get cancer because of testing. Death, even, perhaps especially, on a mass scale, is really beyond the imagination of mankind. Constant predictions of cosmic disaster produce a yawn. No one really believes in the possibility of his own death.

Fear of death has rarely stopped a common brawl, much less a war. But everybody is nervous about having to go to the doctor. Peace propaganda rested—and this is a lesson we have yet to learn—on a vastly oversimplified psychology. Just as the vivid portrayal of hellfire in old-fashioned

[1] It was not a gut issue with Kennedy, as it was with Stevenson. "In the early stages of his public career," Theodore C. Sorensen, his other official biographer, says in his Kennedy (Harper & Row, 1965), "His foreign policy speeches had a militant ring. Defense, in his view, was the bulk of diplomacy and disarmament was only a dream. But with increased perspective and responsibility came a renewed commitment to peace. Nothing gave him greater satisfaction in the White House than signing the Nuclear Test Ban treaty."

gospel evangelism only gave sin an extra dimension of zest, so subconsciously the doomsday theme had an appeal to man's love of excitement and horror. It was like turning on another TV thriller, and it was as unreal.

Despite worldwide fear of fallout, the limited nuclear test ban might never have been signed were it not for some extraordinary circumstances. It is doubtful whether the force of public opinion alone would have brought it about. One was the shock of the Cuban missile crisis, which only a few months earlier had brought the two superpowers and the world for the first time to the brink of nuclear war. The second I believe was the political desperation of Khrushchev, soon to be deposed, and striving desperately for a way out of the arms race and its heavy cost for Russia; his destalinization campaign could only survive if international tension could be lightened and the standard of living in the Soviet Union dramatically raised. Roger Hilsman summed it up neatly in his memoirs of the Kennedy Administration[2] when he wrote:

The Soviets put missiles into Cuba in an attempt to solve a set of problems—a strategic imbalance, the exigencies of the Sino-Soviet dispute, and the impossible combination of demands on their limited resources made by defense, their space program, their peoples' appetite for consumers' goods, and the drain of foreign aid needed to support their foreign policy. When the crisis was over, the missiles withdrawn, the same set of problems remained. The irony is that these same problems, which brought the world so close to nuclear war, later brought about the so-called *détente*—a relaxation of Cold War tensions. For it was the same pressure that led the Soviets to put missiles in Cuba that later led them to take up Kennedy's proposal for a treaty banning nuclear testing.

For five years, ever since the formal nuclear test ban negotiations began in 1958, the Soviets had insisted that they would never accept an accord which did not ban all nuclear testing, in all environments, underground included.

---

[2] *To Move A Nation: The Politics of Foreign Policy in the Administration of John F. Kennedy* (New York: Doubleday, 1967), p. 228.

Khrushchev backed down on this, as he backed down on the
Cuban missiles and as he had backed down in 1955 on the
Austrian treaty, which was the admission price to a summit
on Germany and disarmament. For these backdowns he got
nothing, nothing but a temporary change of international
atmosphere.

Potentially, this was worthwhile, for in the changed atmosphere agreement on substantive issues became possible.
But they were never forthcoming. The West took what
Khrushchev had to offer but gave nothing in return. This I
believe is the key to his downfall, and perhaps part of the
explanation for the more rigid, cautious, and unimaginative
policies of his successors. Khrushchev all too soon after the
signing ceremonies in Moscow must have begun to look like
an easy mark and a dupe. For when the treaty had to be
sold to the U.S. military bureaucracy and the U.S. Senate, it
was sold not as a victory against the arms race but as a victory in it, *an acknowledgement by Moscow of American
superiority and a new way to maintain it*. This is why no
substantive disarmament agreement followed, though many
the world over hoped for it in the détente the treaty created.

There was another reason Khrushchev accepted the
treaty on Western terms. That lay in the growing tension
between Moscow and Peking. Moscow was at a crossroads
of policy in 1963. This was dramatized by two negotiations
in Moscow, which overlapped in time but faced in totally
different directions. Talks with the Chinese began there
July 5. Talks with the U.S. and Britain on a test ban agreement opened July 15, while the negotiations with Peking's
representatives were still under way. In an open letter to
Peking released the day before the talks with the West
began, the Central Committee of the Soviet Communist
party declared it[3]

[3] Senator George McGovern, *A Time of War, A Time of Peace*
(New York: Random House, 1968), p. 44. A first-rate summary of the
Sino-Soviet factor in the achievement of the treaty from his memorable
speech in the Senate, Sept. 16, during the ratification debate.

. . . a necessary duty to tell the party and the people with all frankness that in questions of war and peace the Chinese Communist party leadership is based on principle differences with us. . . . The essence of these differences lies in the diametrically opposite approach to such vital problems as the possibility of averting a world thermonuclear war, peaceful coexistence of states with different social systems, and interconnection between the struggle for peace and the development of the world revolutionary movement.

In the overlapping negotiations "the Soviets clearly gave more attention to the test ban group, and no doubt intended this as a deliberate slap at the Chinese and a deliberate effort to emphasize that they were opting for a policy of détente with the West, even if it would be at the expense of a further disintegration in Sino-Soviet relations." [4] A study at the cold-warrish Hoover Institute found that the test ban treaty was "perhaps the final straw that brought the schism into the open." For Peking, "symbolically" it represented "Moscow's joining what Peking deemed an imperialist conspiracy, not only to try to block China's nuclear program, but to oppose her political advance in the third world." [5] For Washington the treaty was a political coup, solidifying the split in the world communist movement. Even so Khrushchev had to pay a high price for it.

The American University speech, in which Kennedy announced the three-power agreement to hold the Moscow test ban talks, was one of Kennedy's best. It was published in full next day in *Izvestia*. Khrushchev later told Harriman it was "the best speech by any President since Roosevelt." [6] But the Administrations' psychological warriors could hardly have been unaware that its new tone of friendliness to Moscow would whet the suspicions of Peking and nourish the growing split. According to Sorensen, who drafted the speech,[7] Kennedy was skeptical about the possibility

[4] Morton H. Halperin and Dwight H. Perkins (East Asian Research Center), *Communist China and Arms Control* (Harvard, 1965), p. 169.

[5] Walter C. Clemens, Jr., *The Arms Race and Sino-Soviet Relations* (Stanford, Calif.: Hoover Institute, 1968), p. 50.

[6] Sorensen, *Kennedy*, p. 733.

[7] *Ibid.*, p. 730.

that the talks would succeed. Moscow was still insisting on an agreement banning tests in all environments. Kennedy seemed to regard the speech in part at least as an exercise in political propaganda. In preparing for it, he "valued in particular," Sorensen relates,[8] "a letter from Norman Cousins" suggesting that "the exposition of a peaceful posture prior to the May meeting of the Soviet Communist Party Central Committee, even if it could not deter a new rash of attacks on U.S. policy, might at least make those attacks sound hollow and hypocritical outside the Communist world."

Kennedy's first move after the speech was to visit and reassure the ever-nervous Germans. Sorensen's account of Kennedy's feelings on the eve of the Moscow talks is revealing:[9]

The Adenauer government still took an alarmist attitude about the whole matter. But the trip to West Germany had improved popular as well as official feeling in that country about our intentions, the President told his negotiators [i.e., before they left for Moscow], "and I am willing to draw on that as much as necessary, if it's worthwhile. I don't, however, want to do what we did in the Berlin talks, getting the Germans suspicious if the Russians aren't going to agree to anything anyway." *Inasmuch as even a limited test ban treaty required a Soviet acceptance of permanent American superiority in nuclear weapons,* he refused to count too heavily on the success of the Moscow meetings (my italics).

But on July 2, three days before the talks with China were to open and thirteen days before the test ban talks with the West began, Khrushchev reversed the Soviet's past position and agreed to accept the West's proposal for a ban on tests in the atmosphere, outer space, and underwater, but not underground. This was not only to accept "permanent inferiority" but to leave the door open to a form of testing in which the U.S. was far more proficient and for which it could more easily bear the expense. He asked in return only that it be linked with a non-aggression pact between NATO

[8] *Ibid.,* p. 730.
[9] *Ibid.,* p. 734.

and the Warsaw powers. This would have made the Chinese feel that he was thereby protecting his rear in the West in the event of a conflict with them in the East.

But Kennedy was in no mood to pay this price even though Sorensen says there was "apprehension that Khrushchev would insist on both or neither." [10] The negotiators were instructed, before leaving for Moscow, to stall on the request for a non-aggression pact. Such a pact was always a bugaboo with Adenauer, who still dreamed that the cold war, the arms race, and the rearmament of Germany would some day force the Russians to accept its reunification on Western terms. The negotiators finally threw Khrushchev a very slim bone. He had to be satisfied with a noncommittal paragraph at the end of the Agreed Communiqué on the treaty which mentioned his proposal only to bury it in diplomatic double-talk: [11]

The heads of the three delegations discussed the Soviet proposal relating to a pact of non-aggression between the participants in the North Atlantic Treaty Organization and the participants in the Warsaw Treaty. The three governments have agreed *fully* [My italics. A delicate touch of humor in that adverb, since they had agreed to nothing!] to inform their respective allies in the two organizations concerning these talks and to consult with them about continuing discussions on this question with the purpose of achieving agreement satisfactory to all participants.

That was the last anybody heard of any such discussions. In any case, if the reader will look at the skillful wording again, the communiqué did not promise discussions but only consultations (i.e., with the Germans) on *whether* to discuss the Pact. This was exquisite conmanship.

The final sentence of the communiqué, cryptic and inconsequential as it appeared to be at the time, marked the burial of Khrushchev's other hopes. "A brief exchange of

[10] *Ibid.*, p. 736.
[11] Text on p. 8 of the Senate Foreign Relations Committee hearings on the Nuclear Test Ban Treaty, August 12–27, 1963.

views also took place," the communiqué ended, "with regard to other measures directed at a relaxation of tension." The "other measures" Khrushchev had in mind were indicated in a speech he made July 20, five days before the treaty was finally initialed, and in an interview with *Pravda* and *Izvestia* as soon as the final agreement was reached.[12] It was the year before Khrushchev's ouster, and these two declarations show the central role of disarmament in his domestic and international program. He quoted Lenin in support of the policy of coexistence and to attack those who saw in war the final victory of socialism. He defended destalinization by citing Hungary as an example of what happens when "the cult of personality" alienates the masses. He said people would judge socialism "by what it gives them" in the way of better living standards. He hoped the limited test ban would make it possible to freeze or reduce military budgets and he suggested among ways to lessen tension that each side reduce its troops in Germany and that the Western powers post inspectors in the East and the Warsaw powers in the West at airfields, railway junctions, and airports as assurance against surprise attack. "After all," he added in the July 26 interview after the treaty had been initialed, "it is necessary to keep clearly in mind that the ban on nuclear weapons tests does not mean the end of the arms race . . . does not do away with the burden of armaments. . . . Let us now advance further . . . toward liquidating the 'cold war.'" But all this was exactly what the Adenauer regime and our military feared.

I see no reason to believe that Kennedy did not feel the same way. Sorensen's account reveals how tightly Kennedy held the reins of the negotiations in his own hands: "All communications to the delegation were cleared through Kennedy. Frequently he altered or rewrote completely the daily cable of instructions prepared in the State Department."[13] Sorensen provides no clue to the differences this

[12] For the former see the *Current Digest of the Soviet Press*, Vol. XV, No. 29. The latter is in Vol. XV, No. 30.
[13] *Op. Cit.*, p. 735.

implies between the departmental drafts and the final White House orders. The former could hardly have been more hard-line than Kennedy's proved to be. The delegation was instructed sharply to limit the agreement in Moscow to a limited ban on testing. If Kennedy had wanted progress on further and broader issues, if he had wanted to lay the groundwork for a more general armament agreement or political settlement, Khrushchev seemed more than ready for it. At a bare minimum, Kennedy could have had a final communiqué promising wider arms talks in the future. Instead he got a hard and narrow bargain, and it must be assumed that this is all he wanted.

Khrushchev got nothing concrete in return for accepting his terms for a limited test ban treaty. Seen from within the Kremlin, where opposition was brewing, Khrushchev's failure to win some relaxation of the arms race must have made the treaty seem another humiliating defeat for his policy of wooing Kennedy, as the U-2 was for his policy of wooing Eisenhower. I believe these sealed his political fate.

Both leaders had two constituencies, the universal two-party system of mankind, whether it lives under freely chosen representatives or imposed regimes: the hard-liners and the soft, the tough and the conciliatory. In Moscow the advocates of heavy (military) industry and a return to the heavy hand this entailed were waiting in the wings to take over. In Washington the hard-liners were preparing to use a minority veto—the constitutional requirement of a two-thirds vote in the Senate for treaty ratification—to block Kennedy unless he met their terms. In both capitals there was a military-industrial complex, buttressed by the same paranoia and cave-man instinct. In both there were factions which saw the only hope for peace in the extermination of the other side.

The Neanderthals on both sides, with touching faith in science, still hoped that in the arms race they could acquire (but they alone) a new magic weapon which would keep nuclear extermination from being mutual. In both countries there was also a public concerned with the costs and dangers of the arms race, but its strength never matched its numbers.

The difference is that Khrushchev, as leader of the weaker nation, returned from the signing of the treaty with nothing but atmospherics as his trophy. Kennedy could offer the opposition the assurance of another period of American military predominance, and the maintenance for a longer period of the American position as the senior firm in the world atomic oligopoly.

For the treaty was also the first non-proliferation pact. The other nations, in signing it, were pledging themselves never to test except underground, which was very difficult and expensive. Some of them might be close to building a bomb of their own, but adherence to the treaty put up another barrier to their becoming nuclear powers. The treaty also gave both superpowers an excuse not to share the secrets of the new weaponry with importunate allies. As Kennedy said in his TV address the night after it was signed, "This treaty can be a step toward preventing the spread of nuclear weapons to nations not now possessing them." [14]

Kennedy had a right to feel that he had brought quite a prize package home from Moscow. Trouble was nevertheless building up in the Senate. "Congressional Republicans," Sorensen relates, "had consistently bombarded the President with attacks on his 'fuzzy-minded disarmament advisers.' " Predictably, leading members of the Joint Committee on Atomic Energy, a watchdog that had become a Pentagon poodle, were saying that anything other than "a reasonably sound-proof test ban agreement . . . could be a greater risk to the national security than an arms race."

Senator Jackson, the Democratic party's leading liberal advocate of perpetual arms race, was "skeptical" even after Khrushchev accepted Kennedy's terms. Senator Russell, chairman of the Armed Services Committee and the military's most prestigious ally in the Senate, opposed the treaty from the beginning and (unlike Jackson) was one of the nineteen who voted against it. Conservative congress-

[14] *Public Papers of the Presidents: John F. Kennedy, 1963,* p. 604.

men and newspapermen charged that Kennedy had made a "secret deal" with Khrushchev in Moscow.[15] Whatever the "gaps" between America and Russia, the two nations were obviously neck-and-neck when it came to paranoid politicians.

The biggest obstacle was the Joint Chiefs of Staff. Sorensen tells us that the President had been careful to obtain their approval in advance of the negotiations. "But their agreement," he adds, "had assumed that a test ban, *like all other disarmament proposals*, was only a diplomatic pose unlikely to achieve reality" (my italics). When they found themselves confronted with an actual agreement, "they hedged." [16] Phil G. Goulding, in his newly published memoirs of his years as the Pentagon's top press officer,[17] gives us a description of how McNamara went over the treaty point by point with the Joint Chiefs in sessions that lasted several days and took many hours each day. "When they were finally finished," Goulding reports, "the Joint Chiefs agreed with McNamara's own basic position—that the treaty carried with it certain risks, but that the alternative risks of continued atmospheric testing were far more grave, both from the moral standpoint of the health of unborn generations *and from the hard military standpoint that unlimited testing on both sides was allowing the Soviet Union to narrow the gap*" (my italics). That obviously was the clincher.

Part of the price which had to be paid, nevertheless, for the support of the Joint Chiefs, was that we would use the advantage given us by the treaty to widen that gap by intensified underground testing. This was imperfectly understood at the time. When Kennedy, the day after the treaty was initialed, made his eloquent TV address for public support,[18] he said the treaty would not "prevent this nation from testing underground" but he also added that "unlim-

[15] Sorensen, pp. 736–37.

[16] *Ibid.*, p. 738.

[17] P. G. Goulding, *Confirm or Deny: Informing the People on National Security* (New York: Harper & Row, 1970). See pp. 173–74.

[18] *Public Papers of the Presidents: John F. Kennedy, 1963.* Text begins at p. 601.

ited competition in the testing and development of new types of destructive nuclear weapons will not make the world safer for either side." No one could have guessed from this that we were on the verge of an intensified period of underground testing designed to enable us to pull far ahead technologically of the Russians.

This was one of the main selling points in the Senate hearings on the treaty. "By limiting Soviet testing to the underground environment, where testing is more difficult and more expensive and where the United States has substantially more experience," McNamara said in his opening presentation,[19] "we can at least retard Soviet progress and thereby prolong the duration of our technological superiority." He added—but to this the senators seem to have paid little attention—"A properly inspected comprehensive test ban would, of course, serve this purpose still better."

It was not our intention merely to retard Soviet progress while maintaining our margin of superiority. This would have been a freeze, stabilizing the level of destructive capacity and putting a ceiling on the arms race. To reread McNamara's presentation on the treaty August 13, 1963, to the Senate Foreign Relations Committee (along with senators from Armed Services and the Joint Committee on Atomic Energy) is to see why the better atmosphere created by the signing of the limited nuclear test ban treaty was never used for substantive negotiations to stabilize or reduce the burden of armaments. For what McNamara outlined that day was a program for a sharp step-up in the arms race, both qualitatively and quantitatively.

First, the quantitative. McNamara said the U.S. then had "more than 500 missiles—Atlas, Titan, Minuteman, Polaris" and planned to more than triple the number in the next two years "to over 1,700 by 1966." Though McNamara did not say so, this was the goal originally set by the Kennedy Administration in its first budget preparations in the fall of 1961. Obviously he and Kennedy saw no reason to change it because of the nuclear test ban treaty.

[19] Senate hearings already cited, p. 105.

McNamara estimated that the Soviets had "only a fraction as many ICBM missiles." Perhaps he did not give a concrete figure because it would have shown a missile gap so lopsidedly in our favor as to make the planned step-up look fantastic. The 1962–63 edition of the annual Military Balance issued by the Institute for Strategic Studies in London credited the Soviet Union with "75+" as of early 1963. If this figure is correct then we had more than six times as many ICBM's as the Soviet Union at the time that McNamara announced that we would more than triple the number by 1966. As for submarine-launched missiles, McNamara said those of the Soviets were "short range, require surface launch, and generally are not comparable to our Polaris force." McNamara said that by 1966 "our ballistic missile numerical superiority will increase both absolutely and relatively." [20] When that testimony was read in the Kremlin, the gathering opposition must have felt that Khrushchev had lost his mind in believing that the treaty was a step toward lightening the burden and danger of the arms race.

McNamara dealt next with plans to improve the quality of our nuclear weapons. In four pages of testimony,[21] some of it opaque to protect classified information, McNamara indicated the wide variety of improvements we could and would make by underground testing. The only field in which the Soviets were ahead was in large-yield weapons. They had tested a 60-megaton "device" (he did not say bomb) and he thought it could be turned into a weapon of 100 megatons. But they had no missile that could carry such a monster and it would be "suitable only for vulnerable high altitude or suicide low level delivery," i.e., against our air defenses.

The U.S., McNamara said, could "without any further testing" develop a warhead of 50 to 60 megatons for B-52 delivery. But the U.S. believed that smaller bombs, with greater accuracy, were far more efficient. The key improvement, as admitted throughout the hearings, was in weight-to-yield ratios, i.e., packing more punch into smaller warheads.

We know now in retrospect that this was essential for the next great breakthrough, which was to put more warheads on each missile (MRV) and then target them separately (MIRV). With these we are now on the verge of multiplying the number of warheads on these 1,700 missiles by three in the case of Minuteman, and by ten in the case of Poseidon, the most stupendous expansion yet in nuclear delivery power.

It is even more extraordinary to reread those pages which concern the ABM. McNamara outlined what we could and would do in developing "penetration aids" to confuse any enemy ABM, and techniques to make it difficult for the enemy to counter any ABM of our own. "The ABM warhead designs we now have," McNamara said that day, "or can develop through underground testing will provide a high probability of killing Soviet warheads *even if they incorporate advanced technology far beyond what now exists*" (my italics).[22]

Against this background one can now better understand the full significance of the "safeguards" on which the Joint Chiefs of Staff insisted and to which Kennedy and McNamara agreed before the Chairman of the Joint Chiefs, General Taylor, would tell the Senate that "while there are military disadvantages to the treaty, they are not so serious as to render it unacceptable." [23] They ensured an intensified arms race. The safeguards, as given by General Taylor in the Senate hearings, read like a meticulously spelled-out treaty between the military and the Kennedy Administration, an agreement between two bureaucratic superpowers. It proved more significant than the treaty itself. The terms are worth looking at in full text as a warning for the future, since the peace movement tended euphorically to skip over them as a kind of bone thrown the military. The bone

[22] Senate hearings, p. 103.
[23] Senate hearings, p. 275.

proved to be the giant skeleton for a new stage in the arms race. Here are the safeguards Kennedy promised the Joint Chiefs:

(a) The conduct of comprehensive, aggressive, and continuing underground nuclear test programs designed to add to our knowledge and improve our weapons in all areas of significance to our military posture for the future.

(b) The maintenance of modern nuclear laboratory facilities and programs in theoretical and exploratory nuclear technology which will attract, retain, and insure the continued application of our human scientific resources to these programs on which continued progress in nuclear technology depends.

(c) The maintenance of the facilities and resources necessary to institute promptly nuclear tests in the atmosphere *should they be deemed essential to our national security* or should the treaty or any of its terms be abrogated by the Soviet Union.

[The italics are added. In other words, the military was promised that we would abrogate the treaty—and resume atmospheric tests if we felt that necessary to national security— even if the Soviets were abiding by it.]

(d) The improvement of our capability, within feasible and practical limits, to monitor the terms of the treaty, to detect violations, and to maintain our knowledge of Sino-Soviet activity, capability and achievements.[24]

This has the precise and wary wording of a treaty between two powers in which one at least, in this case the military, wholly distrusts the other, in this case the civilian—ostensibly and constitutionally the superior power. The military might well have mustered that one vote more than one-third which is all that the Constitution requires to block a treaty. They had the power and they exacted their price. Even so there were nineteen negative votes to eighty yeas in the Senate when the treaty was ratified September 24, 1963. During the debate Senator McGovern emphasized to the doubters "the repeated assurance of our President and our military leaders that underground testing will be energetically pushed and that we will be prepared to re-

[24] Senate hearings, pp. 274–75.

sume atmospheric tests if that becomes necessary." Then he added, in an exasperation events have justified beyond even his apprehensions at the time:

Indeed, Mr. President, the Administration has been called upon to give so many assurances of our continued nuclear efforts after treaty ratification that a casual observer might assume that we are approving this treaty so that we can accelerate the arms race and beef up the war-making facilities of our country! [25]

In retrospect this proved to be exactly what the treaty did. A month earlier, in the first flush of enthusiasm over negotiation of the treaty, Senator McGovern made a memorable address in the Senate (August 2) proposing that $5 billion be diverted from strategic weapons to social needs at home. He asked that plans be drawn up for the conversion of war industry to peacetime needs. McGovern said our nuclear stockpiles already represented a huge overkill capacity. "How many times," he asked the Senate, "is it necessary to kill a man or a nation?" He quoted from a story leaked to the *New York Times* June 30 of that year which said the Kennedy Administration was considering (this was before the treaty talks) a substantial cutback in the production of nuclear weapons. A "policy-making official" was quoted as saying, "We have tens or hundreds of times more weapons than we would ever drop even in an all-out war, and we have had more than we needed for at least two years."

If that was a Kennedy Administration viewpoint, it was not shared by McNamara. I believe the story represents the surfacing in the news of conclusions reached by certain arms-study groups Kennedy had appointed early in his Administration. The closely guarded secret of their existence has slowly become known over the years to some reporters, including myself, but only on an off-the-record basis, so we still are unable to reveal or independently confirm the participants or the conclusions.

They were kept under wraps because they upset the Pen-

[25] From p. 40 of his speech of Sept. 16, 1963, as reprinted in his book *A Time of War, A Time of Peace* already cited above.

tagon and because, if they had become known at the time, they would have cut the ground from under the 1,700-missile expansion which emerged from the first Kennedy-McNamara military budget in late 1961. Maybe some of the participants will some day tell us more in their memoirs, for they were men of weight in both the scientific and general community.

McGovern seems to have touched a tender nerve with his speech, particularly since it was caustic about McNamara's latest rationalization for so many missiles—the "controlled counterforce" or "no cities" doctrine unveiled in the Ann Arbor speech of June, 1962. The idea was that we needed so many missiles because, if the Russians spared our cities in a first strike, hitting only our missile bases, we would not hit their cities in retaliation but only *their* missile sites. This required an enormous amount of missiles. It also required a lot of addlepated computerism. McGovern blew this nonsense sky-high with two questions in his August 2 speech:

If the United States were aiming at the effective destruction of Russia's nuclear forces, how could we apply such a strategy unless we knocked out the Soviet missiles before they were launched from their silos? What military objective could we achieve by knocking out missile launchers after their rockets had hit American targets?

The silly doctrine was custom-made for missile salesmanship. It is significant that when McNamara compiled his principle speeches and reports on leaving the Pentagon in 1968 in his book, *The Essence of Security*, the Ann Arbor speech was omitted. There isn't even a reference to it in the index.

But when McNamara appeared before the Senate hearings to ask ratification of the test ban treaty, eleven days after that plea by McGovern to reduce spending on missiles, he was in no mood for second thoughts. When Senator Symington asked him about McGovern's speech, McNamara insisted that he was holding the defense budget "to an absolute minimum." McNamara submitted a formal memorandum declaring that any such cuts as McGovern proposed would represent "a substantial risk to our national security." [26] As for McGovern's charge of overkill capacity in our nuclear weapons inventories, McNamara replied cryptically, "I think it is possible to say that we have more weapons than would be utilized in a particular war situation, without concluding that our inventories are excessive." Such was the evasive nonsense McNamara was still uttering after the treaty offered an opportunity to freeze or reduce the inventories on both sides. I believe he would agree today with the unnamed officials the *New York Times* quoted in that news story of June 30, 1968, as fearing that the production of atomic weapons was "coming to be based more on the capabilities of the Atomic Energy Commission to manufacture them than on the actual requirements of the military." Yet this mindless momentum continued despite the treaty, and McNamara was its prisoner and tool.

When Senator Aiken asked McNamara what effect approval of the treaty might have on the military budget during the next few years, McNamara was discouraging:

McNAMARA: I believe the treaty *per se* should not lead to a reduction in the budget. As I mentioned, I think we should all be concerned lest we be lulled into a false sense of security and act to reduce the budget for our military forces.

AIKEN (*still trying to be hopeful*): Do you think it might have some tendency perhaps to stabilize the budget at about the present level?

McNAMARA: No, sir; I really don't believe that the treaty by itself will have any, should have any, important influence on the budget.

AIKEN: It would have no effect whatsoever?

McNAMARA: No, sir.[27]

When the Joint Chiefs appeared before the senators a few days later they were blunter:

26 See pp. 146–50 of the Senate hearings.
27 Senate hearings, p. 128.

SENATOR CURTIS: If the safeguards that you favor are adequately carried out, is this test ban, would this test ban, then be a money-saver?

GENERAL WHEELER: On the contrary I would say, Senator, if I may offer my opinion first. As I look at it, the military threat to our security from the Soviet Union specifically and from the Communist bloc in general is not lessened in one degree by this treaty. The safeguards, also, in my opinion, are going to cost sums of money over and above the sizable military budget that the chairman pointed out this morning.

GENERAL LEMAY: I would agree that the military budget will probably go up as a result of the treaty, not down.

SENATOR CURTIS: I see.[28]

Earlier that same day Senator Morse had asked the Joint Chiefs an untactful question. In the Pentagon it must have seemed downright indecent, almost pornographic.

MORSE: Now, you gentlemen have close contact with the large defense contractors of this country. What has been their view generally of this treaty?

GENERAL LEMAY: I certainly have no idea. I have not discussed it with any of them.

MORSE: Any of you know of any opposition by the defense contractors?

GENERAL LEMAY: I don't know of any.

GENERAL WHEELER: I would like to speak for myself, Senator, I have no contact with the large defense contractors of the country and I, too, have not discussed it with any of them.

ADMIRAL McDONALD: I haven't discussed it, nor have they discussed it with me.

GENERAL SHOUP: I have no contacts with them.[29]

How reassuring that after so many years in the services every member of the Joint Chiefs of Staff would turn out—so to speak—to be a virgin! But what need was there for seduction by industry, when the insiders so obviously planned to permit no letup in the arms race in the wake of the treaty?

It is startling now to check back and see how our testing has increased since it was "limited" by treaty. I phoned the

28 Senate hearings, pp. 404–5.
29 Senate hearings, p. 369.

Atomic Energy Commission April 3, 1970, as this was being
written and asked for the figures on testing as of that day.
Its press officer told me there had been ninety-eight U.S.
tests from 1945 until the treaty went into force on August
5, 1963. Since then there were 210 U.S. tests, or more than
twice as many in the seven years since the treaty as in the
eighteen years before it. When I asked for the costs, I was
given year-by-year figures including those for the next fiscal
year in the new budget. The total cost of testing for those
eight years will be $1,834 million, an average of more than
$200 million a year. It was some $206 million in fiscal 1964,
the year the treaty went into effect. It will be $226 million
in fiscal 1971. I have never seen these figures published before.

On the other hand the AEC's figures on Soviet testing
show a sharp decline. It credits the Soviet Union with 126
tests in the years before the treaty, including one underground. It lists only three Soviet tests since. But these figures, like so much else the AEC does, are tricky, indeed
doubly so. For the AEC also lists what it calls thirty-five
"seismic signals" from known Soviet proving grounds.
These are announced in this form: "The U.S. has today recorded seismic signals which originated from the Soviet nuclear test area in the Semiplatinsk region. The signals are
equivalent to those of a nuclear test in the low-intermediate
range."

When I asked the AEC why these were not listed as Soviet tests, the answer was that we could not be sure they
were tests without actually digging a hole on the site where
it took place. When I asked how they could be sure of the
three Soviet underground tests they do list as such, the answer was that these "vented" and threw radioactivity into
the air which we detected in the same way as we detect
atmospheric tests.

All this is part of a phony charade in which the AEC has
been engaged ever since talk of a nuclear test ban began in
the fifties. It is designed to support the AEC's view that we
could never be absolutely sure an underground test had

taken place without on-site inspection. In a sense, of course, this is true. But the standard of absolute assurance on which the AEC and the other opponents of a comprehensive test ban have always insisted goes beyond normal experience and scientific necessity. If bridegrooms sought the same degree of assurance in marriage, every bride would be put into an iron chastity belt immediately after the ceremony and followed for the rest of her life by two detectives, both eunuchs.

There have always been two ways to approach the statistics on the probability of test detection. The probability has always been high and has grown higher. Today they are probably 98 chances in 100. One can then shake one's head sadly as the AEC does and say there *is* a 2 percent chance of evasion. The other, the normal and sensible way, is to say that any power which set out to evade the treaty would have to do so knowing that there were 98 chances in 100 that it would be caught out. This is more assurance than one gets in the normal transactions of life.

The seismic signal nonsense is only one of the ways in which the AEC's statistics are tricky and understate the volume of testing on both sides since the treaty. The other way is that its figures—the Soviets give out none—are only for what it calls "announced" tests. We do not announce all our tests, in order to confuse the other side's monitors, and we do not announce all the tests or "seismic signals" we detect on the other side, in order to hide from them just how sensitive *our* monitoring facilities are. All this has another dividend, of course, in hiding from the public the full extent of testing since the treaty.

Fortunately there are independent sources which also monitor tests, and these indicate that the number of "unannounced" tests is very large indeed. The Swedes have a very sensitive seismic recording station at Upsala. "The Swedish Research Institute for National Defense," the new *Yearbook on World Armaments* for 1968–69, issued by the Stockholm International Peace Research Institute[30] notes,

---

[30] New York: Humanities Press, pp. 245–46.

"has for each year since the Moscow treaty reported about twice as many Soviet tests as the U.S. Atomic Energy Commission," i.e., twice as many as the three radioactively monitored tests plus the thirty-five "seismic signals." The Swedish station also reports that there were at least thirty more Soviet atmospheric tests in the years before the treaty than the AEC announced.

The compilers of the Yearbook believe that U.S. testing has been similarly understated by the AEC. "A search was made," it says, "in the Bulletin of the International Seismological Centre, Edinburgh, Scotland, for the period 16 January to 14 April 1964. This indicated thirteen [seismic] events whose location in the Nevada test site indicates that they were U.S. tests. During this period the AEC announced only five tests." The Yearbook concludes that "the true figure" on the number of tests by the two superpowers "could be anything up to twice as large" as those the AEC has announced.

One final touch on this bitter comedy: The day before the limited nuclear test ban treaty was ratified, Richard Nixon gave it his qualified endorsement, but warned against any further agreements with the Soviet Union. He said the treaty signaled the beginning of "the most dangerous period in the cold war." [31] Perhaps it would have been more precise to say arms race rather than cold war. But he could hardly have realized how true that was, though not in the sense he intended. For in this underground testing we were to develop the multiple independently targeted warheads and the anti-ballistic missiles, the extensive penetration aids and improved missile accuracy, that now threaten to destabilize the precarious balance of terror.

May 7, 1970
New York Review

[31] *Facts on File, 1963,* p. 335 A2.

PART VII

That Barroom Brawl with the Lights Out Revisited

ALL WE REALLY KNOW
IS THAT WE FIRED
THE FIRST SHOTS

A major, if inadvertent, revelation in McNamara's new testimony on the Tonkin Gulf affair has been overlooked. If there was indeed an attack involving two U.S. destroyers on the night of August 4, 1964, we began the attack, we opened fire first. Indeed the only shots we are completely sure of beyond any shadow of doubt even at this late date are those which came from our own vessels. McNamara's new version of the attack contradicts the melodramatic account he gave four years ago, two days after the incident, behind the closed doors of a joint executive session of the Senate's Foreign Relations and Armed Services Committees. It was this graphic, but (as it now appears) untrue version which helped stampede the Senate into voting the Tonkin Gulf resolution.

That earlier testimony was given August 6, 1964. When the transcript of that hearing is now compared with the new one held by the Senate Foreign Relations Committee, one can begin to get some idea of the full dimensions of the mendacity by which the Johnson Administration obtained that resolution which was its blank check for war in Southeast Asia. "The attack," McNamara told the Senate committees four years ago, "occurred at night. It appeared to be a deliberate attack in the nature of an ambush. Torpedoes were launched, automatic weapons fire was directed against the vessels [the *Maddox* and the *Turner Joy*]. *They returned the fire*" (my italics).

The Secretary put it even more vividly when Senator Lausche asked him, "Do you know how many of the torpedoes were set in motion and what small arms were used?"

SECRETARY MCNAMARA: It is difficult to estimate. This was a very dark night. The attack was carried out during the night, the hours of darkness. It was a premeditated attack, a pre-planned attack. It was described as an ambush in the reports from the commanders, but because it was night it is very difficult to estimate the total amount of fire.

SENATOR LAUSCHE: The shots were again initiated by the North Vietnamese?

SECRETARY MCNAMARA: Yes.

GENERAL WHEELER: That is correct.

Thus was drawn a picture of "unprovoked aggression." It was magnified and emotionalized by President Johnson when he went on TV after the attack and declared "This new act of aggression, aimed directly at our own forces, again brings home to all of us in the United States the importance of the struggle for peace and security in Southeast Asia." This was echoed in the same high dramatic vein by Adlai Stevenson at the UN Security Council next day: "Without any shadow of doubt . . . planned deliberate military aggression against vessels lawfully present in international waters" was Stevenson's description. The rhetoric made it sound like a new Pearl Harbor.

But when McNamara appeared before the Senate Foreign Relations Committee on February 20 he knew that the Committee had in its possession documents from Defense Department files which cast doubt on every aspect of that earlier version. He had to tone down his own presentation to fit. So in his prepared statement, as given out to the press that day, he gave a very different picture from that drawn four years ago:

At about 9:39 P.M., both *Maddox* and *Turner* opened fire on the approaching craft *when it was evident from their maneuvers* [my italics—not from any shots but from their maneuvers] that they were pressing in for attack positions. At about this time, the boats were at a range of 6,000 yards from *Maddox* when the radar tracking indicated *that the contact had turned away and begun to open in range* [my italics]. Torpedo noises were then heard by the *Maddox*'s sonar. A report of the torpedo noise was immediately passed to the *Turner Joy* by inter-ship radio and both ships took evasive action to avoid the torpedo. A torpedo wake was then sighted passing abeam *Turner Joy* from after to forward.

Even this scaled-down version was still a deceptive picture of what actually had transpired. McNamara released his statement during the noon recess of the February 20 hearing, which was held behind closed doors. He thus jumped the gun on the Committee by getting his version out first, perhaps hoping that it might be some time before the Committee could publish the full transcript.[1] Fortunately Senator Morse, to whom the country owes so much in this whole affair, courageously defied security regulations and in a Senate speech next day made public much of the intramural Pentagon messages obtained by the Committee. This and the Committee's anger over McNamara's tricky action in releasing his own testimony brought about the swift publication of the whole record, with some security deletions.

If the transcript of the two hearings and the text of McNamara's prepared statement are now placed side by side, it is quite clear that he and Secretary Rusk and General Wheeler lied—there is no other word for it—to the Senate committees four years ago, and that McNamara is still trying hard to lie about it now. His whole performance is the shameful climax of what many had believed to be an honorable record as Secretary of Defense. He withheld from the committees then—and in his prepared statement tried to withhold from the public now—many crucial facts which cast doubt on the whole story of the August 4 attack. You have to go from his tricky language to the Morse speech and to the hearing transcript to learn that three or four hours after the supposed attack, the task force commander on the *Maddox* cabled a warning that "freak weather," an "overeager sonarman" and the absence of any "visual sightings" cast doubt on the attack stories and called for "com-

[1] Pentagon and State managed to tie up the transcript of the August 6, 1964 hearing in so many security snafus that it was not finally released, until more than two years later, on Nov. 24, 1966—Thanksgiving Day, when it was calculated to attract as little attention as possible.

plete evaluation before any further action." No one would
know from his accounts then or now that no debris had been
found, though we claimed to have sunk two and possibly
three enemy vessels, and that we ordered our retaliatory attack without waiting to learn the outcome of a belated order
to search for debris.

You have to go back to that master of shyster lawyer
language, John Foster Dulles, to match McNamara's performance. If an attack occurred, how is it that every single
captured North Vietnamese naval man, including one who
was very cooperative, denied knowledge of any such attack?
How is it that Hanoi, which boasted of the August 2 attack, has always denied the August 4 attack? If Hanoi attacked on August 4, in the face of Johnson's warning after
August 2, how is it that its entire tiny fleet was caught by
surprise in our retaliatory attack the next day? "Why," as
North Vietnam asked in its own White Paper, which has
been kept from the U.S. public, "does this small country
with its negligible naval forces embark on a systematic
provocation of the U.S. Seventh Fleet with its 125 vessels
and 650 airplanes?" And then take no precautions against
a counter-attack?

Fake incidents are hardly new in the history of military
bureaucracies. The Japanese military staged one near Mukden in 1931 to begin its seizure of Manchuria despite parliamentary disapproval. The *Pueblo* incident illustrates another notorious military tactic: they play incidents up or
down like an organist depending on whether they want to
make or avoid war. Faked or exaggerated, the Tonkin incidents were used for a war buildup the White House and
Pentagon wanted. The full truth is still hidden and we ap-
plaud Senator Gruening's demand that the staff study prepared by the Fulbright Committee be released. We are told
that McNamara urged "a decisive commitment" in Vietnam on Johnson a few days after the Kennedy assassination.
If the Foreign Relations Committee digs further, it will find
that both the bombing of the North and the commitment
of combat troops to Vietnam were planned at the Pentagon

several months before the Tonkin Gulf incidents, that the Tonkin Gulf resolution was prepared beforehand, and that the course pursued beginning in July, 1964, was calculated to create some kind of incident sooner or later, *to justify the expansion of the conflict already decided upon.* A Rostow Plan No. 6 for "PT-boat raids on North Vietnamese coastal installations and then by strategic bombing raids flown by U.S. pilots under either the U.S. or South Vietnamese flags" was disclosed in *Newsweek* as early as March 9, 1964. The coastal raids began in July, 1964, by vessels we supplied the South Vietnamese, with crews we trained, backstopped by intelligence our planes and ships provided. The collection of such information was the business of those "routine patrols" on which we sent our destroyers.

We cannot claim freedom of the seas for such missions. If Russian vessels backstopped Cuban naval attacks on Florida, we would take counter-action even if they stayed outside our three-mile limit. There are no territorial limits in war, and this would be war. We merely compounded the offense and assured an "incident" by instructing our destroyers to ignore North Vietnam's 12-mile limit. McNamara in his prepared statement fell back on the disingenuous argument that we had no "official documentary" evidence of this 12-mile limit. Even the Geographer's Office at the State Department admitted to us in a telephone inquiry that it had always been assumed that North Vietnam's limit, like China's and North Korea's, was 12 miles. What was McNamara waiting for—an affidavit from Ho Chi Minh? Men who can so twist the truth are a menace to national security.

March 4, 1968

McNAMARA AND TONKIN BAY:
THE UNANSWERED QUESTIONS

The big surprise at the Tonkin Gulf hearing held by the Senate Foreign Relations Committee was the attitude of Secretary McNamara. Chairman Fulbright greeted him with affection and respect. "I for one," Fulbright said, "regret to see you leave the Government at this very perilous time in our history." The Committee's mood was nostalgic. Even Morse, McNamara's sharpest interrogator, called him "one of the most dedicated public servants I have experienced in my twenty-eight years in the Senate." Fulbright assured the Secretary that in seeking to establish the truth about the Tonkin Gulf incidents of August 2 and 4, 1964 "the purpose is not to assess blame on anyone, certainly not upon you." It was "simply to review the decision-making processes of our Government in time of crisis."

At the beginning of the hearing Fulbright was characteristically gentle and philosophical. He expected McNamara, in this last appearance before a Senate committee after seven years as Secretary of Defense, to enter into the investigation in the same spirit. Fulbright was encouraged in this expectation by McNamara's manner the previous Sunday on *Meet The Press*, when the Secretary referred sadly if cryptically to the many mistakes made in Vietnam and volunteered a confession of personal responsibility for those committed at the Bay of Pigs. Fulbright said he had long since admitted his own shortcomings in connection with the Tonkin Gulf affair. "I am a firm believer," Fulbright said, "in the idea that to acknowledge my mistakes of yesterday is but another way of saying I am a wiser man today." He expressed the view that it might be helpful to future Senators and Secretaries "and even future Presidents" if the way decisions were reached in the Tonkin Gulf affair was reviewed. "Mr. Secretary," Fulbright said, "I believe all of us here share your own desire that the United States profit from its mistakes—not repeat them."

But McNamara came on not as a fellow philosopher, ready to reminisce on the common errors of the past, but— as one staff member later phrased it—"like a 10-ton tank." At no point was he prepared to admit that *any* mistake had been made in the Tonkin Gulf affair. He showed no readiness for reflection, much less contrition. The Pentagon's own internal communications on the Tonkin Gulf incidents, as obtained by the Committee, were confused and murky. The full truth about the incidents, which triggered the first American bombing raids upon North Vietnam, is unlikely ever to be uncovered. But in McNamara's version they were evaluated with accuracy, beyond a shadow of a doubt, and responded to with precision. This was neither dove nor hawk but a fighting cock, insisting that he had had everything at all times completely under control. It was as if the Committee had touched the most sensitive depths of his pride, and perhaps also threatened to open up aspects of the story McNamara preferred to remain untold. In retrospect his belligerence may prove as significant as it was unexpected.

Very early in the hearing McNamara indicated that he was going to play rough. He was examined in executive session, and at the very beginning Fulbright expressed the wish that McNamara withhold his prepared statement from the press "until after the Committee has gone through the hearings" and decided what to do about its own staff report on the Tonkin Gulf incidents. "I thought it would be much fairer," Fulbright said, "if we could arrange to release them simultaneously." McNamara seemed to agree, but added, "I doubt very much that we will be able to withstand the pressures of the press today without releasing it." The Pentagon is not exactly inexperienced in the ways of withholding information it does not wish to release. Sure enough, during the luncheon recess it seized upon a remark by Senator McCarthy to the UPI as an excuse to release McNamara's prepared statement to the press, jumping the gun on the Committee and getting McNamara's version into the papers first. McNamara told Fulbright when the executive session resumed after lunch that McCarthy told the UPI McNamara had admitted that one of our destroyers had penetrated North Vietnam's twelve-mile limit. "That is just contrary to what I said this morning," McNamara said. "I cannot stand by without having what I said in my statement issued." McNamara could not have hung his release on a more finely split hair. Indeed the difference between what McNamara said and what McCarthy said he said does not speak well for McNamara's candor.[1]

The real purpose served by the release of the statement even before the executive session was over was not to correct McCarthy but to make the headlines with the counter-attack with which McNamara ended his prepared statement. "As a final point," McNamara said,

I must address the insinuation that, in some way, the Government of the United States induced the incident on 4 August with the intent of providing an excuse to take the retaliatory action which we in fact took. I can only characterize such insinuations as monstrous . . . I find it inconceivable that any-

[1] McCarthy said McNamara had admitted that the *Maddox* had invaded North Vietnam's twelve-mile territorial limits. What McNamara said (page 13 of the hearing) was that "at no time . . . did the *Maddox* depart from international waters. It had been instructed to approach the North Vietnamese coastline no closer than eight nautical miles and any offshore island no closer than four nautical miles." This invasion of the twelve-mile limit was defended by the Secretary on the grounds (1) that the U.S. "recognizes no claim of a territorial sea in excess of three miles" and (2) that there is "no official documentary confirmation" of North Vietnam's claim to twelve miles. Presumably, even if there were such a claim, we would not recognize it. Four years ago McNamara simply deleted from the first Senate hearing (pages 32–33) the fact that our destroyers were instructed to penetrate North Vietnam's twelve-mile limit in order to keep this provocative action from public knowledge. Morse's Senate speech of February 29 (at the bottom of col. 1 p. S1948 of the *Congressional Record*) disclosed a portion of the orders to the *Maddox* which McNamara did not mention. The destroyers were instructed *not* to approach the Communist Chinese coast any closer than 15 miles. Why did we honor Peking's twelve-mile claim and not Hanoi's? Obviously we were willing to risk provoking the North Vietnamese but not the Chinese Communists.

one even remotely familiar with our society and system of Government could suspect the existence of a conspiracy which would include almost, if not all, the entire chain of military command in the Pacific, the Chairman of the Joint Chiefs of Staff, the Joint Chiefs, the Secretary of Defense, and his chief Civilian Assistants, the Secretary of State, and the President of the United States.

Put in this question-begging form, of course it was monstrous. Nobody had implied any such widespread conspiracy to bring about the incident—real or alleged—of August 4. But the more one studies the evidence so far available the more one does begin to see the outlines of a conspiracy, not to fabricate the incident of August 4, but to plan and to put into motion a sharp escalation of the Vietnamese war in the very year Johnson was campaigning for election as a man of peace. The aerial deployments necessary, not for the one retaliatory strike which followed the Tonkin Gulf affair, but for the continuous bombing of North Vietnam which began in February, 1965, were ordered and accomplished— as was the alerting of combat troops—in the very year Johnson was promising *not* to widen the war. This was the conspiracy and this *was* monstrous and this is what will fully appear if the Senate Foreign Relations Committee finishes its job. One major and one minor aspect of this conspiracy are left tantalizingly unexplored in the record of the new hearing at which McNamara testified.

The major aspect involves the steps taken to widen the war *before* the Tonkin Gulf incidents which provided the public excuse for them. As these steps began to figure in Fulbright's examination of McNamara, it was curious to see how McNamara—who remembered so much and so exactly at other points in the hearing—suddenly suffered from lapses of memory. Fulbright cited an article by Hanson Baldwin in the *New York Times* in July of 1964—a month before the Tonkin Gulf incidents—saying that Pentagon sources were then arguing for extension of the war into the North. "Were there in fact," Fulbright asked, "recommendations by the U.S. military at any time from late 1963 until July of 1964 to extend the war into the North by bombing or any other means?" This was hardly a minor question, especially for an executive like McNamara who prided himself on a detailed knowledge of what was going on at the Pentagon. Suddenly the super whiz kid went blank. "Mr. Chairman," McNamara said, "I would have to check the record on that." He couldn't recall any such recommendations but he would be happy to check his records and supply an answer. The answer as supplied and inserted in the printed record at page 22 was amazingly cryptic and inconclusive. It consisted of two short sentences saying, "We have identified no such recommendation. A check of the records of the Joint Chiefs of Staff is continuing." Will the Committee drop the matter, or will it insist on an answer?

Fulbright turned at this point from McNamara to General Wheeler, Chairman of the Joint Chiefs of Staff, and asked, "I wonder if General Wheeler knows at this time?" The General's answer will repay careful study. "I don't believe so, Mr. Chairman," General Wheeler began. This was a curious reply. A witness asked if he knows something will usually reply (1) yes, or (2) no, or (3) that he can't recall. The General came up with a new one. Asked if he "knows at this time," he replied "I don't believe so." What does it mean when a witness says he doesn't believe he knows something? That he is waiting to go home and interrogate himself more closely? The rest of his reply, in its odd qualifications, indicates that the General was not being frank with the Committee. "I think that the proper answer would be," General Wheeler continued, "that there were certain intelligence activities [deleted] but to the best of my knowledge and belief during that period there was no thought of extending the war into the North *in the sense of our participating in such actions, activities*" (my italics). He too promised to check for the record.

Now, in one of the three speeches Morse made on the

Senate floor after the hearing (on February 21, 28, and 29) one may find the key to what Wheeler meant by saying "there was no thought of extending the war into the North in the sense of our participating in such actions." In those three speeches Morse courageously "declassified" most of the hitherto secret material the Foreign Relations Committee obtained from Pentagon files in its investigation. In his speech on February 29 Morse threw new light on the program for commando raids on the North, known as OPLAN 34A, which figured in the background of the Tonkin Gulf incidents. He revealed for the first time that this was initiated as early as February, 1964 jointly by the South Vietnamese forces and the U.S. military advisory group in Saigon. Under this program Morse told the Senate,

U.S. personnel were assigned to provide advice, training and assistance for South Vietnam maritime operations against North Vietnam. A U.S. Navy detachment was assigned to train and advise the South Vietnamese. For the first few months in 1964, the operations consisted of intelligence and interdiction missions. In July of 1964—the same month the *Maddox* began its patrol—the U.S. made available eight fast patrol craft to the Government of South Vietnam. The new craft permitted an extension northward of the attacks on North Vietnam.

From this account it appears that General Wheeler was being disingenuous when he said "there was no thought of extending the war into the North in the sense of our participating in such actions." If General Wheeler interrogates himself more closely he may come to believe that he knows more than he believed he knew when he was before the Committee.

While this secret extension of the war northward was going on, the State Department was not idle. It was drawing up that blank check resolution for a wider war in Southeast Asia which has come to be known as the Tonkin Gulf resolution. This was drawn up well in advance of the Tonkin Gulf incidents. Here again McNamara suffered a lapse of memory. When Fulbright asked him whether he had ever seen the draft resolution before the Tonkin Gulf incidents,

McNamara said, "I don't believe I ever saw it." McNamara added that he called William P. Bundy, Assistant Secretary of State for Far Eastern and Pacific Affairs, "to ask him if he had any recollection that I ever saw it. He states that he has no recollection that I did, and he believes that I did not. But I can't testify absolutely on that. My memory is not that clear." What followed in the interrogation shows how even the best of our human IBM machines can on occasion falter:

THE CHAIRMAN: Mr. Bundy told this committee that this draft was prepared some months before the Tonkin incidents in the hearing. You know that.

SECRETARY McNAMARA: I know that, but I don't think he said I saw it.

THE CHAIRMAN: No, I was asking you, you don't think you saw it?

SECRETARY McNAMARA: I don't believe I saw it, and he doesn't believe I saw it.

THE CHAIRMAN: Isn't it customary for the State Department to consult you on a matter of this kind?

SECRETARY McNAMARA: Well, if it were a working paper and that is apparently what it was, no. It hadn't advanced to a point of decision within the Government.

Presumably "the point of decision" was the August 4 incident. It is hard to believe that a Secretary of Defense as famous for his memory as McNamara would recall so little. The war was being extended northward through these new South Vietnamese activities under American auspices, and a resolution was being readied to authorize the President to widen the war any way he saw fit. Yet McNamara cannot recall that he ever heard of it.

The same kind of amnesia appeared when Fulbright went on to open up the most important question of all. This was whether the aerial and troop deployments announced under cover of the Tonkin Gulf incidents were actually made *before* those incidents occurred. This is where the body is buried and this is where the Senate Foreign Relations Committee owes the country an obligation to complete its job.

To understand the tricky story of these deployments one must go back to Secretary McNamara's appearance before the Senate Foreign Relations and Armed Services Committees on August 6, 1964—the original hearing on the Tonkin Gulf resolutions. In his formal statement at the joint hearings, the Secretary said "the President and his principal advisers" had decided "that additional precautionary measures were required in Southeast Asia" and that "certain military deployments to the area are therefore now underway." Six measures were announced, including "movement of fighter-bomber aircraft into Thailand" and "the alerting and readying for movement of certain Army and Marine forces." In retrospect this was the signal that the Johnson Administration was getting ready for the bombing of the North (which could only be done on a heavy and continuous scale by using Thai bases) and for the dispatch of combat troops to South Vietnam. But this was not discussed with the Senators at the joint session nor did it figure in the Senate debate on the Tonkin Gulf resolution. If known, it would have alerted the Senate and the public to what was being cooked up under cover of the incidents and the resolution. It would also have ruined Johnson's image as a peace candidate against Goldwater. So this information was withheld. It was included in McNamara's prepared statement and inserted later in the hearing record, but this record was so tied up in security snafus by the Pentagon and the State Department, and by other forms of delay, that it was not finally released until more than two years later, on November 24, 1966. Even the date was skillfully chosen, for that was Thanksgiving Day, when it was likely to attract little public attention.

By that time the hearing record looked like ancient history to the press anyway, and nobody noticed the significance of the military deployments disclosed in McNamara's prepared statement. I myself never read it until several weeks later when I began to do the research for the three-

part series on Senator Fulbright which I wrote for *The
New York Review*. It was in the second installment of that
series, published in *The New York Review* January 12,
1967,[2] that public attention was first called to the significance of those carefully buried revelations. I later learned
that although the prepared statement was passed around at
the hearing, no member of either committee seems to have
had time to read it and ask questions while McNamara was
on the stand. Later, other Senators could only have noticed
it if they had taken the trouble to come to the committee
hearing rooms and read the record there, for as a classified
document it was not—until November 24, 1966—available
elsewhere *and it was not available to the staff assistants on
whom Senators depend.* This was perhaps the most ingenious devise ever hit upon to make a record which could
effectively be kept secret while allowing the Administration
afterward to claim that they had disclosed it.

The transcript of the new hearing of last February 20
shows that McNamara and his military aides are still unwilling to be wholly frank about these deployments. The Mc-
Namara statement of four years ago said that because of
"the unprovoked and deliberate attacks in international
waters . . . certain military deployments are now underway." This gives the impression that the deployments were
a result of the Tonkin Gulf incidents, even though—as any
sharp reader will notice now—they were taken *before* the
passage of the Tonkin Gulf resolution, which was Johnson's
authority for widening the war. But now the Senate committee found neither McNamara nor Wheeler ready to assure it that the deployments did in fact follow the incidents.

When Fulbright could get only a fuzzy reply from Mc-
Namara on the deployments, he turned to General Wheeler
and said, "Maybe you are more familiar with military
equipment. Is it not true that fighter-bombers were moved
into Vietnam and Thailand immediately after this [the incident of August 4] took place?" General Wheeler replied,

[2] The series may be found reprinted in my book *In a Time of Torment* (Random House). See pp. 343-4.

"We moved some bombers in 1964, but I don't have the exact dates." But Wheeler had not been asked for exact dates, but only whether the deployments followed the second incident. So now Fulbright asked him, "Were these units alerted to impending movement prior to the Tonkin Gulf incidents?" The question, prepared by staff, reflected the fact that the Senate committee had collected considerable evidence that certain units *had* been alerted for movement before the incidents. Wheeler's reply was wary:

GENERAL WHEELER: To the best of my knowledge, not, Mr. Chairman, but I will check that also, and make sure.

THE CHAIRMAN: Would you check whether or not you considered sending these units to South Vietnam and Thailand prior to the Tonkin incidents?

GENERAL WHEELER: I will check that particular point.

At this point in the printed record there is a notation, "The following information was later supplied: We have not identified any air unit which had been alerted for movement into South Vietnam or Thailand prior to the Tonkin Gulf incidents. A check of the records is continuing." This is not a very responsive reply. It does not answer the question of whether such movements were "considered" before the incidents. The phrasing is odd and in one respect revealing. It does not say that *no* units were alerted. It says only that it has not "identified" any "*air* unit" so alerted. The reply is confined to air units. The key to this may lie in a fact to which John McDermott first called attention in his penetrating review of Roger Hilsman's *To Move a Nation*.[3] McDermott noted a series of steps taken in the first half of 1964 to escalate the Vietnamese conflict, including the announcement on July 27, just six days before the first Tonkin Gulf incident, that we were sending another 5,000 troops to South Vietnam. Oddly enough no discussion of this appears in the Committee hearing. Were the "selected Army and Marine forces" to which McNamara referred in his statement of August 6, 1964 in addition to this 5,000? If so, were

[3] *The New York Review*, Sept. 14, 1967.

the new combat troops alerted before the incidents? Why
this nonsense about "a check of the records is continuing,"
as if we were dealing here with some obscure disappearance
of a recruit or a mislaid shipment of rifles? Could men as
able as McNamara and Wheeler really be so ignorant of so
important a matter? Why were they unable by unequivocal
answer to scotch a suspicion most damaging to them and the
Administration?

Morse interrupted at this point in order, as he said, to
"help" the Secretary refresh his memory, and read McNamara his own description of these deployments in his prepared statement of four years ago. McNamara replied:

I will be very happy to determine when those movements were
first initiated, when the units were put on alert, and whether it
occurred before the Tonkin Gulf incidents. I don't recall that
information.

This was followed by a veritable cascade of non-recalls
by a Secretary who is otherwise famous for his phenomenal
memory:

THE CHAIRMAN: Mr. Secretary, if there had not been a Ton-
kin Gulf resolution would you have recommended to the Presi-
dent and Congress that the U.S. step up its military assistance to
South Vietnam . . . ?
SECRETARY McNAMARA: Mr. Chairman, I think it is a specu-
lative question. . . .
CHAIRMAN FULBRIGHT: But to be more specific, was there
any plan for such an intensification of the U.S. involvement?
SECRETARY McNAMARA: No, not that I can recall.
CHAIRMAN FULBRIGHT: Did it then include the bombing of
North Vietnam?
SECRETARY McNAMARA: Not that I know of, Mr. Chairman.

The Secretary seemed a little nervous about that last non-
recall, for he hastened to add, "I don't mean to say that
contingencies and targets hadn't been examined, because
they had been, prior to that time, but there was no plan for
further buildup that I can remember, and no plan for the
bombing of the North." So he did remember that "contingencies and targets" had been "examined." In that case in

what special sense did he mean that there was "no plan for the bombing of the North"? Any lawyer will agree this was not a very frank witness. The information he offered to supply was not forthcoming in time for the published record. Nine days later McNamara stepped down as Secretary of Defense. Will the committee insist on the full answer promised it?

I now want to bring up a matter I cannot prove, though I am willing to give the Committee the name of the witness who will confirm it. This is that a few days after the assassination of Kennedy, Secretary McNamara, with the support of McGeorge Bundy and Secretary Rusk, urged on the new President the need for "a decisive commitment" in Vietnam, and insisted—over Johnson's reluctance to be rushed quite that fast into so important a decision—that it had to be made quickly. This is known to quite a few insiders, and it is perhaps one reason why in an earlier period Senator Morse—who is, I might say in passing, not the source of this information—used to call it "McNamara's war." The Committee ought to recall McNamara and insist that he clear up the whole question of just when this major step-up in the war was initiated. For all this goes back to the question not just of decision-making in a crisis *but of crisis-making to support a secretly pre-arranged decision.* Here the war-making power of Congress was clearly usurped by a private cabal in the executive department, which was soon to confront Congress and the country with a *fait accompli,* and to do so within a few months after Johnson was elected on the pledge not to do what this inner circle had already decided he would do.

Now we come to a related matter which the Committee has left unexplored, though it goes to the very heart of how the incident came about that was used to cover and to authorize the deployments for a wider war, for the bombing of the North and for the commitment of combat troops in the South. This other "buried body" may be found in Mc-

Namara's prepared statement for the February 20 hearing. Its significance has escaped attention, perhaps because it could not be fully understood except against the background of the new revelations made by Morse in his Senate speeches of February 2, 28, and 29. The country and future historians owe Morse an enormous debt for those speeches, as for those four years ago on August 5 and 6, 1964, in which he first began to lift the bureaucratic curtain of secrecy surrounding the Tonkin Gulf incidents.

In his prepared statement McNamara made an admission which must have cost his pride a good deal. It shows that he was not in full control of his own Department at a crucial moment. The fact that he disclosed it himself would lead a trained lawyer to believe that he knew or feared that documents in the hands of the Committee's staff had already disclosed this, and that he thought it best to slip the fact into his statement to protect himself under interrogation. This is what the Secretary said: "I learned subsequent to my testimony of August 6, 1964, that another South Vietnamese bombardment took place on the night of August 3–4." And at page 90 of the printed record, under interrogation by Senator Cooper, McNamara added a supplementary revelation. "At the time of the specific incidents of August 4," he admitted to Cooper, "I did not know of the attack by the South Vietnamese, but we knew of the operations, and some senior commanders above the level of the commanders of the task force did know the specific dates of the operations." This seems to mean that certain senior commanders knew something McNamara still did not know three days later when he appeared before the Senate committees on the Tonkin Gulf resolution four years ago.

To appreciate the import of this revelation one must turn to the Morse speeches, and to the classified messages and information he courageously made public in them. If we look at Morse's speech of February 29 we will see that the patrols on which the *Maddox* was engaged were far from "routine," not only in the sense that they were electronic espionage missions, but that, when the first attack occurred on the *Maddox* August 2, 1964, it was only the third occasion since 1962—or within two and a half years—on which an American naval ship had approached the North Vietnamese coast. "The appearance of an American destroyer along the Vietnam coast," Morse disclosed on the basis of the Pentagon documents obtained by the committee but still classified, "was highly unusual." The next point to be noted is that the first attack on the *Maddox* followed by 40 hours the first coastal bombardment of North Vietnam by the raiding vessels we had supplied the South Vietnamese.

Now we can understand the significance of McNamara's revelation. On August 2 the *Maddox* was attacked for the first time. On August 3 the President warned of serious consequences if that attack were repeated and announced that we were not only sending the *Maddox* back into those waters but a second destroyer, the *Turner Joy*, with it. That night, the night of August 3–4, there was a second coastal bombardment, the knowledge of which—so McNamara says—was kept from him though it was known to certain higher naval commanders and presumably arranged by the joint South Vietnamese and MACV headquarters in Saigon, which we now know from this new hearing directed these naval attacks. It was the night after this second bombardment—the night of August 4–5—that the alleged second attack on the *Maddox* and the new destroyer accompanying it took place. Whether the second attack actually took place or not—and this is still unclear—that new coastal bombardment was a provocation likely to make a second clash more probable, and therefore to trigger the retaliation Johnson had already threatened.

The Committee cannot close its books on its investigation without determining who was responsible for so provocative a move at so tense a moment, why it was not disclosed to the Secretary of Defense, and whether it was known to the White House. This is the kind of provocation military bureaucracies have often committed in the past to set off a war against the wishes of civilian authorities; a well-known example was the Mukden incident in which the Japanese military themselves blew up one of their own troop and supply trains to give them the excuse they wanted in 1931 for war on China and the annexation of Manchuria. If Chairman Fulbright really wants to explore decision-making in a crisis, he cannot leave these questions hanging.

One final but intensely important point ought also to be explored. *The Politics of Escalation*[4] shows that the Tonkin Gulf incidents occurred just when,

within a two-week period, proposals for a Geneva-type conference on Vietnam and, more largely, Southeast Asia had emanated from three important sources—U Thant, France and the USSR—and had been favorably received in Hanoi and Peking. None of these proposals, it should be noted, specified conditions or "preconditions" in urging that a solution be sought for the Indo-Chinese crises.

On July 24, the day after De Gaulle urged reconvening the Geneva conference, Johnson rejected it as a conference "to ratify terror," and declared "our policy is unchanged." But pressure for negotiations was rising. A bright chance for peace was torpedoed in the Tonkin Gulf that August night four years ago, and the Senate Foreign Relations Committee has a duty to find out how and why.

March 28, 1968
New York Review

THE SUPINENESS
OF THE SENATE

"It was on the dignity of the Senate that Augustus and his successors founded their new empire. . . . In the adminis-

---

[4] By Franz Schurmann, Peter Dale Scott, and Reginald Zelnik; Foreword by Arthur Schlesinger, Jr. (Fawcett, 1966).

tration of their own powers, they frequently consulted the great national council, and *seemed* to refer to its decision the most important concerns of peace and war. . . . The masters of the Roman world surrounded their throne with darkness, concealed their irresistible strength, and humbly professed themselves the accountable ministers of the Senate, whose supreme decrees they dictated and obeyed. . . . Augustus was sensible that mankind is governed by names; nor was he deceived in his expectation, that the Senate and the people would submit to slavery, provided they were respectfully assured that they still enjoyed their ancient freedom" (italics in original).

—Gibbon's *Decline and Fall
of the Roman Empire*

A major item of business for the Senate in the session now beginning is finally to act upon Resolution 187. More than any other single piece of proposed legislation, it reflects the widespread revulsion in Congress against foreign adventures created by the Vietnamese war. It would express "the sense of the Senate" that in the future no President should commit the United States to use its armed forces abroad without "affirmative action" by Congress. The intent is to prevent future Vietnams.

The resolution was introduced by Senator Fulbright in 1967. Nothing he has done in years won such instant and wide support. It was unanimously approved, within his Senate Foreign Relations Committee, by Republicans and Democrats, doves and hawks. It was also endorsed outside the Committee by Democrats as conservative and influential as Russell of Georgia and McClellan of Arkansas, and by Republicans as far to the right as Allott of Colorado and Young of North Dakota. Its passage, overwhelmingly, by the Senate seemed assured. Yet it was somehow kept off the floor all through the 1968 session.

The Johnson Administration opposed the resolution, as did the military bureaucracy, and managed without protest from Fulbright or any other Senator to keep it from a vote. Mansfield, who had voted for the resolution in committee, turned around and put it on the shelf as majority leader, but promised to let it come to a vote this year. The resolution takes on added importance as a possible restraint on the new Administration. Nixon showed his interventionist tendencies as early as 1954 in Vietnam, and his Secretary of Defense, Melvin R. Laird, in his book *America's Strategy Gap: A House Divided*, thought Eisenhower was too weak in the Hungarian revolt and Kennedy at the Bay of Pigs. The excuse for putting off a vote at the last session was that it might upset the peace talks on Vietnam, though the resolution clearly applies only to future commitments. The Paris talks, dragging on, may provide a similar excuse this year. So easily is the Senate deflected from its purposes.

The terms of the resolution were intended to shore up the fast disappearing Constitutional right of Congress to decide when the United States shall go to war. When the Foreign Relations Committee after extensive hearings[1] sent the resolution to the Senate in 1967, it did so with a report[2] which spelled out the reasons why the framers of the Constitution gave the power to declare war exclusively to Congress. It also spelled out step by step the steady usurpation of that power by the Presidency since 1900 and particularly since the Korean war in 1950, the first full-scale war in which the United States ever engaged without a declaration of war by Congress.

The essence of the story is that in the case of America, as of Rome, imperial adventures abroad weakened constitutional controls at home. "The use of the armed forces against sovereign nations without authorization by Congress," the committee reported, "became common practice

[1] "US Commitments to Foreign Powers," Senate Foreign Relations Committee Hearings on Senate Resolution 151, August 16–23 and September 19, 1967. [This later became Senate Resolution 187.]

[2] "National Commitments: Report No. 797," 90th Congress, First Session, November 20, 1967, Senate Foreign Relations Committee.

in the twentieth century." It began with Teddy Roosevelt's use of the Navy against Colombia in the Panama affair, and continued with the military interventions of Taft and Wilson in the Caribbean and Central America. The trend, the report said, was "accelerated by Franklin Roosevelt" and "continued at a rapid rate" under Truman, Eisenhower, Kennedy, and Johnson, "bringing the country to the point at which the real power to commit the country to war is now in the hands of the President."

When the committee contrasted this practice with American constitutional principles, its stately old-fashioned language seemed to be invoking a past as irretrievable as Rome before the Caesars:

There is no uncertainty or ambiguity about the intent of the framers of the Constitution with respect to the war power. Greatly dismayed by the power of the British Crown to commit Great Britain—and with it the American colonies—to war, fearful of the possible development of monarchical tendencies in their new republic, and fearful as well of the dangers of large standing armies and military defiance of civilian authority, they vested the power to commit the United States to war exclusively in Congress. This power was not, like certain others, divided between the executive and the legislature; it was conferred upon Congress and Congress alone.

"The dangers of large standing armies and military defiance of civilian authority" are not antiquarianisms. To put the war power in the hands of the President is to put decision-making behind the closed doors of the White House and the Pentagon where the sheer inertial power of our huge standing armed forces may count for more than public opinion, and secrecy fosters "military defiance of civilian authority." This is how Presidents, though elected, can become Caesars, and like them the masters and the pawns of the imperial legions.

Nuclear weapons invest the process with terrifying dimensions. "The executive, by acquiring the authority to commit the country to war," the committee said in a grave and eloquent conclusion, "now exercises something approaching absolute power over the life and death of every living American—to say nothing of millions of other people all over the world." It warned that unless the constitutional checks on the war-making power were restored, "the American people will be threatened with tyranny or disaster." It is not often that so sedate a committee speaks so strongly.

The incident which occurred, or is supposed to have occurred, in the Gulf of Tonkin three years earlier, and unleashed our first bombings of North Vietnam, weighed heavily in the making of that Committee report. It called Lyndon Johnson's Tonkin Gulf resolution of August, 1964 "the extreme point in the process of constitutional erosion [of the Congressional war-making power] that began in the first years of this century." Yet, as often happens, the judicious gravity of the words bears little relationship to the Senate Committee's haphazard, grasshopper-minded tendency to leave the most serious matters hanging, forever unfinished, in mid-air. Its chairman, Fulbright, and its staff—whether with or without the concurrence of its members, we are not told—have just brushed its five-year-old off-and-on-again investigation of the Tonkin Gulf affair under the rug, uncompleted. This is the one story which, fully disclosed, might have dramatized for the country the dangers on which that "no more Vietnams" resolution dwelt and thus mobilized the popular support required to push it through the Senate this year.

For some unexplained reason this inquiry has instead been brought to a sudden end with a twenty-page document so obscurely put together that its wider significance went unnoticed and few newspapers paid it any attention at all.[3] The timing of the release, just five days before Christmas, with Congress out of session and most Committee

[3] For three that did, see Walter Pincus in the *Washington Post,* Joseph R. L. Sterne in the *Baltimore Sun,* and a shorter, less comprehensible dispatch in the *New York Times,* all on December 20.

members home for the holiday, and the form—an exchange
of letters between Fulbright and the Pentagon with the
scantiest explanation—were alike calculated to attract as
little attention as possible.

This hasty burial is of special interest to readers of *The
New York Review of Books*. When this writer, in the issue
dated March 28, 1968, called attention to the questions left
skillfully unanswered by Secretary of Defense McNamara
and by General Wheeler, chairman of the Joint Chiefs of
Staff, in the hearing held by the Committee on the Tonkin
Gulf affair in February, 1968, Senator Fulbright put the
article into the *Congressional Record* (March 22, 1968),
with a compliment to the writer ("one of the most indus-
trious and perceptive journalists I know") and a pledge to
get the answers. "I can assure Senators," Fulbright told the
Senate that day, "that the Committee intends to continue to
press the Department of Defense for the information we
have thus far not received."

The only result, however, is the flimsy little "Part II"
released by Fulbright in December. The Committee in this
document fails to explain what it did get and to pursue what
it didn't. The military bureaucracy, with adeptness and
effrontery, has left the Committee's main questions and requests as unanswered as they were in the hearing a year ago.
How can Congress, and particularly the Senate, pick up the
reins given it in the Constitution over war-making when the
Senate Foreign Relations Committee, its main reliance in
foreign policy, proves so slack?

The Tonkin Gulf episode provides a model of how *not*
to run an investigation. The first hearing was little more
than a rigged affair, held jointly by the Foreign Relations
and Armed Services Committees of the Senate. It was designed to help the White House stampede the Senate into
voting a blank check for wider war in Southeast Asia, as it
did next day, with only two negative votes, those of Morse
and Gruening, both tragically lost in the last election. Ful-

bright in that hearing, as in the Senate debate, ran interference for the Administration.

A second hearing was held secretly in May, 1966, after Fulbright became disillusioned, but the record has never been released; indeed its very existence is little known. I verified the fact that it had taken place after noting some scattered references to it by Senators in later years. A third, and it now appears the final, hearing was held last February 20, and a censored text released shortly afterward. So the only hearing made public which can really be called investigatory was limited to a single day and heard only the two official witnesses, Secretary McNamara and General Wheeler. At the close of that hearing Senator Gore was so exasperated by the evasions and contradictions that he told Fulbright, "I think we must plow forth and get to the full truth and make a report to the public." [4] But the plowing has ended in mid-furrow. Fulbright and the Committee have written finis to the investigation without making *any* report.

A considerable number of participants in the Tonkin Gulf affair were so antagonized by what they considered the falsities in the official accounts that they volunteered, at considerable risk to their careers, to tell what they saw. Some that night were on board our destroyers in the Tonkin Gulf. Others were in the command and control center at the Pentagon through which a series of frantic messages passed before the President went on the air and ordered our reprisal raids on North Vietnam.[5] But none of them was ever put on the stand to testify before the Foreign Relations Committee, and Fulbright has never explained why.

In his brief Preface to Part II, released in December, Ful-

[4] February 20, 1968 Hearing, p. 109.

[5] The AP had a special team digging out and interrogating these witnesses and sent out an extensive story on what they had to say. But few papers published it. The fullest version we have seen appeared in the Arkansas *Gazette*, July 16, 1967, and may be found at Page S1888 of the *Congressional Record* last February 28. See also the interviews with participants by David Wise in his penetrating account for *Esquire* in April of last year.

bright acknowledges that "several participants in the Tonkin incidents—or individuals in some way associated with the incidents—have voluntarily offered information." But he says, without giving the reasons for it, that the Committee "decided early during our reexamination of this incident to limit published material to that related directly to official documents or communications." To do so was to limit the public record to the documents the Pentagon could be prevailed upon to supply, and to the testimony and examination of the two official witnesses. So one-sided a procedure gave the advantage to the Administration. Fulbright says defensively in the closing sentence of his Preface to Part II that "nothing of an unofficial nature which came to the Committee's attention would, in my opinion, alter in any significant way any conclusion which might be reached by a careful examination of the printed record." What conclusion? That the August 4 incident never happened? That it was a fraud? Fulbright owes the Senate and the country something better than this coy and cryptic teaser.

The first stage in smothering the Tonkin Gulf affair appears in retrospect to have been Fulbright's decision not to publish his staff study even of the documents supplied by the Pentagon. This was circumvented in part by Morse, who put most of them into the *Congressional Record* as part of the speeches he made on February 21, 28, and 29. These courageous analyses will stand as the closest thing to a final report. But his disclosures were no substitute for the staff study itself. Few people will know that Morse's source was the staff study. We are left without the benefit of the staff's own conclusions and of the Committee's considered judgment.

The second and final step in blanketing the investigation is embodied in the so-called Part II released in December. This acquiesces in the Pentagon's refusal to deal with the questions left unanswered by McNamara and Wheeler in February. Fulbright could have taken his fight for the answers to the Senate floor this session. He could, as a minimum, have drawn public attention strongly to the Pentagon's unwillingness to give the Senate anywhere near the full truth. He has done neither.

By far the most important document the Committee wanted last February was the "command and control report" which covered the flow of messages through the Pentagon and the White House the night the decision was made to attack North Vietnam. That such a report existed was kept from the Committee's staff investigators when they asked the Pentagon for relevant reports and documents. Its existence became known only through an anonymous letter dated December 26, 1967, which Morse put into the record of last February's hearing (pages 84–5). "I doubt that all the power of the United States Senate," the anonymous letter said, "could ever penetrate far enough into the super-secret world to learn much about what goes on." The letter said the situation was so bad that "right now the JCS [Joint Chiefs of Staff] is refusing materials in their field wanted by people working on Vietnam for the Secretary of Defense, most obviously because they are fearful it would serve the Secretary of Defense's purposes, not theirs."

Such are the Byzantine labyrinths created by the size and secrecy of the military establishment. The anonymous letter gave the full title of the command and control study so the Committee could ask for it. The anonymous letter said the document would show that "after the first report of the attack there was a report there probably had not been an attack at all. But the President was to go on the air to address the nation about the retaliatory attacks *that had already been planned* . . ." (my italics). The President would have missed out on prime television time if the decision had been held up for confirmation. The attacks already planned would have had to be called off if further investigation had shown that no attack occurred.

This is where the body is buried. The Joint Chiefs of Staff, according to an article published by Hanson Baldwin in the *New York Times* a month before the Tonkin Gulf incidents, had been arguing for an extension of the war into North Vietnam. All was ready for the bombings. This was a case study in instant crisis. It shows how easily Congress can be stampeded and how readily the truth may be hidden. The Senate Committee had some powerful levers at its disposal to obtain that report or to learn its contents. A colloquy on page 77 of the February hearing disclosed that there were forty copies extant and Senator Gore said, "You will find some at the Rand Corporation." If the Pentagon refused to supply a copy, one could have been subpoenaed from Rand. The same page disclosed the name of the man who wrote the report, a man identified only as Ponturo. It took only a telephone call on our part to locate a John Ponturo at the Institute for Defense Analysis, and to learn from him (1) that he was employed by IDA in 1964 at the time it made this report for the Joint Chiefs of Staff, (2) that the report was still classified, and (3) that no one from the Foreign Relations Committee ever contacted, much less questioned, him.

The same page of the hearing last February contains a similarly vague reference to a man identified only as "Fubini." The context indicates that he was a Pentagon official who was dubious about the August 4th incident. Fulbright even got McNamara to say that he had no objection to Fubini's being called as a witness. McNamara said that Fubini, at the time of the Tonkin Gulf incident, was Deputy Director of Research and Engineering. There is reason to believe Fubini saw the excited exchange of messages that night. He too was never called as a witness, though his background would have made his appearance before the Committee impressive. Instead he is left buried in this shadowy reference in last February's hearing.

When we checked the *New York Times* index, we found that Dr. Eugene G. Fubini, a brilliant Italian-born physicist who served as an electronics expert with our

armed forces in World War II, became Deputy Director of
Research and Engineering at the Pentagon in March, 1961,
and was made an Assistant Secretary of Defense by Kennedy in June, 1963. He resigned in June, 1965, to become a
vice-president in charge of research for International Business Machines Corporation, but stipulated that he would
not work on any military business for IBM.[6] A *New York
Times* story of July 4, 1965 said he had become an abomi-
nated " 'no' man" at the Pentagon because he had so often
vetoed proposed military research projects. Fubini also was
never questioned by the Foreign Relations Committee or its
staff. What a way to run an investigation!

The tactics used by Fulbright in dealing with the Pentagon in the wake of last February's hearing—as newly disclosed in Part II—were extraordinarily weak. It turns out
from the first document, Fulbright's letter of request to
Secretary Clifford, dated last March 1, that he did not
really ask for the command and control report. He merely
asked about "*the status* of the command and control report
evaluating the Tonkin Gulf incidents" (my italics). So
flaccid an approach invited the rejection it evoked. Acting
Secretary of Defense Paul C. Warnke replied last April 4
that "the study is not considered appropriate for dissemina-
tion outside the Department." The excuses given were that
it was "an internal study," that it "was not intended to be
. . . a comprehensive evaluation of the incidents themselves," and that it "was not prepared for review by the
Chairman of the Joint Chiefs of Staff." One wonders how
much would have been left of the report if the Chairman
had "reviewed" it.

Fulbright not only took this lying down but did not even
refer to the command and control report and the Pentagon's refusal to release it in the brief Preface, little more
than a page in length, with which he introduced Part II.
There is much in these few extra documents released last
December which was worthy of explanation. They provide

6 In January 1966, he was appointed to a four-year term on the Defense Science Board.

further evidence that we knew North Vietnam claimed a twelve-mile limit when we ordered our destroyers to penetrate it before the "incidents." There is a page which shows that the destroyer *Maddox* carried sixteen electronics experts, four from Taiwan, in addition to its regular crew, convincing evidence of its espionage mission.

From the tortured and disingenuous language of the Pentagon's replies to Fulbright, an expert—but only an expert —can learn just how spurious was that ultra top-secret information which McNamara several times showed the Committee—after clearing the hearing room of its staff, on the excuse that staff members had no security clearances higher than top secret! [7]

This was supposed to be an intercepted message which proved that the enemy attack of August 4 did take place. Now it turns out, from an assertion which Fulbright made in a letter of May 29, and which the Pentagon reply did not deny, that this "source never said that there had been an attack on August 4," and that all this source did was give the Defense Department "the name of a man already known."

It is a pity this revelation of official mendacity is buried so deeply and obscurely that few will ever be aware of it. One can also learn for the first time from Part II that a cooperative captured North Vietnamese naval officer who earlier told U.S. naval interrogators that there *was* an attack on our

[7] We call attention, for its amusement and enlightenment value, to the colloquy which occurred at this point in the hearing last February. The hearing was held behind closed doors, with press and public barred. But that was not enough for McNamara. He wanted the committee staff barred also:

THE CHAIRMAN [Fulbright]: The staff . . . are cleared for top secret information. . . .

MR. [CARL] MARCY [Committee Chief of Staff]: All of the members of the staff who are here submitted renewal requests for top secret clearance recently and, so far as I know, all of these requests have been granted.

SECRETARY MCNAMARA: But that is not the issue. Clearance is above top secret for the particular information involved in this situation. [February Hearings, p. 36]

Apparently the bigger the whopper the higher the classification.

destroyers August 2 but *not* August 4 was able to speak
with authority. He was second in command of the enemy
squadron which was supposed to have made the second attack!

There are also vital lessons to be learned from the exquisite samples in Part II of the rich double-talk the military
bureaucracy can fabricate to hide the facts from civilian authority. These merit attention in future crises and deserved
comment and explanation by Fulbright and his Committee.
One of the unanswered questions—and hardly a minor one
—was whether any air units had been alerted for the bombing of the North even before the alleged attack on August 4
occurred. The answer supplied was brief, crisp, and
opaque:

The Joint Chiefs of Staff have not identified any air unit which
had been alerted for movement into South Vietnam or Thailand
prior to the Tonkin Gulf incidents.

One answer might have been that no air units *were* alerted
before the bombing; another answer might have been that
they were. If the Joint Chiefs of Staff cannot answer yes or
no to that simple question, there is something seriously
wrong with their control of the armed forces. To reply instead that they have not "identified" any units alerted before the incidents is an obvious evasion. The Joint Chiefs of
Staff doesn't even say they *cannot* identify such units.
    Fulbright let them get away with a similar bit of bureau-
cratic obfuscation in reply to another key question. This, as
Fulbright put it in his letter of last March 1, was "whether
recommendations were made by the Joint Chiefs of Staff
[before the Tonkin Gulf incidents occurred] to extend the
war to North Vietnam." This also could have been answered "yes" or "no." Instead the Joint Chiefs of Staff reply
was that (1) while the Joint Chiefs of Staff during "the first
part of 1964" before the August incidents had "examined
several possible types of military action against North Viet-

nam in order to deter that country from continuing its aggression against South Vietnam" and (2) "contingency planning for these actions was taken," "no *definitive* recommendations for extending the war to the North had in fact been made by the Joint Chiefs of Staff" (my italics). What does "definitive" mean? Why "definitive" instead of "definite"? Could it be that there was a definite recommendation but the "definitive" orders to attack were waiting for the incident?

Fulbright not only accepts these evasions but fails to comment upon them in his dry and equivocal Preface. He says the new documents have been made public "because of the possible historical interest"! And he adds that his purpose was not "to revive the controversy over the incidents in the Gulf of Tonkin but to complete, to the best of the committee's ability, the public record."

What a sham!

February 13, 1969
New York Review

PART VIII

Endless War

WHY NOT TIMBUKTU
OR EASTER ISLAND?

Lyndon Johnson does not give the impression of a man eager to reach the peace table. He seems, on the contrary, sorry that he ever brought the matter up. Little more than a year ago in his letter of February 6, 1967, to Ho Chi Minh, Johnson suggested that peace talks might be held in Moscow. Now he balks even at Pnom Penh or Warsaw. He seems to have Walt Rostow feverishly thumbing through the geography books for places Hanoi would be most likely to turn down. The presence of an embassy and adequate communications are among the conditions sprouting up all around Mr. Johnson's often repeated "anywhere, any time." But the latest batch of 10 suggestions are all countries in which Hanoi has no embassy. And in two of them the only places remotely describable as cities—Kabul in Afghanistan and Katmandu in Nepal—may not even have a telegraph office. Only Timbuktu or Easter Island could be more exotic. Lyndon Johnson is willing to show up anywhere Ho Chi Minh won't go.

In that earlier letter to Ho, Johnson suggested "bilateral discussions." Now he is beginning to give out invitations wholesale. Each invitation adds another obstacle to the choice of a site, and if talks ever do get under way the more kibitzers the less the danger of reaching an agreement. One of the newer conditions is adequate press facilities. Johnson normally is not so tender of the press. He is no goldfish-bowl operator. When he really wants to make a deal, he gets his prospect alone and pulls down the blinds. In his letter to Ho last year suggesting peace talks in Moscow, Johnson felt sure of rejection because Hanoi had insisted all along on complete and unconditional cessation of bombings as a precondition. He must have felt equally secure on

March 31 when he asked Hanoi to talk while bombing
went on between the 17th and 20th parallels. It must have
been a harrowing experience when this time Ho tricked him
by accepting. The White House may be piling up conditions to protect it from a similar surprise in the future.
Johnson would like to go on getting credit for making
peace offers so long as he can be sure nothing will come of
them.

"Everything is unclear," U Thant told the AP as he left
New York for Paris April 20. This succinctly summarizes
the situation. I see several significant strands as I try to un-
ravel what Johnson has been weaving. One is that anti-
aircraft defenses around Hanoi and Haiphong had made
bombing in that area prohibitively expensive. Roger Hilsman, Assistant Secretary of State for Far Eastern Affairs in
1963–64, reported in the April issue of *Foreign Affairs*
quarterly that "as of several months ago" the bombing of
the North was estimated to have cost the U.S. $6 billion
"while the dollar value of the facilities destroyed in the
North is estimated to be $340 million." On this basis, Hils-
man said, "Some experts argue that an end to the bombing
might actually result in a military gain rather than a loss."

Hilsman said the targets are few and most of them easily
repaired. He quotes one discouraged pilot as saying, "The
hell of it is that we fly through all that flak for what? To
attack a two-bit bridge that we've already knocked down
five or six times. The damned center spans are now made of
wood, and they put them up again in hours." In any case
the weather above the 20th parallel has been bad; the monsoon in that area won't lift until May. So in the haggling
within Administration councils, it was decided to limit the
bombing to the Panhandle, where there has been little anti-
aircraft. As an extra dividend to the hawks, it was decided
to try and do as much bombing in that narrow coastal strip
as had previously been done in all of North Vietnam.

The second strand in the policy shift was to borrow a
favorite cliché of the Kennedy brothers and propose to
shift more of the war to the South Vietnamese. Johnson

always likes to steal the opposition's thunder, and this was
the easiest way out when confronted with Westmoreland's
demand for 200,000 troops. This made General Creighton
Abrams the logical candidate to succeed Westmoreland,
since he has been working with the ARVN forces, and has
been their advocate in asking for more and better weapons.[1] As Secretary Clifford explained at his press conference April 11, the ARVN forces are to be given "a degree
of preference" in the supply of "our most modern weapons" because we want to "work ourselves into a posture
where the South Vietnamese will take over the war."

This is *really* clutching at a straw. There wouldn't be a
half million U.S. troops in South Vietnam if the Saigon ruling clique over the past decade hadn't demonstrated its
utter political and military incapacity. They themselves
know it. "We are not going to press for real all-out mobilization," one Senator blurted out during the new draft law
debate in the Saigon legislature (*Washington Post*, April
18), "we have to appease American public opinion by
showing we are trying to do something." A day after Robert Kennedy said that if elected President he "would try to
bring American troops home and substitute South Vietnamese soldiers," Peter Braestrup reported from Saigon
(*Washington Post*, April 15), "Few U.S. or South Vietnamese military men see this as a practical proposition." He
reported that if the U.S. troops pulled out, the ARVN
forces would have to abandon the five northern provinces
including Hué and Danang "just to hold their own farther
South." This realistic if gloomy estimate illustrates the continued and wondrous capacity of the U.S. government to
adopt policies which a substantial portion of its own military and diplomatic bureaucracy privately think make no
sense.

Nevertheless this decision to shift the burden of the war
to the South Vietnamese must have decisive impact on the

[1] From a different point of view we can't see much sense in putting
a World War II tank general into command of a war that calls for political finesse.

third strand of policy—to make another try at winning by
peace talks what the U.S. has been unable to win by military means, and that is an "independent," non-Communist
South Vietnam.

Johnson's new "peace" offer and his "abdication" served
to disarm the opposition and throw the peace movement off
balance. (McCarthy has proven much smarter and abler
than Kennedy in seeing through it.) The best guess is that
he did not expect Hanoi to accept his offer, which would
give him a chance to have both credit for a peace move and
later an excuse (when the monsoon ends) to resume full
bombing of the North if he wants to. Hanoi by its qualified
acceptance put the ball back into his court. But how can
Johnson pursue the policy of handing over the war to the
South Vietnamese, how can he get Thieu to mobilize more
men, if at the same time he agrees with Hanoi's demand that
all bombing end before peace talks begin?

As I reconstruct the scenario of events, Thieu must ask
Washington for two or three years leeway to prove that he
can take over the war. To stop the bombing and enter on
talks now would pull the rug from under the Saigon military regime and Mr. Johnson's hopes. A coalition or a neutralist regime would seem to Johnson that "fake solution"
he says he will never accept. So Johnson must stall as long
as he can before going to the conference table, and seize on
every possible way to delay a conclusion when he gets
there. If there are no talks or the prospect of talks breaks
down too early, his popularity will go down again and his
credibility gap widen as never before. This is the bind in
which Hanoi has put him.

But Johnson is no Joshua to bid time stand still. The
shadows of three crises lie ahead. One is military. The U.S.
military is doing splendidly again—in the field of public
relations. Khesanh is advertised as a victory for airpower
and "Operation Complete Victory" (What will they call
the next one? Operation *Even More* Complete Victory?) is
sweeping the enemy victoriously away from Saigon. But
the steady resumption of shelling day after day at Khesanh

indicates the enemy didn't withdraw very far in that area. And on the night of April 16, for the first time since Têt, the Viet Cong bombarded a South Vietnamese Reserve Officers School on the outskirts of Saigon, killing four and wounding 30 of the Saigon military; there were also heavy civilian casualties in the adjoining quarters for officers' families. This attack took place not far from the powerful U.S. air base at Bien Hoa and in the very heart of the area supposedly cleaned up by "Operation Complete Victory."

One of the most experienced war correspondents in South Vietnam, François Nivolon, in reporting this attack (*Le Figaro*, April 18) said, "It has proved anew, and this will surprise no one here, that it is almost impossible to assure the security of the capital of South Vietnam and its environs." M. Nivolon recalled that after the Têt offensive representatives of the U.S. military command estimated that it would take ten divisions to guarantee absolutely the security of Saigon. That is roughly half the strength of the U.S. Army. It is clear that the enemy can still strike almost anywhere he chooses and that surprises may lie ahead. One cannot exclude a new offensive strong enough to unseat the Saigon regime, and replace it with Buddhist and other non-Communist elements willing to negotiate peace.

April 29, 1968

PLAYING FOR TIME
TO CONTINUE THE WAR

A high (and hawkish) Pentagon official told a friend of mine recently, "The purpose of the partial bombing pause and the talks in Paris is to reduce the fighting to a level the American people will tolerate for a long time without giving up our basic aim," i.e., an "independent" South Vietnam. This remark I believe is the best key to the confused and tangled talks in Paris. A similar clue may be found in Max Frankel's dispatch from Austin in the *New York Times* June 2. "It was primarily," he wrote, "to buy time at home to keep waging the war's military and diplomatic battles abroad that Johnson accepted the dovish counsel of at least a partial halt in the bombing on March 31 and threw in his retirement for good measure." Frankel added, "So far the tactic has worked better than he dared to hope. The bitter controversy has abated and the political candidates have been muted." The purpose is to defuse the peace issue during the election campaign, to tread water until after it is over.

I thought at one time that Johnson would make peace as the best way to undercut Bobby Kennedy, whom he hates, and elect Humphrey, or perhaps even run for reelection himself as the man who made peace. But I think I underestimated Johnson's craftiness. His strategy is to undercut McCarthy and Kennedy by *appearing* to seek peace. This political strategy fits his immediate and urgent economic needs. The U.S. cannot escalate the war, adding another 200,000 men to those already in Vietnam, without imposing the kind of wartime taxes and economic controls which would be dangerously unpopular in an election year. *The campaign dictated a pause*. But there is no sign that Johnson has given up his ultimate aims nor changed his deep emotional attachment to this imperialist crusade in Southeast Asia. He was speaking from the heart when at the Korean Consulate in Honolulu April 17 he forecast a continued American protectorate over "the New Asia"—what a euphemism for Chiang Kai-shek and the corrupt oligarchies under our wing! "I deeply believe," Johnson said, "that my successor—whoever he may be—will act in ways that will reflect America's abiding interest in Asia's freedom and in Asia's security." This will certainly prove true if his successor is Humphrey or Nixon, Rockefeller or Reagan.

Much that may seem puzzling falls into place if the peace

talks and the limited bombing pause are viewed as a tactic for a breathing spell. There are, for example, beginning to percolate through Washington bits and pieces of off-the-record talks which preceded the Paris conference. The U.S. negotiators seem to have done very little thinking or planning for any kind of a compromise political settlement. The U.S. is ready for mutual de-escalation, but mutual de-escalation in the absence of a political settlement merely means that the other side give up the revolt and the war and leave the military junta in power in Saigon. This seems to be the shape of that "satisfactory solution" for which, as Humphrey told students at St. Paul May 27, we should be willing to stay at the conference table "for months and if necessary for years." This is what Senator McCarthy sensed in his interview with Frank McGee of NBC June 2, when he said the government wasn't saying or doing anything different from what it had been saying or doing "before the negotiations supposedly began"—

We're still saying no coalition government—Dean Rusk is—no recognition of the National Liberation Front, accelerate the war, call up more troops. There is no pullback, there is no limitation on the search and destroy missions.

There is no change because no real change has taken place.

Jeremy Campbell from Washington in the London *Evening Standard* May 8, and Stuart H. Loory from Washington in the *Los Angeles Times* May 31, both reported that Johnson's March 31 "abdication" address was preceded two weeks earlier by a dramatic reversal of opinion on the part of Johnson's non-official advisers on the war. A panel which includes retired generals Bradley, Taylor and Ridgway, Douglas Dillon, McGeorge Bundy and George Ball, had always before been for vigorous prosecution of the war, the only dissenter being Ball. After their meeting March 18—so goes this story—they startled the President by reporting that continued escalation, intensified bombing and increased American troop strength "would," so Loory writes, "do no good." But there is no indication that these somber military conclusions had any firm political impact. Far from preparing the public mind for compromise, the Administration has shut the door firmly on talk of a coalition. Westmoreland was allowed to use the forum of a Presidential press conference at the LBJ ranch May 30 for another of those silly performances that build up the illusion that a military victory is possible. And now we learn that on May 6 a secret directive was issued by Westmoreland to U.S. commanders in Vietnam calling for "a major breakthrough to a military victory." You don't waste more lives if you're really serious about peace.

June 10, 1968

THE WILLFUL BLINDNESS
OF McGEORGE BUNDY

McGeorge Bundy's speech at De Pauw University is a victory for the peace movement and a justification for those of us who will vote for neither Nixon nor Humphrey. It is a victory in that one of the chief architects of our Vietnamese policy now says that we must end the bombing of the North and deescalate the American military effort, irrespective of what Hanoi does. The speech is also a justification for the election cop-out because this Republican, who was in charge of foreign policy at the White House for Kennedy and Johnson, this symbol of the bi-partisan prowar Establishment, sketches out a new consensus for a new Administration which would neither get us out of the Southeast Asian quagmire nor forestall more Vietnams elsewhere.

The logic of Bundy's position is withdrawal. The man who advised Johnson three years ago to bomb the North now says the bombing is futile and that the war cannot be won no matter how much we escalate it. He says an annual cost of $30 billion, a yearly toll of 10,000 American lives, "the increasing bitterness and polarization of our people," and "the growing alienation of a generation which is the best we have had" are "now plainly unacceptable. So we must not go on as we are going."

But then he turns around and says that "we should cut back—but we need not and should not give up." This man who was so arrogant and smug three years ago in rejecting the anti-war protests of his old academic colleagues is still unprepared to change our basic course or to admit any mistakes. But until those mistakes are clearly faced we are bound to repeat them. He even reminds those who favor the bombing and escalation that his own shift of position does not spring from "moral outrage or political hostility to the objective." This is a confession of moral callousness and willful political blindness.

This is a preview of the best we can expect from either candidate. It is not good enough. Bundy wants us to cut back but to get ready to keep troops indefinitely in Vietnam. He proposes the withdrawal of 100,000 to 150,000 troops in 1969 with a saving of $5 to $8 billion, and a comparable reduction in 1970. These puny half-measures will not free the funds or moral energies we need to meet our racial and urban crises. The Pentagon can swallow up those few billions saved and grab for more on the excuse that we must give our fighting men, especially since their numbers have been reduced, the very best and newest equipment. Bundy would have us dig in for a long war by military reforms which would make it possible to keep combat troops there for longer than the present 12-month rotation. Yet he seriously offers this mishmash as a means by which a new Administration can "reknit the essential relation of confidence between itself and the nation."

To hang around in Southeast Asia is to invite trouble. Without a fundamental revision of policy, we will continue to bleed away our youth and substance in this trap of our own making. Bundy still wants an American protectorate over Southeast Asia. The climax of his folly lies in his assertion that "in a policy of cutback there is still ample room for steadfast support of our friends, and ample guarantee against defeat imposed by the external aggressors . . . ample demonstration for all who live in the area not only that we keep our commitments but that we know how to change our course with care and clarity." Those conceited words will be read with derision in Saigon, Bangkok and Taipei. What if the withdrawal leads to a series of Dienbienphus as the guerrillas overwhelm our shrunken enclaves? What if the Saigon regime collapses as "our friends" head for Switzerland with the money our troops have spent in their bars and bordellos? What if Thailand erupts into a second Vietnam? Bundy's mini-imperialism is a recipe for new disasters.

All this springs from Bundy's unwillingness to reassess a past for which he bears so much responsibility. That is why we find him saying that though "the burden of this war must now be lifted" that does not mean "it should never have been fought" nor that "we are required now, by our new necessities, to lose what has been gained in the strategic sense." What have we gained? We have made a mess of Vietnam and Vietnam has made a mess of the United States. Yet Bundy is still pursuing that line of policy to which we have several times called attention as the key to Johnson's abdication. *This is to reduce the level of conflict to a point the American people will tolerate for a long pull without giving up the basic aim of restoring a South Vietnam under American control.* This is Macchiavellianism parading as a search for peace. It will not work politically and it will not work militarily. Yet this is the best the Establishment offers for the next four years.

Bundy says that a nation ready "to keep at least 100,000 troops in place for years" cannot be accused of "faithless withdrawal." To whom would we be faithless? Three years ago just before the bombing of the North began he was in Saigon trying to bring peace amid the warring factions on our side. The situation there is worse than ever. The recent rumors of a new coup reflect the fears of the die-hards that Big Minh's return may foreshadow a broader government and peace negotiations. Bundy will not admit publicly that the Saigon regime today, with a military junta and a rigged Constitution, has the same unrepresentative social base as Diem's dictatorship. It is heavily weighted on the side of the 10 percent pro-war Catholic minority against the pro-peace Buddhist majority. It is heavily weighted on the side of the landlords against the peasants. It is heavily weighted on the side of North Vietnamese refugee generals who want to reconquer the North against a South and Central Vietnamese majority *of every class* which is for some kind of compromise with the Viet Cong for the sake of peace.

In the name of "self-determination" we are allowing a minority to prevent the majority from determining its own future. This is the sham Bundy would continue, and this is much the same sham bolstered by our Special Forces and Green Berets and electronic anti-guerrilla sniffers and snoopers and all the vast panoply of our military power in the Third World. The only way to free our resources, financial and spiritual, for that "greater America" Bundy calls for is, to free us from militarist delusions, to cut the Pentagon down to size, to try and build a better world through the United Nations, and not by putting navies on every sea and armies on every continent in the effort at a Pax Americana which can only bring our country's ruin. Only such a New Charter can win the best of this generation back to normal politics.

October 21, 1968

WHY THE CASUALTIES RISE
AS THE PEACE TALKS
GO ON

President Nixon's dismissal of a cease-fire in Vietnam calls
for close examination. It was sophistry to say that a cease-
fire "may be meaningless" in a guerrilla war because of the
difficulty in controlling it. Whatever element of truth this
may contain as a general proposition, the history of past
truces in the nine-year-old Vietnam war shows that the other
side has had little difficulty in enforcing a cease-fire on its
own troops. Cease-fires have been broken by the other side
on any meaningful scale only when they wanted to break it,
as in the Têt offensive last year, or in defensive response
to the aggressive patrolling which has been our military's
own way of getting around cease-fire orders in holiday
truces. Until the bombing pause the U.S. official line was to
call for a cease-fire as the price of a bombing halt. The line
has changed because we hope to exploit the present situation by "clean-up" operations against the guerrillas in the
South. That is why casualties still rise as the peace talks go
on.

A neat bit of censorship is helping to hide the truth. The
Pentagon gives out figures on attacks initiated from our side
but the figures on enemy-initiated attacks are "classified,"
an antiseptic word for censored. One of these censored figures came to light last December 14 when the *New York
Times* in an editorial, "Endangering the Peace Talks," said
"Since the bombing halt, the enemy has initiated only one
battalion-sized assault. By comparison last month American
troops mounted 63 battalion operations and South Vietnam
staged 664 such campaigns." It said the purpose was "to extend South Vietnamese Government control over disputed
areas and territory long controlled by the Vietcong" and

warned that such an effort "to upset the balance in Vietnam in advance of a settlement in Paris is bound to produce a reaction sooner or later" and risk a flareup "that could wreck the chance for a negotiated peace."

In the wake of the Nixon press conference, we went over to the Pentagon to check the *Times* figures and bring them up to date. We found the tempo of offensive operations from our side had gone up about 25 percent in December over November. The figures on battalion-sized operations from our side in December were 824 South Vietnamese, 84 U.S. and 48 combined, or a total of 956 as against the 727 figure the *Times* gave for November. But when we asked for the figures on enemy-initiated actions of battalion size, we were told that all the figures on enemy-initiated actions were in classified tables. We went to two different sources and finally put in a formal question on why such figures were classified, but we're still waiting for an answer. The *New York Times* assertion was not challenged.

One officer explained that any paper with a man in Saigon who kept a sharp eye on the daily communiqués could get figures on enemy-initiated attacks. Obviously the totals on enemy attacks do not keep any information from the enemy he does not already know. This is political not military censorship, designed not to confuse the enemy but to hide what is going on from the American public. We hope some members of Congress will insist that these figures be released.

The course in Vietnam becomes clearer if one compares it with U Thant's original three-point plan for peace. At his press conference January 28, the Secretary General noted that two of the points had been put into effect—the bombing of the North had ended and talks among all the parties involved had begun. U Thant's third point was a gradual de-escalation of the fighting. Instead of de-escalating in response to the considerable de-escalation on the other side, we have been stepping up both ground and aerial action in the South, as we have the bombings over Laos.

Tacitly or explicitly, it is now becoming clearer, Johnson exacted a sharp price when he ended the bombing of the

North. He imposed severe restrictions on enemy activity while making it possible for us to increase ours. The Nixon Administration is carrying on the strategy of Johnson's. This strategy has two elements. The first is to threaten resumption of the bombing in the North if the other side should resume substantial forays or shellings from the DMZ or should attack the larger cities. The second is to take advantage of these military limitations on the other side to move considerable forces from the northern part of South Vietnam where they had been on guard against a possible invasion from the DMZ. These forces have been moved south, for "pacification" operations in the Mekong Delta. This has been a guerrilla stronghold since the earliest days of the uprising against the French. The aim is to reconquer the Delta for the Saigon regime.

The bombing of the North ended November 1. The escalation from our side began at the same time. In the three months since, more than 2,000 Americans have lost their lives. White House orders explain the rising .casualty lists. Clark Clifford lifted the curtain on them last November 24 when he said, "General Abrams has specific instructions to maintain constant and intensive pressure on the enemy." The fight-and-talk strategy was ours. Our Madison Avenue-minded military invented a new soap ad phrase to sell this accelerated warfare. They renamed it "accelerated pacification." Clifford added loyally that this was "the right psychology and the right strategy to follow now," but he expressed the hope that when "we begin to make progress in Paris" and agreement "in certain areas" was reached, "then instruction could be given by Hanoi to their battlefield commanders, and instruction could be given here by President Johnson to General Abrams to withdraw from contacts with enemy forces." The enemy began withdrawing from contact and trying to evade battle months ago. But there has been no de-escalation on our side. Three weeks later on *Face the Nation,* Clifford declared himself "inordinately impatient with the continued deaths of American boys in Vietnam" and urged a cease-fire. Neither Johnson nor Nixon seem to share this impatience. Nixon can cut the casualties any time he orders de-escalation and a defensive strategy, as proposed by Senator McGovern in a speech February 3 to Clergy and Laymen Concerned About Vietnam.

The premise of negotiations is that neither side can win a military victory. If we are negotiating, why go on killing? If we hope to achieve our aims in South Vietnam by a step-up in the killing, why negotiate? The cynical answer is that the negotiations serve as a smokescreen. Neither the U.S. military nor the Saigon regime ever wanted to negotiate. The Paris talks for them only make it easier to continue the war. There is a steady flow of optimistic stories from Saigon on how well the war is now going. One by Charles Mohr in the *New York Times* January 3 put its finger on a crucial, though nonmilitary factor. "One important factor on which present optimism is based," Mohr wrote, "is the hope that a decision to continue to prosecute the war can be reconciled with the domestic American desire 'to ease the pain.' "

Few noticed the realities reflected in the last AP weekly casualty report from Saigon (*Washington Post*, January 31). The report covered the week ended January 18 (196 U.S. dead and 1,277 wounded) and the week ended January 25 (190 U.S. dead and 1,224 wounded). Why are casualties still so heavy? The AP explained that while "there has been no sustained large-scale fighting since last fall . . . thousands of U.S. and government troops carry out daily operations in search of the elusive enemy." It added that "pushes are also being made into areas long held by the Vietcong, and in these, even when no opposition is encountered, there are casualties from mines and booby traps." How long can these offensive operations go on without a counter-offensive from the other side? As we write, for the first time in three months, there have been three battalion-sized enemy attacks in the past few days. It is time to make the U.S. public aware of all this before fighting flares up again in full fury.

It is nonsense to say that you cannot have a cease-fire in Vietnam. Fighting ended in the first Vietnamese war when a cease-fire was negotiated at Geneva in 1954. Then it was part of the general settlement. The question is one of policy, not feasibility. The Viet Cong and Hanoi oppose a cease-fire until there has been a political settlement. The U.S. and Saigon don't want a cease-fire until there has been a military "settlement." They cling to the old hope that the war will end with the enemy "fading away," a favorite phrase of Henry Cabot Lodge, whom Nixon resuscitated to be his chief negotiator at Paris. The U.S. military seem to be making their plans on the assumption that there will be no settlement in Paris. They plan a prolonged American occupation, though on a reduced scale. "From those most deeply involved in overall strategy" in Saigon and Washington, *U.S. News & World Report* January 27 reported that our military foresee a slow reduction of U.S. forces in Vietnam to 200,000 men by the end of 1971. They set that level as "the basis for a long-haul, low-cost effort in Vietnam that could continue indefinitely." On such a scale "low cost" could still mean $5 or $6 billion. The military men *U.S. News* interviewed regard Korea as a precedent. There we still have 50,000 men 15 years after the shooting stopped. We also have no peace treaty, a continued trickle of casualties and the ever-present danger that the war may break out again at any time. That is not a comforting precedent.

For the Vietnamese people the end of bombing in the North has meant an intensified terror from the skies in the South. B-52's are employed like buckshot, spreading destruction over wide areas, often on the edge of the cities, wherever we think a few guerrillas may be hiding. Nobody but the victims has any conception of what this horror means. It is not strange that in Saigon, despite press control and the thousands imprisoned for peace agitation, the cry for a cease-fire has been rising, though little reported in the U.S. press. Both *Le Monde* (January 28–29) and *Le Figaro* (January 29) report that elements which have hitherto strongly supported Thieu have joined the militant Buddhists in demanding a cease-fire. They quote Father Ca Van Lau, head of the Dan-Tien bloc in the Saigon Chamber of Deputies, as calling for a cease-fire now, as have two leaders of the Don Xa and the Grand Union Forces, organs respectively of the Hoa Hao sect and one faction of the Catholics. Both parties demonstrated last November in favor of Thieu. Now both parties have swung over to the Buddhist demand for an immediate cease-fire. In this, as in so much else, we are very poorly informed as to what ordinary Vietnamese think. To call for peace is still to risk jail in Saigon. The ungagged voice of popular sentiment may be better expressed in a manifesto issued in Paris (*Le Monde*, January 30) of a Movement of the Free Forces of Vietnam, representing both civilian exiles and former Vietnamese officers who fought in the army organized by the French. It terms the present regime "nothing but a prolongation of the Fascist regime of Ngo Dinh Diem," which "governs by terror." It calls for its replacement by a provisional government which can negotiate in Paris with the Viet Cong and Hanoi.

This parallels the position taken by Hanoi and the NLF in the Paris peace talks. The NLF spokesman called for the formation of a broadly representative provisional government in Saigon which would organize "free general elections in South Vietnam" and be prepared to deal with the NLF in the Paris talks as an independent and equal party (see texts in *Le Monde*, January 28). "Although they speak of negotiations for peace," the NLF delegate to the Paris talks said, "the United States continues to intensify the war," and "still does not wish to renounce their aggressive aims in South Vietnam." We are paying heavily in American lives in an effort to impose the Saigon regime by force on the South Vietnamese. That is why the casualties rise as the peace talks go on.

February 10, 1969

THE BEST-KEPT SECRET
OF THE VIETNAM WAR

It is hard to imagine a document less candid and more opaque than General Westmoreland's report on the Vietnamese war. He was in command in the years of its greatest escalation, and his account is about on a par with a complacent author reviewing his own book. It was—in his own considered opinion—a continuous triumph, a military marvel, in which any shortcomings and the singular lack of a final victory were all due to other factors—the limitations imposed on him by his political superiors and the impatience of the U.S. public. His account nevertheless contains an inadvertent revelation, and this in turn shows how effectively the U.S. military can close the shutters on an "open society" and keep the American people from knowing what is really going on. The revelation concerns the year 1965, when Westmoreland took over and made Vietnam an American war. This was the year we began to bomb the North and to put combat troops into the South.

It has always been assumed that we committed our troops again to an Asian ground war at the request of the Saigon government to save it from defeat. It now appears from Westmoreland's narrative that the commitment of U.S. combat troops was a unilateral decision by our military, that the South Vietnamese were not only reluctant to see our combat troops enter the country but when they did arrive tried to restrict their deployment and keep them as far as possible from Saigon and other populated areas. It is easy to imagine the uproar in Congress and the country if this had not been kept hidden at the time. If it had been known that the Saigon regime itself feared "Americanization" of the war, this would have strengthened the demand that we negotiate instead of escalate—that we do then what we are finally doing now after four years of futile bloodshed. It is heartbreaking to look back and notice that on February 1, 1965, just before we took over the war, only 258 Americans had been killed in Vietnam.

It is strange how, with all the correspondents there were in Vietnam, Saigon's misgivings were kept from public knowledge. This, the best-kept secret of the Vietnamese war, can now be pieced together from three passing references in Westmoreland's account. The first is on pages 98–99 in his chapter on 1965 as "The Year of Commitment." There he says that by the late spring of 1965 he was convinced that the Saigon government could not survive for more than six months unless the U.S. put in "substantial numbers" of combat troops. He nowhere says Saigon asked for them, only that *he* became convinced of their need. The troops began to arrive in July and the first combat commitment put the 1st Cavalry Division (Airmobile) into the Central Highlands. Saigon "concurred" in the decision to deploy the 1st Cavalry in the Highlands. "In fact," Westmoreland discloses, "they suggested that all deploying U.S. combat forces be concentrated in this comparatively remote area *in order to minimize the impact upon the South Vietnamese economy and populace*" (My italics). That sounds as if Saigon were less fearful of defeat than of American "invasion."

Westmoreland reveals that he decided to override Saigon's objections. He says he felt it "essential" that U.S. combat units "be available to reinforce and stiffen South Vietnamese forces in the critical areas of high population density." He adds, "Consequently, I planned to build up U.S. forces in an arc around Saigon and in the populous coastal areas *and not to restrict U.S. troops to the Central Highlands*" (My italics). To ignore Saigon's wishes was, clearly, to treat South Vietnam as a colonial possession, where we made the final decisions, just as the French had. This does not keep Westmoreland, eight pages later, from referring blandly to "the enemy's absurd claim that the U.S. was no more than a colonial power"!

When one checks back on what was happening in Saigon
at the time, one begins to wonder whether Westmoreland
may not have had other contingencies in mind when he insisted on deploying U.S. troops around Saigon. In 1965,
peace sentiment surfaced strongly in South Vietnam. In
February the Buddhists launched a campaign for a negotiated settlement, demanding the withdrawal of both U.S.
and Communist forces. In March the Saigon police broke up
an attempt by the smaller but powerful Cao Dai sect to
begin a similar campaign. In May, Catholic die-hards accused Saigon's last civilian government, that of Phan Huy
Quat, of secretly conspiring with the Buddhists to purge the
military and negotiate peace. In June they forced the civilian
regime to resign and brought in the Thieu-Ky military dictatorship. The military made its debut by ordering all of
Saigon's thirty-six Vietnamese-language papers suspended
for "purification," no doubt of peace sentiment. Was Westmoreland anxious to put U.S. troops around Saigon so they
would be ready to intervene if a government committed to
negotiating peace had come to power?

Even after the military takeover in Saigon, the South
Vietnamese regime still wanted to confine U.S. combat
troops to areas remote from population centers. This is
indicated on page 114 in Westmoreland's chapter on 1966
as "The Year of Development." [1] There he tells how he
positioned U.S. combat troops around Saigon. "This again
affirmed my conviction," he writes, "that the combined
U.S.–South Vietnamese military effort must begin in the
critical areas in which the population was concentrated."
Apparently the South Vietnamese government still disagreed with him, even though Ky was now Premier. For
Westmoreland adds, "Secretary McNamara, on a visit to
Saigon, supported me in my opposition *to yet another South
Vietnamese suggestion* that U.S. forces be deployed only
to remote areas such as the Central Highlands" (My italics).
In this carefully sanitized narrative, we are not told *why*
Saigon persisted in its "suggestion." One reason may appear

[1] I.e., military development.

on page 132. There, in discussing 1967 as "The Year of the Offensive," Westmoreland says that while half of our combat troops continued to be deployed "in close proximity to the heavily populated areas of the country," the other half were used as highly mobile "fire brigade" forces. Westmoreland says "their tremendous fire power made it vastly more desirable that they fight in remote, unpopulated areas if the enemy would give battle there. *This would enable the full U.S. fire potential to be employed without the danger of civilian casualties*" (My italics).

This is what Saigon feared. In discussing Psychological Operations/Civic Action, Westmoreland says on page 239, "Even though reports indicated that civilian losses ran well behind those experienced in World Wars I and II and Korea, I continued to emphasize the efforts to keep losses at a minimum." But the world wars were *total* wars, and the Korean war after the first few months was waged largely in North Korea, which was enemy territory and where we leveled just about everything. South Vietnam was not supposed to be an enemy country. Jonathan Schell, the *New Yorker* correspondent, spent several weeks flying over Quang Ngai Province in South Vietnam in the spring of 1967 in the two-seater FAC (Forward Air Control) planes which helped to find targets for air strikes. He found that 70 percent of the villages in the province had been destroyed, that about 40 percent of the population lived in "refugee camps" and that another 40 percent lived underground beneath their destroyed homes in areas that were shelled regularly by artillery fire. In his book *The Military Half*, Schell reported "the overriding fantastic fact that we are destroying, simply by inadvertence, the very country we are supposedly protecting."

Saigon also feared the effect of U.S. combat troops—as Westmoreland writes—"upon the . . . populace." Foreign troops always stir resentment, not only as an occupying power but even as an ally, largely because in an immemorial fashion they turn so many of the women into whores. But there was a special reason why Saigon had to fear the impact on its people. The "Americanization" of the war meant that a decade after the French had left, here was another, white man's army, taking over in South Vietnam. For so nationalistic a people as the Vietnamese, this was bound to impair the "face" of the Saigon regime, to make it seem a puppet again, and to drive more of the youth into disaffection or the rebellion.

Westmoreland writes (page 71) that on his arrival in South Vietnam the "strong and direct connection between military and political problems was quickly impressed upon me." In an appendix on "Psychological Operations/Civic Action" (on page 239) he speaks of Vietnam as "a politically sophisticated war." But there is very little evidence that he understands the politics of the war. Politics at bottom are people, and people are not Westmoreland's specialty. There is no sign in him of humor or humanity, even in dealing with our own troops—much less the enemy. I do not mean to imply that the general is an inhumane man; the best word to describe him is "wooden"—I first heard it from someone who knew him well in Vietnam. For him as for Admiral Sharp, who was in charge of the air and naval bombardment of the North, the war was an Operation Bulldozer, the application of overwhelming power to punish and to terrorize into submission, what the Germans in World War I called *Schrecklichkeit*.

The two main political problems were the fierce nationalism of the Vietnamese and the land hunger of the peasantry. You will find no light on either in the 350 double-columned pages of the Westmoreland-Sharp report on the war and the bombing. The nationalistic factor is what General Giap had in mind when he said that when the U.S. had a million men in Vietnam, the National Liberation Front would have won the war. We would have been well on the way to that million now if Johnson had given Westmoreland the 200,-000 more men he wanted instead of kicking him upstairs to Army Chief of Staff. The land question was summed up in a captured Viet Cong document first published in Saigon in

1966.[2] "The essence of the national problem," it said, "is the farmer's problem. The basic problem of the farmers is land. This is a strategic problem we can never neglect."

Land Reform is the No. 1 unmentionable in the Westmoreland report. His appendix on pacification talks of the "revolutionary development" teams, but he never explains what, if anything, was revolutionary about them. We are told they help the peasants improve "hygiene, sanitation, education and medical facilities." They ask for land and we give them latrines! The Army's Area Handbook for South Vietnam (1967 edition, page 319) says 2.5 percent of the landowners held half the cultivated land "and more than 80 percent of the land was cultivated by peasants owning no land at all" whom the landlords could dispossess "without cause." The peasant helped the Viet Cong because their defeat would mean the return of the landlords. This is the key to the war, and Westmoreland talks (page 242) of the "wealth of counterinsurgency experience" we have amassed in the war. But this, the basic lesson, he has never learned. Indeed a story probably lies buried behind his silence on this issue. Former Secretary of Agriculture Orville Freeman told a reporter recently (Richard Critchfield in the Washington *Star*, March 16) that in 1966 the U.S. Embassy in Saigon "informed Washington it opposed land reform on the grounds it would create political instability"!

Westmoreland no more understands the politics of the war at home than he did the politics of the war in Vietnam. In his first posture statement as Army Chief of Staff to the Senate Armed Services Committee on March 25 he said, "There are disturbing indications that deliberate efforts are being made to introduce the divisiveness found in our society into the Army." "Divisiveness" is what a free society is all about. If we are divided about Vietnam it is because the

[2] Page 28 of the report on Land Reform in Vietnam by the Stanford Research Institute for AID. It appeared originally in an August 1966 JUSPAO report on "The South Vietnamese Communists and Rural Vietnam."

country is waking up to the lack of candor and the lack of competence in the way he and the military have been running the war. The draftees reflect this same disillusion and dismay, and the same fear that our military are endangering the American economy and the stability of our society.

Even in his final report on the war Westmoreland is still relying on the body count as his primary index of military progress. He wages war by computer. "Since January 1, 1961," he reported to the Senate Armed Services Committee, "the NVA and VC have lost almost four times as many men killed in battle as have the South Vietnamese and Free World forces." This ratio, he added, "includes the figures for 1968, when the enemy lost 5.67 men killed for each allied soldier killed." The precision verges on caricature. Body-count statistics have long been a bitter joke among the troops, but Westmoreland takes them as seriously as a baseball box-score. Asia is no place for body-count warfare. Even with a 4-to-1 ratio in our favor, we could easily run out of American bodies long before we had made a dent in the teeming millions of Asia.

April 21, 1969

IMMEDIATE WITHDRAWAL
BECOMING A BANDWAGON

Whom the gods would destroy, they first drive inane. At the press conference last week it was hard to distinguish Nixon from Agnew. He implied that to criticize his slowdown in Southern school desegregation—15 years after the Brown decision—was to ask for "instant integration"! He could see no ethical problem in replacing Fortas, the judicial moonlighter, with Haynsworth, the judiciary's most absent-minded stock speculator. He said there were no American combat troops in Laos, except maybe in certain activities he did not care to discuss. He denied there was any numbers game in picturing the cancellation of 50,000 draft calls for November and December as a sign of approaching peace in Vietnam, although from June to October he had drafted 56,000 *more* men than last year and four days earlier the Pentagon had announced as an economy move that it would be taking 70,300 *fewer* men into the armed services. He rejoiced that at the UN he had found "no significant criticism" of U.S. policy in Vietnam; the Secret Service must have rushed him through the delegates' lounge pretty fast. He is against the Goodell bill to remove all U.S. troops from Vietnam by December 1, 1970 because he wants to get them out sooner, but it is better not to let the enemy know because that would destroy his incentive to negotiate. All we need to bring peace, he said, is a "united front" at home. The united front hasn't been advocated so openly since the 1937 convention of the Communist party. As for the student moratorium of October 15 and the other antiwar demonstrations planned for this fall, Nixon said "under no circumstances" would he "be affected whatever." Before making that remark, he should have phoned that man down on the ranch.

Either the wiretaps at 1029 Vermont Avenue have broken down or Nixon hasn't caught up with the transcripts. That has suddenly become the busiest place in Washington. On the tumultuous eighth floor, with 17 telephones and 11 outside lines, veterans of the McCarthy movement, led by David Hawk and Sam Brown, are swamped by the response to the Vietnam moratorium, a campus study-stoppage for peace on October 15. On the floor above, the more politically unkempt but equally vigorous New Mobilization Committee to End the War in Vietnam is having trouble coping with public response to its November 15 "March Against Death" to Washington and its "No Peace for Nixon" drive, aimed to make his public appearances uncomfortable until all U.S. troops are out of

Vietnam. The best index of the response is that even the bucolic state college in South Dakota where Nixon last June 3 could safely attack student dissent has defected; the names of the Vietnam dead will be read there on October 15 and a "tree of life" planted.

When Howard Zinn in *The Nation* a few years ago first proposed immediate and unconditional withdrawal, he was a political leper. Now this is becoming a bandwagon. When Congressman Allard K. Lowenstein, the founding father of the dump-Johnson movement, called a press conference last week to demand immediate withdrawal, he was flanked by spokesmen for organizations as sedately respectable as ADA and SANE. The next day Senator Goodell, once solidly right-of-center, called a press conference to launch S3000, to cut off all funds for U.S. military personnel of any kind in Vietnam after Dec. 1, 1970. Goodell named it "the Vietnam Disengagement Act." It is his bold move to build a peace and left-of-center constituency for re-election in the face of Republican New York Old Guard unwillingness even to renominate him. The bill brought an anguished cry from Rockefeller, who appointed Goodell to the Senate last year and wishes he hadn't. The Goodell bill gives the peace movement a focus and a target date. It also raises the ante for former Justice Goldberg, Goodell's most probable opponent, who will have to be explicit to match S3000.

Morse and Gruening would hardly recognize the Senate these days. Four Senators, Goodell, Hatfield, McCarthy and McGovern, have already endorsed the October 15 Moratorium. Senator Harris, the chairman of the Democratic National Committee, met with eleven other Senators and twelve Congressmen to extend the moratorium into the halls of Congress. There is talk of a movement to stay away that day and deny both houses a quorum. Senator Fulbright has promised hearings on the Goodell bill; these should provide a continuous antiwar forum. The most striking evidence of the rising rebellion came when Senator Cooper offered an amendment to the $20 billion military authorization bill to forbid any funds for U.S. combat troops in Laos or Thai-

land. This threw the Pentagon into a dither. Normally the
bill would easily have been voted down, but Stennis was so
afraid of a vote he decided to sweet-talk it instead. He said
he approved its purpose, but sought to de-fang the bill by
interpreting it as applicable only to funds available in the
$2.5 billion military aid bill. He then voted for it, precipitat-
ing unanimous approval, eighty-six to zero. This was the
first time in history that the leadership could only block a
measure by marshaling a unanimous vote *for* it, albeit trick-
ily reinterpreted. But the maneuver, even if effective, leaves
the door wide open to a less ambiguous amendment when
the military appropriation bill reaches the Senate.

October 6, 1969

LESSONS FOR NIXON

The United States may have yet to lose a war, but it is an
illusion to believe that it has never suffered defeat. Vietnam
is our third in Asia, as Castro's Cuba is our second in Latin
America. In his book *The Limits of Intervention*, Townsend Hoopes tells us that Johnson, after campaigning as a
peace candidate in 1964, ordered combat troops into Vietnam in 1965 because he did not wish to become "the first
American President to lose a war." Nixon nine months after
his election said the same thing to Steward Alsop of
Newsweek, to the joy of Brother Joe.

But Vietnam is not the first example of the limits on our
power to intervene. The Chinese Nationalists were driven
off the mainland despite a small army of American military
advisers, arsenals stocked with American arms and several
billion dollars in aid. In the Korean war, primitively armed
Chinese Communist "volunteers" pushed us back from the
Yalu to the thirty-eighth parallel and reoccupied North

Korea even after we had completely crushed the North
Korean armies and leveled just about everything above
ground. In the perspective of Asia, these were victorious
stages in the ebb tide of white imperialism, which began
with Japan's defeat of Russia in 1905. In the perspective of
American policy, China, Korea, and Vietnam are warnings
that we cannot add Asia to Latin America as our imperial
sphere of influence.

Even in the contiguous areas of Latin America, we have
not had everything our own way. Long before the Green
Berets and the CIA, U.S. Marines and operatives, whether
governmental or from U.S. business, dominated the political life of Central America and the Caribbean. Yet Mexico
was a series of defeats for the military-economic warfare an
earlier generation of American anti-imperialists called gun-
boat and dollar diplomacy. From the bombardment of Vera
Cruz in 1913 under Wilson to the world-wide blockade we
imposed on Mexican oil under FDR, we were unable to
stem the successive stages of a nationalist and peasant revolt
that seized—and kept—millions of dollars in U.S. land
and oil properties. Fidel was not the first to defy Yanqui
imperialism and get away with it. Wilson, Roosevelt, Truman, Eisenhower, and Kennedy—at the Bay of Pigs—had
to swallow the bitter pill of political-military defeat, and
did so rather than gamble on a longer and wider war. Nixon
will be in good company if he has to do likewise in Vietnam.

The adjustment to reality is always painful, the recovery
from illusion is never smooth, and relapses are normal.
Hoopes spells out the process brilliantly in his account-
from-within of how Johnson was finally led to de-escalate
the war, and then began to regret it, as Nixon seems to be
doing now. His memoir is given added value because
Hoopes is a defector who had two decades of intimate association with the buildup of the military juggernaut which
has come a cropper in Vietnam. "I too," he writes, "was a

child of the cold war." In 1947–48 he was assistant to the Chairman of the House Armed Services Committee, the military's chief outpost on Capitol Hill. He went from there to the Pentagon, as an assistant to James Forrestal, the first Secretary of Defense, a fanatical cold warrior. He stayed on in the Pentagon as young man of all work for his three successors, Louis Johnson, General Marshall, and Robert Lovett. In 1957 he became secretary to the Military Panel of the Rockefeller Brothers Special Study Project and, with Henry Kissinger, he was a principal draftsman of its report on military policy. He calls this "the pioneering effort" to replace massive retaliation with "the concept of graduated deterrence and flexible response."

This was also, though he does not say so, a blueprint for the military requirements needed to police the world and protect American business and other interests against a wide range of threats, in a time of revolutionary turmoil. Symbolically and practically it came naturally from a study project set up by the Rockefeller Brothers, for it was tailored to the needs of the private empire Standard Oil and Chase Manhattan administer. For them it made no sense to have a muscle-bound military machine which could only threaten a universal nuclear Doomsday when somebody made a pass at their oil wells in Peru.

They finally got from the Democrats what the economy-minded Eisenhower Administration denied them. Under Kennedy and McNamara the armed forces were reshaped to meet the varying levels of violence required for a Pax Americana, and it was under McNamara that Hoopes returned to the Pentagon in 1965 as Deputy Assistant Secretary of Defense for International Security Affairs, i.e., No. 2 man in the Pentagon's own little State Department. This gradually, and his story shows how and why, became infested with doves while the State Department under Rusk remained a nest of hawks. He then moved up to Under Secretary of the Air Force during 1967–69. Thus his return to the Pentagon coincided with Johnson's decision to Americanize the Vietnam war, and he stayed on under Clark

Clifford and helped to turn that policy around. It is quite a conversion when a man of this background describes the Vietnamese war as the beginning of the end for the Pax Americana, though he phrases it less bluntly—

as the probable high watermark of America's tidal impulse to political military intervention in the period following the Second World War.

He sees the war also as marking the end of "a doctrinaire anti-Communism, a social evangelism forming around the idea of American-financed economic development in the Third World and an unquestioning faith in the ultimate efficacy of military alliances and of U.S. military power."

Vietnam was our biggest war of intervention. It cost easily $100 billion. It tied down close to 800,000 men in and around Southeast Asia. It cost more casualties than any war except the Civil War and the two world wars. It is not strange that the disillusion should also have momentous dimensions, though this has only begun to dawn on the principal actors and even on some of the dissenters, who still regard Vietnam as no more than a blunder.

Perhaps the most important lesson to be drawn from the experience is that the bigger and more diverse a nation's military establishment the bigger and more diverse the troubles it will get that nation into. Iceland may be indignant over what is happening in Southeast Asia but it is fortunately helpless to do anything about it. Johnson got into Vietnam when and because we were ready to get in. "By 1965," Hoopes writes, "McNamara's prodigious labors to strengthen and broaden the U.S. military posture were about completed . . . U.S. 'general purpose' forces were now organized to intervene swiftly and with modern equipment in conflicts of limited scope, well below the nuclear threshold."

The Rockefeller Brothers report on military policy had

recommended the reorganization of the armed services into functional commands, which combined naval, air, and army contingents. One such was to be a strike command, framed for swift and distant interventions. Accordingly STRIKE-COM—another of those Pentagon acronymic monsters— had been set up, directly under the Joint Chiefs of Staff, and ready at the President's hand, like the thunderbolts of a new Jove.

This new military capability, Hoopes writes,

had been designed precisely to arrest or restore those deteriorating situations in the world where important or vital U.S. interests were judged to be engaged, to deal with ambiguous subversion-aggressions characterized by little warning and a low silhouette, to blunt national liberation wars.

(How antiseptic it all sounds in the vocabulary of the Pentagon!) Hoopes continues, "To a rational activist like McNamara, with a very thin background in foreign affairs, it seemed entirely logical to employ a portion of this immense U.S. power if that could arrest the spreading erosion in South Vietnam." In retrospect, what McNamara lacked was not a firmer background in foreign affairs, but in human and political understanding. To McNamara the outcome seemed certain. "Surely," as Hoopes explains, "the use of limited U.S. power, applied with care and precision, but with the threat of more to come, would bring a realistic Ho Chi Minh to early negotiations." How do you quantify for a computer the irreducible logic and power of men willing to die?

So the means lay at hand for Johnson's natural pugnacity, and we plunged into the quagmire. What I want to suggest here is that one may deduce from the experience some fundamental axioms of statecraft and history. One is that a large military establishment must justify its existence by finding work to do. The other is that nations which have spent huge sums on a large military establishment will react to complex economic, social, and political problems by trying to solve them with force. What's the good of all those billions spent on such highly perfected military instruments if you don't use them? So if you have a STRIKECOM, you are bound sooner or later to have a Vietnam.

Hoopes's disillusion began early. At the end of 1965 he sent a memorandum to the late John T. McNaughton, then his superior as Assistant Secretary of State for International Security Affairs, which showed an insidious skepticism. He expressed his doubts about the view held "by Lodge, proably Westmoreland and maybe McNamara" that the Viet Cong would just "fade away" when they realized they could not win, making negotiation unnecessary. This is still Secretary Rogers's favorite bedtime story, as it was Rusk's. Hoopes thought the USSR and China too deeply committed to allow the U.S. any such clear-cut victory. He had the temerity to suggest that were the situation reversed and 150,000 Chinese Communists in Mexico, "it seems reasonable to believe the U.S. would be determined to fight for decades and even generations to expel them."

Such objectivity was downright subversive, but it began to spread. By the spring of 1967 McNaughton came back from a White House conference on the war to tell him acidly, "We seem to be proceeding on the assumption that the way to eradicate the Viet Cong is to destroy all the village structures, defoliate all the jungles, and then cover the entire surface of South Vietnam with asphalt."

Hoopes recorded a similar satiric comment in late 1967 from the famous Major Be, a South Vietnamese officer who got himself fired because he really tried to win "hearts and minds" to the detriment of province chiefs more interested in getting their rake-off from "pacification." "Everyone is a Communist," Major Be said of the methods used to "pacify" the villages. "Using the police way, every Vietnamese [in the countryside] would have to be killed and our villages repopulated with Americans." There was nothing wrong in Southeast Asia which could not be cured by removing Vietnam and the Vietnamese.

Later that year, in his testimony before the Senate Armed Services Committee on the futility of bombing the North, McNamara jolted Johnson into complaining, "That military genius, McNamara, has gone dovish on me." He found himself promoted to head of the World Bank, although its directors had just voted to keep George Wood in office for another year until the end of 1968. "The most Byzantine of American Presidents," Hoopes comments, "had given McNamara a fast shuffle, and had gauged his man's character, inner ambivalence and fatigue well enough to be confident that he would go quietly and suffer the indignity in silence." Thus do men put their loyalty to their bureaucratic team over their loyalty to their country.

It was not safe in the Pentagon to speak one's doubts aloud until the Têt offensive in February, 1968. It showed the idiocy of Westmoreland's view that war was neither strategy nor art but simply extermination, as in termite control. "The doctrine of search-and-destroy," Hoopes writes, "had resulted in scattering U.S. forces all over uninhabited border lands; the Têt offensive had made blindingly clear the fatuousness of Westmoreland's ground strategy."

Têt led to a miniature rising in the halls of the Pentagon. The offensive, Hoopes reports, "performed the curious service of fully revealing the doubters and dissenters to each other, in a lightning flash." Even that veteran "Prussian" cold warrior, Paul Nitze, who had succeeded Cyrus Vance as No. 2 man in the Pentagon, suddenly spoke out— i.e., within the Pentagon—on "the unsoundness of reinforcing weakness" and the need to review Vietnam in the light of American commitments elsewhere. Paul Warnke thought Têt showed our military strategy was "foolish to the point of insanity." Alain Enthoven of the Systems Analysis office used to explain to reporters how a certain quantity of military input would produce an equally certain quantity of guerrilla "output" until the computer curve happily reduced them to zero. Now he began to say, "I fell off the boat when the troop level reached 170,000." The revolt had spread from the Mekong to the Potomac.

The man who precipitated the turnaround on Vietnam
was General Westmoreland, with his request in February,
1968, for 206,000 more troops, 100,000 of them in sixty
days. This had the full support of the Joint Chiefs of Staff.
At a Pentagon conference called by McNamara—his last—
to discuss this request, the body count nonsense finally
boomeranged in a big way. Secretary of the Navy Paul
Ignatius wanted to know why Westmoreland needed so
many men in a hurry when we were supposed to have killed
30,000 enemy troops since Têt.

The cost estimates were shocking. McNamara figured
that to meet Westmoreland's request would require calling
up 400,000 more men for military service and adding $10
billion a year to the $30 billion already being spent on the
Vietnam war. Worst of all, there was little reason to believe
even these sharp increases would bring victory any closer.
In a memorandum to McNamara's successor, Clark
Clifford, Hoopes pointed out that based on the manpower
ratios in three years of war, the enemy could neutralize an
increase of 206,000 in our forces by adding a mere 50,000
to his own.

The final blow was delivered by Dean Acheson, whom
Johnson trusted as a veteran cold warrior and hardliner.
"With all due respect, Mr. President," Acheson told him in
a remark which should serve as a warning to all future in-
cumbents of the White House, "the Joint Chiefs of Staff
don't know what they're talking about." This salutary discovery had by then cost $100 billion and some 30,000 lives.

By now the story of how hawks like McGeorge Bundy,
Cyrus Vance, and Douglas Dillon among Johnson's senior
advisers lost faith in the war has been sufficiently told,
though the task of distilling its lessons has hardly begun and
not only Acheson but even Clifford has been drawn to
some extent into Nixon's camp.[1] The debacle and the

[1] In a disturbing speech (Washington *Star*, October 15), Clifford attacked the Goodell resolution for withdrawal of all troops, combat and

belated awakening were only the latest variant in the old fairy tale about the Emperor's clothes. Is it inevitable in any bureaucracy that few men will be found willing to risk advancement or influence by speaking the truth until the disaster has reached such proportions it can no longer be ignored even by the cowardly and self-serving? How do you design a system for courage? What levers can be substituted for the pull of careerism?

Even now the more important part of the story, because it continues under the Nixon Administration, is that "these prodigious efforts," as Hoopes writes, "did not really change President Johnson's mind about the Vietnam war." In retrospect the period between March 31, 1968, when Johnson de-escalated the bombing of the North, to November 3, 1969, when Nixon threatened to re-escalate the war, appears as a rearguard action to appease antiwar sentiment at home while hoping for victory, military or political, abroad.

The Joint Chiefs may not know what they're talking about, but virtually the same Chiefs remained at Johnson's elbow and at Nixon's. General Wheeler, who also wanted 206,000 troops sent to South Vietnam, is still Chairman, and the only change is hardly for the better—Westmoreland is now Army Chief of Staff, a post to which he was promoted by Johnson. There is no sign that the quality or the tenor of their advice has changed. The civilian rebels have left the government, their job half-done, but the same military bureaucrats are in power, still hoping to snatch a political victory from a military stalemate, or even to escalate the conflict again if they cannot get it. The prestige and future of our huge military establishment is at stake, and its managers

support, by the end of 1970 as "unrealistic and impractical," said it would lead to a "bloodbath" in South Vietnam, and declared the country had "a moral obligation" to support Vietnamization of the war. The speech, in a local Washington school, was meant to be off the record but was reported by a Washington *Star* reporter who happened to be present. One result of the speech seems to have been that it torpedoed Fulbright's plan for hearings on the Goodell resolution with Clifford, Harriman, and Cyrus Vance as the first witnesses. The hearings were called off after it became clear that Clifford would oppose the resolution.

may prefer to gamble on a wider war rather than admit that the biggest military machine in human history couldn't win a third-rate war against ill-armed guerrillas with no air force or napalm.

The whole story of Johnson's limited bombing halt has yet to be told. In retrospect, Hoopes notes, it appears that the hardliners "assumed that Hanoi would give a negative response" since it had always insisted on a total halt as a condition for talks. Hoopes does not say so, but a rejection of the Johnson offer could have been made a new excuse for wider bombing. Hanoi surprised Washington by agreeing to talk on the basis of the limited bombing halt, though insisting the talks could only be to arrange a full cessation.

Maxwell Taylor, with the support of Rostow and the Joint Chiefs, began to bombard the President with memoranda on how serious were the military consequences of the limited bombing halt, while Clifford, Harriman, and Vance pressed for a total halt in the bombing of the North since the other side refused to negotiate until it ended. The controversy was bedeviled by the fiction that the bombing halt increased casualties, though as Hoopes wrote in a letter to Clifford, "Present U.S. casualty levels are a function of the U.S. ground strategy in the South; they are only distantly related to the bombing."

Johnson delayed the start of negotiations more than a month by a ludicrous squabble over where to meet, though he had often said he was ready to "meet anywhere, at any time." By autumn, Hoopes reveals, Johnson was telling Clifford "that his primary purpose was now to leave his successor with 'the best possible military posture in Vietnam' "! This was not the remark of a President who took negotiations seriously or had stopped listening to the Joint Chiefs of Staff.

"Clifford argued," Hoopes discloses, "that, for the sake of the President's ultimate standing before the bar of history, he ought to want something much broader and more positive, namely, to leave his successor, 'an ongoing, substantial negotiation, firmly committed to ending the war

and reducing the American involvement in Vietnam.'"
Though Johnson finally ordered a total halt in bombing the
North in October, it was followed by a sharp step-up in the
bombing of Laos and the South, and in offensive operations
on the ground to extend the areas under Saigon's control.

Hoopes says that as the Johnson Administration left
office, ambivalence was at the heart of its Vietnam policy.
"Were we in Paris," he asks, "to negotiate a political compromise on the clearly accepted premise that military
victory was infeasible? Or were we there to stone-wall
Hanoi in the belief that, given enough time, we could grind
out something resembling a military victory in South Vietnam and thus avoid the dangers, and the further affronts to
our prestige, that would attend a compromise political
settlement?" The ambivalence has developed into something worse with Nixon's November 3 speech. Clearly the
second alternative is his aim. He still seeks a political victory, and says he is willing to re-escalate if necessary to get
it.

The strategy of victory through de-escalation began to be
formulated many months before the Têt debacle. As far
back as November, 1966, Westmoreland in Saigon told
Tom Braden, then editor of the Oceanside, California,
Blade-Tribune, that war weariness at home might be dealt
with by reducing U.S. combat operations to 100 a week, or
about the level—the general added charmingly—of the annual toll from auto accidents. An unnamed general I now
believe to have been Westmoreland said in an off-the-record
briefing of correspondents here in Washington more than a
year ago that the fighting would be reduced to a level the
American public would tolerate for a long pull.

A secret scenario by Herman Kahn for appeasing the
peaceniks while holding out for victory began to circulate
in the capital last year. Its main outlines were indicated by
his article "If Negotiations Fail" in *Foreign Affairs* for
July, 1968. There he proposed to "reduce U.S. forces in the

next two or three years to between two and three hundred thousand men," while building up the capacity of the ARVN forces to counter hostilities "with air, artillery and logistic support" by the United States. "To deter a resumption of major hostilities," Kahn also proposed, "the U.S. stations one or two divisions in South Vietnam for a considerable period." That sounds like a preview of Laird's "residual force" and Nixon's "Vietnamization."

In retrospect there appears to be a clear continuity between the Johnson and Nixon Administrations. The theme of "Vietnamization" appeared in Johnson's "abdication" address of March 31, 1968, though little noticed at the time. "We shall accelerate the re-equipment of South Vietnam's armed forces," Johnson said, "in order to meet the enemy's increased firepower. This will enable them progressively to undertake a larger share of combat operations against the Communist invaders." Johnson's warning that we would not accept "a fake solution" foreshadowed Nixon's insistence that a political settlement must include acceptance of the Thieu-Ky regime.

Even the new Agnew-Nixon campaign against dissenters can be traced back to Johnson. It recalls his ferocious attack before the National Farmers Union in Minneapolis on March 18, 1968, on those who would "cut and run" and "tuck our tail and violate our commitments." In that speech, like Agnew and Nixon more recently, Johnson pictured a plot to divide America and obtain by treachery here what the enemy could not win on the battlefield. So long as the enemy, Johnson said, "feels that he can win something by propaganda in the country—that he can undermine the leadership—that he can bring down the government—that he can get something in the Capital that he can't get from our men out there—he is going to keep on trying. But I point out to you that the time has come when we ought to unite, when we ought to stand up and be counted. . . ." This is the same nonsense Nixon elaborated when he said, "Let us be united for peace. Let us be united against defeat. Because let us understand: North Vietnam cannot defeat or humiliate the United States. Only Americans can do that."

This is a new stab-in-the-back myth to absolve the Joint Chiefs and the military bureaucracy for their military and political incompetence. From this common Johnson-Nixon premise, it is a step to Agnew's call at Harrisburg, Pa., October 30, for the polarization of the country and for separating these insidious traitors "from our society—with no more regret than we should feel over discarding rotten apples in a barrel." Even the so-called Guam Doctrine may be traced to Johnson. Less than a month after his "abdication," he was telling General Park of South Korea at their meeting in Honolulu (April 17, 1968), "We wish to see Asia—like Europe—take an increasing responsibility for shaping its own destiny. And we intend and we mean to help it do so."

The Hoopes book shows how isolated Johnson had become, and how hard it was for contrary opinion to get past the Rostow barrier. Nixon is similarly situated, and the hawks are at his ear and elbow, too. William S. White is a credible witness on this point, for he is himself a hawk. In a recent column (*Washington Post*, October 4) he said word had passed to Senate hawks like Tower and Goldwater "that if remorselessly driven to it by final enemy refusal to talk reason and by unbroken dove assault upon the present American posture of marked conciliation, the President has a clear option." This, White went on, "would be not only a halt the process of troop withdrawal but also to order American offensive action on a scale far heavier than is currently seen." A month later just such a threat appeared in the November 3 speech when Nixon said, "If the level of infiltration or our own casualties increase . . . I shall not hesitate to take strong and effective measures to deal with that situation." If this means anything at all, it is a threat to re-escalate.[2]

[2] A glimpse of what the Nixon Administration may be planning can be read in a curious recent Gallup poll (*Washington Post*, October 19). This tested public reaction to a proposal which had not hitherto been broached publicly: "The U.S. would keep aircraft carriers off the coast of Vietnam, to help insure that North Vietnam does not send troops or

White was skeptical about re-escalation but felt there were "certain objective and undeniable realities that point in this direction." The first and greatest of these, White wrote, is the fact that "those members of the White House palace guard who are openly hawkish are far closer to his [Nixon's] elbow every time the hard outlines of this dilemma are put down on the table for discussion than are those more or less dovish members of his entourage." "To be specific," White said, "the big men on foreign crisis" are never Secretary of State Rogers or Under Secretary Richardson. "Always they are, instead, such as Henry Kissinger . . . and a man not much connected with foreign affairs, Attorney General John Mitchell." If the Nixon policy creates more dissent, Mitchell is the man to deal with it and the men he has gathered around him in the Justice Department do not seem likely to let the First Amendment stand in his way.

While Rostow kept telling Johnson he was just like Lincoln, somebody—probably Kissinger—has been suggesting to Nixon that he is Woodrow Wilson. The November 3 speech escalated the rhetoric of the war. It is now another war to end war, with Ho Chi Minh cast as the Kaiser. The Nixon dramaturgy recalls Marx's famous remark in the *18th Brumaire* that history repeats itself, first as tragedy and then as farce. But it may be a costly farce, if Nixon is not forced to cool it.

His November 3 speech began by distorting the origins of the Vietnamese war and ended by distorting the significance of Ho Chi Minh's final private letter to him. Any un-

war material into South Vietnam." Where did Gallup get this ominous idea? It was presented as part three of a new three-part peace plan (internationally supervised elections and withdrawal of "troops"—combat only? —within twelve months, were the other two provisions). The plan won 54 percent approval. Equally tantalizing and perhaps related are certain brief items in the news recently about U.S. aircraft carriers steaming out of various ports here and abroad so rapidly that part of their crews were left ashore.

wary listener would be led to believe that the Vietnamese war began fifteen years ago with a Communist aggression to which Eisenhower replied with the first U.S. commitment of aid. The fact is that fifteen years ago Nixon was doing his best to keep peace from breaking out in Indochina. This has been Nixon's pet war for a long time. In the fall of 1953 he went to Indochina and tried to persuade the French not to negotiate. Fifteen years ago, just before the Geneva Conference opened, Nixon told the American Society of Newspaper Editors—in a famous "not for attribution" speech that leaked—that we ought to "put our boys" into Indochina if necessary to prevent a peace settlement from being made.

The interventionist plans of Nixon, Admiral Radford, and John Foster Dulles were vetoed by Eisenhower, after an astringent report from General Ridgway. "Having avoided one total war with Red China the year before in Korea when he had United Nations support," Sherman Adams comments in his memoirs, "he [Eisenhower] was in no mood to provoke another one in Indochina." It was a measure of Nixon's fanaticism, or cynicism, or both that he was asking Eisenhower to plunge into a second Asian land war only a year after Ike had been elected—and kept his pledge—to end another. Nixon showed himself no man to wait for majorities, silent or otherwise. An Indochina war on the heels of Korea would have torn this country apart.

Nixon's speech was as deceitful in discussing the letter he sent to Ho Chi Minh last summer and the letter with which Ho replied a few days before his death. Nixon read his letter but not Ho's on TV, saying that Ho "flatly rejected my initiative." But there was no initiative in Nixon's letter and no flat rejection in Ho's.

The latter, as Muskie pointed out in a little-noticed Senate speech November 7, was couched in conciliatory language and embodied distinct negotiating concessions. It referred to the ten points of the NLF as a "logical and reasonable basis" for settlement rather than as the "only correct basis" as many earlier statements from Hanoi had done. It

referred to "the right of the population *of the South* and of
the Vietnamese nation to dispose of themselves without
foreign influence" (my italics). This was not too different, Muskie pointed out, from Nixon's insistence that "the
people of South Vietnam" have "an opportunity to choose
their own future." Ho's concluding sentence—"with good
will on both sides, we might arrive at common efforts in
view of finding a correct solution to the Vietnam problem"
—was as Muskie said "probably as forthcoming a generality
as the old revolutionary had ever addressed to a Western
leader at any time in his long lifetime."

Muskie also gave Nixon low marks for discretion. "I cannot see how the goal of a negotiated peace," he told an
almost empty Senate chamber, "is promoted by the publication of private diplomatic exchanges. I cannot see how Ambassador Lodge's task of getting meaningful private discussions under way is served by revealing the eleven times he
has been able to meet with the Communist representatives to
date."

One can only conclude that Nixon does not want successful negotiations, for these would involve political compromise. Hoopes spelled out the course Nixon is trying to
avoid. In a memorandum to Clifford shortly after the latter
took office, Hoopes proposed "a cessation of the bombing
to get talks started, as soon as we have regained our military
poise [i.e., after Têt]; a shift of our forces to the primary
task of protecting the population centers; willingness to talk
to the NLF and to accept a coalition government; organization of the international community, including especially
the Soviet Union, to guarantee the military neutralization
of Vietnam, Laos and Cambodia; and ultimately the phased
withdrawal of U.S. forces."

To focus solely on a peacemeal and suspiciously indefinite withdrawal, as Nixon does, is to dodge the hard issues
of negotiation and lull the U.S. public into believing that

peace is on the way. "Vietnamization" means handing over
the future of South Vietnam not to its people but to a dis-
credited military junta, one that jails or brushes aside those
very elements that are ready to negotiate with the NLF.[3] It
is not a new policy, a thoughtful reaction to America's military and political defeat, but an effort to retreat to earlier
policies, though these have already proved a failure. It was
because a decade of "Vietnamization" under Diem and his
successors failed to work that we finally took over the combat operations from which we would now like to disengage.

It is to Hoopes's credit that unlike Clifford he argues that
there is no real alternative to complete withdrawal, not only
of combat troops but also of the 200,000 or more support
and air forces Clifford would leave in indefinitely. Hoopes
sees partial withdrawal as "a prescription for an intermi-
nable war, partially disguised by the declining level of U.S.
participation." He concludes by warning that it would "in
fact require our country to sustain a continuing burden of
war casualties and heavy dollar costs that would become
explicitly open-ended as we leveled off our forces at
100,000 men or thereabouts."

Sooner or later, he says,

the American people would reawaken to the fact that they
were still committed to the endless support of a group of men
in Saigon who represented nobody but themselves, preferred
war to the risks of a political settlement, and could not remain

[3] A substantial non-Communist pro-peace grouping seems to have made
its appearance in Saigon and among the exiles in Paris under the leadership of General "Big" Minh and Senator Tran Van Don, the general
who led the overthrow of Diem and won a larger vote than any other
candidate in the Senate elections. He is head of a Front of National Preservation which could form the basis of an alternative government. In
Paris, where the peace forces can speak more freely, its tenor was indicated by a manifesto issued on November 1, South Vietnam's National
Day, which celebrates the overthrow of Diem. "It is only by a broad
union of forces," the manifesto said, "that we can clearly show the government of the United States that for patriotic Vietnamese the card of
anti-Communism has long lost its power in the face of the suffering of
the South Vietnamese population under American bombardment" (*Le
Monde*, November 1).

in power more than a few months without our large-scale presence.

These are lessons Nixon still refuses to learn.

December 4, 1969
New York Review

THE ATROCITIES NIXON
CONDONES AND CONTINUES

The Pinkville massacre falls into perspective if we remember that from the first days of the struggle against the
French, General Giap's strategy has been to fight a "People's
War." Without our ever fully realizing it, ours has become
an "Anti-People's" war. Some years ago an American
colonel, who was never identified, put it very plainly. Mao
Tse-Tung, the foremost theoretician of the People's War,
said that the guerrilla swims among the people as a fish does
in the sea. The U.S. colonel said we would "dry up the
sea." Our strategy has been to destroy the villages and the
crops, to drive out or kill the people, wherever we suspect
Viet Cong. We set out to create a desert where no "fish"
could live. The soldiers at Pinkville may not have been ordered to kill women and children but they were certainly
ordered to burn down the village and kill the livestock, to
destroy their homes and their food supply. If the main target of a "People's War" is to win the confidence and support of the peasantry, the main target of an Anti-People's
War is to uproot or destroy the peasantry the guerrillas
may have won over. From such a strategy Pinkvilles come
naturally.

In the rules of war, soldiers and civilians used to be separate categories. The strategy of the Anti-People's War has
given us that legal monstrosity we now read about—the

"innocent civilian." This implies that some civilians are innocent and some are guilty. The latter are not only fair game, but the safe rule when in doubt is to shoot first and investigate later, or just add them to the body count. Horrible as this may sound, it has its logic and the logic grows stronger as the spiral of hate mounts on both sides. The guerrillas use civilians in their area—like the home population in any war—for many auxiliary tasks. The civilians—including women and children—take up those tasks ever more willingly as they see their homes and livestock, their menfolk and ancestral graves, destroyed by indiscriminate bombing and artillery fire and by "search and destroy" missions like the one in Pinkville. Relations are not improved by calling them "gooks" or—more politely, as in Lieutenant Calley's indictment—"Oriental human beings." They retaliate with home-made mines and booby traps, including the "ponji," the sharpened stick coated with excrement. The biggest and dirtiest booby trap of all is the filthy pit of this war itself, from which we emerge stinking in the nostrils of mankind.

There is a flurry of stories from Saigon about "reindoctrinating" troops on the humane treatment of civilians. But we are dealing here not with an occasional atrocity but with a deliberate policy. What a fear-crazed and hate-filled GI may do in occupying a hostile village can be put down to the brutalization of war. The real crime is higher up. When the President announced that he was revising our chemical and bacteriological warfare program and sending the Geneva Protocol to the Senate for ratification, it looked like a gesture of contrition. It turned out to be the most hypocritical kind of public relations. For it excepted from these restrictions the two weapons of gas and chemical warfare from which the civilian population of Vietnam suffer most. These are the tear and lung gases which drive them out of their home-made bomb shelters into the open where our B-52's and fragmentation "anti-personnel" bombs can destroy them, and the herbicides which kill their crops and threaten—like Thalidomide—their unborn children.

How can we convince the world that we have not turned barbarian when a White House announcement, designed to take the curse off Pinkville and demonstrate our concern for international law, perpetuates a gross violation of it? We refer to the use of crop-killers. It is said that the Geneva Protocol banning chemical warfare does not mention herbicides. True. But earlier treaties to which we are a party do. The Army Field Manual (FM27–10) in paragraph 37 cites that provision of the Hague Convention of 1907 which says, "It is especially forbidden . . . to employ poison or poison weapons." The Army interpretation which follows says this "does not prohibit measures . . . to destroy, through chemical or bacteriological agents, harmless to man, crops intended *solely* [my emphasis] for consumption by the armed forces (if that fact can be determined)." But even this tortuous sophistry admits we may not destroy crops just because we believe *some* of the supplies may feed guerrillas, and that we may not employ chemical or bacteriological agents which *are* harmful to humans.

Two years ago the Japan Science Council[1] released a report on anticrop warfare in Vietnam which said nearly 1,000 peasants and more than 13,000 livestock had been killed by it. Han Swyter, a former aide to Secretary McNamara, told the House Foreign Affairs Committee December 2 that since 1962 we have sprayed about 100 million pounds of herbicides over four million acres, an area the size of Massachusetts. He said that since late 1967 there have been increasing reports and pictures in the Saigon press of a new kind of abormality in newly born children. These reports have found confirmation in a still secret report for the National Cancer Institute (see *Scientific Research*, November 10) which found that one herbicide, 2,4,5-T was "probably dangerous" and 2,4-D "potentially dangerous" as teratogenic agents, i.e., capable, like Thalidomide, of producing gross birth defects if ingested by pregnant women. As a result the Pentagon has "restricted" the use of the first,

[1] P. 153 of Seymour M. Hersh's indispensable recent book *Chemical and Bacteriological Warfare* (New York: Bobbs-Merrill).

but not the second, substance to areas remote from human population. But how much reliance can be placed on this restriction remains to be seen and the crop-killing itself goes on. So will the civilian-killing, via the tear-gas route. The government's position is that the Geneva Protocol does not cover tear gas. The Protocol itself speaks of "asphyxiating, poisonous or *other* gases" (my italics). The British government ever since 1930, like many other signatories of the Protocol, has held that tear gases, too, are outlawed. Congressman McCarthy (D. N.Y.) told a Montreal audience December 1 that when in London he heard the U.S. government was pressuring the British government to change its position on tear gas. This is not academic in Britain. Imagine the massacre during the blitz if the Nazis had been able to flush people out of the subways and other shelters with tear gases before the bombing, as we do in Vietnam.

The enormous quantities of tear and lung gas we use in Vietnam—almost 14 million pounds since 1964, or more than half the total weight of the mustard gases used by both sides in World War I—testify how far we have gone from exceptional use in "riot-like" circumstances to routine application before bombardment. These are the atrocities Nixon condones and continues.

December 15, 1969

NIXON, INFLATION
AND THE WAR

Like Lyndon Johnson, Nixon plays the numbers game. In his TV address on the Health, Education and Welfare veto, he said the new budget for fiscal 1971 would call for "a smaller percentage of federal spending for defense than in

any year since 1950." This tricky wording is deceptive. In
fiscal 1950 total federal spending was $76.7 billion and the
military took $13 billion, or about 16 percent. The fiscal
1971 budget on the other hand will be in the neighborhood
of $198 billion. The best information available (*Aviation
Week*, January 26, 1970) as this is written, almost a week
before the new budget is to be published, places the military's portion at $71.1 billion. That is about 35 percent of
total federal outlays, or twice the percentage in 1950, and
the total is five and a half times as great. It is $20 billion—
or 40 percent—larger than military spending in the most
costly year of the Korean war, and less than $20 billion be-
low the peak year of the Second World War. That is
not much to boast about when Vietnam is supposed to be
tapering off.

Despite a flood of figures about cuts, military spending is
tapering off very slowly. So is the Vietnam war. Although Defense Department appropriations for the current
fiscal year are $5.3 billion below last year, this has yet to be
reflected in actual spending. The latest Treasury cash dis-
bursal figures show that on January 22, after almost seven
months of this fiscal year, total Department of Defense
spending was almost $400 million *greater* than in the corre-
sponding period of fiscal 1969. If the current rate is projected for the rest of the fiscal year, actual spending would
be almost $78 billion, or $6 billion more than has been budgeted. This is possible because (as the House appropriations
report on fiscal 1970 noted) the military has almost $40 bil-
lion in unexpended balances from past years. From an inflationary point of view, it is the spending that counts. This
spending record makes the disputed extra $1 billion on the
Health, Education and Welfare bill look like a minor matter.
It is indeed about one-half of one percent of the total
budget and one-tenth of one percent of Gross National
Product. In stressing it, Nixon was straining at a gnat while
swallowing a camel.

The main source of the inflation is military spending, and
the biggest single item is still the Vietnam war. If Nixon

were seriously preparing to get out of it as soon as possible, he would be emphasizing this. Instead the veto broadcast, like the State of the Union message, distracts attention from the role of the war in inflation, and seeks instead to blame the inflation on general Democratic spending policies. This is the impression created when he said the inflation was caused by a cumulative $57 billion deficit in the decade of the sixties. This again gives a false picture. Deficits have been the rule during the past two decades. The Republicans under Eisenhower and Nixon only balanced the budget in three of their eight years in office, and their biggest deficit, $12 billion in fiscal 1959, and 50 percent greater than any Democratic deficit until Johnson plunged into the Vietnam war in 1965.

Truman, by raising taxes and imposing excess profits taxes, kept deficit financing within bounds during the Korean war. Johnson used deficit financing for three years without objection from the Republicans either to the war or to his failure to prevent inflation by raising taxes to meet the cost. The result was a cumulative deficit of almost $38 billion for the first three years of the war, from fiscal 1966 (which began July 1, 1965) through fiscal 1968. This was the biggest inflationary shot in the arm for the economy since World War II. By the Pentagon's own latest figures, the Vietnamese war by next June 30 will have cost us $104.5 billions in 5 years, or an average of $25 billion a year. It is this stupendous and wasteful expenditure which provided a stock market boom for the well-to-do and set off the inflation eating into the average family's budget. This is why we are paying now with a business contraction and an unemployment rise to get the inflation under control. The poor pay the most, but every family pays some of these hidden "taxes" which inflation and deflation impose. The cause is the Vietnam war.

The latest Pentagon projection for the cost of the war in the fiscal year beginning July 1 is $17 billion. This is $6.2 billion less than the projected cost this fiscal year. If this "peace dividend" were made available to civilian needs,

then the new Department of Defense budget ought to be
$6.2 billion below the $71.6 billion budget for fiscal 1970.
The figure which leaked from the Pentagon to industry
sources for fiscal 1971, however, is $71.1 billion. If this is
correct then the Pentagon gets all but half a billion of that
"peace dividend." So while Nixon is picking a major political fight over $1 billion more for education, and represent-
ing this as somehow crucial in the battle against inflation,
the military is quietly adding to its expenditures $5 billion
or more in expected savings on the Vietnam war.

*Nixon is playing down the significance of the Vietnam
war in the inflationary picture because he is in no hurry to
bring it to a close.* He has been encouraged in this by public
apathy, and the comfortable belief that the war is practically over. In this connection I want to call attention to pas-
sages in the State of the Union message which are most disturbing. These repeatedly emphasized a "just peace." Just
what Nixon means by a just peace was nowhere made clear.
He wants "our generation" to be remembered "not so much
as the generation that suffered in war" but for "the courage
and character" to win "the kind of a just peace that the next
generation was able to keep." Courage and character are
only necessary if the struggle is to be long drawn out. This
is an echo of the Johnson-Rusk rhetoric which portrayed
the leader of a tiny Southeast Asian country as if he were
Der Feuhrer of a major Western military power which
threatened world conquest. Any compromise in this perspective was "Munich" all over again, a case of appeasement, buying peace now at the expense of war later. If
Vietnam is of that importance, it is our duty to stick until
we have won victory. That's how Johnson and Rusk saw it.
Is that how Nixon sees it too?

What is a "just peace" in Vietnam? Is it "just" to keep
this divided country plunged into bloodshed until we have
shown that the Pax Americana dare not be challenged?
Does a just peace mean continuing the fighting, whether we
carry the main military burden or the South Vietnamese
army does, until South Vietnam is firmly established like

South Korea in the American sphere of influence? Is it a just peace to impose a military dictatorship on the South Vietnamese people in the process? Is it just to support a regime which denies them freedom of press and political activity? Is it just to avoid any compromise which would bring the terrible bloodshed to an end? What does Nixon mean by "justice" in this context? What is he asking us to show "courage and character" for? Was he afraid to use the plainer term "patience" to a country impatient for an end of the fighting? Is it "just" to ask the American people to go on tightening their belts, eschewing urgent reforms, postponing necessary social expenditures to pursue the same Johnson-Rusk dream of a final political (and therefore military) victory in a far-off Asian country?

There are other indications that Nixon is settling down for a long pull in Vietnam. Stuart H. Loory in the *Los Angeles Times*, January 20, called attention to one. In his December 8 press conference, Nixon said "We have a plan for the reduction of American forces in Vietnam, for removing all combat forces from Vietnam, regardless of what happens in the negotiations." But on January 19, three days before the State of the Union message, his press secretary, Ron Ziegler, told the press the goal was "to remove American troops from a combat role in Vietnam." As Mr. Loory pointed out, "There is a big difference between removing troops from a combat role, while possibly leaving them in Vietnam, and removing combat troops from the country altogether." But in response to questions Mr. Ziegler three times repeated the same formula. It fits with earlier indications that the plan is to leave sufficient combat troops in Vietnam to protect the installations from which our air, artillery and other auxiliary forces would operate in support of the South Vietnamese army. Obviously we don't have enough faith in "Vietnamization" to trust these installations to the protection of the ARVN troops.

To "remove American troops from a combat role" is to move them into enclaves, not enclaves in preparation for a cease-fire, as in the Gavin plan, but into enclaves which would be fortresses from which our support troops would help ARVN continue the war until they get what Nixon and Thieu consider a just peace. Since our half-million troops were about equally divided between combat and support forces, this new formula could easily mean a minimum of 300,000 troops in South Vietnam for a protracted stay. The peak year of Vietnam expenditures was fiscal 1969, Johnson's last, ending June 30, 1969. The Pentagon, which doesn't overestimate these things, figures the cost that year at $28.8 billion. Half that would be $14 billion. A force of 300,000, or 50,000 more than half, could easily cost $17 billion, which is what the Pentagon figures for the next fiscal year. That's a lot of money when we're pinching everything else.

Nixon's State of the Union message reminded me of so many mediocre sermons I covered years ago as a cub reporter. It had the same innocuous "inspirational" rhetoric, firmly against sin—in this case pollution—but not so specifically as to alarm any rich parishioners. It is appalling that all this self-congratulatory purple prose is taken so seriously by our communication media. It served only to hide a reality the country must face. Until the Vietnam war is over, the fight against inflation cannot be won. Until that fight is won, every effort at ending pollution and our other social ills is doomed by high interest rates, constricted credit and a business slowdown. Peace in Vietnam is the first priority. Withdrawal is the first necessity. "It is time," Nixon said of the litter in the cities, "for those who make massive demands on our society to make some minimal demands on themselves." This a dirty dig at the blacks and the poor in the ghettoes. It will be much appreciated in white Southern country clubs.

We would like to turn the dig around. Who makes the most massive demands on our society? The Pentagon. It is time the military was forced to make the minimal acknowledgment that the Vietnam war is not worth its enormous cost from any point of view, and that we cannot face the problems crowding in on us until we get our troops out. Until then, talk of ending the pollution of our air and water, the erosion of our resources, the decay of our cities and the racial polarization of our country is just the kind of Billy Graham hot air in which Richard Nixon loves to indulge.

February 9, 1970

===

NIXON'S IRON CURTAIN
ON THE COST OF THE WAR

Nixon's new budget takes secrecy in government two steps beyond LBJ. Nixon has blacked out the cost of the war in Vietnam and he has also blacked out military spending from his budgetary projections for the next four years. "A budget," Nixon said in his message, "must be a blueprint for the future." In his blueprint these two main parts are missing. "In the past," Nixon said about his new four-year projections, "the federal government has been unwilling to pull all the pieces together and present the results of projecting Government finances into the future." He said this was essential for "an enlightened discussion of public policies even though precise figures are, of course, impossible." Why then omit expenditures which eat up more than half the general revenues of the government?

Contradictory explanations have been given for blacking out the cost of the war. In the press briefings which preceded the release of the budget, the Pentagon briefers disagreed with the Budget Bureau briefers. The Pentagon briefers said the figures had been left out deliberately, so as not to tip off the President's plans. Budget Director Robert P. Mayo, on the other hand, implied that no such figure had been calculated. A Pentagon official put it bluntly to a persistent newsman, "I didn't say there wasn't a dollar figure. I am saying I am not going to tell you what it is." The clearest statement on the record is hidden away on page 81 of the main budget volume. "We expect," it says—

that further troop withdrawals can be made in the future. However, U.S. actions depend upon the actions of the other side in Paris and on the battlefield, as well as progress in Vietnamization. Consequently estimates are not shown for either the size or the timing of our future actions. Because of the need to maintain the security of the plan, certain information included in recent budgets does not appear this year.

The first part of this statement implies that there is no timetable because this depends on Hanoi and Saigon. The final sentence implies that Nixon does have one but is keeping it secret so as not to tip his hand. We expect this will confuse the enemy as much as it will the Congress.

Until now the only items known to be kept secret in the U.S. budget have been the expenditures of the CIA and the various military intelligence agencies. Now the Vietnam war has been added. This should be an issue for the Democrats. Yet the statement on national priorities just issued by the Democratic Policy Council, their more militant or less pusillanimous wing, does no more than say weakly that while it welcomes the cuts announced in the Pentagon budget, "the Administration's figures on expenditures make it difficult to assess the nature and extent of the military reductions which have been proposed." Protest could hardly be worded more feebly. This is what happens when certain lobbyist-lawyers double in brass as Nixon advisers and liberal Democrats.

The blackout hides the size of the peace dividend. The Administration would like to expunge even the phrase. Budget Director Mayo referred to it scornfully as a "rather oddball concept." The decision to keep it secret must have been taken at the last moment. About ten days before the budget was released the Pentagon information office was still telling reporters that the cost of the war during the next fiscal year would be about $17 billion. When Secretary Laird first gave out this figure in October, 1969, he said this would mean a $13 billion saving over the $30 billion the war

cost in fis   al 1969, ...   k. Total military costs in 1969
("defense   ...   were \$81.2 billion. But total mili-
tary cost: ...budget...   scal 1971, instead of being \$13 bil-
lion less tha..   ...   68.2 billion) are \$73.5 billion, or
only \$7.7 billion less. 1 his means that non-Vietnam military
spending is *up* by \$5.3 billion. This *increase* in non-Vietnam
military spending is itself more than twice as large as total
outlays budgeted for natural resources (\$2.5 billion) includ-
ing air and water despite all Nixon's "now or never" rhetoric
on pollution.

This may understate the realities. Proxmire in a Senate
speech February 10 estimated that the Pentagon "has heisted
\$10 billion of the peace dividend." He takes into account not
only Laird's predicted cut in Vietnam war costs but his announcement last October 16 that henceforth the Pentagon
would plan its level of forces for one major and one minor
war instead of two major and one minor wars, as it has since
the Kennedy-McNamara period. Proxmire said the money
thus saved is going to strategic hardware, including the second phase of the ABM, conversion of Polaris into the
MIRVed Poseidon, on which the overruns are now \$3 bil-
lion; into MIRVed Minuteman III, where the overruns are
also about \$3 billion; into the Navy, which is getting \$2.6
billion to modernize the fleet, an increase of \$1 billion over
1967–69 expenditures; and into a huge AWACS, over-the-
horizon warning system. "Some \$18 billion has already
been spent for SAGE and AWACS," Proxmire said of
these two anti-bomber systems, "even though the Russians
have no modern intercontinental bomber. These huge
funds were expended to meet a non-existent threat." This is
hardly austere military budgeting.

This brings me to the related blackout the Nixon Administration is imposing on military spending and planning.
"We have learned," Nixon said in the economic report,
"that 1-year planning leads to almost as much confusion as
no planning at all." He said that was why he was opening
up the books, and making long-range projections "that will
enable the people to discuss their choices more effectively."

He published a four-year projection which shows, among other things, that Nixon's new civilian initiatives including welfare and pollution will go up from $3 billion in the first year to $18 billion in the fourth. Yet there are no similar projections on the military side.

When Budget Director Mayo was on *Meet The Press* February 8, Edwin L. Dale, Jr., of the *New York Times* said, "Your four-year projection of the grand total of government spending under current programs of something like $240 billion is hard to make sense of unless you have an idea of what the defense assumptions are." Mr. Dale asked whether the grand totals assumed "the current force levels, the pre-Vietnam force levels, the levels at the end of the new fiscal year? What?" The Budget Director replied, "We preferred not to be too specific." Mr. Mayo would disclose no more than that the overall four-year projections assumed "a considerable lessening of the expenditures for Vietnam" and also "the effect of higher prices on all weapons systems" though at a lower rate of inflation. "We have also worked in," he added as a final concession, "what we think is a reasonable projection on the military side." But both the details and the totals on the military side were blacked out.

There is an interesting revelation in this connection at page 77 of the annual report of the President's Council of Economic Advisers. It shows that elaborate studies and projections *have* been made on the military as well as the civilian side. It says—

Among the most important steps in this direction have been the interrelated studies conducted through the National Security Council and the Cabinet Committee on Economic Policy. These studies examined alternative defense strategies with their associated costs and alternative nondefense programs. Various defense strategies were translated with rough accuracy into a large number of possible forces and budgets. Similarly alternative nondefense federal programs were developed.

How can Nixon say that he is making long-range four-year projections available to "enable the people to discuss their choices more effectively" when the military side of these projections—by far the biggest single share—is hidden from them? "We must become increasingly aware," Nixon also said in the Budget Message, "that small decisions today often lead to large cash outlays in the future." Of no part of the budget is this more resoundingly true than the military sector. A speech by Congressman Reuss in Milwaukee February 10 provided a swift glimpse of such "small decisions" and the large cash outlays they entail. "There is a $1.5 billion item for the ABM," Reuss said of the new budget, "expected ultimately to cost anywhere from $10 to $50 billion. There is $87 million for AWACS, a new airborne radar system with an ultimate $15-billion price tag. There is almost a billion dollars for continued deployment of the Navy's new F-14 fighter plane, with an expected total program cost of up to $36 billion. There is $370 million in the budget for a start on the F-15, the Air Force's new superiority jet fighter. Costs of this program are expected to exceed $25 billion." These programs impose a heavy mortgage on future budgets, but these are among the military commitments blacked out.

If the budget were candid, the public would see that all the projected spending on welfare and pollution are peanuts compared to the military outlays. Of the grand four-year total of $240 billion, the military portion must be somewhere between a third and a half, or between $80 and $120 billion. These colosssal sums imply a continuation of the arms race, indeed a new spiral in it, for that is what the go-ahead decisions on ABM and MIRV mean. The military only has to drag its heels a few months longer and it will be too late for the SALT talks to be anything more than futile palaver.

The budget presentation is shot through with deceit. "For the first time in two full decades," Nixon boasted in the message, "the federal government will spend more money on human resource programs than on national defense." This was illustrated with a pie chart showing 41 cents of the budget dollar going to human resources and only 36 cents to national defense. But if the government's huge social security and other trust fund receipts are deducted, we can see that the military spends 53 cents of every dollar of the general revenues.

If the huge social security payments and other trust funds are deducted from the "human resources" account, then we see that these get only seven cents of every dollar of general revenues. Even so, "human resources" are padded by including in them $8.5 billion of veterans benefits, although up to now these have been on the national defense side of the budget as part of the cost of fighting past wars. As for the fight against pollution, this is buried in "natural resources," which altogether get one and two-tenths cents of every dollar in the consolidated budget, *one-tenth of a cent less than last year*. The total appropriations asked to fight pollution of the air ($106 million) and water ($465 million) next year total $571 million. In a budget in which 53 cents of every general revenue dollar goes to the military, only four-tenths of a cent will go to save the air we breathe and the water we drink though it may soon be too late to save them. Nixon's anti-pollution rhetoric is miles from his budgetary realities.

February 23, 1970

ONLY THE BUMS CAN
SAVE THE COUNTRY NOW

The race is on between protest and disaster. Despite the first four martyr "bums" of Nixon-Agnewism at Kent State, the college shutdown their deaths precipitated, the outpouring of student and other protesters here last weekend, the campus lobbyists beginning to flood the halls of Congress, the Senate resolutions to limit or end Indochinese military operations, and the smoldering near-revolt within the Nixon Administration itself, we are still on the brink. We are in the first stages of a new and wider war from which withdrawal will be difficult. The military holds the reins and can precipitate new provocations and stage new alarms. The only hope is that the students can create such a Plague for Peace, swarming like locusts into the halls of Congress, that they stop all other business and make an end to the war the No. 1 concern it ought to be. Washington must no longer be the privileged sanctuary of the warmakers. The slogan of the striking students ought to be "Suspend Classes and Educate the Country." I see no other visible and adequate means to stop the slide into a conflict that may sweep very suddenly beyond the confines of Indochina if the man who gambled on Cambodia ends by gambling on the use of nuclear weapons.

In a dispatch from a landing zone in Cambodia, Jack Foisie of the *Washington Post* (May 8) described GIs jumping from helicopters under enemy fire with derisive denunciations of the war scrawled on their helmets. One of those he copied down sums up the situation of the whole country in this war. "We are the unwilling," it said, "led by the unqualified, doing the unnecessary, for the ungrateful." As usual the country is not being told the truth about why we went into Cambodia. In his war address of April 30 Nixon pictured the attack across the border as a preemptive exercise to hit an "enemy building up to launch massive attacks on our forces and those of South Vietnam." It was described as a swift preventive action from which we would soon withdraw and which was not part of any broader intervention in Cambodian affairs.

But thanks to the indiscretion of one Congressman, we now have the private—and more candid—version given members of Congress at special State Department briefings. This puts the origins and purpose of the Cambodian action in a very different light. The Congressman is Representative Hamilton Fish (R. N.Y.), a right-winger who has long questioned the logic of our heavy commitment in so peripheral an area as Southeast Asia. In a letter to constituents

released May 13, Mr. Fish summarizes a private briefing by
Under Secretary of State Richardson for selected members
of Congress. Nixon said we moved across the border to nip
enemy plans for an imminent attack. But from Richardson's
briefing, Mr. Fish reports, "It was clear that the present
military thrust into Cambodia hinged largely on the report-
edly surprise overthrow of Prince Sihanouk." Nixon said in
his April 30 speech that for five years "neither the U.S. nor
South Vietnam moved against those enemy sanctuaries because we did not wish to violate the territory of a neutral
nation." But Richardson gave the Congressmen a different
story. He told them, "U.S. intelligence had known for years
of those enclaves from which attacks on South Vietnam
have been launched" but we had never attacked them before "because it was feared that Sihanouk would counter
any invasion by allowing NVA [North Vietnamese
Army] forces to enlarge their occupied areas."

Sihanouk was trying to maintain a precarious neutrality
by playing one side against the other. Nixon was deceitful
when he said in the April 30 speech that our policy since the
Geneva Conference of 1954 "has been to scrupulously respect the neutrality of the Cambodian people" and added
—as proof of our virtue—that since last August we have
had a diplomatic mission in Pnom Penh "of fewer than 15"
and that for the previous four years "we did not have any
diplomatic mission whatever." The truth is that Sihanouk
ousted our mission and broke relations in 1965 because he
claimed the CIA had been plotting against him for years
and even tried twice to kill him. Sihanouk was especially
resentful of the Khmer Serei (Free Khmer) mercenaries the
CIA and our Special Forces had enlisted from among Cambodians living in South Vietnam and Thailand to act as an
anti-Sihanouk commando force. The CIA gave it facilities to
broadcast anti-Sihanouk propaganda from Saigon.

"For the past five years," Nixon said with bland hypocrisy, "we have provided no military assistance and no economic assistance whatever to Cambodia." He did not explain that Sihanouk threw out our military mission because

he said it had been trying to turn his armed forces against him, and gave up economic aid, too, rather than have it used as a cover for U.S. agents trying to overthrow him. This was not a figment of Sihanouk's imagination. As far back as 1958, in a police raid on the villa of one of his generals, Sihanouk found a letter from President Eisenhower pledging full support to a projected coup and to a reversal of Cambodian neutrality. This was part of a "Bangkok plan" worked out between the dictators of South Vietnam and Thailand (Diem and Marshal Sarit Thanarit) to dismember Cambodia and instigate civil war (see William Worthy's account in the York, Pa., *Gazette & Daily* of April 30). When Sihanouk resumed relations last August, in his desperate see-saw between the two sides, his condition was that the U.S. mission be kept small. He didn't want too many CIA agents roaming around.

That was poor Sihanouk's mistake. Cambodia neutrality was ended when the military we had long wooed finally overthrew Sihanouk on March 18. The most complete account yet published of the events leading up to the coup is to be found in *Le Monde Diplomatique* for April. It is by Daniel Roy, a Frenchman with 15 years' experience in Indochina who was for a time press attaché to Prince Sihanouk. He claims that funds for the coup were provided by a Cambodian adventurer turned banker in Bangkok who was associated in the enterprise with the notorious Son Ngoc Thanh, puppet President of Cambodia under the Japanese occupation. The latter fled to Thailand after the war and according to M. Roy is "today in the service of the CIA." M. Roy also charges that the coup was prepared by Khmer Serei forces who went over the border with their arms and wives and pretended that they were defecting to Sihanouk. They infiltrated the army and the police as a Trojan Horse for the CIA.

Let us now return to Congressman Fish's account of the private State Department briefing. "Following the fall of Sihanouk," the Congressmen were told, "the new anti-Communist government cut all supply lines [of the NVA and Viet Cong] except the Ho Chi Minh trail" which, of course, lies largely outside Cambodian territory. *"To re-secure their severed supply routes,"* the account in the private briefing continued, *"VC and NVA began moving out of the enclaves, thereby threatening the overthrow of the Cambodian government"* (my italics). It is "against this background," Representative Fish's account of the briefing concludes, "that the American-South Vietnamese strikes into Cambodia were ordered."

The sequence is quite different from that given publicly by Mr. Nixon. Instead of preparing an attack on our forces in South Vietnam, the enemy was reacting to an attack on its supply lines. This upset the status quo, and risked a complete take-over of Cambodia by the other side. We intervened to save it from the consequences. Did our government give the new Lon Nol government of Cambodia assurances that we would defend it if its action in cutting all the supply routes precipitated an attack upon it?

It is true that at the State Department briefing "it was stressed that the present attacks were not aimed at either the confrontation of the estimated 40,000 to 50,000 VC and NVA believed operating in Cambodia or the defense of the present government of Cambodia. The raids were described as strictly 'spoiling actions,' aimed at supply, bunker and communication network destruction" and to give the South Vietnamese army additional time while the enemy rebuilds its supplies. But you have to be pretty feeble-minded to accept this at face value. What if Sihanouk, with NVA and Peking support, is restored to power, this time not as a precarious neutral but as an ally of the other side? What if we are then faced with the prospect, not just of restoring the old supply lines and bases but of Cambodia turning into one big enemy base? Who can believe that the Nixon Administration will stand by and let this happen?

This is the wider war which lies ahead. The overthrow of Sihanouk was a grave political mistake. It gave the other side a new ally with legitimacy and mass support, basic necessities for the Indochinese People's War which has already been proclaimed against us. The situation inside Cambodia was succinctly summed up in an interview which the pro-Nixon and pro-war *U.S. News & World Report* for May 18 held by cable with its correspondent, James N. Wallace, in Pnom Penh:

Q. Have the allied attacks in eastern Cambodia saved the rest of the country from a Communist take-over?

A. No. Unless the allied drive completely overwhelms the Communists, Cambodia's position remains about the same . . . the short-run result is even more chaos and confusion . . .

Q. Did the Cambodians welcome the Allied move?

A. Again, no. Cambodians do not like . . . the idea of South Vietnamese troops' rolling across Cambodia . . .

Q. What kind of reception would Sihanouk get?

A. Almost certainly he would receive more popular support than the Lon Nol government cares to admit. Sihanouk still is popular among a great many of Cambodia's 5.5 million peasants, who respected his traditional status as a god-king and liked his earthly personal relations with villagers.

The French journalist Max Clos, who has been covering Indochina for years during both the French and U.S. wars, foresees (*Le Figaro*, May 2–3) a Cambodian resistance based on peasant support, doing in their country what the Viet Cong have done in Vietnam and creating a "liberated zone" from which in time they will be able to take over Pnom Penh. "Mr. Nixon," M. Clos wrote, "hopes to withdraw his troops from Cambodia in a month and a half. Even if he succeeds, it is safe to predict he will have to send them back again."

The political folly of our latest move is not limited to Cambodia. The newly enlarged war must add to the shaky character of the Thieu regime, which has had to close down all the South Vietnamese schools in a rising student revolt much like our own. The idea of South Vietnamese troops being used to bolster a government which has been massacring Cambodian citizens of Vietnamese origin must add to Thieu's unpopularity. The bitterness between the Viets and the Khmers of Cambodia is incomparably older and more

bitter than the recent animosities of the Russo-American
cold war. It is only two centuries since the Viets seized the
Mekong delta from the Khmers. Sihanouk, unlike his successors, never stirred up the mob against the Vietnamese
and the VC and NVA intruders, unlike our forces, did
not bomb and devastate Cambodian villages. This new shift
strengthens the forces opposing our puppets on both sides.

This has been a political war from its very beginning
against the French. We go on believing as they did that a
political problem can be solved by military means. The annals of their war, like ours, is full of sensationally billed
search-and-destroy operations which were finally going to
cripple the rebels, like this latest "Operation Total Victory" across the Cambodian border. The Communists
under Ho Chi Minh seized national leadership in the war
against the French, as the adroit Sihanouk did in Cambodia.
Now they both are allied against us. Sihanouk will now
make it possible for the other side to implement the basic
strategy of a People's War on a wider scale. The strategy is
to force maximum dispersion upon the hated foreign in-
vader to make him widen the area of his activity and stretch
his lines of communication so that the guerrillas can pick
and choose the most advantageous weak points for their
concentrated attacks. We have picked up their treacherous
gambit by invading Cambodia and sooner or later unless we
get out of Indochina altogether, we must send ground
troops into Laos and Cambodia, perhaps even into North
Vietnam where a fresh army of 250,000 or more awaits our
landing. Nowhere has airpower, however overwhelming
and unchallenged, been able to win a war.

What will happen when the country wakes up to find
that instead of withdrawing troops we are going to send in
fresh divisions? What happens to inflation, the budget and
the stock market? To student and racial unrest? Nixon, in a
mood of self-pity, complained in his April 30 address that
past war Presidents did not have to face a nation "assailed
by counsels of doubt and defeat from some of the most
widely known opinion leaders of the nation." He seems to

attribute this to some perversity. He takes it as personal. He does not stop to consider why this war has aroused so much more opposition than any past war, and done so in every class and every region and every age-group, from Wall Street financiers to campus radicals. Even National Guardsmen give the V-sign to students, and soldiers go into battle with peace amulets around their necks. He seems to think there is something wrong with the critics. He will not face up to the possibility that there is something wrong with the war. Certainly this generation of Americans would prove no less patriotic and brave than any other if our country were really in danger.

It is a measure of our stupid leadership that the Cambodian war was started on the phoney pretext that just across the border was a kind of enemy Pentagon and that we could cripple the enemy by smashing it. One measure of the mendacity may be found in an intelligence briefing the *New York Times* reported April 4, two weeks after Sihanouk's overthrow. It said COSVN, the enemy HQ, had been moved from Cambodian to South Vietnamese territory. The story even carried a map showing the old location at Mimot—which figures in recent accounts of the Cambodian operation—in the "fishhook" and the new location in a thick jungle area described as "virtually inaccessible to ground troops" and "probably not seriously vulnerable to air attacks." It is difficult to believe that Nixon and his aides are such idiots as not to be aware of this intelligence information.

The Eichmann trial taught the world the banality of evil. Nixon is teaching the world the evil of banality. The man so foolish as to talk to protesting students about football and surfing is the same man who (like Johnson) sees war in the puerile terms of "humiliation" and a challenge to his virility. He doesn't want us to be a "helpless giant" (which we are in Indochina) so he is plunging us into a wider quagmire where we will end up more helpless than ever.

The past week is the week in which the Nixon Administration began to come apart. Letters like Hickel's showed how isolated he is even from members of his own Cabinet, where there seems to be a silent majority against him. The antiwar round robin signed by more than 200 employes of the State Department shows how deeply the Cambodian affair has stirred even the most timid, conformist and conventional section of the bureaucracy. Nothing Nixon says can be taken at face value. Even when he said on April 20, in his troop withdrawal announcement, that a "just peace" was at last in sight, he must have been planning this expansion of the war. Indeed, General Westmoreland as Army Chief of Staff had already begun to lobby for a Cambodian invasion in off-the-record briefings.

There were two remarks of the deepest significance in the Nixon press conference of May 8. One was that if we withdraw from Vietnam "America is finished insofar as the peace-keeper in the Asian world is concerned." This revealed that he is still committed, despite that vague "low posture" talk on Guam, to a Pax Americana in Asia. If we are to police Asia we are in for many years of war and internal disruption. The folly is as great as if China were to try and become the "peace-keeper" of Latin America. The other remark was that unlike Johnson he would not escalate step by step but "move decisively." This is the Goldwater-LeMay thesis that we could have won the Vietnam war if we had smashed Hanoi and Haiphong in one great blow, perhaps with nuclear weapons. Hanoi, especially after the recent big bombing raids, expects something of the kind. Moscow and Peking are already trying to patch up their differences in expectation of it. If Nixon goes to nuclear weapons, the end result may well be World War III. Unless an army of students can fan out to the grass roots and make the country aware of these dangerous possibilities, terrible days may lie ahead.

May 18, 1970

PART IX

The Mideast

HOLY WAR

Stripped of propaganda and sentiment, the Palestine problem is, simply, the struggle of two different peoples for the same strip of land. For the Jews, the establishment of Israel was a Return, with all the mystical significance the capital R implies. For the Arabs it was another invasion. This has led to three wars between them in twenty years. Each has been a victory for the Jews. With each victory the size of Israel has grown. So has the number of Arab homeless.

Now to find a solution which will satisfy both peoples is like trying to square a circle. In the language of mathematics, the aspirations of the Jews and the Arabs are incommensurable. Their conflicting ambitions cannot be fitted into the confines of any ethical system which transcends the tribalistic. This is what frustrates the benevolent outsider, anxious to satisfy both peoples. For two years Jean-Paul Sartre has been trying to draw Israelis and Arabs into a confrontation in a special number of his review, *Les Temps Modernes*. The third war between them broke out while it was on the press.

This long-awaited special issue on *Le conflit israélo-arabe* is the first confrontation in print of Arab and Israeli intellectuals. But it turns out to be 991 pages not so much of dialogue as of dual monologue. The two sets of contributors sit not just in separate rooms, like employers and strikers in a bitter labor dispute, but in separate universes where the simplest fact often turns out to have diametrically opposite meanings. Physics has begun to uncover a new conundrum in the worlds of matter and anti-matter, occupying the same space and time but locked off from each other by their obverse natures, forever twin yet forever sundered. The Israeli-Arab quarrel is the closest analogue in the realm of international politics.

The conditions exacted for the joint appearance of Israelis and Arabs in the same issue of *Les Temps Modernes* excluded not only collaboration but normal editorial mediation or midwifery. Claude Lanzmann, who edited this special issue, explains in his Introduction that the choice of authors and of subjects had to be left "in full sovereignty" (*en toute souveraineté*) to each of the two parties. The Arabs threatened to withdraw if an article was included by A. Razak Abdel-Kader, an Algerian who is an advocate of Israeli-Arab reconciliation. When the Israelis objected that *Les Temps Modernes* at least allow Abdel-Kader to express himself as an individual, the Arabs insisted on an absolute veto: there would be no issue if Abdel-Kader were in it.

In his Preface Jean-Paul Sartre lays bare the conflicting emotions which led him to embark on so difficult a task as to attempt the role—in some degree—of peacemaker between Arab and Israeli. They awaken the memories of his finest hours. One was that of the Resistance. "For all those who went through this experience," M. Sartre writes, "it is unbearable to imagine that another Jewish community, wherever it may be, whatever it may be, should endure this Calvary anew and furnish martyrs to a new massacre." The other was Sartre's aid to the Arabs in their struggle for Algerian independence. These memories bind him to both peoples, and give him the respect of both, as the welcome he received in both Egypt and Israel last year attests. His aim in presenting their views is, he says wistfully, merely to *inform*. His hope is that information in itself will prove pacifying "because it tends more or less slowly to replace passion by knowledge." But the roots of this struggle lie deeper than reason. It is not at all certain that information will replace passion with knowledge.

The experiences from which M. Sartre draws his emotional ties are irrelevant to this new struggle. Both sides draw from them conclusions which must horrify the man of rationalist tradition and universalist ideals. The bulk of the Jews and the Israelis draw from the Hitler period the conviction that, in this world, when threatened one must be prepared to kill or be killed. The Arabs draw from the Algerian conflict the conviction that, even in dealing with so rational and civilized a people as the French, liberation was made possible only by resorting to the gun and the knife. Both Israeli and Arabs in other words feel that only force can assure justice. In this they agree, and this sets them on a collision course. For the Jews believe justice requires the recognition of Israel as a fact; for the Arabs, to recognize the fact is to acquiesce in the wrong done them by the conquest of Palestine. If God as some now say is dead, He no doubt died of trying to find an equitable solution to the Arab-Jewish problem.

The argument between them begins with the Bible. "I give this country to your posterity," God said to Abraham (Gen. XV: 18) "from the river of Egypt up to the great river, Euphrates." Among the Jews, whether religious or secular mystics, this is the origin of their right to the Promised Land. The opening article in the Arab section of *Les Temps Modernes* retorts that the "posterity" referred to in Genesis includes the descendants of Ishmael since he was the son of Abraham by his concubine Ketirah, and the ancestor of all the Arabs, Christian or Muslim.

All this may seem anachronistic nonsense, but this is an anachronistic quarrel. The Bible is still the best guide to it. Nowhere else can one find a parallel for its enthnocentric fury. Nowhere that I know of is there a word of pity in the Bible for the Canaanites whom the Hebrews slaughtered in taking possession. Of all the nonsense which marks the Jewish-Arab quarrel none is more nonsensical than the talk from both sides about the Holy Land as a symbol of peace. No bit of territory on earth has been soaked in the blood of more battles. Nowhere has religion been so zestful an excuse for fratricidal strife. The Hebrew *shalom* and the Arabic *salaam* are equally shams, relics of a common past as Bedouins. To this day inter-tribal war is the favorite sport of the Bedouins; to announce "peace" in the very first word is a necessity if any chance encounter is not to precipitate bloodshed.

In Biblical perspective the Jews have been going in and out of Palestine for 3,000 years. They came down from the Euphrates under Abraham; returned from Egypt under Moses and Joshua; came back again from the Babylonian captivity and were dispersed again after Jerusalem fell to the Romans in 70 A.D. This is the third return. The Arabs feel they have a superior claim because they stayed put. This appearance side by side in *Les Temps Modernes* provides less than the full and undiluted flavor of an ancient sibling rivalry. Both sides have put their better foot forward. The Arab section includes no sample of the blood-curdling broadcasts in which the Arab radios indulge; the Israeli, no contribution from the right-wing Zionists who dream of a greater Israel from the Nile to the Euphrates (as promised in Genesis) with complete indifference to the fate of the Arab inhabitants. On neither side is there a frank exposition of the *Realpolitik* which led Arab nationalists like Nasser to see war on Israel as the one way to achieve Arab unity, and leads Jewish nationalists like Ben Gurion and Dayan to see Arab disunity and backwardness as essential elements for Israeli security and growth. No voice on the Arab side preaches a Holy War in which all Israel would be massacred, while no voice on the Israeli side expresses the cheerfully cynical view one may hear in private that Israel has no realistic alternative but to hand the Arabs a bloody nose every five or ten years until they accept the loss of Palestine as irreversible.

The picture, however, is not wholly symmetrical. There is first of all the asymmetry of the victorious and the defeated. The victor is ready to talk with the defeated if the latter will acquiesce in defeat. The defeated, naturally, is less inclined to this kind of objectivity. The editor, Claude Lanzmann, speaks of an "asymmetry between the two collections of articles which derives at one and the same time from a radical difference in their way of looking at the conflict and from the difference in the nature of the political regimes in the countries involved." Even if not expressly authorized by their governments or organizations to participate, M. Lanzmann explains, all the Arabs except the North Africans wrote only after consultation and defend a common position, while the Israelis, "as is normal in a Western-style democracy," speak either for themselves or for one of their numerous parties. But this diversity may be exaggerated. On the fundamental issue which divides the two sides, no Arab contributor is prepared to advocate recognition of the state of Israel, while only one Israeli contributor is prepared to advocate its transformation into something other than a basically Jewish state.

The depth of this nationalistic difference may be measured by what happened to Israel's Communist party. Elsewhere national centrifugal tendencies have made their appearance in the once monolithic world of communism. In Israel the same nationalist tendencies split the Communist party into two, one Jewish the other Arab. The days when Arab Communists faithfully followed Moscow's line straight into the jails of Egypt, Iraq, Syria, and Jordan by supporting the 1947 partition plan have long passed away. Today Arab and Jewish Communists no longer find common ground.[1] It would be hard to find an Arab who would agree with Moshe Sneh, head of the Jewish Communist party (Maki) in Israel, when he told *L'Express* (June 19–25), "Our war is just and legitimate. What united the 13 Arab States against us, irrespective of their regime, was not anti-imperialism but pan-Arabism and anti-Jewish chauvinism." He added boldly that Moscow in supporting the Arabs had "turned its back on the politics of the international left and on the spirit of Tashkent." But even Sneh's bitter rival, Meir Vilner, the Jewish leader of, and one of

[1] The relative strength of the two since the split may be seen from the fact that the Jewish branch was able to elect only one deputy while the Arab branch, which draws the largest vote among the Arab minority, elected three, two Arabs and one Jew.

the few Jews left in, the Arab Communist party (Rakka)
expresses himself in *Les Temps Modernes* in terms with
which no Arab contributor to it agrees. M. Vilner is for the
return of all the refugees who wish it, for full equality to
Arabs in Israel and for a neutralist policy, but he defends
the existence of Israel as a legitimate fact and denies that
"one can in any way compare the people (of Israel) to Algerian colons or the Crusaders." The comparisons rejected
by the leader of the Arab Communist party in Israel are the
favorite comparisons of the Arabs outside Israel. The diversity of viewpoint on the Israeli side thus ends with the basic
agreement on its right to exist, and to exist as a Jewish state.
This is precisely where the Arab disagreement begins.

The gulf between Arab and Jewish views becomes even
clearer when one reads two supplementary pieces contrib-
uted by two French Jews, Maxime Rodinson, a distinguished sociologist and Orientalist, and Robert Misrahi, a
well-known writer of the left. The former takes the Arab
and the latter the Zionist side. But while M. Misrahi's article
appears with the Israelis, M. Rodinson's contribution—by
far the most brilliant in the whole volume—appears alone.
He refused, for reasons of principle, to appear in the Arab
ensemble. It is not hard to see why. For while M. Rodinson
gives strong support to every basic Arab historical conten-
tion, he is too much the humanist (and in the last analysis
no doubt the Jew) to welcome an apocalyptic solution at
the expense of Israel's existence. There is still a gulf between M. Rodinson's pro-Arab position and the most moderate view any Arab statesman has yet dared express, that of
Tunisia's President Bourguiba. Bourguiba's famous speech
in Jericho, March 3, 1965, is reprinted in an appendix by
Les Temps Modernes, along with an interview he gave *Le
Nouvel Observateur* (April 15) a month later. But Bourguiba's speech, though it created a sensation by its relative
moderation, merely suggested that the Arabs proceed to regain Palestine as they did Tunisia, by a series of more or less
peaceful compromises. When *Le Nouvel Observateur* asked
him whether this did not imply the progressive disappear-

ance of the State of Israel, he would not go beyond the cryptic reply, "That is not certain."

The Arab section of the symposium is nevertheless far from being uniform. A Moroccan, Abdallah Larouia, professor of literature in Rabat, not only ends by saying that the possibilities of peaceful settlement must be kept open because a war would settle nothing, but even goes so far as to express the hope that the time may come when a settlement is possible without making a new exile, i.e., of the Israelis, pay for the end of another exile, i.e. of the Arabs from Palestine. He even suggests that under certain conditions, a Jewish community "with or without political authority"—a most daring remark—may prove compatible with Arab progress and development.

When we examine these conditions, we come to the heart of the fears expressed by the Arabs in this symposium. The Palestinian Arabs, from the first beginnings of Zionism, foresaw the danger of being swamped and dislodged by Jewish immigration. Neighboring Arab states feared that this immigration would stimulate a continuous territorial expansion at their expense and create a Jewish state powerful enough to dominate the area. The relative size and population of Israel when compared to its Arab neighbors are deceptive and may make these fears seem foolish, but historically the Middle East has often been conquered and dominated by relatively small bands of determined intruders. Even now, as the recent fighting showed, tiny Israel could without difficulty have occupied Damascus, Amman, and Cairo, and—were it not for the big powers and the UN—dictated terms to its Arab neighbors.

It was the attempt of the British to allay Arab apprehension by setting limits on Jewish immigration that precipitated the struggle between the British and the Jews. The 1917 Balfour Declaration, when it promised a "Jewish National Home" in Palestine, also said—in a passage Zionists have always preferred to forget—"that nothing shall be

done which may prejudice the civil and religious rights of
the existing non-Jewish communities in Palestine." British
White Papers in 1922, in 1930, and again in 1939 tried to
fulfill this companion pledge by steps which would have
kept the Jews a permanent minority. It is this persistent and
—as events have shown—justifiable Arab fear which is reflected in M. Laroui's article. In calling the Palestine problem "A Problem of the Occident" his basic point is that if
the Occident wipes out anti-Semitism, or keeps it within
harmless proportions, making refuge in Israel unnecessary
for the bulk of Jewry, and Israel divorces its politics from
the Zionist dream of gathering in all the Jews from Exile,
this will end the danger of an inexorable expansion in search
of *"lebensraum"* at the expense of the Palestinian Arabs,
and finally make peace possible between the two peoples.
Since immigration into Israel has dwindled in recent years,
this Arab fear seems at the moment less a matter of reality
than of Zionist theory and of a past experience which leads
them to take it seriously.

The suggestion that Israel abandon its supra-nationalist
dream finds its only echo on the other side of this collection
of essays in Israel's No. 1 maverick and champion of Arab
rights, Uri Avnery. Avnery was born in Germany in 1923
and went to Palestine at the age of ten, the year Hitler took
power. He began his political career on the far nationalist
right, as a member of the Irgun terrorist group in the struggle against the British, but has since swung over to the far
left of Israeli opinion, to the point where he is considered
anti-nationalist. In the wake of the first Suez war, he supported the Egyptian demand for evacuation of the Canal
Zone and in 1959 he formed an Israeli committee to aid the
Algerian rebels. At one time he organized a movement
which asserted that the Israelis were no longer Jews but
"Canaanites" and therefore one with the Arabs, forcibly
converted remnants of the same indigenous stock. When
this far-out conception attracted few Jews and even fewer
Canaanites, he formed a "Semitic Action" movement which
has now become "the Movement of New Forces." This

polled 1.2 percent of the vote in the 1965 elections and by virtue of proportional representation put Avnery into Parliament. Avnery has been more successful as a publisher. He has made his weekly *Haolam Hazeh* ("This World") the largest in Israel by combining non-conformist politics with what the rather puritanical Israelis call pornography, though that weekly's girlie pictures would seem as old-fashioned as the *Police Gazette* in America.

Avnery writes in *Les Temps Modernes* that he would turn Israel into a secular, pluralist, and multi-national state. He would abolish the Law of Return which gives every Jew the right to enter Israel and automatically become a citizen. Avnery says this pan-Judaism of Zionism feeds the anti-Zionism of pan-Arabism by keeping alive "the myth of an Israel submerged by millions of immigrants who, finding no place to settle, would oblige the government to expand the country by force of arms."

Yet Avnery, who asks Israel to give up its Zionist essence, turns out to be a Jewish nationalist, too. After sketching out a plan for an Arab Palestinian state west of the Jordan, Avnery writes, "The Arabic reader will justly ask at this point, 'And the return of Israel to the limits of the UN plan of 1947?'" Since Israel in the 1947–48 fighting seized about 23 percent more territory than was allotted to it in the 1947 partition plan, this implies a modification of frontiers in favor of the Arab state which was supposed to be linked with it in an economically united Palestine. But to this natural Arab question Avnery replies,[2] "Frankly we see no possibility of this kind. The Arab armies are already 15 kilometers from Israel's most populous city (Tel Aviv) and at Nathanya are even closer to the sea." The Arabs may feel that Avnery is as unwilling to give up the fruits of conquest as any non-"Canaanite." Avnery is as reluctant as any conventional Zionist to see his fellow Canaanite too close to Tel Aviv.

It is easy to understand why neither side trusts the other.

[2] Avnery was writing, of course, before the new outbreak of warfare had again changed these borders to Israel's advantage.

In any case M. Sartre's symposium is a confrontation
largely of moderates and leftists, and on neither side do
these elements command majority support. Another complexity is that while in settled societies the left tends to be
less nationalistic than the right, in colonial societies the revolutionary left is often more nationalistic than the native
conservative and propertied classes.

The overwhelming majority opinion on both sides, even
as expressed in a symposium as skewed leftward as this one,
shows little tendency to compromise. The Arabs argue that
Israel is a colonialist implantation in the Middle East, supported from the beginning by imperialist powers; that it is
an enemy of Arab union and progress; that the sufferings of
the Jews in the West were the consequence of an anti-
Semitism the Arabs have never shared; and that there is no
reason why the Arabs of Palestine should be displaced from
their homes in recompense for wrongs committed by Hitler
Germany. M. Laroui alone is sympathetic enough to say
that if the Jewish National Home had been established in
Uganda, the Arabs who felt compassion for the sufferings
of the Jews of Europe would have shown themselves as un-
comprehending of the rights of the Ugandans as the West
has been in Palestine. At the other end of the Arab spectrum
a fellow Moroccan, a journalist, Tahar Benziane, ends up in
classic anti-Semitism, blaming the Jews themselves, their
separatism and their sense of superiority, for the prejudice
against them. Benziane sees the only solution not just in the
liquidation of Israel but in the disappearance of world
Jewry through assimilation. His would indeed be a Final
Solution. This bitter and hateful opinion, widespread in the
Arab world, explains why Nazism found so ready an echo
before the war in the Middle East and Nazi criminals so
welcome a refuge in Egypt. It also disposes of the semantic
nonsense that Arabs being Semite cannot be anti-Semitic!
  The Zionist argument is that the Jewish immigration was
a return to the Jewish homeland. Robert Misrahi even goes
so far as to argue that the Jews had an older claim to Pales-

tine than the Arabs since the Jews had lived there in the
ancient kingdom of the Hebrews long before the Hegira of
Mohammed! Misrahi argues the familiar Zionist thesis that
their struggle against Britain proves them to be anti-
imperialist, that their colonies are socialist, that their enemies are the feudal elements in the Arab world, and that the
Arab refugees are the moral responsibility of the Arab leaders since it was on their urging that the Arabs ran away.

There is a good deal of simplistic sophistry in the Zionist
case. The whole earth would have to be reshuffled if claims
2,000 years old to *irredenta* were suddenly to be allowed.
Zionism from its beginning tried to gain its aims by offering
to serve as outpost in the Arab world for one of the great
empires. Herzl sought to win first the Sultan and then the
Kaiser by such arguments. Considerations of imperial strategy finally won the Balfour Declaration from Britain. The
fact that the Jewish community in Palestine afterward
fought the British is no more evidence of its not being a
colonial implantation than similar wars of British colonists
against the mother country, from the American Revolution
to Rhodesia. In the case of Palestine, as of other such
struggles, the Mother Country was assailed because it
showed more concern for the native majority than was pal-
atable to the colonist minority. The argument that the refugees ran away "voluntarily" or because their leaders urged
them to do so until after the fighting was over not only rests
on a myth but is irrelevant. Have refugees no right to return? Have German Jews no right to recover their properties because they too fled?

The myth that the Arab refugees fled because the Arab
radios urged them to do so was analyzed by Erskine B.
Childers in the London *Spectator* May 12, 1961. An examination of British and U.S. radio monitoring records turned
up no such appeals; on the contrary there were appeals and
"even orders to the civilians of Palestine, *to stay put*." The
most balanced and humane discussion of the question may
be found in Christopher Sykes's book *Crossroads to Israel:*

1917–48 (at pages 350–5). "It can be said with a high degree of certainty," Mr. Sykes wrote, "that most of the time in the first half of 1948 the mass exodus was the natural, thoughtless, pitiful movement of ignorant people who had been badly led and who in the day of trial found themselves forsaken by their leaders. . . . But if the exodus was by and large an accident of war in the first stage, in the later stages it was consciously and mercilessly helped on by Jewish threats and aggression toward Arab populations. . . . It is to be noted, however, that where the Arabs had leaders who refused to be stampeded into panic flight, the people came to no harm." Jewish terrorism, not only by the Irgun, in such savage massacres as Deir Yassin, but in milder form by the Haganah, itself "encouraged" Arabs to leave areas the Jews wished to take over for strategic or demographic reasons. They tried to make as much of Israel as free of Arabs as possible.

The effort to equate the expulsion of the Arabs from Palestine with the new Jewish immigration out of the Arab countries is not so simple nor so equitable as it is made to appear in Zionist propaganda. The Palestinian Arabs feel about this "swap" as German Jews would if denied restitution on the grounds that they had been "swapped" for German refugees from the Sudetenland. In a sanely conceived settlement, some allowance should equitably be made for Jewish properties left behind in Arab countries. What is objectionable in the simplified version of this question is the idea that Palestinian Arabs whom Israel didn't want should have no objection to being "exchanged" for Arabic Jews it did want. One uprooting cannot morally be equated with the other.

A certain moral imbecility marks all ethnocentric movements. The Others are always either less than human, and thus their interests may be ignored, or more than human, and therefore so dangerous that it is right to destroy them. The latter is the underlying pan-Arab attitude toward the Jews; the former is Zionism's basic attitude toward the Arabs. M. Avnery notes that Herzl in his book *The Jewish*

State, which launched the modern Zionist movement, dealt with working hours, housing for workers, and even the national flag but had not one word to say about the Arabs! For the Zionists the Arab was the Invisible Man. Psychologically he was not there. Achad Ha-Am, the Russian Jew who became a great Hebrew philosopher, tried to draw attention as early as 1891 to the fact that Palestine was not an empty territory and that this posed problems. But as little attention was paid to him as was later accorded his successors in "spiritual Zionism," men like Buber and Judah Magnes, who tried to preach *Ichud*, "unity," i.e., with the Arabs. Of all the formulas with which Zionism comforted itself none was more false and more enduring than Israel Zangwill's phrase about "a land without people for a people without a land." Buber related that Max Nordau, hearing for the first time that there was an Arab population in Palestine, ran to Herzl crying, "I didn't know that—but then we are committing an injustice." R. J. Zwi Werblowsky, dean of the faculty of letters at the Hebrew University, in the first article of this anthology's Israeli section, writes with admirable objectivity, "There can be no doubt that if Nordau's reaction had been more general, it would seriously have paralyzed the *élan* of the Zionist movement." It took refuge, he writes, in "a moral myopia."

This moral myopia makes it possible for Zionists to dwell on the 1,900 years of Exile in which Jews have longed for Palestine but dismiss as nugatory the nineteen years in which Arab refugees have also longed for it. "Homelessness" is the major theme of Zionism, but this pathetic passion is denied to Arab refugees. Even Meir Yaari, the head of Mapam, the leader of the "Marxist" Zionists of Hashomer Hatzair, who long preached bi-nationalism, says Israel can only accept a minority of the Arab refugees because the essential reason for the creation of Israel was to "welcome the mass of immigrant Jews returning to their historic fatherland!" If there is not room enough for both, the Jews must have precedence. This is what leads Gabran Majdalany, a Baath Socialist, to write that Israel is "a racist state founded

from its start on discrimination between Jew and non-Jew."
He compares the Zionists to the Muslim Brotherhood who
"dream of a Muslim Israel in which the non-Muslims will be
the gentiles, second-class citizens sometimes tolerated but
more often repressed." It is painful to hear his bitter re-
proach—

Some people admit the inevitably racist character of Israel but
justify it by the continual persecutions to which the Jews have
been subjected during the history of Europe and by the massacres of the Second World War. We consider that, far from
serving as justification, these facts constitute an aggravating circumstance; for those who have known the effects of racism and
of discrimination in their own flesh and human dignity, are less
excusably racist than those who can only imagine the negative
effects of prejudice.

When Israel's Defense Minister, Moshe Dayan, was on
Face the Nation June 11, after Israel's latest victories, this
colloquy occurred:

SYDNEY GRUSON (*New York Times*): Is there any possible
way that Israel could absorb the huge number of Arabs whose
territory it has gained control of now?
GEN. DAYAN: Economically we can; but I think that is not
in accord with our aims in the future. It would turn Israel into
either a bi-national or poly-Arab-Jewish state instead of the
Jewish state, and we want to have a Jewish state. We can
absorb them, but then it won't be the same country.
MR. GRUSON: And it is necessary in your opinion to maintain this as a Jewish state and purely a Jewish state?
GEN. DAYAN: Absolutely—absolutely. We want a Jewish
state like the French have a French state.

This must deeply disturb the thoughtful Jewish reader.
Ferdinand and Isabella in expelling the Jews and Moors
from Spain were in the same way saying they wanted a
Spain as "Spanish," (i.e., Christian) as France was French. It
is not hard to recall more recent parallels.

It is a pity the editors of *Les Temps Modernes* didn't
widen their symposium to include a Jewish as distinct from
an Israeli point of view. For Israel is creating a kind of
moral schizophrenia in world Jewry. In the outside world

the welfare of Jewry depends on the maintenance of secular, non-racial, pluralistic societies. In Israel, Jewry finds itself defending a society in which mixed marriages cannot be legalized, in which non-Jews have a lesser status than Jews, and in which the ideal is racial and exclusionist. Jews must fight elsewhere for their very security and existence—against principles and practices they find themselves defending in Israel. Those from the outside world, even in their moments of greatest enthusiasm amid Israel's accomplishments, feel twinges of claustrophobia, not just geographical but spiritual. Those caught up in Prophetic fervor soon begin to feel that the light they hoped to see out of Zion is only that of another narrow nationalism.

Such moments lead to a reexamination of Zionist ideology. That longing for Zion on which it is predicated may be exaggerated. Its reality is indisputable but its strength can easily be overestimated. Not until after World War II was it ever strong enough to attract more than a trickle of Jews to the Holy Land. By the tragic dialectic of history, Israel would not have been born without Hitler. It took the murder of six million in his human ovens to awaken sufficient nationalist zeal in Jewry and sufficient humanitarian compassion in the West to bring a Jewish state to birth in Palestine. Even then humanitarian compassion was not strong enough to open the gates of the West to Jewish immigration in contrition. The capitalist West and the Communist East preferred to displace Arabs rather than to welcome the Jewish "displaced persons" in Europe's postwar refugee camps.

It must also be recognized, despite Zionist ideology, that the periods of greatest Jewish creative accomplishment have been associated with pluralistic civilizations in their time of expansion and tolerance: in the Hellenistic period, in the Arab civilization of North Africa and Spain, and in Western Europe and America. Universal values can only be the fruit of a universal vision; the greatness of the Prophets lay in their overcoming of ethnocentricity. A Lilliputian nationalism cannot distill truths for all mankind. Here lie the roots of a growing divergence between Jew and Israeli; the former with a sense of mission as a Witness in the human wilderness, the latter concerned only with his own tribe's welfare.

But Jewry can no more turn its back on Israel than Israel on Jewry. The ideal solution would allow the Jews to make their contributions as citizens in the diverse societies and nations which are their homes while Israel finds acceptance as a Jewish State in a renascent Arab civilization. This would end Arab fears of a huge inflow to Israel. The Jews have as much reason to be apprehensive about that prospect as the Arabs.

It can only come as the result of a sharp recrudescence in persecution elsewhere in the world. Zionism grows on Jewish catastrophe. Even now it casts longing eyes on Russian Jewry. But would it not be better, more humanizing, and more just, were the Soviet Union to wipe out anti-Semitism and to accord its Jews the same rights of cultural autonomy and expression it gives all its other nationalities? The Russian Jews have fought for Russia, bled for the Revolution, made no small contribution to Russian literature and thought; why should they be cast out? This would be a spiritual catastrophe for Russia as well as Jewry even though it would supply another flow of desperate refugees to an Israel already short of Jews if it is to expand as the Zionist militants hope to expand it.

Israel has deprived anti-Semitism of its mystique. For the visitor to Israel, anti-Semitism no longer seems a mysterious anomaly but only another variant of minority-majority friction. *Es is schwer zu sein eid Yid* ("It's hard to be a Jew") was the title of Sholom Aleichem's most famous story. Now we see that it's hard to be a goy in Tel Aviv, especially an Arab goy. Mohammad Watad, a Muslim Israeli, one of the five Arabic contributors to the Israeli side of this symposium, begins his essay with words which startlingly resemble the hostile dialogue Jews encounter elsewhere. "I am often asked," he writes, "about my 'double' life which is at one and the same time that of an Arab and that of an Israeli citizen." Another Arab contributor from Israel, Ibrahim Shabath, a Christian who teaches Hebrew in Arabic schools and is editor-in-chief of *Al Mirsad*, the Mapam paper in Arabic, deplores the fact that nineteen years after the creation of Israel "the Arabs are still considered strangers by the Jews." He relates a recent conversation with Ben Gurion. "You must know," Ben Gurion told him, "that Israel is the country of the Jews and only of the Jews. Every Arab who lives here has the same rights as any minority citizen in any country of the world, but he must admit the fact that he lives in a Jewish country." The implications must chill Jews in the outside world.

The Arab citizen of Israel, Shabath complains, "is the victim today of the same prejudices and the same generalizations as the Jewish people elsewhere." The bitterest account of what they undergo may be found in an anonymous report sent to the United Nations in 1964 by a group of Arabs who tried unsuccessfully to found an independent Socialist Arab movement and publication. Military authorities, despite a Supreme Court order, refused to permit this, and the courts declined to overrule the military. Their petition is reprinted in the Israeli section of this symposium. Though the military rule complained of was abolished last year, and police regulations substituted, it is too soon—especially because of the new outbeak of warfare—to determine what the effect will be on Arab civil liberties. Israelis admit with pleasure that neither in the Christian villages of Central Galilee nor in the Muslim villages of the so-called "Triangle" was there the slightest evidence of any Fifth Column activity. Those Israelis who have fought for an end of all discrimination against the Arabs argue that they have demonstrated their loyalty and deserve fully to be trusted.

It is to Israel's credit that the Arab minority is given place in its section to voice these complaints while no similar place is opened for ethnic minority opinion in the Arabic section. Indeed except for Lebanon and to some degree Tunisia there is no place in the Arab world where the dissident of any kind enjoys freedom of the press. There is no frank discussion of this in the Arab section. One of the most vigorous and acute expositions of the Arab point of view, for example, is an article by an Egyptian writer, Lotfallah Soliman, who has played a distinguished role in bringing modern ideas to the young intellectuals of his country since World War II. His autobiographical sketch says cryptically, if discreetly, "He lives presently in Paris." I stumbled on a more candid explanation. In preparing for this review, I read an earlier article in *Les Temps Modernes* (August–September 1960) by Adel Montasser on *La répression anti-démocratique en Egypte*. Appended to it was a list of intellectuals imprisoned by Nasser. Among them was Lotfallah Soliman. Obviously it's hard to be a free Egyptian intellectual in Nasser's Egypt. Many of those then imprisoned have since been freed, but it is significant that a writer as trenchant and devoted as Soliman has to work in exile.

It is true that the full roster of Arab minority complaints in Israel had to be presented anonymously for fear of the authorities. But in the Arab section of this book no place was allowed even anonymously for the Jewish and the various Christian minorities to voice their complaints. As a result the Arab contributors were able to write as if their countries, unlike Europe, were models of tolerance. They hark back to the great days of Arabic Spain where (except for certain interludes not mentioned) Christian and Jew enjoyed full equality, religious, cultural, and political, with the Muslim: Spain did not become synonymous with intolerance, Inquisition, and obscurantism until the Christian Reconquest. But today no Arab country except, precariously, Lebanon, dimly resembles Moorish Spain. As a result the Jews from the Arabic countries tend to hate the Arab far more than Jews from Europe who have never lived under his rule, which often recalls medieval Christiandom. A glimpse of these realities may be found in the most

moving article in this whole symposium. This is by Attalah
Mansour, a young Christian Arabic Israeli novelist of peasant origin who has published two novels, one in Arabic and
the other in Hebrew, and worked as a journalist on Avnery's paper *Haolam Hazeh* and on the staff of *Haaretz*,
Israel's best and most objective daily paper. M. Mansour
knows doubly what it is to be a "Jew." He is as an Arab a
"Jew" to the Israelis and as a Christian a "Jew" to the
Muslims. He tells a touching story of an accidental encounter in (of all places) the Paris Metro with a young man who
turned out like him to be Greek-rite Christian though from
Egypt. They exchanged stories of their troubles, like two
Jews in the Diaspora. "We in Egypt," the young stranger
told him, "have the same feelings as you. There is no law
discriminating between us and the Muslims. But the governmental administration, at least on the everyday level,
prefers Mahmoud to Boulos and Achmed to Samaan"—i.e.
the man with the Muslim name to the man with the Christian. "Omar Sharif, the well-known movie actor," the
Egyptian Christian added, "is Christian in origin. But he
had to change his Christian name for a Muslim to please the
public." In Israel, similarly, Ibrahim often becomes Abraham to pass as a Jew and to avoid widespread housing discrimination.

If in this account I have given more space to the Arab
than the Israeli side it is because as a Jew, closely bound
emotionally with the birth of Israel,[3] I feel honor bound to
report the Arab side, especially since the U.S. press is so
overwhelmingly pro-Zionist. For me, the Arab-Jewish
struggle is a tragedy. The essence of tragedy is a struggle of
right against right. Its catharsis is the cleansing pity of seeing how good men do evil despite themselves out of un-

---

[3] I first arrived in Palestine on Balfour Day Nov. 2, 1945, the day the
Haganah blew up bridges and watch towers to begin its struggle against
the British and immigration restrictions. The following spring I was the
first newspaperman to travel with illegal Jewish immigrants from the
Polish-Czech border through the British blockade. In 1947 I celebrated
Passover in the British detention camps in Cyprus and in 1948 I covered
the Arab-Jewish war. See my *Underground to Palestine* (1946) and *This
is Israel* (1948). I was back in 1949, 1950, 1951, 1956, and 1964.

avoidable circumstance and irresistible compulsion. When
evil men do evil, their deeds belong to the realm of pathol-
ogy. But when good men do evil, we confront the essence
of human tragedy. In a tragic struggle, the victors become
the guilty and must make amends to the defeated. For me
the Arab problem is also the No. 1 Jewish problem. How
we act toward the Arabs will determine what kind of
people we become: either oppressors and racists in our turn
like those from whom we have suffered, or a nobler race
able to transcend the tribal xenophobias that afflict mankind.[4]

Israel's swift and extraordinary victories have suddenly
transmuted this ideal from the realm of impractical sentiment to urgent necessity. The new frontiers of military
conquest have gathered in most of the Arab refugees. Zionism's dream, the "ingathering of the exiles," has been
achieved, though in an ironic form; it is the Arab exiles who
are back. They cannot be gotten rid of as easily as in 1948.
Something in the order of 100,000 have again been "encouraged" to leave, but the impact on public opinion
abroad and in Israel has forced the state to declare that it
will allow them to return. While the UN proves impotent
to settle the conflict and the Arab powers are unwilling to
negotiate from a situation of weakness, Israel can to some
degree determine its future by the way in which it treats its
new Arab subjects or citizens. The wrangles of the powers
will go on for months, but these people must be fed, clothed,
and housed. How they are treated will change the world's
picture of Israel and of Jewry, soften or intensify Arab

---

[4] In September [1967], Black Star will publish a vigorous little book
The Aryanization of the Jewish State, by Michael Selzer, a young Paki-
stani Jew who lived in Israel. It may help Jewry and Israel to understand
that the way to a fraternal life with the Arabs inside and outside Israel
must begin with the eradication of the prejudices that greet the Oriental
and Arabic-speaking Jews in Israel who now make up over half the population of the country. The bias against the Arab extends to a bias against
the Jews from the Arab countries. In this, as in so many other respects,
Israel presents in miniature all the problems of the outside world. Were
the rest of the planet to disappear, Israel could regenerate from itself—as
from a new Ark—all the bigotries, follies, and feuds of a vanished mankind (as well as some of its most splended accomplishments).

anger, build a bridge to peace or make new war certain. To establish an Arab state on the West Bank and to link it with Israel, perhaps also with Jordan, in a Confederation would turn these Arab neighbors, if fraternally treated, from enemies into a buffer, and give Israel the protection of strategic frontiers. But it would be better to give the West Bank back to Jordan than to try to create a puppet state—a kind of Arab Bantustan—consigning the Arabs to second-class status under Israel's control. This would only foster Arab resentment. To avoid giving the Arabs first-class citizenship by putting them in the reservation of a second-class state is too transparently clever.

What is required in the treatment of the Arab refugees Israel has gathered in is the conquest both of Jewish exclusivism and the resentful hostility of the Arabs. Even the malarial marshes of the Emek and the sandy wastes of the Negev could not have looked more bleakly forbidding to earlier generations of Zionist pioneers than these steep and arid mountains of prejudice. But I for one have a glimmer of hope. Every year I have gone to Palestine and later Israel I have found situations which seemed impossible. Yet Zionist zeal and intelligence overcame them. Perhaps this extraordinarily dynamic, progressive, and devoted community can even if need be transcend its essential self.

I was encouraged to find in this volume that the most objective view of the Arab question on the Israeli side was written by Yehudah Harkabi, a Haifa-born professional soldier, a brigadier general, but a general who holds a diploma in philosophy and Arabic studies from the Hebrew University and from Harvard. He has written a book on *Nuclear War and Nuclear Peace*. His article "Hawks or Doves" is extraordinary in its ability to rise above prejudice and sentiment. He does not shut his eyes at all to the Arab case. He feels peace can come only if we have the strength to confront its full human reality. "Marx affirms," he concludes, "that knowledge of the truth frees man from the determinism of history." It is only, General Harkabi says, when Israel is prepared "to accept the truth in its entirety that it will find the new strength necessary to maintain and consolidate its existence." The path to safety and the path to greatness lies in reconciliation. The other route, now that the West Bank and Gaza are under Israeli jurisdiction, leads to two new perils. The Arab populations now in the conquered territories make guerrilla war possible within Israel's own boundaries. And externally, if enmity deepens and tension rises between Israel and the Arab states, both sides will by one means or another obtain nuclear weapons for the next round.

This will change the whole situation. No longer will Israeli and Arab be able to play the game of war in anachronistic fashion as an extension of politics by other means. Neither will they be able to depend on a mutual balance of terror like the great powers with their "second-strike" capacity. In this pygmy struggle the first strike will determine the outcome and leave nothing behind. Nor will the great powers be able to stand aside and let their satellites play out their little war, as in 1948, 1956, and 1967. I have not dwelt here on the responsibility of the great powers, because if they did not exist the essential differences in the Arab-Israeli quarrel would still remain, and because both sides use the great power question as an excuse to ignore their own responsibilities. The problem for the new generation of Arabs is the social reconstruction of their decayed societies; the problem will not go away if Israel disappears. Indeed their task is made more difficult by the failure to recognize Israel, since that means a continued emphasis on militarization, diversion of resources, and domination by military men. For Israel, the problem is reconciliation with the Arabs; the problem will not go away even if Moscow and Washington lie down together like the lion and the lamb or blow each other to bits. But the great powers for their part cannot continue the cynical game of arming both sides in a struggle for influence when the nuclear stage is reached. It is significant that the one place where the Israeli and Arab contributors to this symposium tend to common conclusions is in the essays discussing the common nuclear danger. To denuclearize the Middle East, to defuse it, will require some kind of neutralization. Otherwise the Arab-Israeli conflict may some day set off a wider final solution. That irascible Old Testament God of Vengeance is fully capable, if provoked, of turning the whole planet into a crematorium.

August 3, 1967
New York Review

THE NEED FOR
DOUBLE VISION IN
THE MIDDLE EAST

One way to approach the Middle Eastern crisis is to recognize that Israel is an island in a hostile sea. Its only swift and sure access to the rest of the world is by air. You cannot go by train from Cairo to Tel Aviv's neighboring city, Jaffa, as you still could in 1945 when I first visited Palestine, nor can you take a taxi from Jerusalem to Amman or from Haifa to Beirut, or to Damascus, as I still could in three memorable trips in 1947. There is no exit by land from Israel today; the sea route is slow, and in time of war rendered insecure by Soviet-supplied naval vessels in the hands of the Egyptians and by the new presence of the Soviet navy itself in the Mediterranean.

Only the air is Israel's open door to the rest of the world. More than any other nation today it is the child of the air age. Its swift victory in the Six-Day War last year was a lightning victory by airpower. A major element in its balance of payments, the tourist trade, depends on the air. By air it is only a few hours from New York, London

and Paris. In the days of the Romans and centuries later of
the great Arab empires in North Africa and Spain, it took
slow and arduous months for Jewish pilgrims and poets to
reach the Holy Land. Today only a few hours separates
Israel from its Jewish supporters in the outside world. Perhaps most fundamentally of all, the air alone saves Israel
from the claustrophobia and despair of a nation besieged
ever since its birth 20 years ago.

The new target of the Arab guerrillas is that lifeline. It is
as vulnerable as a man's jugular vein. Israel's national airline,
El Al, owns seven jets. When one was hijacked in Rome
early last year and another attacked in Athens a few weeks
ago, the Arab guerrillas hit Israel's most sensitive point.
This was no sporadic shelling of a border settlement or even
the bombing of a crowded Jerusalem market. The threat,
the repercussions and the possibilities were of a far graver
order. El Al is one of the few national airlines which is in
the black. It would only take a few unsuccessful attacks to
frighten away much of its business; what the Arab guerrillas could not do at Israel's well-guarded main airport in
Lydda, they might do abroad. The next step would be attacks on other airlines which fly into Israel. I can still remember my own desperate feelings in Paris, on my way to
Palestine on the eve of the 1948 war, when the airlines
stopped flying into Lydda and getting there depended on a
chance lift on a special Haganah plane from Genéva. To
cut the air link would be to close an iron ring around Israel.

It is foolish in this perspective to ask why Israel retaliated
against Lebanon, its one moderate Arab neighbor and the
only one which has done little or no fighting against it, the
only neighboring Arab state which has protected its own
Jewish minority from persecution in the blind furies unleashed by three Arab-Israeli wars. The reprisal was not
against the Lebanon. It was against the Arab air lines, and—
to speak frankly—the British companies which insure them
and the American companies which finance them. It was
struck at the nerve center and main air gateway of the Arab
world, the Beirut airport. It sought by damaging the Arab

airlines and their financial links in London and New York to warn the aviation world that airports had best be kept safe for all nations, Israel included. These are the blunt truths of the Beirut affair, and this is a message which had best get a full debate in the air age. For airports can easily become a new and critical nerve point in all the various short-of-war struggles which afflict a cantankerous and quarrelsome mankind.

The price paid by Israel was a political victory for the Arab guerrilla movements. Israel has never been as isolated as it is today in the wake of its unanimous condemnation by the Security Council. The Israeli cabinet, according to reports in Israel's most respected newspaper, *Haaretz*, was deeply split on the eve of the reprisal raid. Its magnitude, despite the sensational success in carrying it off without any loss of life, was bound to seem so disproportionate as to evoke condemnation. To strike at Lebanon, half Christian in population, still substantially French in culture, was bound to arouse traditional protective sympathies in the Vatican and in Paris. It would be just as well for Jewish spokesmen to keep their cool about the reactions of Pope Paul and de Gaulle, and not make more enemies. The feeling of Rome for the ancient Christian communities of the Lebanon is as natural as those of the Jews for Israel. The first point of repair should be with Lebanon, for its success in welding Christian and Moslem communities into a stable nation is a model for what must sooner or later develop in some form between Israel and the Palestinian Arabs if there is to be peace in the Middle East.

Indeed at a time when Ulster's bloody battles between Catholic and Protestant in Ireland show that even the embers of Cromwell's cruel time still smolder, Lebanon seems to be about the only place in the world (look at Belgium torn between Fleming and Walloon, and at French Canada!) where bi-national and multi-national solutions are working smoothly. Something of the sort must come in a reconstructed Palestine of Jewish and Arab states in peaceful coexistence. To bring it about Israel and the Jewish

communities of the world must be willing to look some unpleasant truths squarely in the face, and to rise to heights of
magnanimity which could write the finest chapter in the history of a great people.

One is to recognize that the Arab guerrillas are doing to
us what our terrorists and saboteurs of the Irgun, Stern and
Haganah did to the British. Another is to be willing to
admit that their motives are as honorable as were ours. As a
Jew, even as I felt revulsion against the terrorism, I felt it
justified by the homelessness of the surviving Jews from the
Nazi camps and the bitter scenes when refugee ships sank,
or sank themselves, when refused admission to Palestine.
The best of Arab youth feels the same way; they cannot
forget the atrocities committed by us against villages like
Deir Yassin, nor the uprooting of the Palestinian Arabs
from their ancient homeland, for which they feel the same
deep ties of sentiment as do so many Jews, however assimi-
lated elsewhere.

We made the Palestinian Arabs homeless to make a home
for our own people. That is the simple truth as history will
see it, and until we make amends and resettle the refugees
and create a new political framework in which Jew and
Arab can live together in a new and greater Palestine there
will be no peace. This is a tragic quarrel of brothers, requir-
ing for its resolution that healing double vision which may
at last enable each to see with pity the all-too-human fears
and features of the Other, who is only the mirror image of
ourselves, tightly embraced in hate, where love alone can
free.

Self-pity and self-righteousness, the psychic counterparts
of the siege, can only block a solution. Just as the lofty sky
is Israel's physical way out, so its political and spiritual way
out must be to rise to a higher plane of understanding. To
do so is to clear the way for the political initiatives which
can alone free it from isolation. If Israel wishes to avoid an
imposed solution, then it must come forward with alternative constructive proposals of its own. These should be seen
not as giving away bargaining cards in advance but as a

means of preventing that polarization of sentiment in both the Jewish and Arab communities the die-hards on both sides seek, whether Arab guerrillas or military-minded Israelis. In some form or another this must involve a federated coexistence among Israel, the Palestinian Arabs and the Jordanians, with access to the sea for Jordan and the West Bank. The foundation for such a political settlement must be a major effort to end the Arab refugee problem once and for all time. To this the world Jewish community must show the same generosity we have shown our own uprooted people. So long as more than a million Palestinians live in homeless misery there will be no peace for Israel, and there should be no peace of mind for world Jewry. This is the wrong we must right.

I believe that Charles W. Yost, the American diplomat Nixon has recalled from retirement to act as the U.S. representative at the United Nations, is well suited by experience, insight and humanity to further this cause of reconciliation. I recommend his article on the 1967 war, "How It Began," in the January, 1968, issue of *Foreign Affairs,* and the article he wrote just before his appointment for the January, 1969, issue of *The Atlantic Monthly*, "Israel and The Arabs: The Myths That Block Peace." I agree with the broad outlines of a solution as he has outlined them. A certain hopeful convergence of forces toward a solution is visible in the November, 1967, resolution of the Security Council, the Jarring mission and in the drawing closer of the four big powers toward unified action. "Neither Israel nor the Arabs," *The Times* of London was quite right in warning January 2, "can act as if they were conducting a private vendetta in a vacuum." The Middle East is not Southeast Asia. The Middle East is still the crossroads of the world. Only Berlin could be a more dangerous place for a confrontation of the nuclear superpowers.

Both Washington and Moscow, for all their rivalry, are soberly aware of the dangers. If Israel and the Arabs cannot agree, some solution will have to be imposed which can allow both to live in peace. The die-hards on both sides feel this settlement approaching, and would like to upset it with desperate action. The Beirut affair must be seen in this perspective, too. The fanatical agree only in stalling for time. But it is a myth, as Yost wrote in *The Atlantic Monthly*, to believe that time works in anyone's favor in the Middle East. "A settlement during coming months on the basis of the November resolution may still be feasible," Yost wrote. "Later it may not be. Provocation and counter-provocation may become so shocking and intolerable that compromise will be politically out of the question. If the parties cannot themselves come to a settlement, it will be high time for the UN, with great power backing, to take the initiative. . . . After twenty years, so many dead, so much waste and suffering, world peace more and more threatened, there is no time to lose." To this we can only say Amen.

January 13, 1969

PART X

Pax Americana

HOW THE U.S. PLAYS OUT
A BANANA REPUBLIC
COMEDY IN GREECE

A capsule history would say that German capitalism gambled on Hitler and fell back in defeat on Adenauer. It succeeded (with the help of its opposite numbers in U.S. finance and industry) in regaining power behind the façade of a republic as far to the right as was feasible. To head it West Germany's masters found in Adenauer as authoritarian a figure as ever presided over a parliamentary system. John Foster Dulles, lifelong counsel for German big business interests and an apologist for Nazi expansion, turned up to mold U.S. policy in their favor after the war. He and Adenauer became the Siamese twins of the cold war, a continuation in new guise of Hitler's holy war against Communism. Two major decisions set West Germany's course. In 1949 Adenauer turned to the right, including the far right, rather than to the Social Democrats for the votes he needed to become Chancellor. In 1952 he rejected Soviet proposals for a unified but neutral Reich with an army of its own and chose instead the road of division and NATO. Perhaps the best that can be said of Adenauer was that he was slightly less unlovely than his equally rigid and humorless old antagonist, Ulbricht.

Greece, the first "frontier of freedom" in the cold war and its starting point, is, like West Germany, another example of the U.S. tendency to restore the old order, or as close a simulacrum as possible, under cover of fighting Communism. There the U.S., the world's oldest republic, has been doing its best to maintain Europe's last *un*constitutional monarchy. U.S. propaganda pictures the Greek monarchy as a unifying force between the politically turbulent

Greeks, but its record is one of rightist intrigue. When the monarchy was restored in 1935 after years of republicanism, the King, the present one's uncle, proceeded within a few months to impose a military-Fascist dictatorship on the country which lasted until the Axis invaded in World War II. The pattern seems now to be repeating itself. The monarchist oligarchy ruled Greece with U.S. help until the elections of 1963–64 gave Papandreou's new middle-class liberal Center Union an absolute majority. But the King soon forced him out of office when Papandreou tried to end the system which made the Army officer class the tool of the throne and the preserve of a rightist upper class. Months of intrigue and tension were to have ended with new elections May 28, but the Army has seized power for fear that Papandreou would win them.

One has to be pretty credulous to believe that this coup was pulled off without consulting the King, the U.S. military mission and the CIA. Our guess is that they decided to preserve the appearance of royal detachment. It is reported here that the U.S. Ambassador, in this well-planned charade, even warned the military the U.S. would break off relations if they dethroned the King! There are no reports that we threatened U.S. action unless the Constitution were restored.

May 1, 1967

THE FIRST MILITARY DICTATORSHIP WITH A FREE (BUT SUSPENDED) CONSTITUTION

It is easy to imagine what the U.S. would be saying if the military had seized power in Czechoslovakia, written a Constitution allowing the military junta to suspend indefinitely all basic freedoms, asked the Czechs to vote on that Constitution in an election campaign which allowed no opposition voice, held the plebiscite under martial law, and announced that 99.2 percent of the people had voted approval.

How the Kremlin must envy U.S. technological superiority in arranging such affairs! How clumsy the Kremlin's maneuvers in Czechoslovakia appear beside the smooth operations of the colonels in Greece! The Pentagon's excuse for this extinction of liberty in Greece with U.S. arms is strategic—the need to prevent the rise of a possibly neutralist government on NATO's southern flank. The Kremlin's excuse for the Czech operation is strategic—to prevent the rise of a possibly neutralist regime, outflanking Poland to the north and Hungary to the south. But how few Americans will compare them. The remains of our Old Left is as ready to justify the extinction of liberty in Czechoslovakia as the military and the cold warriors are to justify it in Greece.

The Greek colonels must be given high marks for virtuosity. The new Constitution contains all kinds of democratic guaranties—but leaves it up to the colonels to decide when, if ever, they are to become effective. In the voting, "yes" slips were blue, "no" slips black; there was psychological conditioning in the choice of colors. The voter by dropping or refusing the black ballots could ingratiate himself with the police and military. The two correspondents of *Le Figaro* reported (September 30) they found piles of "no" ballots strewn all over the floor of the balloting places they visited. Many feared reprisals if suspected of voting wrongly.

The early returns were too good. The London *Times* (September 30) carried an *Agence France Presse* dispatch saying the first returns from the north of the country "showed 100 percent in favor." Alfred Friendly in the *Washington Post* (October 1) indicated that the government was embarrassed and holding back early returns which "smacked too much of those traditional to dictatorships." The results from Athens were finally given as 75 percent in favor "compared with 99.8 percent in most rural areas" (*New York Times*, October 1). This reduced the national average to 92.2 percent. It is hard to know how to assess these final figures since the regime did the counting.

The colonels must be spending a fortune on propaganda. "Thirty-five foreign writers, of which five were American," the *Washington Post* reported from Athens (September 29), "have been brought here as guests of the regime with transportation expenses and hotel bills of them and their wives fully paid." Kingsbury Smith of the Hearst press, William F. Buckley and Erwin D. Canham, editor-in-chief of the *Christian Science Monitor*, were among the five. "So confident was the government in the purity of its electoral process," was the way Mr. Canham admitted this in an October 1 dispatch, "that it invited half a hundred news observers, myself included, to be their guests at the voting." With guest-like politeness, Mr. Canham went on to say that he had talked with leading members of the government. "They give the impression," he wrote, "of being dedicated, zealous men."

Similar VIP tours have produced similar compliments from West European parliamentarians. Two British Conservatives issued a statement on their return (London *Times*, September 9) calling the military "dedicated and able" and the people, "in spite of what had been written by hostile writers, happy and relaxed." Six French deputies returned equally euphoric, according to this same story, and declared the Greek economy "wide open to foreign investments."

These happy tidings were interrupted September 21 when a British public relations man, Maurice Fraser, obtained an injunction forbidding the London *Sunday Times* to print a document which had come into its possession. This was a report by Fraser to his employers in the military junta boasting that a British member of Parliament was on his payroll "with the object of influencing other British MP's." A week later, while the injunction was still on appeal, the *Sunday Times* said another British MP was ready to raise the issue in the House of Commons as a breach of parliamentary privilege. The *Sunday Telegraph* the same day named 10 MP's Fraser had flown to Athens with their wives on VIP tours. "During the year," the *Telegraph* added, "six German and six French MP's have also been flown to Athens, as well as numerous journalists, bankers and businessmen."

Freedom's frontier in the Balkans is now the world's first military dictatorship with a free constitution, and the first free constitution which provides indefinite suspension by the military dictators. To the creation of this paradox the U.S. has made no small contribution. Richard J. Barnet has just published a new book, *Intervention and Revolution*. In a chapter on "The Subversion of Undesirable Governments," he quotes a lovely remark by Hubert Humphrey in a happier day during a Senate investigation of the Iranian aid program in 1957. "Do you know what the head of the Iranian army told one of our people?" Humphrey asked. "He said the army was in good shape, thanks to U.S. aid—it was now capable of coping with the civilian population." The same prowess, due to the same aid, is now on display in Greece.

October 7, 1968

PART XI

'It Wasn't for Lack of Spies . . .'

IT WASN'T FOR
LACK OF SPIES THAT
THE CZARS FELL

Our public controversy over the CIA coincides with the fiftieth anniversary of the Czar's overthrow. There couldn't be a better time to remember that it wasn't for lack of spies that the Russian monarchy fell. No government—except Stalin's—had a more widespread network of secret intelligence operatives at home and abroad than the Romanoffs. The Czars felt, as do American apologists for our own network, that they were up against a sinister, Godless and crafty foe, against whom any tactics were justified to save Holy Russia. Those who exposed police practices were regarded as disloyal.

In my library is a book published in 1930 in London on *The Ochrana, The Russian Secret Police*, by its last chief, A. T. Vassilyev, who died in exile. When I read the apologetics being offered for the CIA, I pulled Vassilyev's memoirs off my shelf. I thought the vigorous going-over that press, radio and TV have given the CIA a wonderful manifestation of health in our own body politic. I was appalled to see even so good a liberal as John Kenneth Galbraith turn out a subtle defense of "the Agency" and speak of "the ravening wolves which in Washington pounce on any individual or agency which has problems" (*Washington Post*, March 12). Vassilyev, like Katzenbach whitewashing the CIA, defends the Ochrana's activities as "always strictly legal." Vassilyev attributes its bad reputation to its adversaries. "It is to be ascribed to the propaganda of these scoundrels," Vassilyev wrote, "that the Secret Political Police acquired such an evil reputation, for the revolutionaries naturally did their utmost to bring discredit upon their bitterest enemy." This is the line today of the CIA, the FBI and the ten other assorted if less glamorized spy organizations—a dozen, no less—represented on the U.S. Intelligence Board. We have but scratched the surface of their pervasive and corrupting influence in eroding the foundations of American freedom. These professional hunters of subversion are our No. 1 subversives.

Just as Central Intelligence was established under Truman in 1947 (when the cold war began) to keep the President posted, so the Ochrana was the Czar's eyes and ears. Twice a month the Ochrana provided the Czar with a publication of which only a single copy was ever printed—for his august eyes alone. "His Majesty was always very desirous," Vassilyev recalled, "of being minutely posted on all the details of the revolutionary movement and of the fight being waged against it. He attached great value to complete accounts of the discovery of secret printing presses, of plots, forbidden libraries." The Czar was even supplied with copies of private letters in which Tolstoy "had given expression to his anti-militarist views." For just as the U.S. has "mail-covers" (as Senator Long of Missouri discovered) so the Ochrana had an elaborate system for reading private correspondence, including invisible ink and codes. This practice, Vassilyev assured his readers, "was never directed against orderly subjects of the Czar but only "seditious elements." The "real honest Russians" (like the real honest Americans?) "were really proud of their Police." Critics, whether Russian or American, are *un*.

The Ochrana carried on not only intelligence but cloak-and-dagger activities. It had so thoroughly penetrated subversive and terrorist organizations that in some cases, as in that of the double agent Azef and the murder of the Prime Minister Stolypin, no one knows to this day whether it was the secret police using the terrorists or the terrorists using the secret police. Those who naively marvel at the CIA's use of liberal and left organizations will find that the Czar's operatives were way ahead of it. In nineteenth-century Europe the ranks of the anarchists were so full of Czarist agents that anarchism was regarded as a kind of Czarist

Comintern to subvert Western Europe. Kerensky in his own memoirs, *Russia and History's Turning Point,* complains that the secret police in 1917 were "almost openly supporting the propaganda of Bolshevik defeatist organizations." Vassilyev in turn (like our own J. Edgar Hoover sneering at "pseudo-liberals") scornfully attacks the Russian "liberals" (his quotation marks) for an "intellectualism" which "was absolutely opposed to the national spirit." For him, Kerensky was only a more subtle menace than Lenin.

Vassilyev could boast that his network had informers everywhere, including members of the Russian Duma or Parliament. It could be said of the Ochrana, as it has been said of the CIA, that it knew everything and understood nothing. The cops never see the underlying grievances. For them, their *nigras* are always happy and contented until secret agitators upset them. It is said in our present controversy that CIA should be limited to intelligence and its cloak-and-dagger operations curtailed or ended. But its clearest successes have been its assassinations. There hasn't been a critical situation, from Cuba to Vietnam, in which the President couldn't get a clearer view of the real situation by carefully reading the newspapers (inadequate as they often are) than by reading his CIA reports. The CIA has been consistently wrong. Clarity of insight is not to be expected from the weird collection of renegades, scholar-mercenaries, Ivy League adventurers, superannuated military men, glorified hotel dicks and just plain corkscrew types that bulk so large in all our intelligence services.

If an omnipresent and well-heeled secret police makes for safety, the Czars should still be on their throne. If what the secret police call "naïveté" and others call the democratic or libertarian tradition is the real danger, then the Revolution when it came should have burst out not in Moscow but in London, where the British were "naïve" enough to allow the arch revolutionaries of our time to work, study, write and agitate unmolested. By all the rules of CIA and FBI, Britain could not have made a greater mistake than to give Marx and Engels asylum. The lesson that revolutions are not made by conspiracies, nor stopped by assassins, that you cannot suppress revolutionary agitation without crippling the debate so necessary to healthy change, is one that every generation has to learn afresh. We are back again to fundamentals. The CIA, the FBI and the other networks would exchange those traditions of which the First Amendment is the symbol for the practices that have sickened the younger generation in Soviet society and alienated it, as we are in danger of alienating the best of our own.

March 20, 1967

THE MUJIK AS THE NEGRO OF THE RUSSIAN REVOLUTION

The historic task which faces the best of the new youth in the Soviet Union is how to establish free institutions under socialism. This will require a double revolution, first in thought and then in action. The first must scrap all the evasive banalities of Communist party talk since the Twentieth Congress about "cult of personality"—and embark instead on a reexamination of the Soviet system and its past which spares neither Lenin nor Marx. All idols must be overthrown, all sacred dogmas exposed to criticism, the windows thrown open, the cobwebs swept away. This task will have the value of separating Soviet accomplishments from those cancerous malformations which, 50 years after the Great October Revolution, still keep the Soviet system a dictatorship in which neither worker nor peasant dares speak freely.

For American youth our current racial crisis offers a fresh perspective from which to understand the real roots of what the Twentieth Congress called the "cult of personality." We are learning from bitter experience what a terrible price can be imposed on a society by slavery and its aftermath. Perhaps the most important single fact in understanding Soviet realities is that a century ago most of the people in Russia were little better than slaves. The *mujik*, the peasant, was Russia's Negro. Their emancipations occurred at the same time: Alexander II's edict freeing Russia's slaves was issued two years before Lincoln's. Both left the intended beneficiaries in a limbo somewhere between bondage and real freedom. Russia, like America, though in a different way, failed to provide 40 acres and a mule. The freed *mujik*, like the freed Negro, remained at the mercy of the master class. All the worst traits attributed to the Negro were attributed to the *mujik*. In America little more than a tenth of our people bear the marks of that crippling past. In Russia it is the overwhelming majority that is of peasant or recent peasant origin.

I once described the American Negro as a case of internal colonialism, a submerged people exploited like those of distant colonies for their cheap labor power, an idea which Stokely Carmichael has developed in his book *Black Power*. This is also true of the *mujik*. For the Russian peasant, the Revolution was indeed a dictatorship of the proletariat. The capital the Soviet Union needed for its industrialization was sweated out of the peasantry—by the huge expropriations which accompanied the liquidation of the *kulaks* and the middle peasantry, by the work extracted from them in the huge labor camps to which they were driven in Siberia and the North, and by the low prices at which the poorer peasants were forced to deliver their products from the collectives and state farms into which they were forced. The *mujik* was Bolshevism's internal empire.

The Revolution was consolidated first by letting the peasant keep the lands he had seized and then by taking back the land in order to get the capital for industrialization. The basic fault of the new peasant proprietors was that they were eating well for the first time in their lives and selling less. By 1927 Russia's global production of wheat had recovered to the prewar level, but it produced only half as much for the market and exported only five percent as much as before the war. The problem was how to get more out of the peasant. The right opposition, led by Bukharin, suggested the carrot. He was impressed by American agriculture. He wanted to stimulate greater farm production by offering the peasant more consumer goods and expanding industry on the basis of a prosperous agriculture. The left opposition, led by the Trotskyists, suggested the stick. Stalin adopted the program of the left, but in practice it took on a ferocity not even he had foreseen; it became a new civil war against the majority of the peasants and it was carried out with the clumsy and wasteful brutality characteristic of Russia's past.

The worker as well as the peasant suffered. The war against the peasant brought on a famine. The Russian worker as well as the peasant had to be subjected to Draconian discipline to keep the economy going. The symbol of the change was the internal passport. This was established by Peter the Great to keep the serf tied down on the farm and in the state factories. It had been abolished by the Revolution as "a police instrument of oppression of the masses." At the end of 1932 internal passports were reestablished to keep workers from changing their jobs and peasants from fleeing to the cities. Soviet citizens must still carry them. In America the passport was used—until the Supreme Court ended the practice—to restrict the movement of suspected citizens abroad; in the Soviet Union it is used to keep police control of everybody's movements at home.

This relic of the past is a reflection, like so much else, of the fundamental if disagreeable fact that the collectivization campaign, like the Bolshevik Revolution from the very beginning, was impressed by a minority of the revolutionaries themselves from above and by terror. All those terrible crimes, "distortions of socialist legality" and "departures from Leninist norms" which the Twentieth Congress attributed to Stalin and the cult of personality flow from this

fundamental fact. Until it is recognized no fundamental reform can be achieved. The backwardness of the country led
the Bolsheviks to deal with it by the backward methods to
which it was habituated—reform from above, an omnipresent secret police system, suppression of dissent, denial of the
freedoms of press and speech.

In the view of Marx and Engels socialism was to be the
natural outgrowth of capitalism, the end result of that evo-
lution by which capitalism collectivizes the processes of industry and the sources of capital while clinging to concep-
tions of private property it was itself rendering obsolete.
The propertyless working class created by capitalism was
to be the natural inheritor and administrator of the new society. This was the Grand Design the Communist Revolution was to fulfill. But Lenin at least as early as 1905 said
that the working class left to itself would only develop a
trade union—and not a socialist—consciousness. The Socialist revolution was to be imposed from above by an elite
of professional revolutionaries who knew better than the
workers what they really wanted. This grandiose vision, itself the product of Russian realities and the Russian past,
implied not a dictatorship *of* the proletariat, but *over* the
proletariat. This is where the so-called evils of the "cult of
personality" began, not in Stalin's personal character.

It is true that Lenin and Trotsky, before they took
power, sometimes spoke in terms very similar to that "par-
ticipatory democracy" which our own New Left cherishes.
In *The State and Revolution*, in August, 1917, Lenin
sketched the outlines of a society in which every official,
whether of the factory or the state, would be subject not
only to election but "to instant recall." "Having conquered
political power," he wrote, "the workers will break up the
old bureaucratic apparatus" and move immediately "to a
state of things when *all* fulfill the functions of control and
superintendence so that *all* become 'bureaucrats for a time,
and *no one* therefore can become a bureaucrat.' " But once
Lenin took power, the new state—as Martov, the greatest
of the Menshevik leaders, noted in 1919—showed a "tend-

ency toward the utmost possible strengthening of the principles of hierarchy and compulsion . . . toward the development of a more specialized apparatus of repression . . .
toward the greater independence of the usually elective
functions and the annihilation of the control of these functions by the elector masses."

A year earlier the great Polish Jewish revolutionary, Rosa
Luxembourg, from her prison cell in Breslau also saw what
was coming. Trotsky, she pointed out, had written that in
"the open and direct struggle for governmental power, the
laboring masses accumulate in the shortest time a considerable amount of political experience and advance quickly
from one stage to another of their development." Rosa
Luxembourg wrote that "the very giant tasks which the
Bolsheviks have undertaken with courage and determination" required the fullest possible development and participation of the masses for their accomplishment. "The public
life of countries with limited freedom," she wrote with an
insight rare among those supporting the Communists, "is so
poverty-stricken, so miserable, so rigid, so unfruitful, precisely because, through the exclusion of democracy, it cuts
off the living sources of all spiritual riches and progress."
She said no one knew this better and repeated it more often
than Lenin, yet "the means he employs: decree, dictatorial
force of the factory overseer, draconic penalties, rule by
terror" were depriving the masses of all voice in the process.
"Without general elections," she declared, "without unrestricted freedom of press and assembly, without a free
struggle of opinion, life dies out in every public institution
. . . . only the bureaucracy remains as the active element."
And in words which link the Revolution with Jefferson and
point the way to a free socialism she sketched a reality the
Soviet leadership still refuses to recognize—

Freedom only for the supporters of the government, only for
the members of one party—however numerous they may be—
is no freedom at all. Freedom is always and exclusively freedom
for the one who thinks differently. Not because of any fanatical concept of "justice" but because all that is instructive,

wholesome and purifying in political freedom depends on this essential characteristic, and its effectiveness vanishes when "freedom" becomes a special privilege.

Two years later Bertrand Russell after a visit to Russia described in his *The Practice and Theory of Bolshevism* the consequences of the course which Rosa Luxembourg had deplored. "The necessity of inculcating Communism," he wrote, "produces a hot-house condition, where every breath of fresh air must be excluded: people are to be taught to think in a certain way, and all free intelligence becomes taboo. The country comes to resemble an immensely magnified Jesuit College."

Every regime must take a choice of risks—the risk of freedom with the danger of popular rejection, even misunderstanding, or the risks of a dictatorship which must increasingly, however well-meaning its founders, become rigid, despotic and encrusted with careerist barnacles. The Bolsheviks chose the latter, and so it is that 50 years after the Revolution, there is still neither free discussion nor free press in the Soviet Union. It has become a gigantic caricature of what socialism was meant to be.

The work of the Twentieth Congress has been aborted because the Party and its leaders fear that full discussion of the "cult of personality" must become a menace to their own monopoly of power and to their habits of ruling by coercion rather than persuasion. The bourgeois state borrowed from feudal experience Magna Charta principles which were developed into a means of protecting the individual from oppressive state action. There is no reason why the proletarian state should not borrow from bourgeois experience. There is no reason why habeas corpus should not exist under socialism as under capitalism, why a man's lawyer may not get him out of jail and force the state to explain why he is being held and subject its accusations to public trial. Had this right existed in the Stalin period some of the best Communists might have been saved—for it was the lickspittles who survived, the brave and the concerned who were liquidated. The only reason for denying so fundamental a right is to retain over the heads of the masses and the intellectuals the shadow of the old terror, the fear that arbitrary arrest is still possible.

The most important change of all, if the Soviet Union is to evolve toward a good society, is freedom of the press. I well remember thirty years ago how the Communists boasted that freedom of the press in Russia under the Constitution newly promulgated by Stalin was broader than in the United States because it not only guaranteed freedom of press and assembly but also ensured these rights "by placing at the disposal of the working people and their organizations printing shops, supplies of paper, public buildings, the streets, means of communication and other material requisites for the exercise of these rights." Thirty years later this is still a bitter hoax.

The Soviet regime's vast apparatus for propaganda serves today as in Stalin's time to hide these realities from the outside world and from many of its own people. All that is worst in the practice of the "bourgeois" states exists in magnified form within the Soviet Union. Despite all the promises of law reform since Stalin died, the law of counter-revolutionary crimes—many times worse in its sweep and vagueness than our Smith Act—is still on the statute books and can still be used to stifle any real discussion. It is only in the worst of the "bourgeois" states—in those of a Fascist character like Spain, Greece, South Vietnam, Brazil and Portugal—that writers are exiled, silenced or imprisoned as Sinyavsky and Daniel are in the Soviet Union. Eleven years after the Twentieth Congress, fourteen years after the death of Stalin, "corrective labor" camps are back in operation and two gifted writers are serving savage sentences of seven and five years respectively in them. Characteristically, no one can find out from the bureaucracy whether or not these sentences have been shortened by the limited amnesty declared in commemoration of the Revolution.

It is for a new generation in the Soviet Union to change these realities. Hegel declared the dialectic had ended in the creation of the despotic Prussian state; the Communists say it ended with the creation of the despotic Soviet state. But truly understood the dialectic goes on forever, and the synthesis of the contradiction between socialism and freedom must be a new state which combines the advantages of both. The great Western tradition which comes down from Spinoza and Milton and Jefferson is fully applicable to socialist society and must be combined with it if Soviet man is to be free and if the socialist ideal is to regain its attraction for youth. The Soviet people who have suffered so much and created so much, who in 50 years have made such giant strides, owe it to themselves and the world to strike out boldly on this new road to the freedom which has so long been denied them.

November 13, 1967

THE REBIRTH OF FREEDOM— OR OF FASCISM?

In the middle of the next decade, in 1976, we will celebrate the 200th anniversary of independence. There has never been so much doubt whether on that birthday the United States will still be free. The next decade may see a resurgence of fascism in many countries, as the pendulum swings from the permissive to the repressive. A healthy society requires a balance of freedom with order, and of social change with stability. Everywhere in the world this balance has become more difficult to achieve, as population explodes and life becomes more complex. This breeds violence and frustration, as it does when too many animals are pushed into one cage. Hence the snarling and the quarreling. In our country, on top of the universal problems of pollution, urban sprawl and youthful alienation, we are beginning to harvest in a spreading black revolt the bitter fruit of a century of slavery and another century of humiliation. We cannot cope with these interlocking problems unless in the next few years we can raise sharply the level of political understanding and social sympathy and convince the well-to-do majority of the need to forego private luxury in order to wipe out public squalor.

Over the past few years a series of high-level commissions of inquiry has tried to further this task of public education. The latest is the commission on violence appointed 18 months ago after the assassinations of Robert Kennedy and Martin Luther King, Jr. Its final report says again what so many earlier reports have said—that the way to eradicate crime and violence is to eradicate poverty and racial discrimination. The Commission included men as conservative as Senator Hruska, Congressman Hale Boggs of Louisiana and Cardinal Cooke of New York, military vicar of the U.S. Armed Forces. "As a first step" they called for a reversal of the priorities which have given the military establishment first call on the national resources. Yet even as the report was issued the tides were moving in the opposite direction.

Not a single direct word of comment or even thanks came from Mr. Nixon when the report was presented to him. The chairman, Dr. Milton Eisenhower, could announce only that the President had "authorized" him to say he was "gravely concerned" and would "study it with care." The *Weekly Compilation of Presidential Documents* contains four separate speeches and interviews given by Mr. Nixon that week on football, but not one word about the violence report! The Commission proposed that the government increase welfare expenditures by about $20 billion, partly from a "peace dividend" of reduced military expenditure after Vietnam, partly from increased tax revenues as the Gross National Product grows. But Mr. Nixon had already shown at a press conference a few days earlier how foreign such calculations are to his basic thinking.

A reporter asked the President's comment on the statement that there didn't seem much prospect of a peace dividend after Vietnam, but that this rich country could provide all the funds necessary "for the very big problems at home" any time it was prepared to make the necessary sacrifices so "we might very well do it now and get on with the job." Mr. Nixon did not dispute the statement that the end of the Vietnam war would not release substantial funds for domestic needs—a significant key to his own planning. Nor did he deny that we had ample wealth to meet domestic problems. He took a very different tack, one that seemed to foreclose hope. He said federal, state and local taxes already take 25 to 37 percent of the nation's total income (30 percent is the usual estimate), and that to take more would mean that the nation would lose "its character of a free enterprise economy." This was saying that the maintenance of the "free enterprise system" takes precedence even over social problems that may tear the country apart. He implied that if necessary poverty must go on so that profit can thrive. This is vintage Republicanism. It is also the somber diagnosis of Marxist-Leninist fatalism. No radical has said anything more subversive than Mr. Nixon's few unfeeling words.

All this runs directly contrary to the best advice of the violence commission and its predecessors. The so-called Southern strategy, which has led wags here to call the Nixon White House, Uncle Strom's Cabin, is more than Southern. It aims to mobilize the smug against the concerned, the unthinking wealthy against the despairing poor, bewildered middle age against idealistic youth, and bigoted whites against desperate blacks. This strategy may indeed put Wallace out of the running in 1972, as it is intended to do, and let Nixon ride triumphantly back into power on an undivided Know Nothing vote. But the cost in social turmoil will be high, and the price may make the U.S. in 1976 a police state like South Africa. Here as there the price of racial repression must prove to be everybody's freedom.

Seen through the eyes of the blacks, the events of the year end are sinister. The effort to get rid of the 1965 Vot-

ing Act and to slow down school desegregation looks like a
second post-Reconstruction era, an attempt to solidify
white supremacy again in the South. Law-and-order seems
to translate itself in this Administration only into black repression. In New York City a U.S. Attorney who has been
vigorously prosecuting white-collar crime is under White
House pressure to get out just as his investigations touch
financial interests involved in Saigon black marketing and
the Mafia's Swiss bank operations. Crime in the banks
arouse no such passion as crime in the streets. Worst of all is
the trigger-happy lawlessness of the police themselves as
demonstrated in the Black Panther killings in Chicago and
the shoot-out in Los Angeles. These have stirred terrible
fears.

The Black Panther raids have sent seismic tremors
through a black community which has hitherto had little
sympathy with this revolutionary fringe. It is amazing how
many blacks are obsessed with what happened to the Jews
in Germany. They fear—however horrible this may sound
to decent whites—a similar fate. They see the Black Panther affair in a long perspective. For two centuries, under
slavery and after, the militant has been the special target of
harassment and killing. In the ghettoes today too many policemen treat suspected militants with a hatred they rarely
show drug peddlers or pimps. The Chicago killings look like
the climax in a series of "search and destroy" operations designed to wipe out the Panthers, and as a first step—however wildly exaggerated that may sound—toward genocide
should blacks insist on their rights. If this fear of a bloody
confrontation and a Nazi-style "final solution" be paranoia,
it is up to the white community to dispel it. For these fears
are a menace to our common future.

Normal politics will no longer do. Normal politics is the
Southern strategy. Normal politics is the new tax bill, in
which both parties compete to give tax relief when we require a sharp increase in taxing and spending. We need a
campaign of public education, reaching into every town
and village, carrying to town meetings across the country

the findings and the recommendations of the Kerner commission and the Eisenhower violence commission and all the
other sober counsels of recent years. We need to convert a
benighted into an enlightened majority. We need a small
army of youthful Thomas Jeffersons to bring home again
the lessons of freedom and of social change as the framer of
the Declaration so well understood them. We need a mobilization to make us realize that whatever our differences we
are trapped together, breathing the same air, drinking the
same water, walking the same streets. The rich could buy
no finer luxury than to pay the cost of keeping them clean
and safe. To wipe out poverty and racism would be to
make America really secure. But to get the kind of planning
and spending required we need a revolution in public
understanding. No other revolution will work, for it is the
comfortable majority itself which must be converted. To
bring that about is the truest challenge of the seventies, a
task worthy of our finest youth.

December 29, 1969

WHO ARE THE REAL
KOOKS IN OUR SOCIETY?

It's hard to judge which is worse—the vulgarity or the stupidity of government officials in dealing with the Chicago
conspiracy trial. The U.S. Attorney, Foran, attacks the defendants as "fags," sneaks and scum. The Cook County
sheriff has them sheared of their long hair in jail and exhib-
its the photos at a political rally as an example of "how Republicans get things done." Vice President Agnew calls
them "kooks." If the Administration wants to provoke
more student rioting, this is the course to pursue. Nothing

could make a sizeable portion of our youth more sympathetic to the defendants than forcible hair-cuts, for their hair is the symbol of their revulsion against a society they see as morally bankrupt. The name-calling will sound all too reminiscent of parents too dense to understand the anguish of youth.

Agnew asked that these "kooks . . . demagogues . . . social misfits" be kept off the front pages and the TV screens. If the Administration wanted to keep them off, it should have had more sense than to bring them to trial. An AP dispatch[1] reveals that there were lawyers in the Justice Department who warned that the statute making it a crime to cross state lines to incite a riot was of doubtful constitutionality, that the trial would inevitably become political and that the accused might turn it into a circus which would embarrass the government. Attorney General Mitchell overruled them and now the Vice President seems to want more of the same. He told the Governors Conference in Washington, "Let us react automatically, briskly and effectively to the threat of violent revolution and recognize it for the clear and present danger it constitutes." To call it "a clear and present danger" is to invoke the Supreme Court's rationale for justifying the restriction of fundamental liberties in a time of imminent danger. Only the far-out Weatherman faction of the SDS is kooky enough to join Agnew in imagining that a rash of window-breaking by students puts the government of the United States in imminent danger of overthrow. And nothing would do more to foster blind revolutionary rage on the campuses and in the ghettoes than to start filling the jails with more student and radical leaders.

An Agnew at large poses more danger to social stability than the Chicago defendants. One passage in his appeal to the Governors was the authentic voice of repressionist ideology. He called on the Governors "to withstand the criticism of the liberal community, who are presently so blinded by total dedication to individual freedom that they cannot

[1] Jean Heller, AP, in the *Washington Post*, February 27.

see the steady erosion of collective freedom . . ." To speak
of being "blinded by total dedication to individual freedom" is strange language from an American Vice President
in the capital of the so-called free world. This is not Jeffersonianism. It is a compote of decayed Leninism and left-
overs from the Fascist era. The only meaningful freedom is
individual. "Collective freedom" is the jailhouse liberty the
Communist bureaucracy imposes on dissidents in Moscow,
Warsaw and Prague, and the military junta of Papadapoulos on Athens. There are a few wacky Maoists on the
fringes of the youth movement who sound in this respect
just like Agnew. The Vice President has taken a great leap
forward. . . .

March 9, 1970

WHERE THE FUSE
ON THAT DYNAMITE LEADS

> The search of the youth today is for ways and means to
> make the machine—and the vast bureaucracy of the
> corporation state and of government that runs that ma-
> chine—the servant of man. That is the revolution that is
> coming. That revolution . . . need not be a repetition
> of 1776. It could be a revolution in the nature of an ex-
> plosive political regeneration. It depends on how wise
> the Establishment is. If, with its stockpile of arms, it re-
> solves to suppress the dissenters, America will face, I
> fear, an awful ordeal.
>   *Points of Rebellion:* Justice Douglas.

The *New York Times* editorial Friday March 13 on the
rash of bombings and bomb scares in New York City was
called "Not Idealists: Criminals." This was the standard reaction of a liberal publication, the easy way to clear its

skirts of any suspicion of the slightest sympathy with revolutionary radicalism. But it is a dangerous cliché. Falsely to diagnose the trouble is to move toward the wrong remedies, and the wrong remedies will worsen the disease. Statistics on bombings from cities around the country suggest that we may be entering the first stages of an urban guerrilla movement. A guerrilla movement is a political, not a criminal phenomenon, however many crimes it may commit. Experience has shown over and over again that a guerrilla movement can only be defeated by political means. The effort to treat it simply as a criminal matter, without resolving its political causes, ends by increasing the number of the guerrillas and widening their support in the larger community.

Whether the New York bombings prove to be a spasm in the wake of the Greenwich Village explosion, when a radical arsenal blew up, or the beginning of a serious terrorist movement will now depend on the authorities, and their ability to keep their cool. The first requisite—*and* the second, *and* the third—is understanding.

The Weatherman kids can be seen in various ways, and it is necessary to see them in as many as possible. The Weatherman faction of SDS, whence several different "direct action" splinter groups seem to derive, can be looked at like a distraught child. They can be viewed as spoiled brats, in a tantrum with a world which will not change overnight to suit them. But they are also the most sensitive of a generation which feels in its bones what we older people only grasp as an unreal abstraction, that the world is headed for nuclear annihilation and something must be done to stop it. The Weatherman manifesto from which they take their name is from one point of view a mishmash of ill-digested pseudo-Marxist rubbish, an effort to compete with their bitterest rivals, the "square" sectarian ideologists of that other far-out splinter group, Progressive Labor. The manifesto spurns every normal base of revolutionary support and ends up squarely in the clouds: the middle class is, of course, no good; the working class is corrupted; the college generation will soon sell out; their only hope is in the juvenile Robespierres of the high schools. It sounded like the Children's Crusade come back to life, a St. Vitus dance of hysterical politics.

It is from just such despair that terrorist movements have grown. This recalls the Russian pre-revolutionary *Narodnya Volya* (People's Will) through which a handful of disaffected middle class and noble youths sought by bomb and pistol to overthrow the mighty Czarist order, with roots so deep in the religious reverence of the peasant masses as to seem impregnable. How to overturn their Little Father? A movement which has no faith in the masses seeks out the desperate few idealists willing to sacrifice their lives in gestures they realize may be futile. Some of our young revolutionaries are chillingly sober and disconcertingly sensible. Their criticism of conventional dissenters like myself and our futility, as the war goes on, is hard to rebut. Others in recent months have displayed a morbid development, a tendency to glorify violence for its own sake, as when they make Manson a hero for killing "bourgeois pigs," i.e., people exactly like their fathers and mothers. The ultimate menace they fear is their own secret selves in their own parents. This is what they are acting out on the stage of national politics.

But these psychological aspects are only a part of the whole complex picture. These wild and wonderful—yes, wonderful!—kids also serve quite rational political ends. I became strongly aware of this when I ran into an old friend on an early morning Washington street corner the other day who is working hard in a respectable do-good reformist organization, the very kind the youthful radicals despise. I told him that in talks on various campuses I had tried to talk the young people out of the typically American idea that revolution could be "instant" like coffee or iced tea. "Don't discourage them," was his unexpected plea. "If they stop acting up, we'll never get the Establishment to budge."

From a longer range political point of view, the New Left and the hippies and the Yippies may, in however weird a form, also forecast the future. They see Soviet Communism merely as a further stage of capitalism, a mass production bureaucratic society concentrated on the production of goods rather than the liberation of the spirit. They see the working class becoming "middle class" under it, and the need for a newer revolution against making the individual a *thing* in a mindless industrial process rather than the loving center of a universe meant to be joyous in our brief moment of passage through it. To study their irrationality is to become aware of ours.

The immediate lesson is this: If the police authorities are high-handed and arbitrary in their hunt for the bombers—as some already are—they will turn more moderates into activists. The answer to the revolutionaries is to behave with justice, to demonstrate that the system can operate under pressure in accordance with its own best ideals. *And first and above all to end the war.* Again and again, the over-reaction and panic of an established order has turned a handful of conspirators into a revolutionary movement. This is, of course, exactly what the Chicago trial has done in radicalizing youth and destroying its faith in the courts. What happens on appeal may represent the last chance of winning them back to rational discourse and faith in peaceful change. In these, rather than a blind and volcanic upheaval, I see mankind's only chance. For the problems which confront us lie deep in the conditioning of man and in the power of technology to enslave him. No one is yet wise enough to chart the way out, as the most perceptive of the kids themselves admit. They merely hope something better will turn up out of the ruins. But I do not believe in salvation by holocaust. Hate and hysteria certainly will not create a new man or build a better world. Political suicide is not revolution.

But I must confess that I almost feel like throwing rocks through windows myself when I see Judge Julius Hoffman turn up as an honored guest at the White House and when I see Billy Graham like a smoother Rasputin dishing out saccharine religiosity there: If all Americans would only repeat the Lord's Prayer together, he said, "He could lead us out of our dilemma"—and at no increase in taxes either! I sense in Nixon and his entourage no anguish, no awareness, no real comprehension. When has there been a more inane leadership as storm clouds gather? Not since Marie Antoinette has there been a remark to match Moynihan's "benign neglect."

Between the disaffected white youth and the growing anger of the blacks, we could be on the verge of a wild upheaval. I hold my breath as I go to press waiting to see whether Rap Brown is dead or alive. In the black community here in Washington those who knew Ralph Featherstone best, and remember his efforts only two weeks ago to advise the ghetto youth against violence, do not believe he was transporting explosives. They think he was murdered. They see the police and the FBI engaged in an effort to throw the blame upon the dead men themselves. Hoover's name at the bottom of that cryptic FBI report on the bombing is a provocation to the blacks. For them Hoover is an old ally of the Southern racists in Congress. In the black community, too, the established order is recruiting the forces which threaten it. Until the war in Southeast Asia is ended, until the Pentagon is cut down drastically, until priorities are revised to make racial reconciliation and social reconstruction our No. 1 concerns, the dynamite that threatens us sizzles on a fuse that leads straight back to the White House.

March 23, 1970

PART XII

The Streets

THE RICH MARCH ON
WASHINGTON ALL THE TIME

No other Western country permits such a large propor-
tion of its people to endure the lives we press on our
poor. To make four-fifths of a nation more affluent than
any people in history, we have degraded one-fifth
mercilessly.

Report of the Citizens Inquiry into Hunger

To see the Poor People's March on Washington in perspective, remember that the rich have been marching on Washington ever since the beginning of the Republic. They came
in carriages and they come on jets. They don't have to put
up in shanties. Their object is the same, but few respectable
people are untactful enough to call it handouts. Washington owes its very existence as the capital to a deal for the
benefit of wealthy speculators. They had bought up the de-
faulted bonds issued to finance the revolution, paying as
little as 15 cents on the dollar to the needy original investors. The speculators wanted repayment at full face value.
It was only by promising to move the capital from Philadelphia to a new city to be built on the Potomac that Alexander Hamilton could get enough Southern votes to swing
the deal.

The fiscal and banking system of the new republic was
thus solidly established on the basis of a $20 million handout
to the rich and on the Hamiltonian theory that if the new
government would channel enough of the national wealth
to the top some of it would eventually trickle down. In the
meantime the farmer and the consumer would pay the taxes
and the tariffs to keep the investor fat and happy. Ever
since then the public treasury and the public lands have
been a major source of the great American fortunes, down

to our own day of never-ending oil depletion allowances.
The tax structure and the laws bear the imprint of countless
marches on Washington; these have produced billions in
hidden grants for those who least need them. Across the
facade of the U.S. Treasury should be engraved, "To him
who hath shall be given."

One easy and equitable way to finance an end to abject
poverty in this country would be to end the many tax privileges the wealthy have acquired. A 12-man committee of
industrialists and financiers has just recommended to Governor Rockefeller of New York a form of that guaranteed
income the marching poor will demand. The committee
proposes a negative income tax to raise 30 million of our
neediest above the poverty level. Instead of paying income
taxes they would receive enough from the Treasury to
bring their incomes up to a minimum of $3300 a year for a
family of four. The additional cost would be about $11 bil-
lion a year. That is what the more obvious tax loopholes for
the rich now drain from the U.S. Treasury.[1]

Few people realize that our present tax and welfare structure is such as to encourage the wealthy to speculate and
the poor to vegetate. If a rich man wants to speculate, he is
encouraged by preferential capital gains and loss provisions
which give him a 25 percent cushion against losses and take
less than half as much on his speculative gains as on his normal
earnings. But if a poor man on relief took a part-time job,
he had until very recently to pay a 100 percent tax on his
earnings in the shape of a dollar-for-dollar reduction in his
relief allowance. Even now after a belated reform in the
welfare system, a poor man on relief, after his first $30 a
month in extra earnings, must turn back to the Treasury 70
cents on the dollar while the rich man need pay the Treasury
only 25 cents of every dollar he wins on the market even
when his normal income tax rate is more than 50 percent.
Such is the topsy-turvy morality of the Internal Revenue
laws.

[1] The figure is from a staff study made for Senator Proxmire as chairman of the Joint Economic Committee of Congress.

A heart-breaking report on hunger by a Citizens Board of Inquiry has just lifted the curtain on why the poor are marching. In the richest country in the world people eat clay to still the pains of an empty belly, children come to school too hungry to learn, and the infants of the poor suffer irreversible brain damage from protein deprivation. Much of the crime in the streets springs from hunger in the home. Much of this hunger is also linked to hand-outs for those who do not need them. Some of its roots may be found in subsidy programs designed to encourage farmers to make more money by producing less food. The effect has been to push the poor off the land and into the ghettoes. A program designed 30 years ago ostensibly to help the desperate family farmer has become a source of huge handouts to big farmers and farm corporations.

In 1967 the 42.7 percent of our farmers with incomes of less than $2,500 a year received only 4.5 percent of total farm subsidies paid by the government while the top 10 percent, many of them farm corporations or vertical trusts in food processing, received 64.5 percent of these subsidies. The contrast between these handouts for rich farming interests and the stingy surplus food allotments for the poor is dramatically displayed in the statistical appendices of the Citizens Report on Hunger. In the calendar year 1966 a quarter billion dollars in farm subsidies was paid to a lucky landowning two one-hundredths of one percent of the population of Texas while the 28.8 percent of its population below the poverty line received less than $8 million in all forms of food assistance. Such grotesque maldistribution of federal aid is not limited to the South. That same year the U.S. Treasury paid almost $36 million in farm subsidies to one-third of one percent of the population of Nebraska while only $957,000 in surplus food allotments went to the 26.1 percent of its population which is in poverty. One farm company in California, J. G. Boswell, was given $2,807,633 in handouts by the Treasury that year and the Hawaiian Commercial and Sugar Company got $1,236,355 in federal sweetening.

Such are the huge hogs that crowd the public trough. Other even bigger corporations live on the gravy that drips from the military and space programs. We may never reach the moon—or know what to do with it when we get there —but the race for it has already created a new generation of Texas millionaires. The arms race and the space race guarantee the annual incomes of many in the country club set.

Even before the marchers began arriving, the President at his latest press conference was already inviting them to leave. Their demands would be "seriously" considered, he said, "and then we expect to get on with running the government as it should be." For years, "running the government as it should be" has meant financing and planning these programs which are the welfare systems of the American upper classes. Three-quarters of the poor get no help. Two-thirds of our hungry schoolchildren are not reached by the school lunch program. But finding the money to help them is not part of "running the government as it should be," i.e., with a budget allocated 80 percent to the Pentagon and 10 percent to health, education and welfare.

Ours is a warfare, not a welfare, state. And unless the better conscience of the country can be mobilized, it will wage war upon the poor, too. Only twice before in our history have the poor marched on Washington—Coxey's Army of the jobless in 1894 and the bonus marchers in 1932. Both times they were easily dispersed by force. The last heartless chapter of the flinty Hoover Administration was the attack of General MacArthur's troops upon the encampment of the bonus marchers on the Anacostia flats. This time the shanties will not be burned down nor the poor scattered so easily. A clash could set off the hottest summer yet of our nascent civil war. The poor may prove an irresistible force. The Congress is certainly an immovable object.

At this dangerous juncture we need a crusade of the progressive well-to-do to supplement the efforts of the Poor People's March. We are glad to see that SANE and a group of other organizations is calling for demonstrations of support throughout the country for Saturday, May 25. We need volunteers to stand on street corners and collect money to feed the encampment of the poor in Washington. And we need an army of young white idealists to ring doorbells in the suburbs and awaken the middle class to the crisis the poor may precipitate. What lies ahead may be far more important than the election.

We wish the unaware millions of the suburbs could have heard the extraordinary collection of spokesmen for the poor whom the Reverend Ralph David Abernathy brought to Wesley A.M.E. Church for a preliminary rally here last week. The volcanic despair of our Negroes, Puerto Ricans, Indians, Spanish Americans and poor whites has thrown up new and unknown leaders able to present their case with an untaught and unmatchable eloquence. The descenders of the enslaved, the conquered and the dispossessed have found voices which makes one realize what human resources lie untapped among them. It was also thrilling in a time of rising separation to join hands again with blacks in singing "We Shall Overcome" and to feel how truly this movement stems from Martin Luther King's teaching. If this fails, multi-racialism and non-violence will fail with it. Yet fail it must unless the middle class and the suburb can be aroused to pressure Congress for the steps required to wipe out poverty. "There is nothing," Martin Luther King said, "except a tragic death wish, to prevent us from reordering our priorities, so that the pursuit of peace will take precedence over the pursuit of war." Now is the time for the white and the fortunate to organize themselves for this work of solidarity. This—it cannot be said too often—may be our last chance.

May 13, 1968

THEY PLEADED GUILTY
OF BURNING PAPER
INSTEAD OF CHILDREN

In the days of the New Deal the WPA had something called Living Theatre. Living theatre is what radicals have begun to produce. One example is the black comedy a wild horde of hippies and yippies wove around the House Un-American Activities Committee, driving it to suspend its hearings into the Chicago peace demonstrations. Those shopworn inquisitors did not know what to do with witnesses who acted out the procedure's essential irrationality.

Another example is the morality play the Catonsville Nine have been enacting. They staged their first act on May 17 when they entered a local draft board in Catonsville, Md., and burned up its files, with napalm they manufactured themselves from a recipe in the U.S. Special Forces Handbook. "Our apologies, good friends," said Father Daniel Berrigan, the poet-priest who was one of their leaders, "for the fracture of good order, the burning of paper instead of children."

The second act was in a federal court in Baltimore last week before Chief Judge Roszel C. Thomsen. The Nine are all Catholic, clergy and lay. Their types are recognizable through history: the stuff of which saints are made, moved by a deeper sensitivity to human suffering. They joyfully admitted their guilt, like early brethren preparing for the lions. No legalisms spoiled the second act curtain.

The government, in its own dramaturgy, picked a black man to prosecute them. First Assistant U.S. Attorney Arthur G. Murphy said the morality of the war was not at issue, though he admitted in passing that a reasonable man might think it illegal. The issue, he said, was simply destroying property and obstructing the law. The chief defense attorney, William Kunstler, insisted "The trial is not simple, any more than those of Jesus and Socrates were simple."

Judge Thomsen, like a certain forerunner, kept washing his hands of the affair by allowing the defendants extraordinary latitude in explaining why they did it. The two most wondrous characters among the Nine, the ex-priest Thomas Melville and his wife, the ex-nun, were even allowed to touch on the sufferings they saw in Guatemala which ended by driving them into the arms of the guerrillas and out of the Church. Their quiet sobriety is in strange contrast to the traumas that so transformed their lives.

The trial drew some 2,000 zealots from all over the country. The deepest appeal of the spectacle for them was in Father Daniel Berrigan's testimony when he said, "I was in danger of verbalizing my moral impulses out of existence. I sought a way to defy the state even if I was too old to defy the draft." Of course they were found guilty. Not to acquiesce in murder, the chief and most ancient business of the State, is clearly subversive. On November 8 they will be sentenced. The third and longest act will be when they and their supporters use the appeals to put the show on the road. We cannot think of a finer way to stir the sluggish conscience of the nation.

October 21, 1968

IN DEFENSE OF
THE CAMPUS REBELS

I hate to write on subjects about which I know no more than the conventional wisdom of the moment. One of these

subjects is the campus revolt. My credentials as an expert
are slim. I always loved learning and hated school. I wanted
to go to Harvard, but I couldn't get in because I had graduated forty-ninth in a class of fifty-two from a small-town
high school. I went to college at the University of Pennsylvania, which was obligated—this sounds like an echo of a
familiar black demand today—to take graduates of high
schools in neighboring communities no matter how ill-fitted.
My boyhood idol was the saintly Anarchist Kropotkin. I
looked down on college degrees and felt that a man should
do only what was sincere and true and without thought of
mundane advancement. This provided lofty reasons for not
doing homework. I majored in philosophy with the vague
thought of teaching it but though I revered two of my pro-
fessors I disliked the smell of a college faculty. I dropped
out in my third year to go back to newspaper work. Those
were the twenties and I was a pre-depression radical. So I
might be described I suppose as a premature New Leftist,
though I never had the urge to burn anything down.

In microcosm, the *Weekly* and I have become typical of
our society. The war and the military have taken up so
much of our energies that we have neglected the blacks, the
poor and students. Seen from afar, the turmoil and the
deepening division appear to be a familiar tragedy, like
watching a friend drink himself to death. Everybody
knows what needs to be done, but the will is lacking. We
have to break the habit. There is no excuse for poverty in a
society which can spend $80 billion a year on its war ma-
chine. If national security comes first, as the spokesmen for
the Pentagon tell us, then we can only reply that the clearest danger to the national security lies in the rising revolt of
our black population. Our own country is becoming a
Vietnam. As if in retribution for the suffering we have imposed, we are confronted by the same choices: either to satisfy the aspirations of the oppressed or to try and crush them
by force. The former would be costly, but the latter will be
disastrous.

This is what the campus rebels are trying to tell us, in the only way which seems to get attention. I do not like much of what they are saying and doing. I do not like to hear opponents shouted down, much less beaten up. I do not like to hear any one group or class, including policemen, called pigs. I do not think four-letter words are arguments. I hate *hate*, intolerance and violence. I see them as man's most ancient and enduring enemies and I hate to see them welling up on my side. But I feel about the rebels as Erasmus did about Luther. Erasmus helped inspire the Reformation but was repelled by the man who brought it to fruition. He saw that Luther was as intolerant and as dogmatic as the Church. "From argument," as Erasmus saw it, "there would be a quick resort to the sword, and the whole world would be full of fury and madness." Two centuries of religious wars without parallel for blood-lust were soon to prove how right were his misgivings. But while Erasmus "could not join Luther, he dared not oppose him, lest haply, as he confessed 'he might be fighting against the spirit of God.' " [1] I feel that the New Left and the black revolutionists, like Luther, are doing God's work, too, in refusing any longer to submit to evil, and challenging society to reform or crush them.

Lifelong dissent has more than acclimated me cheerfully to defeat. It has made me suspicious of victory. I feel uneasy at the very idea of a Movement. I see every insight degenerating into a dogma, and fresh thoughts freezing into lifeless party line. Those who set out nobly to be their brother's keeper sometimes end up by becoming his jailer. Every emancipation has in it the seeds of a new slavery, and every truth easily becomes a lie. But these perspectives, which seem so irrefutably clear from a pillar in the desert, are worthless to those enmeshed in the crowded struggle. They are no better than mystical nonsense to the humane student who has to face his draft board, the dissident soldier who is determined not to fight, the black who sees his people doomed by shackles stronger than slavery to racial humiliation and decay. The business of the moment is to end the

[1] Froude's Life and Letters of Erasmus.

war, to break the growing dominance of the military in our society, to liberate the blacks, the Mexican-American, the Puerto Rican and the Indian from injustice. This is the business of our best youth. However confused and chaotic, their unwillingness to submit any longer is our one hope.

There is a wonderful story of a delegation which came here to see Franklin D. Roosevelt on some reform or other. When they were finished the President said, "Okay, you've convinced me. Now go on out and bring pressure on me." Every thoughtful official knows how hard it is to get anything done if someone isn't making it uncomfortable *not to*. Just imagine how helpless the better people in government would be if the rebels, black and white, suddenly fell silent. The war might smolder on forever, the ghettoes attract as little attention as a refuse dump. It is a painful business extricating ourselves from the stupidity of the Vietnamese war; we will only do so if it becomes more painful *not to*. It will be costly rebuilding the ghettoes, but if the black revolt goes on, it will be costlier *not to*. In the workings of a free society, the revolutionist provides the moderate with the clinching argument. And a little *un*-reason does wonders, like a condiment, in reinvigorating a discussion which has grown pointless and flat.

We ought to welcome the revolt as the one way to prod us into a better America. To meet it with cries of "law and order" and "conspiracy" would be to relapse into the sterile monologue which precedes all revolutions. Rather than change old habits, those in power always prefer to fall back on the theory that all would be well but for a few malevolent conspirators. It is painful to see academia disrupted, but under the surface were shams and horrors that needed cleansing. The disruption is worth the price of awakening us. The student rebels are proving right in the daring idea that they could revolutionize American society by attacking the universities as its soft underbelly. But I would also remind the students that the three evils they fight—war, racism and bureaucracy—are universal. The Marxism-Leninism some of the rebels cling to has brought into power a bureaucracy more suffocating than any under capitalism; the students demonstrate everywhere on our side but are stifled on the other. War and imperialism have not been eliminated in the relations between Communist states. Black Africa, at least half-freed from the white man, is hardly a model of fraternity or freedom. Man's one real enemy is within himself. Burning America down is no way to Utopia. If battle is joined and our country polarized, as both the revolutionists and the repressionists wish, it is the better and not the worse side of America which will be destroyed. Someone said a man's character was his fate, and tragedy may be implicit in the character of our society *and* of its rebels. How make a whisper for patience heard amid the rising fury?

May 19, 1969

BITTER BATTLES LIE AHEAD

From my days as an editorial writer on one of the few pro-New Deal papers in the country, I remember how bitterly the Democrats complained about the hostility of the press and radio; they portrayed Roosevelt as a dangerous revolutionary. When he won his landslide victory in 1936 it was over their overwhelming opposition. We felt as the Nixon crowd does now that the news media were one-sided, but there are crucial differences between the two periods. Poor people don't own newspapers. The news media now as then are in wealthy, mostly conservative and largely Republican hands. It takes a lot of steam in the boiler before they turn against a Republican President. Their growing opposition testifies to the unpopularity of the war and the spreading suspicion that Nixon wants to hang on, whatever the cost, until he can get a political victory. Nixon might as well

complain about the unfairness of the stock market. It has
been going down steadily since it sized up the November 3
speech as the signal for a prolonged war. Nothing Huntley
ever said to Brinkley is as subversive as the Dow-Jones
ticker. Wall Street—the citadel of the GOP—has lost confidence in Nixon and in Nixon's war.

Nixon's real complaint is that the news media don't agree
with him. Since the First Amendment doesn't require the
press to agree with the President, he doesn't dare say this
openly and instead charges unfairness. It is remarkable how
little evidence of this the Administration is able to cite, after
gathering transcripts from every TV station on what they
said about the November 3 speech. When Agnew—Nixon's
Papadapoulos and official cleanser of the U.S. media—went
on TV ten days later, all he could offer was a scurrilous attack on Averell Harriman and a colorful but curiously
vague bill of particulars. He complained about "a raised
eyebrow, an inflection of the voice, a caustic remark dropped
in the middle of a broadcast." What caustic remark? What
insidious inflection? Whose raised eyebrow? Couldn't Klein
find anything more specific? Is this Athens where the cops
even watch eyebrows?

Equally feeble in its vagueness was Agnew's attack a
week later on the *New York Times* and the *Washington
Post*. You'd think Agnew could do better than complaining
about one story which missed the early edition and that the
Pope's support for Nixon made page 11 instead of page 1. Is
that all the White House researchers could find? Agnew
was so desperate he made like a liberal at one point and attacked "monopolization of the news." We welcome him to
the fold. But neither New York nor Washington are one-
newspaper towns. In New York the pro-Nixon *Daily
News* circulation is far bigger than the *Times* and the *Post*
combined. In Washington, both the *Daily News* and the
Star are conservative and pro-Nixon (as is the *Washington
Post* quite often, most recently on Haynsworth and, alter-
nate days, on Nixon's war policy). It is true that just three

days after Agnew spoke a Washington paper had the impudence to write—

From the first announcement of the Mobilization plans, the Administration reacted by building a wall of indifference and hostility between itself and the demonstrators. The opposition was generally classified as the product of either stupidity or subversion. There was little attempt to reason, and a massive effort at rejection.

But that was an editorial in the conservative *Star* (November 23).

We are seeing a marriage of paranoias. Nixon has always felt (remember his outburst after he lost the Governorship in California) that the media were against him. The military and its supporters in the State Department and the White House have been grumbling about press coverage ever since the Vietnam intervention began. The animosity deepened every time the reporters were proven right and the generals wrong. The baldest and most recent expression of the bureaucracy's delusions came when General Walt of the Marines told a press conference in Danang (*Washington Post*, November 23) that the war would have been over a year ago if the American people had supported Lyndon Johnson! He criticized the news media for failing to present a "positive" picture of the conflict and said how long the war lasts would "depend in lots of respects on how good treatment it gets from our news media." So the main obstacle to victory is the First Amendment, and Jeffersonianism will soon be un-American again.

In Saigon the regime is cracking down on the press as dissatisfaction rises. Here the Administration is trying to make independent reporting seem unpatriotic. In the events of the tumultuous last two weeks, the Administration has been demonstrating its incompetence on many levels; to give it freedom from criticism would be an invitation to mismanagement. The Haynsworth affair was one example. We cheer the outcome but note that it was a self-inflicted defeat. The Attorney General was slipshod in his preliminary inquiry; the White House was crude in its pressure tactics. The low point was the crass attempt at political blackmail—the threat to impeach Mr. Justice Douglas if the nomination were rejected. The revolt in the Northern Republican leadership showed the bankruptcy of the Southern strategy and its corollary, the attempt to compete with Wallace in Know Nothingism. Such hands at the wheel of state are a safety hazard.

The handling of the Mobilization missed disaster by a hair's breadth. Until the intervention of Mayor Washington, the Administration was on the verge of denying a parade permit and doing a Daley. At the Pentagon, on the eve of the Mobilization, a Mass in the south concourse, where it blocked no traffic, was broken up by the police (all black for the occasion) and an Episcopal Bishop and the peaceful celebrants arrested just as it drew to its close. It was an ugly scene a modicum of good sense would have avoided. Before the Mobilization, the Administration ostentatiously moved troops into the capital, as if for an uprising, and filled the press with alarms. It reminded me of the days when Hoover called out the troops under MacArthur and drove the Bonus Marchers out of town in a glorious military victory. It sealed Hoover's defeat in 1932. The Republicans are trigger-happy again.

Despite the incendiary forecasts, the Mobilization proved as pacific as the Moratorium. The March of Death was a masterpiece of dramaturgy. Thanks to an army of marshals, and logistic preparations few armies could match, Saturday's parade went off without incident, the greatest outpouring of its kind in U.S. history. It was quite a contrast to the sparse turnout and screwball tone of the pro-Nixon demonstration four days earlier. Even so, when the Mobilization drew to its close, the police roughed up departing citizens on the Monument grounds and outside churches where buses were being loaded, as if someone higher up regretted the absence of violence. In the same spirit the Attorney General over-reacted to the Justice Department demonstration against the Conspiracy Trial by drenching the downtown areas with tear gas and locking up passersby and two reporters with imbecile impartiality.

Nothing is more dangerous than weak men who think they are tough guys. The resignations of Lodge and Walsh at the Paris peace talks, coming after the threat to re-escalate in the November 3 speech, indicate that the Administration is getting ready to be "tough" in Vietnam as at home. There is no sign that it is heeding the repeated warnings of the Gallup organization that its good showing in the public opinion polls is predicated on the expectation that Nixon "will remove U.S. troops from Vietnam within a reasonable time" (*New York Times*, November 23). That "silent majority," if any, will evaporate if this expectation is disappointed. This is where Nixon is most vulnerable. It is the job of the peace movement to fan out into the country with a campaign of education while it can. This Administration is capable of suicidal folly. It may resume the bombing of the North. It may try another witch hunt at home. We believe that if it tries either it will be swept away in a landslide in 1972, as Hoover was 40 years ago. But there are bitter battles ahead. We had better get ready for them.

December 1, 1969

INDEX

Abdel-Kader, A. Razak, 412
Abernathy, Ralph David, 97, 99, 113, 477
ABM, see anti-ballistic missile system
Abrams, Creighton, 345, 356
Abshire, David M., 167
Acheson, Dean, 261-63, 376
Adams, Sherman, 383
Adenauer, Conrad, 289, 441
Agnew, Spiro G., 43-44, 381, 463-65, 484-85
Aiken George, 300
Albert, Carl, 46
Aleichem, Sholom, 22
Allen, Richard V., 166-67
Alliance of National, Democratic and Peace Forces, 37
Allison, Royal B., 244
Allott, Gordon, 327
Alsop, Joseph, 208-9
Alsop, Stewart, 369
American Anti-Slavery Society, 26
Americans for Democratic Action, 12
American Socialist Party, 8
American Sugar Refining Company, 5
AMSA, 213-15
Amory, Robert, 166
Anti-ballistic missile system (ABM), 96-98, 155-59, 199-200, 204-6, 232-33
  budget and, 221-25
  military-industrial establishment and, 213-15
  Nuclear Test Ban and, 283, 296
  SALT and, 231-33, 239-48
Anti-Communism, 134-35
  two-party system and, 9-11
Anti-imperialism, 14, 17-18
Anti-Imperialist League, 14
Anti-Semitism, 101-8
Anti-war movement, see Peace movement

Apple, R. W., Jr., 63
Arab guerrillas, 434-38
Arab-Israeli conflict, see Israeli-Arab conflict
Arms control, 241-48
  see also Disarmament
Arms race, 169-230
  budget and, 230-34
  as corporate welfare, 97-98
  Kennedy, J. F., and, 272-73, 275-98
  Nixon and, 169-77, 180, 190, 207-23
  Nuclear Test Ban Treaty and, 282-304
  SALT and, 230-33, 239-48
  see also Disarmament
Arnett, Peter, 59-60
Atomic Energy Commission, 302-4
Australia, 130-32
Aviation, Israel and, 433-35
Avnery, Uri, 418-19, 422-23
Azef, 450

Bacteriological warfare, 387-89
Baldwin, Hanson, 315, 335
Balfour Declaration, 417-18
Ball, George, 52, 349
Barnet, Richard J., 445
Barr, Joseph, 100
Baruch, Bernard, 262
Baruch Plan, 261-64
Be, Major, 374
Beals, John Robinson, 267
Beard, Charles, 22
Beecher, William, 232
Beirut affair, 434-38
Beisner, Robert L., 14n, 17
Ben Gurion, David, 414, 427
Benson, Robert S., 129
Bentre, 86-87
Benziane, Tahar, 420
Berrigan, Daniel, 478-79
Big Business, see Business
Black, Hugo, 114
Black Panther Party, 462

Black revolt, 93
  two-party system and, 19-21
  Vietnam war affects, 88-90
  in Washington, D.C., 93-96
Blacks, 481-83
  open admissions and, 135-36
  persecution of, 462
  Republican party and, 28-29
  Vietnam war and, 85, 88-90
  see also Slavery
Boeing Aircraft, 174-75, 178-80
Boggs, Hale, 460
Bombings, 465-69
Bourguiba, President, 416-17
Braden, Tom, 379
Bradley, Omar, 155, 349
Braestrup, Peter, 345
Brown, George, 69
Brown, Harold, 171-73, 182, 188,
  243-47
Brown, Rap, 469
Brown, Sam, 367
Brownell, Herbert, 9
Bryan, William Jennings, 17
Buber, Martin, 423
Buckley, William F., 444
Budget, 121-30
  armament and, 97-100
  arms race and, 207, 209-30
  military, 230-34, 238, 289-90
    Nuclear Test Ban and, 300-1
    Rockefeller on, 37-38
    Vietnam war affects, 395-400
    see also Vietnam war, costs
  pollution and, 400
  Vietnam war and, 215-16, 218-21
Bukharin, N., 454
Bundy, McGeorge, 323, 349-53, 376
Bundy, William P., 82-83, 318
Burger, Warren, 114-15, 135
Burke, Arleigh, 166
Bush, Vannevar, 262
Business
  Republican party and, 29-31
  two-party system and, 4-5
Byrd, Robert C., 94-95

Calhoun, John C., 16
Cambodia, 84-85, 139-41, 238, 401-8
Campaigns, political, 212-13
Campbell, Jeremy, 349
Campbell, Leslie, 104-5

Campus revolts, 479-83
Canham, E. D., 444
Canning, Secretary, 15-16
Carmichael, Stokely, 453
Carswell, Harold, 112-14
Casey, William J., 248
Catonsville Nine, 478-79
Ca Van Lau, 359
Cease-fire, 354-59
Censorship, *see* Media, censorship
  of
Central Intelligence Agency, 449-52
  in Cambodia, 402-3
Chemical warfare, 387-89
Chicago Conspiracy Trial, 463-65,
  468
Childers, Erskine B., 421
China, 286-89
Churchill, Randolph, 250
Citizens Board of Inquiry, 475
Citizens' Report on Hunger, 475
Civil liberties, 114-15
  in Soviet Union, 453-59
  Vietnam war and, 74-75
Clark, Joseph, 158-59, 224
Clark, J. Reuben, 5n, 6
Clark, Tom, 9, 135
Class, *see* Socioeconomic class;
  Working class
Clemens, Walter C., Jr., 287n
Clifford, Clark, 147-48n, 376,
  384-85
  arms race and, 191, 193, 196-97,
  199, 203-4, 213-14
  Vietnam war and, 345, 356-57,
  378-79
Clos, Max, 405
Cobden, Richard, 250-51
Coffey, Raymond R., 61-63
Coffin, William, 82
Cold war, 40-42
  see also Arms race
Communist Control Act of 1954, 10
Communist party, Israeli, 415-16
Conant, James B., 262
Concentration camps, U.S., 9-10
Conference for the Reduction and
  Limitation of Armaments
  (1932), 256
Constitution, U.S.
  Nixon and, 114-15
  war declaration powers in, 328

Cooke, Cardinal, 460
Cooper, John Sherman, 10, 140, 223, 324, 368-69
Cooper-Church amendment, 138-41
Cousins, Norman, 288
Crime, 460-62
Critchfield, Richard, 365
Cuba, 13
  missile crisis, 285
  Monroe Doctrine and, 15-16
Cult of personality, 452, 455, 457
Curtis, Senator, 171, 173, 175, 179, 211, 301
Czechoslovakia, 442-3

Dale, Edwin L., Jr., 398
Daley, James, 44, 46-48
Davidson, James, 69
Dayan, Moshe, 414, 424
Debs, Eugene, 9
Defense Marketing Service, 223-24
Dellinger, David, 45
Democratic party
  anti-Communism and, 9-11
  anti-imperialism and, 17
  composition, 19-20
  imperialism and, 15-17
  1968 Convention, 45-49
  property and, 4-8
  reform and, 3
  socialism and, 8
  see also Two-party system
Democratic Party Council, 396
Detention camps, U.S., 9-10
Dillon, Douglas, 349-376
Disarmament
  history, 248-59
  SALT and, 230-33, 239-48
  see also Nuclear disarmament
Disraeli, B., 250
Dominican Republic, 13
Douglas, William, 466, 486
Draft resistance movement, 82, 85
  see also Peace movement
Dulles, John Foster, 207-8, 383, 441

Earth Day, 237-40
Eberstadt, Ferdinand, 262
Eckardt, Bob, 94
Einstein, Albert, 260

Eisenhower, Dwight D., 21
  ABM and, 156
  arms race and, 280
  Indochina and, 383
  on military-industrial complex, 146
  nuclear disarmament and, 267-70
  on Rockefeller, 38
Eisenhower, Milton, 460
El Al, 434
Engels, F., 455
Enthoven, Alain, 375
Ernst, Harry W., 6n
Ervin, Sam, 114-15, 179
Erasmus, 481

F-111, *see* TFX airplane
Farley, Philip J., 244
Farm subsidies, 475
Featherstone, Ralph, 469
Fish, Hamilton, 9, 401-4
Flood, Daniel J., 98
Foisie, Jack, 401
Food stamp program, 109-10
Foot, Michael, 69
Foran, Thomas, 463
Foreign policy, Republican party and, 161-62
Foreign Relations Committee, Senate
  Resolution 187 and, 328-30
  Tonkin Gulf incident and, 307-9, 312-26, 330-39
Forrestal, James, 371
Foster, John S., 186-87, 205
Frankel, Max, 348
Fraser, Maurice, 444-45
Freeman, Orville, 365
Free soil party, 26
Friendly, Alfred, 443-44
Fubini, Eugene G., 335-36
Fulbright, William, 83, 368, 377n
  Resolution 187 and, 327-28
  Tonkin Gulf affair and, 312-23, 326, 330-39

Galbraith, John K., 449
Gallup polls, 21, 31, 381-82n
Gas warfare, 387-89
Gavin, James M., 147
General Dynamics, 170, 172, 174-81, 209-11

Geneva Protocol, 387, 389
Giap, General 364, 386
Gilpatric, Roswell, 178
Godkin, Lawrence, 14
Goldberg, Arthur, 52, 68, 368
Goldwater, Barry, 39, 43, 247
Goodell, Charles, 368
Goodman, Leon, 103-4
Gore, Albert, 132, 332, 335
Gorton, John Grey, 130-32
Goulding, Phil G., 293
Graham, Billy, 119-20, 468-69
Great Britain
  Israel and, 417-18
  nuclear relations with, 264
  war scares in, 249-53
Greece, 441-45
Green, Edith, 98-99
Grey, Edward, 255
Groves, Leslie R., 262
Gruening, Ernest, 310, 331
Grumman Aircraft, 180
Gruson, Sydney, 424
Guam Conference, 72-75
Guam Doctrine, 139-40, 381
Guaranteed income, 474
Guatemala, 13
Guerrillas, U.S., 465-67

Ha-Am, Achad, 423
Hague Disarmament Conferences,
  253-55
Halperin, Morton, 287n
Hamilton, Alexander, 473
Hancock, John, 262
Hansen, Clifford P., 138
Harcourt, William, 252
Harding, Warren G., 9
Harkabi, Yehudah, 431-32
Harriman, Averell, 378
Harris, Fred, 47, 368
Harris, William, 106
Hatfield, Mark, 233, 368
Hawaiian Commercial and Sugar
  Company, 475
Hawk, David, 367
Hay, John, 253
Hayden, Tom, 45, 49
Haynsworth, Clement, 112-14,
  485-86
Heller, Jean, 464
Hersh, Seymour M., 388n

Herzl, Theodor, 422-23
Hess, Karl, 164, 247
Hickel, Walter, 407-8
Hill, Robert C., 166
Hilsman, Roger, 285, 321, 344
Hippies
  1968 Democratic Convention and,
    47-48
  HUAC and, 478
Hirst, F. W., 251
Ho Chi Minh, 383-84
Hoffman, Julius, 468
Hofstadter, Richard, 7
Hoopes, Townsend, 369-85
Hoover, Herbert, 21, 23, 256
Hoover, J. Edgar, 9, 451, 469
Hosmer, Craig, 166
House Un-American Activities
  Committee, 478
Hruska, Roman, 460
Humphrey, H. H.
  anti-Communism and, 10-11
  on business, 5-6
  civil liberties and, 10-12
  Iranian aid and, 445
  and Johnson, 12-13
  Mundt-Nixon bill and, 9-10
  at 1968 Democratic Convention,
    48
  on Nixon, 50
  Vietnam war and, 17-18, 49-53,
    72-73, 349
Hunger, 475
Hunter, Lloyd, 106

ICBM, 195-99, 228-30
Imperialism, 13-17
  see also Anti-imperialism
Indochina, 383
Inflation, 390-95
Iron Triangle campaign, 58-60
Israeli-Arab conflict, 411-38

Jackson, Andrew, 7
Jackson, Henry, 167, 240, 292
James, William, 24
Jefferson, Thomas, 7
Jenkins, Percy, 105-6
J. G. Boswell Company, 475
Johnson, Frank M., 113
Johnson, Lyndon B.
  arms race and, 213

Blacks and, 112-13
budget and, 123, 125-28, 215-19
credibility gap, 70, 79-80
inauguration, 119-21
on McNamara, 375
1968 Democratic Convention and,
  46-47
Rockefeller on, 41-42
Tonkin Gulf affair and, 308
Vietnam war and, 12-13, 18,
  51-52, 60, 132
  bombing halt, 378-79
  bombing resumption, 60, 67,
    78-79, 81-82
  civil liberties, 74-75
  escalation, 83
  financing, 391
  McNamara and, 323
  opposition to, 375-81 *passim*
  peace talks, 343-44, 346, 348-50,
    378-79
  propaganda, 77-78
  Têt truce violations, 70
  Vietnamization, 344-45, 380
Johnson, Luci, 78-79
Joint Chiefs of Staff, 293, 296-97,
  300-1
Judd, Walter, 166
Junction City, 67, 69

Kahn, Herman, 167, 379-80
Kaysen, Carl, 212-13*n*
Kefauver, Estes, 10
Kellock, Alan, 105
Kempton, Murray, 107
Kennedy, John F.
  anti-Communism and, 10
  arms race and, 207, 272-73,
    275-98 *passim*
  Cuba and, 13
  inauguration, 120
  McNamara and, 150-54
  nuclear disarmament and, 272-98
    passim
  Rockefeller on, 40-41
  TFX airplane and, 181
  Vietnam war and, 13
Kennedy, Robert F., 12, 30, 33, 345
Kerensky, A., 451
Kerr, Walter, 267
Khesanh incident, 87-88
Khmer Seri, 402-3

Khrushchev, N., 154, 285-93, 295
King, Martin Luther, Jr., 89-90,
  93-94, 477
Kissinger, Henry A., 132, 166-67,
  371, 382
Klein, Herbert G., 208-9, 242
Korean war, 369-70
Korth, Fred, 178-79
Kropotkin, P., 480
Kunstler, William, 479
Kuznetsov, V. V., 154-55, 274

Laird, Melvin R., 119, 125*n*, 163-69,
  190, 237-38, 248, 277-78, 281, 328
  arms race and, 196, 214, 217, 218*n*,
    219-20, 225-30
  SALT and, 240
  TFX airplane and, 210
  Vietnam war costs and, 396-97
Land reform, 72-74, 365
Lanzmann, Claude, 412, 414-15
Laos, 84, 328
Lapp, Ralph, 97-98, 152, 157
Laroui, M., 418, 420
Larouia, Abdallah, 417
Latin America, 370
Lausche, Frank, 307-8
Law and order, 462
Lawrence, David, 133
League of Nations, 255-57
Lefevour, Joseph J., 47
Lehman, Herbert, 10
LeMay, Curtis, 193-94, 205-6, 301
Lenin, 455-56
Levinson, Naomi, 103
Liberty party, 26
Lilienthal, David E., 261
Limited Nuclear Test Ban Treaty,
  282-304
Lincoln, Abraham, 26-27
Lincoln Park, 47-48
Lindsay, John V., 22, 101-2, 108
Lodge, Henry Cabot, 120, 358
Long, Edward, 450
Loory, Stuart H., 349-50, 393
Lowenstein, Allard K., 12, 48, 368
Lownds, Col., 87
Luther, Martin, 481
Luxembourg, Rosa, 456-57

McCarthy, Congressman, 389

McCarthy, Eugene, 11-12, 32-34, 313-14, 349, 368
McClellan, John, 175, 327
McClosky, Robert, 62
McCloy, John J., 262, 281
McCloy-Zorin agreement, 258-59
McConnell, General, 171, 173, 187, 189
McCoy, Rhody, 106
McDermott, John, 321
McDonald, Admiral, 301
McGee, Frank, 349
McGovern, George, 78, 110, 286n, 297-300, 357, 368
McNamara, Robert
  ABM and, 155-59
  on arms race, 191, 194, 200-3, 205-6, 213-14, 293-300
  bombing resumption, 80-82
  fired, 375
  intervention and, 371-73
  Laird on, 168
  military-industrial complex and, 145-59
  missile gap and, 150-55, 276, 279-81, 298-300
  Nuclear Test Ban and, 293-300
  TFX airplane and, 169-82, 186-87, 209-10
  Tonkin Gulf affair and, 307-26, 331-33, 335-37
  Tonkin Gulf resolution and, 317-18
  Vietnam war and, 86, 362
  Westmoreland and, 376
McNaughton, John T., 374

Madariaga, Salvador de, 258
Magnes, Judah, 423
Mahan, Alfred T., 253-54
Mahon, George, 188-89, 206
Majdalang, Gabran, 423-24
Mandracchia, John, 106
Mansfield, Mike, 95, 205, 328
Mansour, Attalah, 429
March of Death, 486
Marcy, Carl, 337n
Martov, Y., 455-56
Marx, Karl, 11, 455
Mass media, see Media
Mayer, George H., 22, 25-26
Meany, George, 50

Media
  censorship of, 74-75
  Nixon and, 483-85
  Têt truce and, 70-72
  see also Press
Melville, Thomas, 479
Mekong Delta campaign, 57-60
Mexico, 370
Military budget, see Budget, military
Military-industrial establishment, 97-98
  budget affected by, 124-25, 128-30, 207, 209-11, 212-30
  campaign funds from, 212-13
  Eisenhower on, 146
  General Dynamics, 170, 172, 174-81, 209-11
  history of, 148
  McNamara and, 145-59
  Nuclear Test Ban and, 301
  Republican party and, 159-62
  Vietnam war and, 180-9
  see also Arms race
Minh, General, 385n
MIRV, see Multiple Independently Targeted Reentry Vehicle
Misrahi, Robert, 416, 420-21
Missile gap, 150-55, 273-82, 298-300
  see also Arms race; Nuclear disarmament
Mitchell, John, 114-15, 163, 382, 464
Mobilization, 486-87
Moch, M. Jules, 266
Mohr, Charles, 357
Mondale, Walter, 109
Monroe Doctrine, 15-16
Montasser, Adel, 428
Morgan, Edward P., 268
Morse, Wayne, 9-11, 12, 301, 309, 312, 314n, 316-17, 322-25, 331, 333-34
Movement, the, 481-83
Moynihan, Daniel P., 469
Multiple Independently Targeted Reentry Vehicle (MIRV), 194-96, 199, 204-6, 231-33, 239-40, 241-47, 283, 296
Mundt, Karl, 134-35
Mundt-Nixon bill, 9-10, 134-35
Murphy, Arthur G., 478-79
Muskie, Edmund, 47, 383-84

Nasser, A. G., 414
National Farmers Union, 72
Negroes, *see* Blacks
Nelson, Gaylord, 97
New Deal, 3
New Left, 45, 47-49, 467-78, 479-83
Newman, Edwin, 82-83
New Mobilization Committee to
    End the War in Vietnam,
    367-68
New York Board of Education,
    105-8
Nguyen Cao Ky, 74
Niemeyer, Gerhart, 166, 167
Nitze, Paul H., 244, 375
Nivolon, François, 347
Nixon, Richard
    as anti-Communist, 134-35
    arms race and, 169-77, 180, 190,
        207-23, 239-40, 242, 248
    Blacks and, 112-13, 115
    budget, 123-30, 207-23, 215-16,
        218-25
    business and, 30
    cabinet, 162-63
    Cambodia and, 139-41, 401-8
    Commission on Violence and,
        460-61
    Humphrey on, 50
    inauguration, 119-22
    Indochina and, 383
    inflation and, 389-95
    judicial philosophies, 112-15
    media and, 483-84
    Nuclear Test Ban and, 284, 304
    open admissions and, 135-36
    peace movement and, 406-8,
        486-87
    Poor People's March and, 476
    poverty and, 109-12, 126-28
    as Republican, 22
    self-image, 28
    TFX airplane and, 170-77, 180,
        209-11
    Vietnam war and, 162, 328, 354,
        357, 366-67, 369-70, 377, 380-86
        Cambodian invasion, 401-8
        costs, 390-400
        opposition to, 380-82
        withdrawal, 136-37
Noel-Baker, Philip, 264, 266, 269
Nordau, Max, 423

Novak, Robert D., 23, 30
Noyes, Newbold, 87
Nuclear disarmament, 261-304
    passim
    Baruch plan, 261-64
    Limited Nuclear Test Ban
        Treaty, 282-304
    Soviet proposals, 264-71, 281-82
Nuclear Non-Proliferation Pact,
    257-58
Nuclear testing, 301-4
    see also Limited Nuclear Test
        Ban Treaty
Nuclear weapons
    in combat, 39
    in Middle East, 432
    in Vietnam war, 87-88
Nutter, G. Warren, 247-48

Ocean-Hill Brownsville, 103-8
Ochrana, 449-51
Olney, Richard, 16
Open admissions, 135-36
Operation Cedar Falls, 58-60
Operation Complete Victory,
    346-47
Operation Dockhouse V, 57-58
Oplan 34A, 317
Oppenheimer, J. Robert, 261
Otepka, Otto, 135

Pace, Frank, 178
Packard, David, 211
Palmer, A. Mitchell, 9
Palmerston, Lord, 251
Papandreou, George, 442
Paris Peace Talks, 52, 347-50, 354-59,
    378-79
Parker, Alton B., 23
Peace movement, 367-69, 400-1
    Catonsville Nine, 478-79
    Mobilization, 486-87
    1968 Democratic Convention and,
        45, 47-48
    Nixon and, 406-8
    Vietnam war affected by, 75-77,
        82-85
    see also Movement
Peace talks
    see Vietnam war, peace talks
Peel, Robert, 249
Percy, Charles, 222*n*

Perkins, Dwight H., 287*n*
Pett, Saul, 147
Phoenix missile, 182, 184
Pincus, Walter, 330*n*
Pinkville massacre, 386
Polaris missile, 195-96
Pollution, 400
Ponturo, John, 335
Poor People's March, 473, 476-77
Poseidon missile, 195-96
Potter, Philip, 78
Poverty, 474-75
  budget and, 126-28
  Nixon and, 109-12, 126-28
  taxation and, 474
President's National Commission on
  Violence, 460-61
Press
  censorship of, 74-75
  at 1968 Democratic Convention,
    45-46
  in Soviet Union, 458
  see also Media
Preventive detention, 9-10, 114-15
Priest, Ivy Baker, 44
Propaganda, 77-78
Property, 4-8
Proxmire, William, 210, 297, 474*n*
Puy, Major General de, 59

Racism, 87-88
Radford, Arthur, 166, 383
Rand Corporation, 335
Raskin, Marcus, 48, 49
Republican party
  anti-Communism and, 9-11
  Blacks and, 28-29
  business and, 29-31
  history, 22-23
  and independents, 21-22
  1968 Convention, 43-44
  platform, 159-62
  property ownership and, 4
  slavery and, 25-28
  social change and, 29, 31
  socioeconomic class and, 28-29
  see also Two-party system
Resolution 187, 327-30
Reston, James, 239
Resurrection City, 96-99
Reuss, Henry, 399
Richardson, Elliott, 383, 402

Ridgeway, Matthew, 349, 383
Rivers, Francis E., 107
Rivers, Mendel, 239
Robb, Roger, 135
Roberts, Chalmers, 133
Rockefeller, Nelson, 368
  Cold War and, 40-42
  Eisenhower on, 38
  foreign policy and, 31
  free enterprise, 30
  on Lyndon Johnson, 41-42
  on John Kennedy, 40-41
  on military budget, 37-38
  nuclear disarmament and, 269-70
  on nuclear weapons, 39
  on Truman, 40
  Vietnam war and, 35-42
Rockefeller Brothers, 371-73
Rodinson, Maxime, 416
Rogers, David, 105
Rogers, William P., 163, 239, 249,
  382
Roosevelt, Franklin D., 3, 7, 8, 482
Roosevelt, Theodore, 23, 254
Rostow, Walt, 130, 154, 167, 274,
  276-77, 311, 343, 378
Rowe, David N., 166
Roy, Daniel, 403
Rubin, Jerry, 45
Rusk, Dean, 61-62, 248, 309, 323, 349
Russell, Bertrand, 457
Russell, John, 250
Russell, Richard, 68, 137, 171, 172-
  73, 175, 224, 225, 292, 327
Russian Revolution, 449-54
Ryskind, Allan, 50

Safeguard, *see* ABM
Salinger, Pierre, 150, 152
Salisbury, Lord, 252
SALT, *see* Strategic Arms
  Limitation Talks
Sartre, Jean-Paul, 411-12
SCAD, 203
Schell, Jonathan, 363
Schlesinger, Arthur, Jr., 152-54,
  273-82
Schurmann, Franz, 326*n*
Schurz, Carl, 254
Scott, Hugh, 133
Scott, Peter Dale, 326*n*
SDS, *see* Weatherman

Searls, Fred, 262
Selzer, Michael, 430*n*
Senate, U.S., 327-30
Shabath, Ibrahim, 427
Shanker, Albert, 102
Sharp, Admiral, 364
Sherrill, Robert, 6
Short Range Attack Missiles
    (SRAM), 203, 226-28
Sihanouk, Norodom, 402-6
Silverman, Sidney, 69
Simpson, Bryan, 113
Slavery
    Republican party and, 25-28
    in Russia, 453
Smith, Gerard C., 244
Smith, Kingsbury, 444
Smith, Richard Austin, 176
Sneh, Moshe, 415
Social class, *see* Socioeconomic class
Socialism, 8
Social Security system, 126-28
Socioeconomic class
    Republican party and, 28-29
    Two-party system and, 24-25
    see also Working Class
Solidarity Day, 98
Soliman, Lotfallah, 428
Son Ngoc Thanh, 403
Sorenson, Theodore C., 284*n*, 287-91
Soviet Union, civil liberties in,
    453-59
SRAM, 203, 226-28
Space program, 476
Spock, Benjamin, 82
Stalin, J., 454
Stassen, Harold, 269, 271
Stennis, John, 94, 137, 183, 198-99,
    369
Sterne, Joseph R. L., 330*n*
Stevenson, Adlai, 284, 308
Stimson, Henry L., 262
Stock market, 484
Stolypin, Prime Minister, 450
Stone, Jeremy, 245*n*
Strategic Arms Limitation Talks,
    230-33, 239-40, 241-48, 258-59
    see also Nuclear disarmament
Strauss-Hupé, Robert, 166, 167
STRIKECOM, 373-74
Subsonic Cruise Armed Decoy
    (SCAD), 203

Subversive Activities Control Board
    (SCAB), 135
Sumner, Charles, 27
Swope, Herbert Bayard, 262
Swyter, Han, 388
Syelard, Leo, 260*n*
Sykes, Christopher, 421-22
Symington, Stuart, 173, 175, 183,
    186-87, 225, 299

Tate, Merye, 250*n*, 254
Taxation, 474
Taylor, Maxwell, 193, 275-76, 296,
    349, 378
Teachers' strike, New York City,
    100-8
Tear gas, 387, 389
Teller, Edward, 38-39, 167
Terrorist movements, 465-67
Têt offensive, 375
Têt truce, 60-72
TFX airplane, 170-89, 209-11, 213-14
Thant, U, 139, 344, 355
Thompson, Llewellyn, 244
Thompson, Robert, 85*n*
Thomsen, Roszel C., 478-79
Tolstoy, Leo, 450
Tonkin Gulf affair, 307-26, 330-39
Tonkin Gulf resolution, 317-18
Ton That Thien, 74-75
Tower, John, 166
Tran Van Don, 385*n*
Tran Van Van, 74
Trotsky, Leon, 455, 456
Truman, Harry, 5, 9, 10, 40, 135, 391
Tuttle, Elbert, 113
Two-party system, 3-5
    anti-Communism and, 9-11
    failure of, 44-45
    prevalence, 24
    property and, 4-5
    social change and, 19-21
    socioeconomic class and, 24-25
    see also Democratic party;
        Republican party
Tydings, Joseph, 238

United Nations (UN), 139

Vagts, Alfred, 252-53
Vance, Cyrus, 200, 375-76, 378
Vassilyev, A. T., 449-51

Vietnam, elections in, 74
Vietnam Disengagement Act, 368
Vietnamization, 380, 384-85
Vietnam moratorium, 367-68
Vietnam war
  Americanization, 360-66
  atrocities, 386-89
  Australia and, 130-32
  Blacks and, 85, 88-90
  bombing resumption in, 60-66,
    70-72, 78-82
  budget and, 128-29, 215-16, 218-21
  casualties, 354-59
  cease-fire, 354-59
  civil liberties, 74-75
  costs, 121, 215-16, 218-21,
    390-400
  de-escalating, 375-86
  escalations (1968), 82-85
  Humphrey and, 17-18, 49-53
  inflation and, 390-95
  land reform and, 72-74
  lessons from, 369-86
  McCarthy, Eugene, and, 33-34
  nuclear weapons in, 87-88
  peace attempts, 35-37, 343-44, 346,
    350-53, 367-79, 378-79, 383-84
    see also Anti-war movement
  peace talks
    casualties and, 354-59
    Paris, 52, 347-50, 355-59, 378-79
    proposals, 82-83
  peace movement affects, 75-77,
    82, 85
  popularity of, 13-14
  Rockefeller, Nelson, and, 35-42
  supply build-ups, 60-72
  Tonkin Gulf affair, 307-26
  two-party system and, 19-21
  Vietnamization, 344, 380, 384-85
  winning, 13, 76-77, 162
  withdrawal, 136-37
    see also Cambodia; *specific entries*
Vilner, Meir, 415-16
Violence, 460
Viorst, Milton, 22-23, 25-27, 29, 30
Vo Nguyen Giap, 85n, 86

Wallace, Henry, 9
Wallace, James N., 405
Walt, General, 485
Warnke, Paul C., 336, 375

War on Poverty, 125, 126
Washington, George, 146
Washington, D.C.
  Black riots, 93-96
  March on, 89-90, 93
  Poor People's March on, 473,
    476-77
Watad, Mohammad, 426-27
Watson, Marvin, 53
Weatherman, 466-67
Webb, Alvin B., Jr., 64
Welfare, 110-12, 126-28
Wellington, Duke of, 251
Werblowsky, R. I. Zwi, 423
West Germany, 441
Westmoreland, William, 13, 75-78,
  86, 350, 360-66, 375, 376, 377,
  379, 408
Wheeler, Earle, 86, 301, 308, 309,
  316-17, 320-22, 331-33, 377
White, William S., 381-82
Wiesner, Jerome, 154, 274, 276-77,
  280
Wiggens, Russell, 52
Williams, John, 123
Wilson, George C., 232
Wilson, Harold, 60-61
Wilson, Richard, 133
Wilson, Woodrow, 7-8, 9, 255
Wood, George, 375
Working class, Republican party
  and, 28-29
Worthy, William, 403
Wu, Yuan-li, 247

Yaari, Meir, 423
Yippies, 467-68
  HUAC and, 478
  at 1968 Democratic Convention,
    47-48
Yost, Charles W., 437
Young, Elizabeth, 264n
Young, Stephen M., 216n

Zangwell, Israel, 423
Zelnik, Reginald, 326n
Ziegler, Ron, 393
Zinn, Howard, 368
Zion, Sidney E., 31
Zionism, *see* Israeli-Arab conflict
Zorin, V., 281
Zuckert, Eugene, 179

About the Author

I. F. STONE was born in Philadelphia in 1907. He launched his first publication in Haddonfield, New Jersey, at the age of fourteen, and dropped out of the University of Pennsylvania in his junior year for a life of newspaper work which he has never left. He has been a reporter, editorial writer and columnist on the Philadelphia *Record*, *PM* and the New York *Post*, the Washington *Star* and the New York *Daily Compass*. He was Washington editor of *The Nation* from 1940 to 1946, and in January 1953 founded his own newsletter, *I. F. Stone's Weekly*, which immediately established itself for its biting opposition to political repression and its exposure of official mendacity. Now published twice monthly, it has acquired a circulation of more than 60,000 as well as an international reputation.

Mr. Stone and his wife Esther live in Washington and get out the *Weekly* together.

Vietnam, elections in, 74
Vietnam Disengagement Act, 368
Vietnamization, 380, 384-85
Vietnam moratorium, 367-68
Vietnam war
   Americanization, 360-66
   atrocities, 386-89
   Australia and, 130-32
   Blacks and, 85, 88-90
   bombing resumption in, 60-66,
      70-72, 78-82
   budget and, 128-29, 215-16, 218-21
   casualties, 354-59
   cease-fire, 354-59
   civil liberties, 74-75
   costs, 121, 215-16, 218-21,
      390-400
   de-escalating, 375-86
   escalations (1968), 82-85
   Humphrey and, 17-18, 49-53
   inflation and, 390-95
   land reform and, 72-74
   lessons from, 369-86
   McCarthy, Eugene, and, 33-34
   nuclear weapons in, 87-88
   peace attempts, 35-37, 343-44, 346,
      350-53, 367-79, 378-79, 383-84
      see also Anti-war movement
   peace talks
      casualties and, 354-59
      Paris, 52, 347-50, 355-59, 378-79
      proposals, 82-83
   peace movement affects, 75-77,
      82, 85
   popularity of, 13-14
   Rockefeller, Nelson, and, 35-42
   supply build-ups, 60-72
   Tonkin Gulf affair, 307-26
   two-party system and, 19-21
   Vietnamization, 344, 380, 384-85
   winning, 13, 76-77, 162
   withdrawal, 136-37
   see also Cambodia; *specific entries*
Vilner, Meir, 415-16
Violence, 460
Viorst, Milton, 22-23, 25-27, 29, 30
Vo Nguyen Giap, 85n, 86

Wallace, Henry, 9
Wallace, James N., 405
Walt, General, 485
Warnke, Paul C., 336, 375

War on Poverty, 125, 126
Washington, George, 146
Washington, D.C.
   Black riots, 93-96
   March on, 89-90, 93
   Poor People's March on, 473,
      476-77
Watad, Mohammad, 426-27
Watson, Marvin, 53
Weatherman, 466-67
Webb, Alvin B., Jr., 64
Welfare, 110-12, 126-28
Wellington, Duke of, 251
Werblowsky, R. I. Zwi, 423
West Germany, 441
Westmoreland, William, 13, 75-78,
   86, 350, 360-66, 375, 376, 377,
   379, 408
Wheeler, Earle, 86, 301, 308, 309,
   316-17, 320-22, 331-33, 377
White, William S., 381-82
Wiesner, Jerome, 154, 274, 276-77,
   280
Wiggens, Russell, 52
Williams, John, 123
Wilson, George C., 232
Wilson, Harold, 60-61
Wilson, Richard, 133
Wilson, Woodrow, 7-8, 9, 255
Wood, George, 375
Working class, Republican party
   and, 28-29
Worthy, William, 403
Wu, Yuan-li, 247

Yaari, Meir, 423
Yippies, 467-68
   HUAC and, 478
   at 1968 Democratic Convention,
      47-48
Yost, Charles W., 437
Young, Elizabeth, 264n
Young, Stephen M., 216n

Zangwell, Israel, 423
Zelnik, Reginald, 326n
Ziegler, Ron, 393
Zinn, Howard, 368
Zion, Sidney E., 31
Zionism, *see* Israeli-Arab conflict
Zorin, V., 281
Zuckert, Eugene, 179

About the Author

I. F. STONE was born in Philadelphia in 1907. He launched his first publication in Haddonfield, New Jersey, at the age of fourteen, and dropped out of the University of Pennsylvania in his junior year for a life of newspaper work which he has never left. He has been a reporter, editorial writer and columnist on the Philadelphia *Record*, *PM* and the New York *Post*, the Washington *Star* and the New York *Daily Compass*. He was Washington editor of *The Nation* from 1940 to 1946, and in January 1953 founded his own newsletter, *I. F. Stone's Weekly*, which immediately established itself for its biting opposition to political repression and its exposure of official mendacity. Now published twice monthly, it has acquired a circulation of more than 60,000 as well as an international reputation.

Mr. Stone and his wife Esther live in Washington and get out the *Weekly* together.